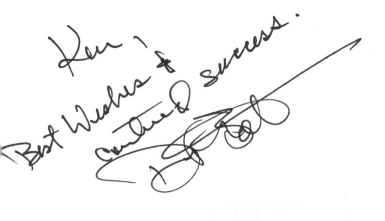

Ken,

Best Wishes +
Continued Success.

D0058423

The Art & Science

of

INVESTMENT MANAGEMENT CONSULTING

&

FIDUCIARY INVESTING

The Art & Science
of
INVESTMENT MANAGEMENT CONSULTING

Daniel R. Bott, CIMC

The definitive book on the evolution, processes, value and responsibilities of the professional Investment Management Consultant

FIDUCIARY INVESTING

Catherine L. Theisen, AIMC

An essential guide for trustees, plan sponsors and investment professionals who have fiduciary responsibilities

THE ART AND SCIENCE OF INVESTMENT MANAGEMENT CONSULTING
The definitive book on the evolution, processes, value and responsibilities of the professional Investment Management Consultant

FIDUCIARY INVESTING
An essential guide for trustees, plan sponsors and investment professionals who have fiduciary responsibilities

This publication is designed to provide accurate and authoritative information in regards to the subject matter covered. It is sold with the understanding that the publisher is not engaged in the rendering of legal, accounting, or other professional service. If legal advice or other expert assistance is required, the services of a competent and licensed professional person should be sought.

From a Declaration of Principles jointly adopted by a Committee of the American Bar Association and a Committee of Publishers.

ISBN-13: 978-0-9790314-0-3
ISBN-10: 0-9790314-0-0

This book is available at quanity discounts when purchased for business, educational, or sales promotional use. For more information, please email/write to:

New Financial Frontiers LLC, Attn. Institutional Book Sales
PO Box 1167
Carefree, Arizona 85377
email: NFF.LLC@earthlink.net

Acknowledgments

Book Acknowledgements:

Dan Bott and Catherine Theisen would like to thank the following individuals and companies for their contributions of time and resources in the production of this book.

Jim Babson, Jim Barksdale, Nancy Bertino, Daniel Bott II, Judy Bott, Steve Chun, Elizabeth Cline, Denise DiLallo, Ross Hawkins, Anne Ruddy, Ron Surz, Timothy Tigges, Brandes Investment Partners, Calamos Asset Management, Equity Investment Corporation, Informa Investment Solutions, Nationwide Financial, Laura Blackford of Ned Davis Research, Oakridge Investments, and Steven Hardy and Kelly Higgins of Zephyr Associates, Inc.

Personal Acknowledgements:

Our lives are shaped and given direction by the people we interface and work with over the years. The following individuals had a memorable impact on my professional career over the past 30 years. I was introduced to the business by my older brother of eight years, Gerald F. Bott (a forty year veteran of the investment business). Jerry introduced me to the great firm of Kidder Peabody were I began my career in March of 1975. During my 10 years at Kidder, Jerry gave me direction and inspiration that has lead to a rewarding financial career. While at Kidder, there were many other people who made their mark, they include Jim Mann, Steve Shirley, Steve Goddard to name only a few.

Before I started to refine my skills as an investment management consultant, I became very interested in the art and science of technical analysis of the capital markets. My deep rooted appreciation for the technical aspect of the markets came from my study and passion of the historical side of the capital markets. During my early years in the business I developed some personal relationships with some notable individuals. Joe Granville was considered a wild and crazy showman and it was Joe that helped me appreciate the importance of understanding the difference between the economy and the stock market when it came to investing. During the early 1980's Joe was a guest in my home, and we did a few TV shows and some traveling together. I was able to witness the real knowledge and talented side of Joe that many never could appreciate. Another early pioneer of technical analysis is Ralph Acampora who was at Kidder when I was just a rookie. It was Ralph that gave me my first taste of the real tools of technical analysis. Ralph went on to become an industry legend and a major driving force behind the growth of the Market Technicians Association. The MTA has created a legitimate forum and educational platform for market technicians. Then there was Bee Dow, a brilliant lady with a great laugh. I talked with her daily for over three years during the early 1980's, learning the finer points of market cycle analysis. Bee was a rare find for me, I can't even begin to remember how many major market bottoms her cycle training helped me recognize.

I want to thank Carl Hulick for giving me the opportunity to be the product manager at Dean Witter in New York during the mid 1980s. While there I was given the opportunity to create the beginning pieces of what became the managed money and consulting program currently in place at Morgan Stanley. That experience allowed me to associate with hundreds of great money managers and focus entirely on the future growth of the consulting business. While at Dean Witter it became very clear that Wall Street brokers needed an educational and industry association to drive the emerging profession of investment management consulting, particularly at the brokerage firm level. So twenty years ago, a small group of people supported my vision to create such an organization. In 1985, Jim Owen, Jack Polley and I, along with some industry leaders, started the Investment Management Consultants Association (IMCA). A couple of years later, I formed the Institute for Investment Management Consultants (IIMC) with the following dedicated group of professionals: Jack Polley, Jim Johnson, Frank Gibb, Marty Jensen, Ephraim Ulmer, Joe Godsey, Jim Awad, Sydney LeBlanc, Drew Washburn, Dave Loeper, John Gepfert, Jay Schmallen, John Calamos, Larry Chambers and Bob Wood, to name just a few. IMCA and IIMC merged and became the leading association representing the investment management consultant with membership into the thousands and a highly respected and flourishing certification program.

In 1987, I re-entered the client servicing side of the business at E.F. Hutton, this firm later evolved into Smith Barney. During those 15 years, I had the pleasure of working with many great professionals, including Len Reinhart, Frank Campanale, Tom Mann, Lee Weiss, Norm Nabhan, Bryson Cook, Dennis White and former business partners Pat Cavallero and Jim Pupillo. As a result of this profession I am honored to have many great relationships with such notables as Charles Brandes and John Calamos. I have developed many close friendships, to numerous to list, but a few that I will mention and call my close friends are Donn Goodman, Joel Kramer, and Sydney LeBlanc. Most recently, I have had the pleasure of working with seasoned professionals at Wachovia Securities, LLC., including Mark Staples, Scott Trent, Burt White, Gavin Raphael, Wayne Morris, David Kowach, John Jetter, David Oberman, John Peluso, Brand Meyer and many other dedicated professionals.

There are four individuals who had an important impact on my career and are no longer with us. Bill Mullen was the executive director of the Institute for Investment Management Consultants for 10 years. Bill and I spent many years working together planning, budgeting and nurturing the growth of the Institute and his dedication could not be more appreciated. Bob Wood introduced me to Charles Brandes when Brandes had less than $100 million under management. Most people will never know how much of the Brandes business success was due to Bob Woods' vision, correctly foreseeing that the brokerage industry would adopt the use of professional money management in a big way. Jack Polley, a close and dear friend, who left us much too soon, had the vision to promote and finance the idea of starting the Registered Rep magazine. He funded the early days of publishing and provided the early support for both IIMC and IMCA. Finally, the late Cathy Ensor, who took a green young broker and gave me my first managed account in 1977, that account and her support was the inspiration to pursue consulting as a profession.

Finally, and certainly not least, I thank both my wife Judy and my son for their patience and support over the past decades, as we made career related moves across the country and supporting my days away from home. During those early IIMC days Judy spent many hours grading student's tests from the private study course offered while I was building a new consulting practice. I want to thank and acknowledge Tim Tigges, for his loyal and skillful support at my side for the past 20 years, and Catherine Theisen, who has taken on projects, such as this book, over the past seven years, with keen attention to detail. I am particularly excited about my son entering the business and the practice full-time; this move has inspired me to increase my focus on the future growth of our consulting business.

Daniel R. Bott

Contents

Forward

When I started out in the investment business more than 30 years ago, I became an educator. The advent of mutual funds had moved investing from the province of the very wealthy to a broader group of clients. To newcomers, the investment world was complicated, complete with a language of its own. I quickly realized that I needed to help educate my clients about investing if they were going to entrust me with their money.

Today, the financial industry is undergoing dramatic change: customer needs are changing, driven by the looming retirement of the biggest demographic wave in our history. Add to that, the fact that many pensions are underfunded and other investment choices can seem quite simply overwhelming.

The Art and Science of Investment Management Consulting is a helpful book for these complicated times. Daniel Bott and Catherine Theisen bring their collective experience to the subject.

Smart financial professionals know they will prosper in the coming years by adopting the approach of providing service rather than selling a product. This book offers helpful information and tools for such a practice. The book is also helpful to those who use or should use investment management consulting. It discusses the role and value of the consultant and the investment management consulting process.

The book provides the reader with the means to understand the investment management process and how to find value in a consultant and/or a portfolio design. The reader will learn what happens behind the scenes, how an allocation is designed and who or what investment vehicles will execute the plan. The book describes how to balance risk and return and how to measure both.

The elements of *Fiduciary Investing,* combined with *The Art and Science of Investment Management Consulting,* are also helpful to those tasked with developing investment strategies and finding solutions for the benefit of others, such as fiduciaries. The book describes how brokerage firms package the idea of managed money and provide strategic and tactical allocation techniques for model portfolios.

There's also information on the benefit of delegating to investment professionals, such as consultants and money managers, as well as how different market cycles and manager styles move in and out of vogue.

The Art and Science of Investment Management Consulting and *Fiduciary Investing* reflect many of the changes that have taken place in the industry during the last decade. Well-written and logically presented, this book is a valuable tool for the smart investment professional.

John P. Calamos, Sr.

Author's Guidance to the Reader

In order to be clear about the descriptions in this book, it is important to understand the terminology used. There are layers of professionals involved in the investment management consulting process and there is often some overlap in the terms used to describe them. The industry may use a technical term, whereas those not directly involved in the industry may use another. For the sake of consistency and better understanding, we have selected specific usages to be used throughout the book.

The **Investment Management Consultant or Consultant** is the individual or group that works directly with the client to develop an investment policy, design an appropriate asset allocation, provide performance analysis for manager searches, recommend money management firms, review performance and reallocate when appropriate. Consultants are responsible for understanding the capital markets and developing strategic asset allocation plans for an overall portfolio and then, continuing to monitor and evaluate the client's needs, the capital markets and the money managers.

Money managers are also referred to as Registered Investment Advisors (RIA) or Investment Advisors, however since "advisor" is widely used for many positions, we will refer to them as money managers in this book for clarity. These firms specialize in an investment style within the capital markets and are very focused in the types of securities that they buy for a client's portfolio. It is the money manager who makes the tactical day-to-day buy and sell decisions within their respective discipline, such as small capitalization value stocks, not the consultant or investor.

We will use the general term **"advisor"** for professionals who give investment advice to clients. These include stockbrokers, financial planners, insurance agents, CPAs, attorneys and perhaps others. In the context of this book, advisors may provide some of the services that a consultant does, however most of these investment professionals are not trained or skilled in the full range of consulting services.

Asset classes are distinct types of securities, such as equities (stocks), fixed income (bonds), convertible bonds, REITs (real estate investment trusts) and cash.

Styles are sub groups of the asset classes. Equities are an asset class, which can be divided into several styles, including small, mid and large capitalization stocks and each of these capitalizations can be further categorized as intrinsic value, relative value, core or growth. An individual style would be "small cap growth." Some limit the term "style" to value or growth, but in this book it is used to differentiate all sub groupings of securities. Fixed income securities include corporate, government, agency, municipals or variable rate securities. Preferred stocks trade on their dividend yield and are usually found in fixed income portfolios. Convertible bonds are bonds that can convert to equities and constitute a specific style. REITs are an asset class that can be broken into styles specific to the type of properties owned by the real estate trust, such as apartments, shopping malls, etc.

Separately managed accounts (SMA) require a process. Investment goals and objectives are established, money managers are recommended and selected, assets are placed with the managers who generally have discretion to buy and sell securities on behalf of the client. The client owns each of the securities individually, unlike buying a number of shares of a mutual fund, thus the assets are managed separately for a specific client. SMAs are also referred to as **wrap accounts,** as all elements of the account are "wrapped" together for a single (bundled) fee.

Market cycles often correspond to the economic clock, with periods of similar patterns at regular intervals. Areas of the capital markets tend to move in three to five year cycles, which generally correspond to valuations. When an area of the markets is out-of-favor, it becomes undervalued as it moves to the bottom of its market cycle. As money begins to move away from overvalued areas that are at the top of their cycle, there is generally a shift in allocations to the undervalued areas of the markets. This reflects the concept of buying value (low) and selling risk (high).

Broker/Dealer is any individual or firm in the business of buying and selling securities for itself and others.

Wirehouses are the larger broker/dealer firms whose branch offices are linked by a communications system that permits the rapid dissemination of pricing, information, and research relating to financial markets and individual securities. The term "wirehouse" dates back to the time when only the largest organizations had access to what was then high-speed communications, the telegraph wire system.

SECTION 1
Understanding Professionally Managed Accounts

1

The Art and Science of Investment Management Consulting

L ong-term, consistent investment returns are the goal of every serious investor; achieving that goal is the challenge of the investment professional. To meet that challenge, many tools and techniques have evolved to control risk, generate alpha, track performance and identify talent. The science of investment management consulting, the mathematical tools designed to analyze markets and performance, has evolved and expanded tremendously over the past three decades, creating volumes of additional data to be interpreted. It is the artisan, the experienced consultant, possessing a blend of experience and analytical understanding, who can bring clarity to this data, and effectively incorporate all elements of the process into a successful, dynamic investment strategy.

As the investment industry continues to expand, adding new offerings and investment platforms at a rapid pace, combined with the globalization of industries and economies, it is incumbent upon investment professionals to continually expand their knowledge-base. Whether you are a practicing consultant, an individual investor, or a trustee with fiduciary responsibility, there will always be a need to learn more about the investment process. Successful investment management is no accident, nor is there a single, fool proof method to achieve consistent results. There are however, time-tested techniques and methods that serve the investment consultant community and investors alike, and we are confident that this book will be a valuable resource for those who seek further insight into the processes of investment management consulting.

In the chapters that follow, many of the industry's tools and methodologies will be described, their merits and flaws discussed, their applications explained, and most significantly, the value that the consulting process offers will be demonstrated. We provide a historical perspective and our thoughts on the future direction of the profession. We believe that describing this evolution will better illustrate the value of a consistent, well thought out approach to the investment process. We will provide direction in selecting the right consultant, one who not only has a full understanding of the consulting process, but one who is appropriate for the needs of the client. It is this individual who will guide the process, therefore selecting the right consultant is the single, most important step in the establishment and maintenance of a successful investment strategy.

The consulting process involves several continuous and interwoven steps, beginning with the Investment Policy Statement. This first step identifies the investor's reason for investing and all investment decisions will be made as a result of these stated goals and objectives. Strategies are then structured to achieve the investor's *long-term* investment objective, which may occasionally be at odds with the short-term perspective of "beating the market." Investors and consultants are human; they have emotions that can, and sometimes do, interfere with good judgment, therefore it is the mission of the consultant to keep the process on track, striving to produce a consistent rate of return that will meet the investor's objectives, while exposing the portfolio to as little risk as practical. This goal was particularly difficult during the mania of the late 1990s, as investors' appetite for risk expanded with each high-flying dot com story. It was up to the consultant to keep the investor out of harm's way, but to do so, he or she had to understand the warning signs, which we describe in some detail in Chapter 11.

The investment strategy drives the asset allocation, which like everything in the industry, can be approached in many different ways. The sophistication of this process has evolved from a static equity/fixed income mix, to the dynamic processes of strategic and tactical overlays that we see today. During the 1980s and 1990s, the acceptance of the Modern Portfolio Theory (MPT) became widespread, as it offered a mathematical approach to producing consistent returns, while moderating portfolio volatility. MPT has its flaws though, and these became very evident by the late 1990s, as money poured into large cap growth stocks. Computer models produced using MPT algorithms rely heavily on past performance and the faulty assumption that a style or sector will continue producing their most recent performance (linear progression). The large cap growth data of the '90s overwhelmed the mathematical capabilities and assumptions of MPT, causing these models to become extremely overweighed in the most dangerous segment of the market, large cap growth. Consultants who were adept in capital market analysis, and who understood the limitations of MPT, were not lured into this trap. This was a challenging time for consultants, as the behavioral psychology of greed and fear caused many investors to abandon their long-term strategy. Consultants who were able to navigate through this difficult time were those who were empowered with the knowledge and tools described in the chapters that follow.

Exposing MPT's vulnerable underbelly on such a large scale, once again reinforced the need for the consulting process and the continual study of the capital markets. During the Bull market of the late 1990s, as the media touted "a new paradigm" for investing, some fundamentalists and a growing number of market technicians were expressing great concern over the market's valuation. This concern was not clearly understood by many within the industry and their clients paid the price. Fundamental and technical analyses are two widely accepted methods of investment analysis used by investment management professionals to identify opportunities and risks within the capital markets. The fundamental approach includes financial analysis, balance sheet analysis, Fed watching, and macro economic and earnings forecasts to name just a few; whereas, technical analysis is focused on the market itself. Technical analysis includes trend analysis, chart patterns, historical cycles and trend patterns, moving averages and momentum indicators. The science of both fundamental and technical market analysis are based on years of theoretical and practical experience, using widely accepted tools and techniques that can, at certain crossroads, find themselves in opposition to one another. Accepting, integrating and using both methods requires a pragmatic, open mind, which is truly an art form in itself. We explore the advantages of understanding both disciplines and describe when and how to integrate their use into a portfolio's design. Investing in the capital markets of the new millennium requires a dynamic approach to asset allocation, which integrates the merits of both fundamental and technical analyses. This approach allows consultants to proactively reallocate away from high-risk areas of the markets and toward areas of opportunity.

There are many approaches to implementing an asset allocation strategy and varying levels of skill within the industry. Many Wall Street firms have chosen to centralize a "think tank" and have hired very talented market strategists to design model portfolios and to make recommendations to the firm's broker/advisors, some with great success. To further this process, most firms have continued to develop platforms that can take advantage of this talent and have encouraged their broker/advisors to leverage this talent by using these structured platforms, most of which incorporate the attributes of separate account management and fee-based relationships. The proliferation of these platforms, as well as the introduction of new products, such as exchange traded funds (ETF), continues to broaden the need for due diligence and an understanding of their features, uses and suitability. We describe these platforms and discuss how to discern value in the format of the platform and, evaluate the skills of the individuals responsible for creating and recommending the model designs. We will also describe the costs associated with these and other types of investing strategies.

Consultants, who do not rely solely on these structured platforms, focus their efforts on market analysis, asset allocation, and the selection and evaluation of professional money managers. The task of finding, selecting, reallocating and terminating money managers has been a primary role of the professional investment management consultant since the 1970s, when the use of money managers was restricted to the institutional-type investor. Now, many of these managers are available to a much broader range of investor through brokerage firm separate (wrap) account platforms. There are thousands of great money managers to choose from, employing many styles and disciplines of portfolio management, such as value, growth, large cap, small cap, domestic and international. The consultant must employ a process of qualitative and quantitative analysis to determine a manager's suitability in an overall portfolio design. This evaluation, once again, requires the science of analyzing performance data, blended with the skill to interpret and integrate the data into a successful, long-term investment strategy.

Every year, there are a number of new or emerging managers that enter the marketplace. As their assets continue to grow, consultants attempting to add value will not overlook these potential diamonds in the rough. The well-known mega managers of today, once brought their entrepreneurial spirit to the industry as emerging managers. This spirit continues to flourish and it is important that consultants continue to explore this segment of the manager space, in order to continually provide the best talent available to their clients.

The manager due diligence process does not stop after the manager is hired; it continues throughout the engagement. There must be an ongoing monitoring and evaluation system in place to detect changes in the manager's structure, performance or style, as well as changes in the capital markets that may affect either a manager's style, or the overall allocation of the portfolio. Money management firms change over time; they may grow too fast to maintain their investment discipline, they may be acquired by a much larger financial services firm causing a change in focus or attitude or, they may lose key personnel. Any internal change that may affect the consistency of management results is a red flag to the consultant.

Markets also change with time. There are times when a specific manager style will work well, and times when it will not. As market cycles mature, they often become overvalued. This can cause the risk profile of the portfolio to exceed tolerances, as they did in 2000. To truly add value, the consultant must act, and proactively reallocate to reduce exposure of dangerously overvalued segments of the markets and increase allocations to areas that offer more opportunity. It is up to the consultant to determine if a manager's performance is the result of being in the right place (style) at the right time or, if the manager adds true value (alpha). Put another way, "Is the manager lucky or good?" If the investor's needs or circumstances change, this too may require reallocation. An effective monitoring and reevaluation process is vital to the long-term success of the investment strategy.

No comprehensive book on investment management consulting would be complete if it did not address the responsibilities associated with fiduciary investing. The rules are complex and the penalties for non-compliance can be harsh. Many people unknowingly become fiduciaries through their involvement with a plan or trust's assets, while many others voluntarily take on the role of fiduciary without fully comprehending their legal obligations or, the consequences of failing to comply with the required standards of care. *Fiduciary Investing* (Section V) is devoted to the fiduciary investor.

Fiduciaries at every level are subject to growing scrutiny and are expected to carry out their duties with ever-increasing levels of skill. The "Prudent Man Rule" has transitioned to the "Prudent Expert Rule," and fiduciaries are now bound to the standards of care set forth in the UPIA and ERISA. These standards, combined with the tenants of the Modern Portfolio Theory, have motivated fiduciaries to seek out investment professionals to assist them in fulfilling their duties, and to minimize their potential exposure to personal liability. The chapters in *Fiduciary Investing* (Section V) provide an overview of the legal requirements for fiduciaries of trusts, as well as those who must comply with the demands of ERISA. Special care and a thorough understanding of these requirements are needed to properly fulfill one's duties as a fiduciary, and are crucial in avoiding unwanted liability exposure.

There is no shortage of individuals wanting to share their investment knowledge and there are hundreds of excellent books written on the subject of making money in the capital markets. Each one focuses on a specific style or approach, and many have proven track records. Professional investment management consultants understand that most investors are not interested in learning how to become a professional money manager or, in risking capital to test an investment strategy. Most serious investors are interested in working with a seasoned professional who will help them achieve their goals at an acceptable level of risk. The consulting process is an effective way to achieve this goal and this book was written to enhance the skills of investors and consultants seeking to increase their knowledge of intelligent investment management.

Some investors believe you have to be lucky to make money in the capital markets. Consultants know otherwise and believe in the popular adage: "Luck is created when you cross opportunity with preparation." The world of investing is no different; the markets are full of opportunity, and the disciplined application of time-tested tools (science), under the watchful eye of a seasoned investment management consultant (art), is the preparation that creates "luck."

2

A Historical Perspective

Separately Managed Accounts, SMAs, had their infancy in the 1970s as Wrap Accounts. Today, they are the primary focus of most brokerage firms. Few are aware of their origins or those who contributed to their development, so in this chapter, we will provide a brief history of the three main elements of SMAs and the pioneers within this industry.

- The account structures and the firms that developed them
- The fee structure
- The changing role of the Consultant

In doing so, the reader will have a better understanding of the structure and flexibility of the separately managed account today. There have been many innovations in the industry, all designed to bring the advantages of separately managed accounts to a wider range of investor. By knowing the evolution of this investment philosophy, one can better select the investment professionals and structure to meet their needs.

Prior to 1974, the only accounts that were separately managed by professional money managers were those in excess of the $5 to 10 million minimums required by the institutional money managers. The money managers and the investor worked directly with one another, although the investor may have employed the services of a consultant. Assets were probably held at a bank trust department and trades were done at the trading desk/s that the managers selected.

In the early '70s, the two firm sponsored managed money departments were Prudential Bache and E.F. Hutton and Company. Prudential Bache began developing a separate account management program and in 1973, with the leadership of James Lockwood, E.F. Hutton and Company formed the Consulting Group with the intent of "wrapping" the process together. The consultant would advise the investor and recommend the managers, and custody, administration and trading would be done at E.F. Hutton. These services were provided for a single "wrapped" fee. Managers were contracted separately (dual contract). Hutton began to offer investment consulting to their retail clients in 1974, but did not begin firm-wide marketing and sales for its brokers until 1976. Another key element in the development of separate account management was May Day. On May 1, 1975, the Securities and Exchange Commission ended the fixed transaction commission schedule, making it possible for per trade commissions to become less expensive. Prior to this change, fee-based accounts would not have been possible.

ERISA passed in September of 1974, and all pension and profit-sharing plans had to be in compliance by the end of 1975. The mandates of ERISA are discussed in *Fiduciary Investing* (Section V). The passing of ERISA was significant in both the growth of professional money management and the need for qualified Investment Management Consultants, because the Modern Portfolio Theory (Chapter 9) could now be applied to pension fund management. Prior to this change, bank trust departments, using a single style, had been the norm for managing these funds, using a buy-and-hold philosophy. Now, active portfolio management and asset allocation could be used. Performance improved and actively managed accounts grew, creating the need for more money management firms and Investment Management Consultants (Consultants).

Consultants took the lead in allocating funds into multiple asset classes that could improve returns and reduce risk. They were also responsible for conducting manager searches, monitoring performance and creating performance benchmarks. These consultants then devised a means of incorporating the use of risk-adjusted returns for portfolio manager evaluation, which has since become a widespread means of performance monitoring. Consultants provided investment guidelines, a means of adjusting asset allocations and promoted innovative new asset classes to corporate boardrooms. The consultants were independent of the money management firms and therefore the plan sponsors felt comfortable that there were fewer conflicts of interest associated with their advice.

These changes marshaled in a process-oriented approach to pension fund management and most would agree that the increasing influence of Investment

Management Consultants had a positive effect on the overall performance of pension funds. It also fostered the development of money management firms that specialized in unique investment styles, since these consultants were able to provide an objective basis by which these new styles could be properly evaluated and incorporated into asset allocation decisions.

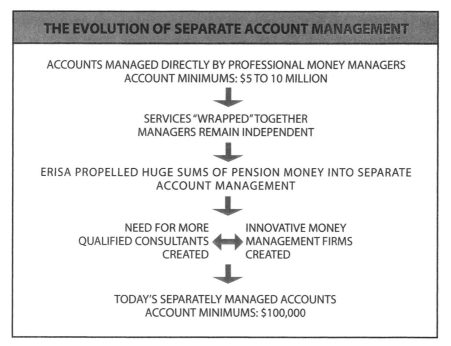

Illustration 2-1

George Ball, then president of E. F. Hutton, considered pension funds an excellent market for their new program to penetrate and indeed, ERISA helped to move their concept to a new level. By the 1980s the assets of E.F. Hutton's Consulting Group exceeded $1 billion and slowly, other firms began to join the party. It was not until 1987 that the other major firms, Merrill Lynch, Dean Witter and Paine Webber, began to test the separate account management waters, launching their own wrap account platforms. The E.F. Hutton program, through many mergers, became the Consulting Group at Smith Barney.

Now, most firms have separately managed account (wrap) programs, and due to the economies of scale derived from the money management firms' association with the brokerage firms, these managers have account minimums of $50,000 to $250,000, with $100,000 being the norm.

We will now look at the incarnation of the major elements of separately managed account, mainly the money managers, the fee structure and the consultant. We believe that describing this evolution will help in understanding the structure of today's Separately Managed Account.

EARLY SEPARATE ACCOUNT MANAGERS

In the 1970s, a few small entrepreneurial money management firms and individuals recognized both the value and opportunity that wrap accounts (separately managed accounts - SMAs) could represent, and began offering them to their clients with minimums of $1 to 5 million, the "smaller accounts." These managers built a comfortable base of business with these smaller accounts and grew rapidly. That original handful of firms grew from a base of $100 million to over $1 billion in just a few short years. A large number of these small firms grew too fast to manage the back office administration that accompanied their growth. Consequently, their initial level of enthusiasm, interest, and client cooperation soon changed—and not for the better. In order to make their growth more manageable, they began to increase their minimum account size, which quickly eliminated the smaller investors...again. The heat was back on for consultants and brokerage firms to find managers who would take on smaller accounts. Finding a solution to these administrative issues was a constant challenge for both the consultant and the industry.

Wall Street finally determined that instead of looking for money management firms that would provide all of the administrative services, and manage the portfolios, the brokerage firms would attempt to solve the administrative problems internally. The brokerage firms would hire the money management firms as sub-advisors, take over client servicing and assume the burden of account record keeping, custodianship, account separation, billing and printing of statements, as well as maintaining the client relationship. This approach would leave the money manager free to focus on their real expertise—investing money. Economies of scale came into play as the money manager now found it easy and attractive to offer their services at reduced fees, as the administrative burden had been lifted. Wall Street had developed a win-win format. The money managers could concentrate on managing portfolios, the minimum account size was more attractive to a wider range of clients, and the consultant could concentrate on client relationships and asset allocation.

ACCOUNT STRUCTURE

Today, there are two basic SMA structures that money management firms and brokerage firms offer to their clients and they both had their roots at E.F. Hutton. The first program that E. F. Hutton offered was "Suggest." There was a direct agreement between the money management firm and the investor. The money manager communicated directly with the investor, and the investor had two separate contracts, one between the investor and the money management firm for the management of the portfolio, and one between the investor and the brokerage firm, which included all recordkeeping and administrative requirements, as well as the consultant relationship. This dual contract arrangement is still popular, but it is used almost exclusively by more seasoned consultants who research money management firms themselves, thus giving them a broader range of investment talent to offer their clients.

The Birth of the Sub-Advisory Wrap Account

The second program that Hutton (soon to become Shearson Lehman Hutton) created was called "Select." Select utilized a single contract between the client and Hutton. In this relationship, Hutton hired the money manager as a sub-advisor and all administration and communications, including client communications, were handled through Hutton. Hutton used several money management firms with whom Hutton already had a strong working relationship, and relied on these managers to provide the best service to their investors.

To implement this approach, Hutton placed computers with proprietary software on-site with each money management firm. Every morning, the independent money manager was informed of new accounts opened by Hutton and then he or she could call the Hutton trading desk to place the orders. Hutton took care of everything from there. They created, in effect, a workable administrative "highway." The brokerage firms then sent their own marketing people around to familiarize their own in-house brokers with these money management firms and the Select program. That move proved to be a very valuable use of resources. In both formats, single and dual contracts, brokerage firms had their own in-house managers, but as the industry grew, this "highway" was made available to independent money management firms, thus broadening the choices available to investors.

When Shearson Lehman Brothers acquired the firm E. F. Hutton in 1988, they became the biggest and the best overnight due, in large part, to E. F. Hutton's initial development of the Select program for wrap fee accounts. Shearson then took the next step and made managed money available to all of its brokers. Although it was a brilliant business decision at Hutton to launch the program, it was Shearson's willingness to mass market the program that made it the success it is today.

Most brokerage firms and advisors today use programs modeled after the Hutton's "Select" prototype. The investor is not the client of the money management firm, but rather the brokerage firm. These programs allow the brokerage firm to maintain some control over the number and quality of managers that are recommended to clients. The brokerage firms review the qualifications of the money management firms and perform the due diligence required before they select participants for their firm's SMA program. The brokerage firm holds the assets and is the custodian of the securities. They are also responsible for all back office and administrative functions, including transactions. Part of this arrangement generally includes reduced fees charged by the money management firm to the brokerage firm due to the large amount of assets that flow to the management firm through the brokerage firm. As brokerage firms bring in more and more managed money accounts, they are able to spread their costs over a larger base and their costs go down accordingly, to the benefit of both the investor and the firm. Brokerage firms have also established their own trading desks for money managers, which helps keep the manager's costs under control. These relationships, and the technology that supports them, have helped put a competitive fee lid on money management firms.

FEE STRUCTURE

In developing the Suggests program, and then the Select program, E. F. Hutton needed to decide how to charge the customer for all of the services involved. Richard Shilffarth was an early pioneer in the "wrap" account development, consulting with many individuals and firms in the development of their "wrap" programs. He worked out the first "wrap fee" program model for E. F. Hutton in 1975. He first calculated the total sum of the "Suggests" Accounts assets.

Next, he calculated the average commissions for all of the accounts and arrived at a figure of 1.9%. He rounded that number to 2% and added a 1% fee to the manager, resulting in an even 3% total on assets under $500,000, and assigned a 2% wrap fee for assets exceeding $500,000. Schilffarth called it a "wrap fee," because it represented wrapping together fees for services, which included: The manager's fee, the cost of executing the trade, clearing the trade, custody of the securities, collecting dividends and interest, paying out dividends and interest, as well as serving the client. The result was an all-inclusive, single fee that was charged to the investor (Illustration 2-2). This fee structure has changed little over the years, although the average fee charged is lower today (Illustration 2-3).

ORIGINAL 1975 WRAP FEE SCHEDULE

Assets	Total Client Fee	Manager	Firm/Broker
$0-500,000	3.0%	1.0%	2.0%
OVER $500,000	2.0%	1.0%	1.0%

Illustration 2-2

Shilffarth believed that there was an inherent conflict of interest when one has the authority to determine how often he or she trades, and stands to earn commissions on those trades. The all-inclusive "wrap fee" effectively solved that conflict, once May Day had opened the door to fee-based accounts.

Today, we see two basic fee structures. The first is the single contract, which is all-inclusive, bundling the money manager fee with the fee paid to the brokerage firm (Illustration 2-3). A single contract is used when the client has a single contract with the brokerage firm and the money manager is contracted with the brokerage firm as a sub-advisor. As the following tables illustrate, the manager fees tend to be lower, due to the brokerage firm's "volume discount" negotiations. The brokerage firm makes a limited number of managers available to its broker network and therefore management firms are likely to receive increased assets through this arrangement (Chapter 4). Consultants who provide independent manager research and recommend managers that are not part of a sub-advisory program, use the second structure, the dual contract (Illustration 2-4).

TYPICAL SINGLE CONTRACT FEE SCHEDULE

Assets	Total Client Fee	Manager	Firm/Advisor
$0-500,000	3.0%	.5%	2.5%
Next $500,000	2.5%	.5%	2.0%
Over $1,000,000	2.0%	.5%	1.5%
Over $5,000,000	1.5%	.5%	1.0%

Illustration 2-3

Dual contracts are used when a consultant recommends a money manager that is not part of a brokerage firm's pre-selected group or when the investor has a direct relationship with a manager and chooses to use the consultant's firm for administrative services, custody and trades. One contract is between the investor and the money management firm, and the other is between the investor and the brokerage firm. When using dual contracts, there are two fees charged and the cost to the client will be slightly higher, as the money manager will charge their customary rate, versus the fees that brokerage firms negotiate with their sub-advisors (Illustration 2-4). Occasionally, particularly with institutional type clients, the fees may be completely unbundled, resulting in separate fees paid to the consultant, custodian, money management firm and commissions for trades (Chapter 5). The industry has adapted to accommodate the needs of most types of clients.

TYPICAL DUAL CONTRACT FEE SCHEDULE

Assets	Total Client Fee	Manager	Firm/Advisor
$0-500,000	3.0%	1.0%	2.0%
Next $500,000	2.5%	1.0%	1.5%
Over $1,000,000	2.0%	1.0%	1.0%
Over $5,000,000	1.5%	.75%	.75%

Illustration 2-4

Both the manager fees and the fees paid to the brokerage firm (which includes the consultant fee), are regressive. The more money that is invested, the lower the overall fee is likely to be. Generally, fees can be negotiated and the ones represented here show no discounts.

THE CONSULTANT

The consultant's role has been evolving since the early '70s, when the pioneering institutional consultants, representing just a few firms, most notably A.G. Becker (later to become SCI), Callan Associates and Frank Russell, targeted the $25 million and higher market. At this time, there were also a handful of broker/consultants targeting middle market institutions, investing $1 to 50 million. In those early years, the broker/consultant conducted manager searches, since there were no research departments available to assist them. In the early '70s, it was unrealistic to think of using a money manager unless the investor had $10 million or more to invest.

It was the evolution of the broker/consultant, which began in 1970 at Butcher Singer, which paved the way to the lower account minimums. Butcher Singer, who through many mergers became Wachovia Securities, became one of the first few financial services firms to offer consulting services. At approximately the same time, a group of individual account executives at Kidder Peabody created their own internal network for exchanging money manager information at lower account minimums in the late '70s, but it was limited to this small group. When E. F. Hutton and Prudential, introduced firm-sponsored programs and made them available to all of their brokers in 1974, a new challenge arose. How do transaction-trained brokers become consultants? Hutton began the first training program in 1976, but the industry needed more.

Investment management consulting became more widespread in the mid to late '80s, as more brokerage firms developed wrap programs. By 1990, those who had maintained a fee-based consulting practice realized that utilizing professional money managers was a much more efficient way to conduct business and retain their client's assets. Still, most retail brokers opted for the big commission tickets, such as tax-sheltered investments and unit trusts. When market conditions changed in the mid to late '80s, and the tax-shelter business dried up, many of those still doing big business were the broker/consultants using wrap accounts, which have evolved into today's separately managed accounts. These early broker/consultants should be credited with putting separately managed accounts on the map and elevating the value and use of investment management consultants to the level of recognition that they enjoy today.

By the late '80s, the industry was growing rapidly. Many brokers, advisors and financial planners had begun selling managed money, but learned that the investment management consulting process was quite different than that of product sales. Both the industry and a growing number of brokers and advisor recognized that there needed to be a way to train consultants. In order to bridge the gap between sales and process, early consultants and industry pioneers, Jim Owen and Daniel Bott, collaborated to form IMCA, the Investment Management Consultants Association in 1985 and later, in 1988, Daniel Bott (co-author of this book) launched IIMC, the Institute for Investment Management Consults.

IMCA focused on providing an association for consultants and later adopted an extension study program from Wharton, catering to product department heads, analysts and a growing list of consultants and money manager sales reps. IIMC provided a six-month private study program designed for all levels of consulting. IIMC was devoted specifically to honing the skills of the practicing consultant and was not open to those who were associated with money management firms. In 2002, under heavy pressure from the money management industry, the two organizations merged to form one industry voice under the name Investment Management Consultants Association and there is no longer a focus solely on the practicing consultant. The new merged group sponsors various conferences where money managers and consultants can network and consultants can attend continuing educational lectures. IMCA provides publications and educational programs and is the sponsor of the CIMA program for its members.

We believe the continued growth of the professional investment management consulting business is assured. Those who are planning to be part of the investment business for the long-term, say for twenty years or more, recognize that they must consistently add value for their clients. Consulting is more labor intensive and perhaps not always as personally satisfying as making the big sale or as exciting as buying a "hot" stock and realizing dramatic gains, but the process does provide the value and consistency that most investors seek. Consistency and process builds the type of relationships between clients and the consultant that enables investment plans to become successful.

CONCLUSION

Separate account management was once available only to institutional sized investors and now, due to the efforts and creativity of many individuals, especially the broker/consultant, these accounts are now available to a much larger marketplace. The combination of the information age and advanced computer technology has created an extremely fast-paced market and the individual investor is in search of the same high quality investment management as the corporate plan sponsor. No matter the size of the portfolio, the investor wants it managed in a manner that will provide the highest probability of success.

The managed money process has continued to grow and evolve to meet that need. At the end of 2004, there was approximately $270 billion in broker-based separately managed accounts and by the end of March 2006, that number exceeded $735 billion dollars[1]. Impressive growth by any standard, with new programs and opportunities being continually offered and explored by all major and most of the smaller brokerage and advisory firms. The institutional account market still dwarfs the broker-based SMA market, and the combination of the two continues to increase the expectations for quality and service from money managers. Many mutual fund providers are also offering SMAs and today the lines between mutual fund companies and SMAs have become less defined. Having an understanding of the evolution of the investment management consulting process, gives the investor the basis for developing an effective investment management plan. We will spend the balance of this book discussing the elements of this process, the types of programs offered and the tools used by the Consultant.

1. Money Management Institute.

3

Differentiating Separately Managed (Wrap) Accounts and Mutual Funds

We have discussed how separately managed accounts have evolved and now we will compare them to mutual funds. Most investors are familiar with mutual funds and know them to be professionally managed and generally diversified within each fund. By combining a bond fund, an international fund and say a blue chip fund, most investors believe that they can be adequately diversified. This approach is reasonable for smaller pools of money, as the minimum investment is often as low as $250 per fund.

When dealing with larger investments however, there are many advantages to investing in separately managed accounts. The investor has the benefit of a consultant, an experienced money management firm and on-going performance monitoring. This level of service generally exceeds that provided when investing in mutual funds. Most brokerage firms now provide platforms to the money management firms that allow them to lower their minimum account size to $100,000 or less. Lower minimums have opened the door for many more investors to consider the advantages and disadvantages that each type of investment presents.

There are many differences between a separately managed account and a mutual fund. We will compare several of the more important differences in this chapter, which include:

- Ownership
- Management
- Transparency
- Performance
- Control and Flexibility
- Costs
- Tax management

HOW MONEY IS SEPARATED AND MANAGED

A mutual fund is a co-mingled pool of assets that is managed by a Registered Investment Advisor (RIA), who is the fund's money manager. The investor owns shares or units of the mutual fund, not individual securities. All investors in the fund own undivided interests in the same portfolio of securities.

A separately managed account is a portfolio of securities, which are owned individually by the investor and are also managed by an RIA. There is no co-mingling of funds or securities allowing the money manager to work solely for the benefit of the individual investor. We will cover several key advantages that separate ownership affords in portfolio management, such as tax management and purchase restrictions.

HOW CAN FUND CHARTERS AFFECT RETURNS?

Most mutual funds have a mandate to remain close to fully invested. During times of mania, the fund manager has to invest new money, regardless of the prices they have to pay. During times of panic, the fund manager must sell (often at the worst time), in order to have cash available to meet shareholder redemptions. Both of these actions might significantly impact the performance of the fund and therefore, the individual investor. The investors in a fund have no say in the matter. The manager of a separately managed account makes buy and sell decisions solely on their merit. The manager is not forced into these emotionally driven decisions.

Returns are affected by the stock selections that make up the portfolio. This is an obvious statement, however what is not so obvious is that the number of different securities in the portfolio can also affect performance. The manager of an SMA will probably achieve better results by screening down to his or her favorite 40 or 50 stocks, while some mutual funds may have to buy hundreds of different stocks to meet the volume and liquidity needs of the fund.

On the surface, mutual funds and separately managed accounts are both managed by professional money managers who make the decisions to buy or sell each stock that is in the portfolio. Both portfolios are generally well diversified and generally, quite liquid. In both cases, the style and philosophy of the money manager is stated, i.e., large cap growth, mid cap value or fixed income, allowing the investor or advisor to allocate between asset classes and styles. But, what goes on behind the scenes may not be what the investor had intended.

WHO IS ACTUALLY MANAGING YOUR MONEY?

Manager turnover in funds can be significant and it is rarely made visible to the public. Commonly, after a well known portfolio manager stops managing a fund, such as Peter Lynch and the Magellan fund, the fund may have to go through several new managers before they find someone (if ever) whose performance is comparable to the manager who left. Funds do not advertise manager turnover. When reviewing funds or separate account management, look for consistency of management, philosophy and style over the years. The historical numbers mean very little if there is someone new at the helm. This information is available if you know where to look.

Many very successful fund managers gravitate to independent firms for better compensation and partnership opportunities. The loss of such a manager may seriously affect the performance of the fund. Separate account managers may leave as well, so part of the investor or advisor due diligence process must address this issue. Remember, someone is managing or directing the management of the portfolio, including the criteria used for buying and selling stocks, to achieve the performance numbers that the investor and/or advisor is reviewing. This person is also responsible for maintaining the firm's philosophy and adherence to investment style. Know everything that you can about this person.

Mutual funds are notorious for style drift. Style drift means that a small cap manager may put a large cap stock in the portfolio because they are chasing performance. There can also be tremendous overlap of securities from fund to fund, so it is important to determine the holdings in a fund, not just the reported style. Style drift and overlap of securities can seriously affect the realities of diversification and proper asset allocation. Managers of SMAs are less likely to style drift due to their transparency, but improper asset allocation to managers with similar styles is likely to result in an overlap of securities.

If the manager is new to the firm, what was his or her performance in their last position? What is his or her background and investment philosophy? Insist on knowing the background and track record of anyone who has been the lead portfolio manager for less than 2 years. Unfortunately, most sales or service representatives of mutual funds do not have this information. Conversely, the representatives of independent money management firms tend to be well informed. Many of these firms have active founder/s, who are often still the portfolio managers, whereas the average age of portfolio managers in the mutual fund industry is under 30 years of age. As a rule, portfolio managers of separately managed accounts have significantly longer track records than those of fund managers. In addition, investors generally have access to the portfolio manager of their SMA, whereas this is not the case with mutual fund managers.

TRANSPARENCY

Separately managed accounts are generally updated daily and a list of holdings and the account activity (buys and sells) are readily available to the investor. Mutual funds generally only provide a listing of holdings once a year with the annual report, although some may also provide holdings with the semi annual report. An individual (investor or advisor) can call the fund at any time and ask about the holdings, but the account-servicing people generally only have the top ten holdings and these are only updated quarterly or occasionally, monthly. Advisors, but usually not individual investors, can sometimes obtain more complete information, but generally the funds only provide the top 10 holdings. Information that is more complete may be available through Morningstar.com, but only with the purchase of their software. Morningstar lists holdings, but the information is only as timely as that which the fund provides.

Who cares? An investor may have chosen a fund because it was heavily weighted in a sector that the investor felt was poised for growth and/or not overvalued, but at some point, the portfolio manager changed strategy and began to chase returns in a highly overvalued area of the market. This quest for higher returns by fund managers can be quite common in markets such as those that in the late 1990s. Many portfolios with few or no tech stocks suddenly became very overweighted in tech. Good or Bad? If the investor was interested in returns without regard to risk, maybe it was all right, however if the fund was chosen specifically for its perceived valuation, style and risk profile, then the intended asset allocation was no longer valid. This change in strategy was common in the late 1990s and many investors got a very bad surprise in the early 2000s.

Knowing the holdings in a portfolio is also important when making asset allocation decisions among different styles. Investors and advisors strive to achieve proper diversification when selecting different managers or funds, which means that there should be little, if any, overlap of the securities that are held by each. Separate account management makes preventing excess overlap very easy, because the list of each manager's holdings is current and readily available. As you can see from the above discussion, this need for transparency can be quite a challenge with mutual funds. We described style drift earlier in this chapter, and saw that the investor cannot rely solely on the name of the fund and the top ten holdings to indicate the content or philosophy of the entire fund. It is common to see significant overlap in separate accounts or funds with similar names (large cap growth), or in funds within a fund family. Three separate accounts or funds, each with a 40% overlap of securities, are not adequate diversification. As you can see, holdings are a key element in proper diversification and asset allocation.

TURNOVER RATE

The average mutual fund turnover rate is approximately 100%[1]. Many funds have a significantly higher rate, while others are lower. The turnover rate is important, because whatever taxable events the fund generates become taxable gains to the investor, even if the investor did not personally have a profit in the fund. We describe how "phantom gains" can occur later in this chapter under "Tax Planning." Also, the fund's turnover rate will affect the transaction costs within the fund and therefore the funds performance.

Comparatively, the securities in separately managed accounts are individually owned, the turnover rate is often much lower, there are no transaction costs and the managers strive to make the taxable gains long-term. Understanding a manager's turnover rate is another area where knowing the fund and manager's investment philosophy can help to achieve investor goals, as some aggressive managers can have substantial turnover.

HISTORICAL PERFORMANCE

Many fall into the trap of looking only at the last few years of performance numbers, without looking deeper. A three-year average return can look good if year-one was great, year-two mediocre and year-three terrible. Unless you look at each year and compare the results to market conditions and an appropriate benchmark, the three-year average can be very misleading. By looking at the

1. Richard Rutner in "The Trouble with Mutual Funds."

last 10 years or 20 years or even since inception, a much different picture may evolve. It is important to know what the performance has been during the bad years, as well as the good, in order to better understand the risk that a manager takes to produce results. Look at the performance in 1987, 1990, 1993, 1994 and 2000 to 2002. Make these comparisons when looking at both mutual funds and SMAs. Style plays a role in performance, because the results may be a matter of being in the right place at the right time. It is when that particular style is out of favor that an investor or advisor can learn the most from performance numbers (Chapter 18).

Most mutual fund companies have numerous funds in their "family of funds." Some companies cleverly run ads about the performance of a single fund and use specific "to and from" dates, which represent a period of particularly high returns. The next year or quarter, they may use a different fund from their family in their ads. Selling the sizzle is not unusual for a family of funds. Thus far, SMAs advertise very little and are very style specific therefore, what you see is generally what you get. Before recommending any manager or fund, a consultant or advisor should go through a thorough process of due diligence to decipher true performance.

CONTROL AND FLEXIBILITY

The portfolio manager has full control over all buy and sell decisions in both types of accounts, as they are both generally discretionary. However, with a separately managed account, the investor can customize the portfolio to more effectively meet his or her needs. The investor can instruct the manager to sell specific securities for personal reasons, such as tax management, or restrict the purchase of certain types of stocks, such as tobacco stocks. Additionally, if the investor has specific holdings in other accounts, i.e., company stock, these can be excluded from the portfolio. Customization is not available with mutual funds, since the investor only owns shares of the fund, not shares of securities. It is only in SMAs that stocks showing loses can be sold to offset gains and thus help to manage tax liabilities. The separate ownership of securities is a great advantage to those who wish to manage their cash flow and tax liabilities.

Mutual funds have a mandate to maintain a tight range of cash as a percentage of the portfolio. A mutual fund must keep a certain amount of cash on hand, un-invested, in case there are fund redemptions. This un-invested money will not perform as well as securities, assuming the fund is doing well and in this case, acts as a drain on the overall performance of the fund. If there are significant redemptions due to market conditions or a panic, the fund will be forced to sell securities to meet these redemptions, whether the fund manager believes it is a wise or tax-efficient move or not. Panics are often the best times to buy, but due to the redemptions, most funds are not able to take advantage of buying opportunities. During manias, or "panic buying," the mutual fund manager must invest the money, regardless of the prices that have to be paid. A separately managed account can remain fully invested, or if market conditions dictate, the manager can hold a large cash position. During times of mania or panic, the manager can act prudently and manage the portfolio in the best interests of the individual investor.

INVESTMENT REQUIREMENTS

An investor can open a mutual fund account with as little as $250 and make small monthly contributions to the fund. This money buys shares or units in the co-mingled fund.

Separately managed account minimums are generally $100,000, which is used to buy individual securities.

COSTS—MUTUAL FUNDS

Different Share Classes

Mutual funds were originally developed to provide professional money management to the smaller investor (under $100,000) and to do so at a moderate expense. Investors are very interested in having professional management and diversification, and are often unaware of any alternatives. Large investors who invest in mutual funds end up subsidizing the smaller investor, since there are no price breaks on the expense ratios. SMAs can offer significant advantages in both fees and flexibility for the larger investor.

The cost structure of mutual funds is complex and to understand the fees and charges, we will review the "alphabet" of mutual funds. It is important to examine and understand the charges within the fund, as these will affect overall performance. It may be interesting to note that industry fees as a whole are rising, not decreasing and comparisons are even more important than ever.

A mutual fund that charges a sales commission is called a load fund and is referred to as an "A" share. The load or sales commission is usually between 3% and 6%, depending on the amount invested and these charges are usually deducted from the initial investment. Refer to the "break points" in the prospectus to determine the sales commission. The more an investor invests with a fund family, the lower the percentage sales commission. In 2003, the mutual fund industry fell under severe scrutiny regarding this point, as well as other practices within the industry. It was determined that an individual investor, for purposes of break points, could include (1) the aggregate amount that was invested by any related person with a single fund family, (2) in any share class or even any product (mutual funds and 529 plans) sponsored by the fund family, and (3) from any number of points-of-sale that were used (different brokerage firms, direct, on-line services). These are all to be combined per fund family to determine the appropriate breakpoints.

"B" shares are funds that do not have up front sales commissions, but there is usually a penalty for early redemption. Because there is no sales commission, they are often erroneously called "no-load" funds, however a true no-load fund has no commission or penalty for early redemption. When a "B" share is sold to an investor, the fund pays the advisor a commission for selling the fund and the fund then expenses the amount of the commission on their books and amortizes the expense out over say 6 to 8 years. Since the fund does not bill the investor at the time of purchase, there must be a mechanism in place to recoup the commission dollars paid out. The funds recoup these dollars by charging additional fees (12b-1) and charging a penalty (CDSC) if the fund is sold before the surrender period has elapsed. After the surrender period, "B" shares can convert to "A" shares, reducing or eliminating the 12b-1 fees, thus reducing the internal costs of owning the fund. Most brokerage firms limit the dollar amount ($250,000 to $500,000) that may be invested in "B" shares by any one client, as the SEC has increased scrutiny on the suitability of "B" shares.

12b-1 fees allow the fund to charge an annual fee for distribution and marketing costs. They allow the fund to develop different options to pay sales charges and provide encouragement to the advisor to sell more shares to the public, but not all funds charge these fees. Rule 12b-1 was adopted in 1980 and although not its original intent, 12b-1 fees provide compensation to the advisor in the form of annual (paid quarterly) trails, for his or her ongoing oversight of the fund and advice to the investor. 12b-1 fees are invisible to the investor and have also fallen under SEC scrutiny. The ultimate goal of the SEC is to make all fees fair and visible to the investor, so many believe that there will be some changes in SEC regulations regarding this issue in the future.

CDSC, contingent deferred sales charge, is the surrender charge for liquidating "B" shares before the fund has recouped the fee that it paid out as a sales commission. There is a penalty schedule for early liquidations, which can be as high as 8% of the net asset value of the fund in the first year. This penalty decreases each year thereafter until it is zero. Remember, the fund paid out the commission when the purchase was made and there will be a surrender charge until this commission is recouped through the 12b-1 fee. It is at this point that the shares can be converted to "A" shares.

"C" shares are something of a hybrid between "A" and "B" shares. There is generally a small load, 1 or 2%, and the surrender period is usually only 12 to 18 months. The surrender charge (CDSC) for early liquidation is generally 1%. These shares will not convert to "A" shares and therefore the internal costs (12b-1) will remain high throughout the holding period of the fund. The advisor or investor should carefully consider the potential holding period of these shares prior to purchase.

SHARE CLASS	LOADS	12b-1 FEES	CDSC
A shares	Front end	Small or none	None
B shares	Back end	Yes, usually 0.75%	Yes
C shares	Small front end and small back end	Yes, usually 0.75%	Yes
Other share classes, such as R, F or I shares	Refer to prosectus	Refer to prosectus	Refer to prosectus
True no-load	None	None	None

Illustration 3-1

"A," "B" and "C" shares are different ways of buying the same fund. The "B" and "C" shares have higher expense ratios designed to recoup the amortized expense of the sales charge and therefore, early redemptions are charged a surrender charge to cover the unamortized expense. Penalties, surrender charges and internal fees can be found in the prospectus. Look for the expense ratio, the 12b-1 fees and the CDSC.

When investing directly in no-load funds, there is no investment advisor to assist in the selection of the most appropriate fund or to provide guidance through market cycles, thus no-load. True no-load funds have no front end or back end charges. No-load is a broadly used term however and it is not always used correctly. It is often used to describe "B" shares, as they do not have a front-end load, but it is an incorrect usage of the term since they have a surrender charge. Always check; do not assume that the often-misused term "no-load" means anything more than a fund with no sales commission.

Funds offer other types of shares, such as institutional shares or those used exclusively in wrap platforms, which have different fee structures. Most mutual funds in wrap programs do not charge a sales commission, CSDS or 12b-1 fees, but some do. Refer to the prospectus to determine the fees.

Redemption Fees

Redemption fees have been instituted by many mutual funds in response to the growing number of market timing transaction made by investors during the late 1990s. Trades were made at ever increasing rates, forcing the fund to redeem shares or purchase shares in response to these demands. This increase in trading frequency was operationally cumbersome, but more importantly, the actions of a few were affecting the performance of the entire fund for all. This fee is charged when fund shares are bought and then sold within a certain (short) period of time. As yet, neither the fee nor the time table are regulated by the SEC, however they are looking at some form of regulation. This fee imposes liquidity constraints that the investor should be aware of prior to purchasing shares in a fund.

Expense Ratio or Operating Expenses

Mutual funds have internal operating expenses, which are referred to as the expense ratio. The expense ratio usually includes manager fees, 12b-1 fees, administrative costs, accounting, legal, marketing, custodial fees (holding the money and accounts), broker/dealer rebates and concessions and any other costs. This charge is reported as a percentage of the total asset value of the fund and is available in the prospectus. The annual fee generally ranges between 1% and 3% and is charged to the fund on a quarterly basis. According to Lipper Analytical Services, Inc. and Morningstar, the average equity fund expense ratio is approximately 1.5%.

Management Fees

Funds also have management fees, which are paid to the portfolio manager. These fees are generally between 0.5% and 1% of the total asset value of the fund and are generally included in the expense ratio.

Transaction Costs

Transaction costs are the commissions paid by the fund to the brokers who buy and sell the individual stocks or securities (turnover) within the fund. These costs usually do not show up in the expense ratio, which makes them almost impossible to pin down. They are absorbed into the purchase and sale price of the securities. The mutual fund adds the commissions to the price of securities it buys and subtracts the commissions from the price of securities that it sells. It is reasonable to assume that the greater the fund's turnover rate, the greater this expense will be to the fund. Burton Malkeil, an economics professor at Princeton University and author of *A Random Walk Down Wall Street,* estimates a portfolio turnover rate of 50% will cost a fund 0.8% to 1% of the asset value of the fund. According to Richard Rutner in *The Trouble with Mutual Funds,* turnover rates have increased from 15-20% in 1950, to over 95% in 2000, so if we assume a turnover rate of 100%, these costs would be an additional 1.6% to 2% of the net asset value of the fund.

By adding the expense ratio and transaction costs, the total annual internal costs of an average no-load fund can actually be 3.1% to 6%. When making an overall comparison, combine loads, CDSC and early redemption penalties with the expense ratio. The website personalfund.com can be helpful in this process.

> **TOTAL COST =** Sales Commission + Expense Ratio + Transaction Costs + CDSC + Redemption Fees

COSTS—SEPARATELY MANAGED ACCOUNTS

Separately managed accounts are generally fee-based and appear on a statement. The fee includes the money manager, the consultant, the brokerage account and transaction costs, all wrapped into one asset-based fee, with no hidden expenses. As we have just seen, in many cases these fees are actually less than most no-load mutual funds and, they are regressive. The larger the portfolio, the lower the percentage fee charged. With mutual funds, the larger investor does not get the same economies of scale, as the $1 million investor pays the same fee ratio as the $10,000 investor. SMA's generally have a single all-inclusive fee, but under some arrangements, the fee is separated or un-bundled. Make sure that you understand the cost structure offered, as there are several delivery and management platforms available (Chapter 4). An all-inclusive fee should not exceed 3%, which is increasingly considered excessive, and the fee is generally regressive. The greater the asset value of the account, the lower the percentage fee assessed. The breakpoints usually occur at $500,000, $1 million and again at $2 million and the fees can generally be negotiated.

TAX PLANNING

Tax liabilities in mutual funds can be difficult to manage. Mutual funds are required to distribute any capital gains and/or income each year to the shareholders (the investors). Capital gains are distributed when, during the course of the year, the fund sells more securities for a gain than can be offset by those that it sells for a loss. Income is derived from interest paid on fixed income securities or dividends paid by companies owned by the fund. Distribution of both or either of these might mean that the investor could, and often does, realize capital gains, which can be short or long-term or, taxable income from dividends or interest, without showing a gain in the fund. The investor can actually lose money on the fund investment and still owe taxes!

How does this happen? The portfolio manager may buy a stock for the fund at say $10 per share and hold it for several years before he or she sells it for say $80 per share, just before you bought into the fund. The fund will have an embedded capital gain that will be realized at the time the stock is sold. This gain will be distributed to investors if it cannot be offset inside the fund by losses. The fund companies usually make this distribution near year-end; if you own the fund at the time of distribution, you will receive the capital gain distribution (phantom gain), a taxable event. Only the owners of shares at the time of distribution pay the taxes. This tax treatment does not apply to losses, as mutual fund tax losses do not pass through to the investor. Phantom gains were common toward the end of the bubble, 1999 through 2001. In 2000, the high-flying Janus Venture fund lost 46%, but distributed a 13% capital gain[2].

Losing money, while still owing taxes can be an unpleasant surprise, but one that can possibly be anticipated or avoided when planning a purchase. Fund companies usually have an idea of when the distributions will be made and in what amount, by the end of the third quarter. Distributions can be made mid year or any time the fund company may choose, so if it is a high turnover fund, this additional possibility should be investigated. If the fund has a high turnover rate of short-term holdings, the fund will generate short-term gains that are taxed at ordinary income rates. Potential distributions from embedded capital gains can be determined prior to making a purchase and may affect the decision to buy into the fund at a certain time or at all. This information may also persuade the investor to sell the fund prior to the distribution. If you do not own the fund at the time of distribution, you will not receive the taxable distribution.

Understanding embedded gains and losses can create opportunity. Although the funds don't distribute capital losses, if the fund has a high level of embedded capital losses, these will be carried forward within the fund and can be used to offset future capital gains. In this case, the investor may benefit from appreciation of the fund, and have the tax benefit from this carry-over of losses, the opposite of the previous scenario. Many funds had embedded capital losses in 2002 and 2003.

Many mutual fund investors employ the practice of fund "swapping" to manage taxes. Funds with like holdings can be swapped (sell one and buy another) in order to capture losses or avoid gains, while essentially leaving the overall asset allocation unchanged. Swapping can also be used to lower one's exposure to embedded capital gains. It is best to swap within a single fund family or among no-load funds to avoid new sales commissions or surrender charges. If a fund has appreciated in value (NAV, the net asset value) since its purchase and it is swapped to avoid a capital gains distribution, the investor will realize a short or long-term capital gain on the sale, depending on the holding period. Calculate both before making a decision. The capital gain or

2. Morningstar 12-31-2000.

loss is the difference between what was paid for the fund (cost basis) and the proceeds from the sale of the fund. This calculation includes all commissions, fees and penalties.

The investor can try to avoid receiving phantom gains, and can employ swapping as a tax management strategy, but he or she is unable to do year-end tax management through tax-loss selling of individual securities. The mutual fund investor only owns shares in the fund, not individual securities. The only strategy available is to sell part or all of the fund to realize a capital loss that can be used to offset other capital gains. As we have seen, the investor has limited control over exposure to potential tax liabilities.

Those who invest in separately managed accounts **can** do this type of tax management, as the manager has the flexibility to balance capital gains with tax loss selling or harvest losses that can be used to offset capital gains that the investor has outside of the portfolio. Tax sensitive investors, through their money managers, can manage the timing of sales to realize long-term versus short-term gains. Since the securities are individually owned, the only taxable gains are those generated by each individual portfolio. There is no risk of receiving unexpected capital gains at the end of the year. In addition, the investor can gift highly-appreciated securities to avoid realizing the gain upon sale or, he or she may be able to deduct management fees and consultant fees.

SEC RULINGS

On August 18, 2004, the SEC acted on 10 new mutual fund rules affecting many of the topics discussed in this chapter. One of the more significant rulings involves "directed brokerage," which we will discuss more in later chapters, but for clarity here, when securities are bought or sold, there is a fee charged by the broker/dealer that executes the trade. Mutual funds trade in high volume, so broker/dealers want to capture that business. Broker/dealers have access to assets and channels of distribution, so mutual funds want to be "featured" by these firms. Herein lays the quid pro quo that has existed between mutual fund companies and broker/dealers for years; mutual funds place trades with those broker/dealer firms that feature or promote them. From a regulatory standpoint, this practice creates the potential for abuse. Mutual funds are required to seek the best execution for their trades, but in an effort to be "featured" by broker/dealers, they may have purchased "shelf space" through directed brokerage. Or similarly, broker/dealers that sell large amounts of a fund are rewarded with directed brokerage. Either way, the best interests of the investor are not the primary motivation for this trading relationship. On August 18, 2004, this practice was banned. The SEC believes that banning directed brokerage will even the playing field for smaller fund families and ultimately benefit the investor. In June of 2005, the NASD began levying fines against broker/dealers that exchanged preferential treatment of certain mutual fund companies for directed brokerage.

Other rulings now force the fund companies to provide the name of the portfolio manager, rather than the common practice of "Team management" and fund managers will be required to disclose their personal investment in the fund/s that they manage. Additionally, the SEC will require that the bonus and incentive schedule of managers be made public. These are significant changes in mutual fund regulation and it is probably just the beginning.

Separately managed accounts are not immune from SEC and industry scrutiny, therefore the actions and fee arrangements of advisors/consultants and money managers must be suitable and fully disclosed, as we will show in the chapters that follow.

CONCLUSION

Separately managed accounts are not for everyone, nor are mutual funds. Some individual investors have the necessary education, current information, skill and time to manage their own investments, and do not want to use either. Some investors do not meet the asset minimums required by SMAs or are unable to adequately diversify using SMAs, as the minimums range from $50,000 to $100,000 per manager for this type of investment program. SMAs generally generate a great deal of paper in the form of statements, confirmation notices (many brokerage firms can have these suppressed), proxies, and annual reports. As strange as it may seem, this alone may make a SMA unsuitable for some investors. For these investors, *well-selected* mutual fund/s can offer an excellent value.

The larger investor, who is able to diversify using separately managed accounts, will realize cost savings from lower proportional fees, more individuality in investment decisions and will have the availability of more tax planning options. Investment activity, holdings and fees are visible and portfolio managers are accessible to the investor. These SMA advantages will generally result in better overall portfolio satisfaction for the larger investor.

As with every investment decision, the pros and cons of each must be weighed for each individual investor. No one investment option is right for everyone, nor does an investor need to make a single investment choice. We believe that the information in this chapter gives the investor the tools to properly compare and evaluate mutual funds and separately managed accounts as investment options and choose that which is most suitable to their circumstance.

4

Differentiating
Fee-Based Platforms

As the financial services industry continues to evolve, it has increased its focus on creating and promoting fee-based platforms. Firms are looking for a more consistent "ever-green" revenue flow, as commission-based or transactional revenue is inconsistent and has been significantly impacted by discount and on-line brokerage. Additionally, fee-based accounts minimize brokerage firms' concerns over churning an account (frequent buys and sells) to generate revenue. However, much has been written about the suitability of fee-based accounts. As with all investment recommendations, fee-based accounts must be suitable for the investor and there are an ever-increasing number of platforms and fee structures to consider.

WRAP FEE ACCOUNTS

Fee-based accounts include "wrap fee" accounts and Separately Managed Accounts (SMAs), which are not necessarily the same. SMAs are wrap fee accounts, but not all wrap fee accounts are SMAs. There are various types of fee-in-lieu-of-commission account platforms available that do not qualify as SMAs. These include:

- Fee-based brokerage accounts
- Mutual funds in fee-based accounts
- Wrap accounts for mutual funds only

Fee-Based Brokerage (Trading) Account

Most firms have developed a platform designed for fee-in-lieu-of-commission trading. These accounts are often referred to as fee-based brokerage accounts. There is a single asset-based fee charged quarterly, instead of a commission for each trade. These platforms usually include most securities and a specific list of mutual funds. This type of account can be used by investors who want to make their own investment choices or by those who want the advice of an advisor. Fees should vary depending on the level of advisor involvement and the types of securities held in the account. Before using this type of account, the investor should compare the fee to estimated trading costs. If the account is fairly active, a fee may be appropriate. If the account is rarely traded, then a commission structure may be more appropriate. The NASD has issued fines to firms that have inactive fee-based brokerage accounts, so suitability issues should always be considered in structuring this type of account.

Many firms are transitioning "fee-in-lieu-of-commission" accounts to "advisory" type accounts, where the fee compensates the advisor or consultant for their portfolio advice and guidance, rather than focusing on trades. The suitability and fee structure of this type of account is dependent on the value of the advice and services provided by the advisor or consultant.

Advisors who have discretionary accounts with their clients often use this type of platform. The advisor acts as the portfolio manager, making all trading decisions on behalf of the client for a single fee. Discretion alleviates the need to contact the client prior to each transaction, but also takes the client out of the tactical decision-making process. The suitability of this type of account is very client-advisor dependent. Expect minimums of $50,000 per account.

Mutual Funds in Fee-Based Accounts

When including mutual funds in fee-based accounts, it is wise to understand all of the costs prior to investing, as there are situations when these accounts are not in the investor's best interest. The funds that are included in these accounts have agreed to sell "A" shares or a close equivalent, for no commission. Load waived "A" shares mean that the client will pay the low "A" share expense ratio (Chapter 3) and no front-end load or back-end load (surrender charge or CDSC), but there may be short-term trading redemption fees. 12b-1 fees may go to the fund for administrative charges or be returned to the value of the fund. The latter is more advantageous to the investor. Some fund companies have issued a specific class of share for fee-based accounts, such as "F" or "I" shares that may have a unique expense structure. Although the eligible funds are load waived, there is still an expense ratio to be paid to the fund, in addition to the wrap fee. This combination of fees makes for a pricey package and should only be used if there are distinct advantages to the investor, such as flexibility. There is generally a different fee structure for

wrap fee
+
fund expense ratio
+
trading costs (turnover)
+
possible redemption fee
+
12b-1 fee

stocks, mutual funds, fixed income and cash, which allows the advisor and client to arrive at an acceptable fee for each.

If it is the investor's intent to buy a mutual fund or funds for a long-term hold, then a wrap account is probably not appropriate. If however, the investor is more proactive in his or her approach to market conditions, then this type of account may be cost effective. It is also important to understand the trading policies of the fund company and brokerage firm prior to selling a fund. The elimination of loads, combined with volatile market conditions, resulted in considerable trading abuses in fee-based accounts and both began to charge redemption fees for short holding periods.

Wrap Accounts for Mutual Funds Only

There are account platforms designed exclusively for mutual funds and these may be presented with different structures. Some firms offer different risk-appropriate blends of mutual funds. A group within the sponsoring firm designs the asset allocation, researches and selects the funds, and replaces funds or rebalances when they feel that it is appropriate. The advisor merely recommends the blend. In other structures, the advisor will select the funds and the account can then be set up to automatically rebalance at specific time intervals or it can be easily rebalanced manually. After considering all of the points made in a previous paragraph about the total cost, the investor can determine the value of this type of account. Wrap accounts can reduce the cost of buying and selling mutual funds, but be sure that there is value added to the overall objective of the portfolio. The minimums are as low as $25,000 per account.

SEPARATELY MANAGED ACCOUNTS

There are many types of separately managed accounts and in an attempt to clarify the choices and distinguish between them, we will describe several common platforms. These delivery platforms may vary somewhat between brokerage firms, as the individual firms tend to add their own features and restrictions, but all share the following characteristics:

- The account is separately managed by a professional money manager, solely for the benefit of the investor
- The securities are separately owned
- The account is fee-based
- Most or all of the fees are wrapped together into one fee, which can include:
  - The consultant
  - The brokerage firm's costs: Custody, trading, clearing and administration, which includes monthly statements and generally quarterly reports
  - The portfolio manager
  - Separate account management can be paperwork intensive

Multiple Strategy Portfolios (MSP)

In 1997, the industry introduced Multiple Strategy Portfolios (MSP). MSP is a somewhat generic term to describe multiple strategies and/or managers in a single separately managed account. MSPs help bridge the gap between a mix of mutual funds and a well-diversified portfolio of independent money managers and offer many of the personalized advantages of separate account management. As you will note, the success of the models described will depend on the skills of the individuals working behind the scenes at the sponsoring firm and not necessarily on those of the advisor. The investor should investigate the backgrounds, skills and track records of whomever is making the investment decisions, just as one would prior to investing in a mutual fund.

Different brokerage firms use different names (MDA, DSP, MSP, DMA and MAP) and generations of this product, depending upon the level of sophistication and complexity that is suitable for the investor. All support the idea of the consulting process, as they begin with an investor profile, invest using risk appropriate asset allocations and monitor the portfolio in accordance with the investment plan. We will describe the generations that have marked the genesis of MSPs, as they move from a single firm structure to one that includes multiple asset classes and independent money managers. These include:

- Turn-key, internally managed accounts
- Internal managers in multiple strategy portfolios
- Independent managers in multiple strategy portfolios
- Unified Managed Accounts (UMA)

Turnkey, Internally Managed Accounts

Many firms are offering "turnkey" products, utilizing their internal strategy departments to determine both the macro-asset allocation (the percent of stocks, bonds, cash, etc.) and the security selection. These are actively managed portfolios designed to meet the risk and return profiles for different types of investors. The basic portfolios offered are Conserva-

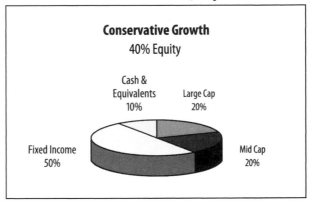

tive Growth, Moderate Growth and Long-term Growth, but depending on the firm, there are likely to be others. We have provided sample asset allocations in this section. Once the risk and return profile is determined and a portfolio model is chosen, the decision making is left to the professionals at the sponsoring firm. This approach is similar to the mutual fund platform previously mentioned, however the securities used in these portfolios can be individual stocks and bonds, as well as closed-end funds and exchange traded funds. Each security is individually owned and therefore the tax management advantage of SMAs is available to investors.

The active management can add value to the portfolio by underweighting vulnerable, overvalued areas within the targeted allocations and taking advantage of opportunities in undervalued areas. The active management of the portfolio's allocation mix has the advantage of being somewhat flexible, however within this platform, it is limited and all portfolio decisions are made solely at the discretion of the portfolio manager. The account minimums are as low as $50,000 per account.

Internal or Affiliated Managers in Multiple Strategy Portfolios

As a rule, the minimum account size for a managed account with a single manager is $100,000, but again, SMAs are a popular concept and the brokerage firms are looking for ways to broaden their use by making them available to a wider range of individuals. In order to diversify adequately with small-

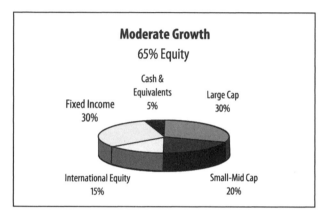

er sums of money, many firms are now offering multiple strategy portfolios. The strategy and/or consulting department of the sponsoring firm develops models to meet various risk and return profiles and then makes all asset allocation and reallocation decisions within each model. They select portfolio managers for each allocated investment style from firm employed or firm affiliated[1] portfolio managers to create the risk-appropriate models. The portfolio managers make the tactical decisions regarding

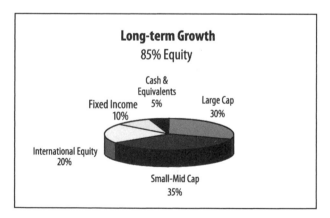

1. Many financial institutions own a variety of companies, including money management firms. All of these companies are affiliates of one another.

individual securities. This platform differs from the previous "turnkey" account, in that this platform utilizes style specific portfolio managers.

The basic models are generally Conservative Growth, Moderate Growth, Long-term Growth and Aggressive Growth, however there may be other allocations offered by the different firms. The advisor has little or no input in the overall asset allocation or management of the portfolio, other than to choose the appropriate model, freeing the advisor to develop client relationships. Minimums vary, but generally start at $150,000.

Thus far, the SMAs that we have discussed have used the talent pool that is directly available to the brokerage or sponsoring firm. We will now look at platforms designed to integrate the expertise of independent money managers. These managers were once out of reach for the average investor, as their account minimums could be $1 to 5 million. Now that the brokerage firms have provided the administrative functions and the consultant or advisor works directly with the investor, these managers are left to do what they do best, manage portfolios. This arrangement has made their expertise available to a much wider range of investors.

Independent Managers in Multiple Strategy Portfolios

Most major brokerage firms offer this type of multiple strategy portfolios. The managers that participate in these programs are generally limited to the firm's sub-advisors, which we will describe later in this chapter. Unlike the previous MSPs, these portfolio managers are independent or non-affiliates of the brokerage or sponsoring firm. This platform allows the managers to use the brokerage firm's trading desk and administrative resources, just as they would for individual accounts. Firms offer pre-determined asset allocation models for the advisor to choose from, constructed and managed by the firm's consulting department, or the advisor can customize the manager and allocation mix. The minimum account size may be as low

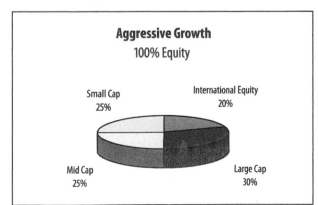

Aggressive Growth
100% Equity

Small Cap 25%
International Equity 20%
Mid Cap 25%
Large Cap 30%

as $150,000. This open architecture increases the investor's access to managers that may otherwise have prohibitive minimums. There are some limitations however. The investor is limited in the number of managers that can be used, depending upon the size of the account. As an example, a $150,000 account may be restricted to two managers. For some investor's, this type of account may be appealing, because it requires substantially less paperwork than separate account management. There can be multiple managers in a single account, utilizing a single new account form, a single statement and a consolidated performance monitor.

Firms offering this account platform often utilize an Overlay Portfolio Manager (OPM). This individual can be associated with the sponsoring firm or be an outside third party. The OPM is 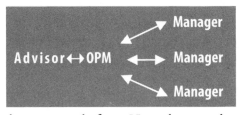 responsible for coordinating the multi-manager platform. He or she may select the managers (on-going manager due diligence); review and execute manager trades, watching for duplication of securities; oversee the tax management of the portfolio, including potential "wash sales;" and rebalance when appropriate. The OPM may also be responsible for asset allocation and reallocations decisions. The advisor need only interface with the OPM, thus freeing their time for building their business.

The models in all of the platforms that we have discussed provide the advisor and the investor with many advantages, such as:

- Multiple strategies in a single account
- Direct stock ownership
- Risk-based portfolio management
- Professionally designed and monitored asset allocations that are periodically re-balanced to stay within the model guidelines
- Extensive due diligence of managers or in some of the platforms, mutual funds
- A disciplined, unemotional process
- Professional money managers
- Tax management
- A diversified team approach
- Consolidated reporting

Unified Managed Account

The Unified Managed Account (UMA) is the next generation of MSPs, combining the multi-manager capabilities of MSPs with any number of additional products, such as exchange-traded funds, alternative investments and bonds, all managed in a single account by either the consultant or advisor or, an Overlay Portfolio Manager (OPM). Consultants or advisors can act with or without discretion, whereas an overlay manager generally acts with discretion. In either case, the investment professional is responsible for the asset allocation, risk management and tax considerations. This innovation will allow the investor and advisor to combine many types of investments (open-end and closed-end funds, ETFs, bonds, Holders, etc.) into this account, using a single investor profile analysis, statement and performance monitor, all for a single fee. The goal is to streamline oversight, while improving risk and tax management and, many UMAs allow investors to broaden their access to asset categories that may not have been available to them in an SMA, such as emerging-market debt. Many firms have launched UMAs, as there is great demand for the efficient simplicity of this type of delivery and oversight; all types of investments in a single account, for a single fee, coordinated and managed to maintain proper diversification and tax efficiency. The success of the UMA depends heavily on the consulting process, as well as back office functionality, which must effectively administer the variety of securities and products that can be used within this platform.

Separate Account Management

As the skills of the consultant advance and the client relationships demand a more sophisticated investment approach, we return to where the industry began in the 1970s; separate account management, guided by consultants and implemented by independent money management firms. As we discussed in Chapter 2, money managers developed relationships with brokerage firms in the '70s and account minimums came down to $100,000. This relationship continues today in the two platforms that we will now describe:

- Sub-advisor groups of independent managers
- Independent outside managers

Sub-advisor Groups of Independent Managers

Money management firms are selected by brokerage firms to become sub-advisors to their SMA programs only after an extensive due diligence process. This process adds a substantial amount of value to investors, as most advisors and consultants do not do their own manager searches. Each money manager selected will pass through an evaluation process that includes firm size, philosophy, management, performance, turnover ratio and trading capabilities (Chapter 15). Once this process is complete and the money manager becomes a sub-advisor to the brokerage firm, they will be one of a limited group of managers available to all of the advisors and consultants within the firm.

After developing an appropriate asset allocation, the advisor or consultant can then choose managers from their firm's sub-advisory group according to their investment style and philosophy. The investor can hire these managers through the firm using a single contract (Chapter 2). Minimums are generally $100,000 per manager. Most advisors and consultants opt for these managers because as we have mentioned, very few advisors or consultants have the skills or time to independently review and select money managers. Many brokerage firms have a dedicated consulting department whose staff selects and monitors these managers and can readily offer support, such as sales materials, research and manager information, to its advisors and consultants.

Behind the scenes, there may be additional criteria required of sub-advisors that may influence the selection in an unintended way. The sub-advisors must be willing to accept a lower fee through one of these programs than they ordinarily would charge when acting independently. Reduced fees are somewhat equivalent to mutual fund companies buying shelf space. Many managers are willing to do this because they expect to receive more assets while expending fewer resources per account, due to their association with the brokerage firm. The brokerage firms limit the number of money management firms that represent each asset class and style and their entire network of advisors have easy access to this limited pool of sub-advisors. This type of distribution, combined with the emphasis that firms are placing on the conversion of transactional business to fee-based business, sets the stage for a substantial flow of assets to the sub-advisory firms. The brokerage firms do the manager screens and due diligence for their advisors and the advisors will place assets with the sub-advisory money management firms. There are advantages to all, from the investor to the managers, but the requirements of the brokerage firms may exclude quality management firms. These firms can be hired as independent, outside managers through the efforts of consultants who do their own manager research.

When reviewing managers and manager styles to complete an asset allocation, the consultant may find a shortage of certain styles within the sub-advisory program. There is generally an over representation of large cap managers and an under representation of small cap managers in most of these programs. This disparity is due to firm size and costs.

To participate in a sub-advisory program the manager often must a) lower their fees and, b) contribute money to sponsor brokerage firm events. Large cap management firms generally have more assets under management than small cap firms, due to the liquidity of the stocks that they buy. This liquidity allows large cap managers to make larger trades for more accounts than small cap managers and therefore many small cap managers choose to have fewer assets under management, as they feel controlling size best serves their clients. Fewer assets under management generate lower fee revenue and it is therefore more difficult for them to accommodate the cost structure required of sub-advisory firms.

Illustration 4-1 is an example of the management styles that brokerage firms are seeking to provide in their sub-advisory programs. If the advisor or consultant is offering his or her firm's sub-advisory platform to diversify a portfolio, ask them to provide their firm's listing of managers and styles. They should also provide a list of balanced and fixed managers if either of these styles is appropriate.

Manager Style	Deep Value	True Value	Relative Value	Core	GARP[2]	True Growth	Aggressive Growth
Large Cap							
Mid-Lg Cap							
Mid Cap							
SMID[3]							
Small Cap							
International							
Global							

Illustration 4-1

2. GARP: Growth At a Reasonable Price.
3. SMID: Small to mid cap portfolio.

Brokerage firms offer model portfolios to their advisors under this platform as well. The advisor has the flexibility to choose any manager combination that they feel fits the investor's profile, or they may leave this decision up to the consulting department. The consulting department is familiar with the managers and they generally work with strategists to develop the asset allocation models. If the advisor's firm has a talented team to provide this guidance, this approach may provide significant value to the investor and advisor.

Consultants, who are skilled in analyzing the capital markets, generally design their own asset allocations. If they also do their own manager searches, they can be more investor-specific and flexible with both their allocations and manager choices.

Separately Managed Accounts Offered by Mutual Fund Companies, Bank Trust Departments and Insurance Companies

The Investment Company Act of 1940 allowed Registered Investment Advisors (RIA), who were providing their services to large institutional level clients, to form mutual fund companies to provide the smaller investor an opportunity to access the same professional money management and diversification. As more money is entering the SMA market, more and more of these investment advisory (money management) firms are using their mutual fund marketing efforts to offer separate account management. They have come full circle in concept, as they are now offering institutional style management to the smaller investor through a variety of separate account management platforms. The portfolio managers are either employees of the mutual fund company or they are sub-advisors to the mutual fund company. The same portfolio manager generally manages the SMA, as well as a similar strategy or clone mutual fund. The account minimums are as low as $50,000 per account.

Bank trust departments still dominate the pension and institutionally sized separate account market, but have also entered the sub-institutionally sized SMA market. Historically, banks have tended to underperform, as their structure is rigid and their primary focus is banking, not investment management. Large insurance companies have used independent money management in the form of mutual fund sub-accounts in their variable products for years and are also entering the SMA market. Look for both of these entities to offer many of the platforms that we have discussed in this chapter.

Independent Outside Managers

For those consultants who do their own manager searches and due diligence, there are many more money management firms from which to choose. There are many smaller "boutique" firms, often referred to as emerging managers, who are still run by their founders and these firms are generally more flexible in working with consultants and investors. Investors are often able to meet directly with the founder/portfolio manager, increasing the level of personalized service and understanding between the two. Consultants who are able to offer this level of service to their clients, are able to provide access to the widest range of managers and investment philosophies to best match the investor's needs. Many are able to accommodate minimums for individual investors of $100,000 to $250,000, as they are still able to use the brokerage firm's trading desk and administrative resources, however minimums of $1 million to $5 million are common. They provide services under a dual contract arrangement, one between the investor and the manager and, one between the investor and the brokerage firm (Chapter 2). Institutions, usually with the help of a consultant, often hire independent money managers directly. The consultant will assist institutions with a variety of functions, including the manager search and due diligence process. Institutional account minimums are generally in excess of $3 million per manager.

SPONSORING FIRM DUE DILIGENCE

Most brokerage firms have a consulting department that is responsible for fee-based accounts. It is important to know how strong that department is, since the advisor or consultant relies on many staff functions in order to provide an efficient delivery system. The real heroes of cost containment in SMA's are the unseen men and women who work in the "back office" of the firm. They are on the front lines day in and day out, fulfilling a myriad of administrative functions. These organizational and technical people are part of the team that must to be in place for a firm to offer a fully integrated, seamless separately managed account platform. Investigating a firm's operational capabilities is another important part of the selection process. The investor needs the assurance that a state-of-the-art system is in place before entrusting their assets to a firm.

In addition to the administrative requirements of SMA platforms, advisors who are planning to use model portfolios must know the qualifications and track records of those responsible for developing and maintaining the asset allocations of the models. These individuals are a key element in the success of your relationship with the client. In order to determine a sponsoring firm's level of commitment to the investment management consulting process, we have provided questions to ask the advisor or consultant regarding the firm under consideration for their money management platform(s).

1. How long has a sponsoring or brokerage firm had a consulting department?

2. How many fee-based platforms does the firm offer and what is the history and make up of these platforms?

3. How many professional consulting support staff members are in the consulting department and how many full-time analysts are there who are designated to conduct on-site manager visitations, account audits, and due diligence evaluations for independent money management firms? Describe these analysts' background.

4. Describe the qualifications and process of the strategy and/or consulting team responsible for developing and maintaining the model portfolios.

5. In the firm's consulting history, how many managers have they thoroughly evaluated through on-site, face-to-face interviews as opposed to mailed questionnaires?

6. How many of the managers in the brokerage firm's database are audited on the manager's premises annually?

7. How many managers are in the firm's sub-advisory group and what investment styles do they represent? What are the selection criteria?

8. Is the firm's database of managers proprietary and self-developed or purchased from another source? There is nothing inherently wrong with either database, although it may imply that firms with a self-developed database have committed more time, energy and resources to their consulting departments.

9. Does the sponsoring firm provide and/or sell research to money managers? It is much more "arms length" if the money managers obtain their information independently, particularly in light of the research analyst scandals of the early 2000s.

10. Are the managers in the database required to purchase research or contribute to the sponsoring firm's events in order to be included that

firm's database? These questions will uncover potential and obvious conflicts of interest. This topic is covered from the money management firm's perspective in Chapter 15.

11. Does the firm have any affiliation with the money manager? It is important that you know all of the financial industry activities or affiliations of your Investment Management Consultant's firm. This information will help determine whether your consultant may face any potential conflicts of interest and what his or her firm's level of commitment is to the services you desire.

CONCLUSION

The type of platform that is best for an investor depends on the assets that will be invested, the investor's profile and the skills or focus of the advisor or consultant. Models provide many advantages to the investor, including the investor questionnaire and profile, and professional management. With the increasing volatility of the financial markets spurred by the information age, securing valuable professional advice through programs like these may very well be the critical element in the financial success of many individual investors.

Investors who require a more individualized approach and have portfolios that can be diversified across a range of independent money managers, often opt for independent money managers and the full range of services offered by a consultant. They are able to discuss their investments with both their consultant and their money managers, creating a sophisticated investment team. Separately managed accounts of all types can be an exceptional value for many types of investors and are a value-added addition to the investment landscape.

5

Deliniating Cost Structures

B rokerage costs and management fees; where is the value and what is actually appropriate?

"How much will this cost me?" is often the first thing that an investor will ask. This question puts the cart before the horse, as costs are an unknown before an investment plan is developed. A better question would be, "Am I receiving a valuable service commensurate with the fee?" Many investors are not familiar with an investment process and therefore can become overly focused on costs, without regard to the value added. That being said, investors today are deluged with opinions and negative press ranging from the fee practices of mutual funds to the excessive costs of separately managed accounts (SMAs). The perceived value of trading costs, the old standard, has been significantly altered with the rise of low cost, on-line trading and discount brokerage firms. As transactional business is rapidly losing market share and a variety of wrap type programs and SMAs take its place, investors need to be armed with the tools necessary to sort out costs and determine value. The key is determining the value that each service adds to the investment process and the bulk of this book is dedicated to revealing where and how that value can be found. We will use this chapter to help the investor uncover the true costs associated with different investments and offer our opinion on what is reasonable. These costs can include commissions, fees, trading costs, expense ratios and tax consequences. In the examples that follow, we will make dollar-for-dollar comparisons. In the chapters that follow, we will show the investor how to determine the value added to the process by the advisor or consultant.

COST OF TRADING AT A FULL-SERVICE BROKERAGE FIRM

We will use a full-service firm for this comparison, where we expect that the value will come from an advisor who has taken the time to develop an investment plan and is skilled in analyzing and diversifying the stocks that make up a portfolio.

Let us assume that in investor has a $100,000, all-equity account and has twenty stock positions. The average cost of each position is $5,000 and the commission for each trade is $125, which is approximately 2.5%. Assume that the account is fully invested and has a 50% turnover during a one-year period, which is not unreasonable. These assumptions mean that 50% or 10 positions of the portfolio were sold and 50% or 10 new positions are bought within that year, resulting in 20 trades and commissions of $2500 or 2.5%. If the portfolio has a 100% turnover, which is reasonable in styles that are more aggressive and in small to mid cap portfolios, the commission is now $5000 or 5%.

In the previous chapter, we discussed the fee-based alternative to trading accounts. If this same $100,000 were in a fee-in-lieu-of-commission account with a 2% annual fee, the charge to the investor would be $2,000. The suitability of the fee-based alternative is determined by the trading activity.

COST OF SEPARATELY MANAGED ACCOUNTS

A common criticism leveled at separately managed accounts is that their fee structure is too high when compared to mutual funds. We believe that this criticism is unfounded and may be the result of superficial reviews of cost structures. All costs associated with SMAs are transparent, itemized on statements and within the body of contracts. The investor sees the actual charges, whereas mutual fund charges can be quite difficult to determine (Chapter 3), as they occur internally; they are not itemized on a statement. Investing in separately managed accounts involves a comprehensive process, not the sale of a single product. Dollar-for-dollar comparisons may be irrelevant or misleading. This is not to say that SMAs are right or even cost effective for everyone. They are not. However, when we open the hood and look at the component costs, the fees are quite competitive.

The standard full price, all-inclusive fee for a managed account is 3%. This figure includes the services of the consultant or advisor, all trading and administrative costs and the manager's fee. The consultant or advisor's services generally include a customized investment policy, asset allocation, manager searches and performance monitoring. The administrative costs include custody, trades, billings and statements. In addition to these administrative services, most firms do a considerable amount of work in their ongoing due diligence of their sub-advisory managers and provide account performance comparisons to industry benchmarks. Most consultants and advisors will discount this fee and the fee is generally regressive. Regressive fees mean that as the account increases in size, the percentage fee of assets under management decreases. We provided typical fee schedules in Chapter 2. The fee schedule is established at the time the account is opened, which places a ceiling on costs, regardless of the trading frequency. According to Cerulli Associates, in 2004, the industry's average account size is $437,000 for individuals utilizing this comprehensive, sub-advisory platform and the average total fee is 1.78%, which is allocated as follows:

Manager fees	48 basis points
Clearing and trading costs	5–20 basis points
Advisory support services	60–70 basis points
Consultant or advisor	60–70 basis points

SMAs include a variety of services and if we were to unbundle them and price each of them separately, the value of the all-inclusive fee becomes more pronounced. Unbundling is only available to institutional sized accounts, which can include high net worth individuals, but it does illustrate the costs of individual services.

Asset allocation studies	$5,000–$15,000
Development of investment policy	$2,500–$10,000
Custodial fees	10–20 basis points
Trading costs	$0.03–$0.10 per share
Manager fees	.50–1%
Multiple-manager searches	$5,000–$10,000 per manager search
Performance monitoring	0.25–0.50%

Individual Account

If we use the same $100,000 account from the previous example and charge an all-inclusive fee of 2.5%, the cost to the investor would be $2,500, regardless of the trading frequency. In addition, the services listed above are included. Some may argue that a qualified transactional advisor will provide all of the same services. We will leave that judgment to the reader's experience. If we make that assumption in this case, the advantages to a SMA are tax management, unlimited trades, the investment expertise of both the advisor and the money manager and the peace of mind that there is no agenda associated with the frequency of trades. An account that is rarely traded may be inappropriate for an annual fee, however there may still be great value associated with this structure. Each account should be evaluated on its own merits and priced accordingly.

Institutional Account

If we assume a $10,000,000 balanced account with an all-inclusive bundled fee of 1.25%, the annual fee would be $125,000. If we unbundled this account and assume annual policy reviews, annual asset allocation studies, a single manager search and performance monitoring, as well as general administrative costs, all charged at the lower end of the ranges, we see the following:

Asset allocation studies	$5,000
Investment policy review	$2,500
Custodial fees	$10,000 @ 10 basis points
Trading costs	$12,500 (250,000 shares @ $0.05 per shr*)
Manager fees	$65,000 @ 0.65%
Single manager search	$5,000
Performance monitoring	$25,000 @ 0.25%
Total annual costs	**$125,000**

*Assume an average turnover rate of 50% for 75% of the balanced portfolio and an average price per share of $30.

By using the above information, the investor can analyze the most optimal pricing structure and negotiate accordingly. The unbundled fee structure will often require additional manpower for monitoring fees and paying invoices and this additional cost should be factored into the analysis.

An additional benefit to all types of investors using an all-inclusive fee is the elimination of a potential conflict of interest. When a transactional advisor recommends securities or products, and his or her compensation is tied to the commissions generated by the sale, there can always be a question of motive, regardless of whether or not the concern is valid. When the fee is fixed, there is no longer this concern.

COST OF BALANCED OR FIXED MANAGED ACCOUNTS

It is important for the investor to realize that balanced and fixed accounts, which generally have a low turnover rate, should be priced below the 3% that was discussed above. A reasonable all-inclusive fee for a $500,000 balanced account that is 50% equity and 50% fixed might be 1.75% to 2%, whereas a $10,000,000 account may be only 1.25%. A reasonable all-inclusive fee for a $500,000 fixed account might be 0.70% to 1%. There are many compositions for these types of accounts, including the equity/fixed ratio and the types of bonds. Pricing should reflect the level of activity and availability of the securities in the account.

Investors, who buy a bond portfolio for income only and intend to hold the bonds until maturity, will probably not benefit from a managed account. Those who invest in bonds for both income and capital appreciation will benefit from professional management, as the bond market has many complexities (Chapter 15). Bonds sold in the retail market have sales credits that range from 0.5% to 3.5% built into the bond's price. This cost varies widely depending on the type of bond, the bond's maturity, the size of the trade and the commission (or discount) that the advisor charges. There is a sale credit when the bond is purchased and sold. There is no sales credit built into the bond's price when purchased by the manager. Trading frequency and the value added by a bond specialist will determine the suitability of a fixed managed account.

COST OF MULTIPLE STRATEGY PORTFOLIOS

The fees vary with the type of MSP used, as they range from the turnkey account that utilizes the skills of the sponsoring firm's staff, to those that use independent money managers. Once again, pricing should reflect the level of involvement of those investment professional managing the account. As a rule, the regressive fee for a turnkey-type account may start at 2.5% to 2%, all of which goes to the sponsoring firm and advisor. When the complexity of the account increases to include style specific management, we see the fees increase, however the money managers are still affiliated with the sponsoring firm and this affiliation should be considered in the pricing negotiation. Finally, those accounts that utilize independent money management firms are the most complex, but are generally not priced above 3%. The following is a guideline of the fees associated with MSPs.

Advisor	1–1.25%
Manager	35–50 bps
Trading & Custody	25–35 bps
Sponsoring Firm	20–50 bps
Total fees	1.8%–2.60%

When comparing costs for all types of SMAs, consider the value-added that a separately managed account offers by determining the quality and level of the service provided by the firm and the advisor or consultant.

COST OF MUTUAL FUNDS

Again, according to Lipper Analytical and Morningstar, the average expense ratio of an equity mutual fund, excluding trading costs, is approximately 1.5%. When trading costs (0.8 to 1.0% per 50% turnover) are added, assuming a 50% turnover rate, the average total cost is now approximately 2.3%. This expense is ongoing and assumes no-loads, penalties or commissions. We covered all of the costs associated with mutual funds in great detail in Chapter 3.

COST OF MANAGED ACCOUNTS THAT USE MUTUAL FUNDS

Since the expense ratio and trading costs of a mutual fund will remain the same regardless of the size of account (no fee regression), we will continue to use the 2.3% annual cost as a starting point. If there is then an additional wrap fee of 1 to 2%, depending on the size of the account, the costs rise to over 3 to 4%. These costs may seem high, however for smaller accounts this may be a very effective investment strategy because of the value added by the advisor. In this situation, the wrap fee provides the advisor with compensation for monitoring and advising on the allocation of funds held in the account. These accounts should be evaluated for suitability, as it is unlikely that they are an appropriate account platform for the buy-and-hold investor.

As described in Chapter 4, funds in mutual fund wrap accounts are usually load waived "A" shares where there is no commission (or load) paid, nor should there be a CDSC, however some funds are now charging redemption fees for short holding periods. The treatment of 12b-1 fees should be understood, as it can affect returns. 12b-1 fees can be returned to the fund's value (NAV) or, they may go back to the fund company or to the sponsoring firm as additional revenue. The latter two are the less favorable options from the investor's point of view, however distribution of 12b-1 fees is not negotiable with the fund. The 12b-1 fees can not go to the advisor in this instance, as advisors are precluded from "double dipping," receiving both the wrap fee and the 12b-1 on the same assets.

CONCLUSION

By understanding the true cost of managing money, the investor is better able to assess the value and suitability of each fee structure. The information provided in this chapter will enable the investor to properly analyze costs and determine the value of the various investing platforms. True consultants who provide exceptional value will stand out from those who sell managed money as a product. This value should be considered when comparing or negotiating fees.

The contents of this book will help the investor determine the level of service and skill that is available in the industry. Insist that your costs are reasonable and comparable to the level of services that you receive. Negotiate the best fee arrangement possible, but do not assume that you will receive the highest level of professionalism and quality for the lowest cost.

SECTION II

Components of the
Investment Management
Consulting Process

6

Investment
Management Consultants

*"Consulting is an active process of capturing opportunity and managing
risk without prejudice to style or specific security."* - Daniel Bott, 1994

Some call consulting an art, some call it a science, but most people can
agree that selecting the right investment consultant is essential to successfully navigating the money management marketplace. The professionals
who specialize in the process of asset allocation modeling, manager selection
and performance analysis are called Investment Management Consultants.
These investment professionals are dedicated to helping both individuals
and institutions meet their investment goals, utilizing professional money
managers and/or other capital market investments to create a diverse, risk-
appropriate investment portfolio. An Investment Management Consultant
is a highly skilled individual who is proficient in market analysis and asset
allocation and has extensive experience with professional money managers
and performance analysis.

The consultant works with the investor to develop a realistic investment
policy, design a suitable asset allocation, select the appropriate money management firms and/or capital market investment alternatives and, regularly review
the performance of the managers and the portfolio. Each step in the consulting process is fundamental in realizing the investor's financial objectives. To be
effective, the consultant must have an in-depth understanding of the investor,
the capital markets, available investment alternatives and the money managers
that they recommend. These professionals carefully match the investor to style

specific portfolio managers whose investment philosophy, style, and performance are consistent with the investor's specific financial requirements, goals and risk profile.

INVESTMENT POLICY	ASSET ALLOCATION	MANAGER SELECTION

• Investor goals & objectives
• Cash flow needs
• Time horizons
• Risk tolerance analysis
• Wealth transfer
	• Investment policy guidelines
	• Market analysis
	  • Fundamentals
	  • Valuation models
	  • Macro-economics
	  • Technical analysis
	  • Market trends & momentum
	  • Cycle analysis
		• Qualitative & quantitative assessment
		• Primary asset class & style
		• Investment Philosophy
		• Risk-adjusted returns & risk management strategies
		• Search for potential conflicts of interest

CLIENT COMMUNICATION, PORTFOLIO MONITORING & REVIEW

- Regular review of the portfolio and the portfolio's risk profile to assess portfolio and manager performance, including risk-adjusted returns, adherence to the investment policy and monitor for conflicts
- Communicate changes in market conditions and/or investor objectives that may warrant changes in allocation or modification of the investment policy.
- Make re-allocation or rebalancing recommendations when appropriate

Illustration 6-1

SELECTING A CONSULTANT

Selecting the correct consultant is the best determinate of the success of any investment plan. This first step is much more important than most investors realize. The success of a portfolio depends far more on proper asset allocation and control of risk, than on stock selection. Therefore, when selecting an Investment Management Consultant, experience matters. It is important that the consultant have extensive experience in the capital markets and, possess the ability to adequately consider multiple factors when developing an asset allocation for the investor. These tools and skills are a critical part of successful allocations and reallocations.

After determining the asset allocation, the consultant will then match the investor to the most appropriate, professional money management firms and/or investment vehicles available and have a monitoring system in place to evaluate the managers and the overall performance of the portfolio as they relate to the investment objectives. Each element of this process is essential in realizing the long-term investment goals and objectives of the investor.

This relationship is ongoing, active, and involves a dynamic process of continuously monitoring the markets and recommending asset allocation changes as warranted. Allocation changes may be in response to changes in market trends or valuations, or they may be in response to changes in the investor's objectives. While striving to achieve the investor's goals, the consultant is vigilant in managing the investor's exposure to risk. During certain market conditions, the most significant contribution that a consultant may make is the preservation of capital.

KEY DRIVERS OF INVESTMENT PERFORMANCE

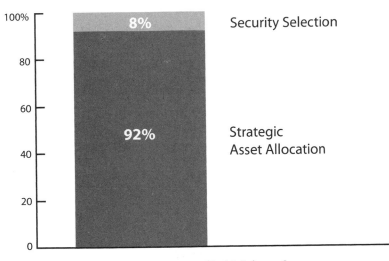

Source: Brinson, Hood and Beebower, "Determinants of Portfolio Performance," *Financial Analysts Journal,* May–June 1991

Illustration 6-2

Basic Role of the Consultant

The consultant brings a comprehensive, disciplined process to the investment plan. Their role can be divided into four major areas and each of these has several components. We have provided a brief discussion of each here and we will discuss each in detail in the succeeding chapters.

- Develop a realistic investment policy, balancing return expectations with risk tolerance
- Design an appropriate asset allocation, taking advantage of low correlation of styles
- Select the most qualified money management firms and/or investment vehicles to achieve the investment objectives through an extensive, on-going due diligence process
- Evaluate the performance of the managers and the overall portfolio on a regular basis, using realistic time horizons and expectations, incorporating an on-going risk assessment of the capital markets into decisions and recommendations

1 ANALYZE
Analyze the client's goals and objectives. Recommend appropriate asset allocation

2 IMPLEMENT
Recommend and hire appropriate money managers to implement the asset allocation

3 EVALUATE
Review money manager performance, client goals and market conditions. (DARP)

4 COMMUNICATE
Explain changes occurring in the economy and capital markets and recommend allocation changes if warranted.

Illustration 6-3

A consultant will analyze the investor's objectives and consider market conditions prior to recommending an overall asset allocation. The consultant will then recommend allocating assets into various investment styles and recommend the most qualified and appropriate money managers and/or investment vehicles available to invest within these styles. As part of this process, the consultant will determine the proper comparative index for monitoring the performance of each manager. Determining proper benchmarks is a key element in reviewing not only performance, but also the value added by each manager. This review is measured against the risk/return objectives set forth in the investment policy. We will cover performance analysis in Chapter 18. Over time, circumstances may change and if either the investor's objectives or market conditions change substantively, a qualified consultant will adjust the allocation and manager mix accordingly.

High net worth investors may wish to develop a comprehensive wealth management plan and if that is the case, the consultant may incorporate the following strategies into the investment plan. Comprehensive management is a valuable service that the consultant may offer, however it is not the focus of this book. We mention them here because they can clearly affect the structure of an individual's investment plan.

- Wealth management and control strategies
- Tax planning and management
- Retirement and educational planning
- Wealth transfer and estate planning techniques

INVESTMENT POLICY STATEMENT

Be wary of the financial advisor who handles the consulting process superficially or one who discusses returns before an investment plan is in place. This approach can signify that the advisor may not have the necessary skills to act as a qualified consultant to the investor. The consulting process begins with the investment policy.

The consultant will help the investor thoroughly analyze and define their values, goals and objectives. These and other discussions constitute an essential element of the professional consulting process, and serve to educate and inform the investor, enabling him or her to make informed and sound financial decisions. The consultant and the investor will establish realistic investment objectives, and implement a plan designed to realize those objectives. Working closely with each investor and in turn, their other advisors, such as their CPA or attorney, the consultant thoroughly examines and evaluates the financial concerns of the investor. They then establish a clear written investment policy statement, which incorporates the investment goals, objectives, risk tolerance, and cash flow needs of the investor. This step is essential in establishing a course of action, and must be periodically reviewed and adjusted as objectives and time horizons change.

Without professional guidance, many investors create a poorly planned portfolio, make decisions based on emotion, react to the media, and take excessive risks. This lack of process typically results in poor performance. Individuals, corporations and retirement plans should all create a well thought out investment plan, centering on long-term objectives, in order to develop an effective investment strategy.

To effectively develop an Investment Policy Statement (IPS) (Chapter 8), the consultant will require a thorough understanding of the following:

- Investor values, goals and objectives
- Cash flow needs
- Risk tolerance and tolerance to market volatility
- Time horizons
- Considerations for wealth transfer

The Role of Risk Management in a Sound Investment Policy

One of the key elements in developing an investment policy is a clear understanding of risk and risk tolerance between the investor and the consultant. As noted in Chapter 9, there are four major types of risk that must be considered and communicated in the development of an investment policy: inflation risk, reinvestment risk, liquidity risk and market risk. Properly evaluating the investor's tolerance to risk is key to a successful investment plan, as their inability to deal with market fluctuations can derail the investment process. A seasoned and qualified consultant will not ignore this ongoing process as the investor passes through the many stages of life. Life is a fluid process; circumstances can and do change, and therefore so can the investor's tolerance to risk and thus, the structure of their portfolio.

It is then imperative to match the money manager's investment philosophy (style) and risk profile to the investor's risk tolerance. If a money manager's philosophy is more volatile than the investor's tolerance, this manager is not suitable for the investor, regardless of the manager's performance. Only a thorough understanding of the money managers, and a well thought out investor profile will allow the Investment Management Consultant to match the most appropriate managers to each of their clients.

No single risk is predominant at all times, and it should be the mission of the consultant to guide investors through various market conditions and life changes, striving always to meet or exceed their client's objectives, while minimizing their exposure to risk.

ASSET ALLOCATION

The techniques used to design and maintain an appropriate asset allocation are covered in Chapters 10 and 12. Again, this process should be flexible, responding to changes in market risk and the investor's risk tolerance. Once the consultant has a thorough understanding of the investor's goal and objectives, as established in the investment policy, he or she can then recommend an appropriate asset allocation. A qualified Investment Management Consultant will use the following market analysis tools, in conjunction with the investor profile, to design and adapt the asset allocation of the portfolio:

- Market analysis
- Fundamental analysis
- Valuation models
- Macro-economics
- Technical analysis
- Market trends & momentum
- Cycle analysis

In Chapter 11, we discuss the various factors that were at play leading up to the Bear market in 2000. This Bear followed a nearly 20-year-long Bull market. Recent history provides us with few chances to compare the skills listed here to an actual seismic market event, so take this opportunity to correlate each of the analytical tools described in Chapter 10 to the events that led up to this significant Bear market. It is the consultant's responsibility to recommend changes to asset allocations, as managers tend to remain invested in their respective styles regardless of market conditions. While interviewing a potential consultant, find out what advice they gave to their clients during this period and why. The answers will tell a lot about the consultant's investment philosophy and approach to asset allocation (Chapter 12).

MANAGER SELECTION

The due diligence process used to screen potential money management firms is described in Chapter 15. Discussing, recommending, and then hiring the most effective money managers that align with the investor's risk profile, and who will most likely meet the investor's goals and objectives, is the next step in the process. Each firm selected will specialize in a specific style within the capital markets, such as mid-cap value stocks and collectively, their styles will complete the overall asset allocation. Style specific managers allow the asset allocation process to have a greater level of confidence in reducing security overlap, however understanding a manager's investment philosophy is more important than a specific "style box." Managers are selected for their skill and suitability for the client and the market environment. There may be other investment vehicles used within a portfolio that should be evaluated using many of the same standards, but we will focus on money managers here. The following criteria will be considered prior to recommending or hiring a money management firm:

- Primary asset class and style
- Management team and decision-making process
- Philosophy and adherence to discipline
- Buy and sell criteria; can it be easily explained
- Upside capture ratio
- Downside capture ratio
- Alpha return

PERFORMANCE MONITORING AND CLIENT COMMUNICATION

Monitoring overall performance should be done quarterly and the results measured against established objectives, which include both return expectations and the risk parameters dictated by the investor's risk tolerance. Both the portfolio as a whole, and each individual money manager, should be evaluated on this basis. Measuring a portfolio's performance against the "market" does not consider the risk profile that is built into the asset allocation and therefore falls short of a meaningful comparison. The consultant must be well versed in performance analysis to properly evaluate the managers and the overall performance of the portfolio in this manner. This skill offers the investor an objective third party analysis of performance. There is a thorough discussion of performance measurement techniques in Section IV.

The quarterly review process allows the consultant and the client to discuss changes in the capital markets and changes in the client's needs or goals. The consultant continuously monitors both the markets and the managers utilizing the criteria listed in the above sections, "Asset Allocation" and "Manager Selection," to determine the continued appropriateness of the asset allocation and the suitability of the managers from a market perspective. The consultant may recommend changes to the portfolio as a result of this analysis. During these meetings, the client has the opportunity to discuss personal changes that should be incorporated into the investment policy and perhaps in turn, the asset allocation. It is through this process that the investment policy remains relevant; the consultant can make appropriate asset allocation recommendations and the client's vision for the future remains on track. Measuring pure performance is actually secondary to meeting the client's goals and objectives in the consulting process.

We will discuss these concepts in greater detail in other chapters, but it is safe to say that a consultant who is able to effectively communicate with the investor will substantially enhance the chances of a successful investment plan.

INVESTMENT MANAGEMENT CONSULTANTS AND MONEY MANAGERS

It is the consultant's role to recommend money managers to the investor; it is the money manager's philosophy and style that drives his or her individual investment choices. It is therefore important for the consultant to make suitable manager choices and for the investor to understand the consultant's process for screening and selecting managers. Aside from the consultant's "track record," the investor will want to know the number of money managers that the consultant and/or their firm works with on a regular basis. It is not necessary or even reasonable for consultants to deal with a large number of firms. It is far more important that the consultant have a thorough understanding of the money managers that he or she recommends, which includes understanding the strengths and the weaknesses of the money manager's style, philosophy and performance. It is only with this information that the consultant can effectively match the most appropriate managers to the client's objectives. This step involves close examination on the part of the consultant, and therefore requires a relatively close relationship between the consultant and the money manager, as opposed to only casual or infrequent contact. This communication must be ongoing, as different managers may be more appropriate at different times throughout market cycles and the manager and client should have compatible investment philosophies.

There are several platforms used to select money management firms. Contrary to the ideal expressed in the previous paragraph, selection is most often made from a limited list of money management firms that are pre-screened by the brokerage firm and the consultant or advisor can simply choose from a "style box," i.e., large cap growth and/or from performance numbers. It is often the case that these consultants or advisors have little or no personal knowledge of the money management firms and will rely on their brokerage firm or third party platform provider to conduct the manager searches and to do the ongoing due diligence monitoring. This selection process can be a valuable service offered by the brokerage firms to support the client-servicing advisor (Chapter 4).

A seasoned consultant will know many money management firms first hand and will use only those who fit the personality, asset allocation guidelines and risk profile of the client. This knowledge of, and interaction between, the consultant and the money manager is very helpful in obtaining the desired result and can be achieved with both independent money managers and sub-advisory managers (pre-screened). Not all large cap growth managers are appropriate for each individual investor, as their style may be incompatible with the investor's objectives. As an example, a large cap growth GARP manager may have an average P/E in their portfolio of 18, whereas a large cap aggressive growth manager may have an average P/E of 48 in their portfolio. It is up to the consultant to go beyond a "style box" analysis to find the best fit. Another benefit of working with a seasoned consultant is his or her ability to negotiate manager fees with a depth of experience and knowledge that few investors possess. Again, experience matters.

The investor should be aware of any financial relationship between the consultant, the consultant's firm and the recommended money management firms. Even though the association may be entirely appropriate, the investor should be aware of how the consultant and his or her firm are paid and/or any other fees that might be paid to outside parties by money management firms being recommended by the consultant. We will delve more deeply into this area when we discuss the relationship between money managers and consultants and this investigation is included in the questions that we have provided at the end of this chapter.

THE VALUE-ADDED CONSULTANT

The consulting process provides the investor with the information, knowledge and understanding to achieve their financial goals. The consultant acts as a trusted, objective third party providing expertise and guidance throughout the investment process. For those with fiduciary concerns, the consultant provides the expertise, structure and accountability that ERISA demands. The consultant must be a good educator, prepared with information, able to deliver the information in an understandable way, confident in recommendations and efficient at implementation. In order to fulfill this role, the consultant should possess the following skills:

Knowledge: The consultant must understand the capital markets and be proficient with the analytical tools required to manage risk and recognize opportunity. These skills are essential in the development of a risk appropriate asset allocation. Implementation of the asset allocation depends on understanding the money manager's investment philosophy and style, and matching the most suitable managers with the investor's investment profile.

Interpreter: The consultant must be able to translate complex market information into a form that the investor will understand. This ability is a very important building block in the investment process. Recapping old market information adds little value. In addition, the consultant must take the time to understand the underlying biases of the investor, such as fear, greed or previous unpleasant investment experiences. The consultant must interpret what the investor says and does not say to best assess what the client needs and wants from their investments. By separating emotion from investment goals, the consultant can help the client develop a realistic, disciplined (yet flexible) investment plan.

Communicator: A consultant must be a good communicator. He or she must describe every element of the process with clarity and in a manner that is simple, visual and to the point. Tying investor objectives to market conditions and the overall asset allocation is described at each meeting, as the portfolio mix is evaluated and critiqued. A well-informed investor is the best investor as they are able and willing to stay the course. Once they understand the process, the short-term vagaries of the markets will not cause them to lose their focus.

Educator: A well-educated investor is an even better investor. They become an informed participant in the decision-making process. Education empowers the investor and helps the consultant develop the trust relationship that is so important to success.

Disciplined Process: The consultant will have a disciplined process in place that includes all of the elements of this chapter. This focus takes "emotional investing" out of the equation. They will understand how to manage the investment process, including the asset allocations, managers and the client's risk and return expectation. They will have an evaluation system in place to select appropriate managers and effectively appraise the progress of the investment plan.

Confidence: The consultant must exude the confidence of a seasoned, experienced professional. If it is an act, the savvy investor will recognize it for what it is. If the consultant lacks confidence in his or her recommendations, so will the client. Consultants should be knowledgeable and confident in their recommendations. Investors expect honesty and quick resolution when recommendations prove to be incorrect.

The ability of a consultant to work with both the investor and the managers will produce a consultant-client relationship of mutual understanding and respect. The investor will continuously gain knowledge about the markets and "smart" investing as the consultant consistently presents straightforward and truthful direction, education and advice. Investing is a process designed to meet goals, not make sudden "killings in the market." A seasoned consultant will be able to present a case to the client that will substantiate a course of action that avoids chasing returns and taking inappropriate risks. In order to stay on course, the consultant must be knowledgeable and able to communicate well enough with the client to overcome the inevitable attempts by the client to "redesign" their goals "on the fly." As we will discuss in Chapter 10, there are times when maintaining an appropriate, risk-managed portfolio can be a considerable challenge. Greed and fear are powerful emotions that the consultant must help the investor overcome. Can the consultant persuade the investor to sell a winning position when it is overvalued and buy into the lagging area of the market when it is undervalued and presents better opportunity? As you might imagine, this feat can require all of the skills listed above.

Many investors are unwilling to let go of the decision-making authority and it is up to the consultant to provide rational, well thought out direction. Those who think that "making the client happy" is a winning formula, will soon find out that serious, long-term investors are more interested in an intelligent process than quick results, despite what they may say. This will build the respect that makes the process work.

Designing and adapting an investment plan, implementing it with the most qualified professionals available, and staying on course, are the hallmarks of an Investment Management Consultant. The consulting process is a dynamic, continual practice of analysis and communication. A consultant who is proficient in the skills discussed in this chapter will provide the value that investors need and want.

Background and Experience of a Consultant

A professional Investment Management Consultant is most often a fully licensed securities professional, but his or her practice generally does not include the management of individual stock and bond portfolios, nor the buying and selling of securities. These are the responsibilities of the money manager. A stock broker, as most apply the term, does employ these investment practices, perhaps in conjunction with the use of money managers however, he or she is not necessarily a qualified consultant. Coming from a transaction-oriented background, not all brokers fully understand or are well versed in the concepts of investment management consulting. Becoming a competent consultant requires a thorough understanding of investment management, as well as a perceptual shift from product-oriented selling to process-oriented service.

As the separately managed account industry continues to evolve and grow and, as transactional business is becoming less desirable to firms and their advisors, the firms are strongly encouraging their advisors to market and sell fee-based accounts, such as SMAs. Many firms are doing so by changing the payout structure to these advisors; a smaller percentage is paid for transactional business and a larger percentage is paid for fee-based accounts. These incentives have resulted in many advisors, trained to sell products and securities, treating and selling managed money like any other product. The investment management consulting process is not a product to be sold, rather an investment philosophy to be integrated into the client's investment plan. A true consultant works solely to achieve the objectives of their client, while minimizing their client's exposure to market risk. A disciplined "process" drives the consultant's actions, not the sale of investment "products."

Today, most Investment Management Consultants are part of a brokerage firm, where their consulting department can provide valuable services. The next largest group, the independent consultant, is not associated with a brokerage firm, but must still have some type of broker/dealer relationship if they provide any sort of transactions. One is not better than the other, but one consultant may be more appropriate for certain investors than another. The institutional sized investor has vastly different requirements than a smaller investor, which may affect the relevance of the consultant's affiliations. As an example, it is cost-prohibitive to unbundle fees for the smaller investor, whereas this is common practice for institutional investors. Therefore, the smaller investor is probably best served if their consultant has access to fee-based platforms.

Individuals who call themselves Investment Management Consultants should have specific training, demonstrate that they have been in the consulting business for a number of years and currently have assets under management. Many are members of professional associations that have standards and/or examinations. The Money Management Institute, formed in 1997, provides educational programs and provides a forum for the managed account industry's professionals to discuss issues that affect this industry and their clients. The Institute for Investment Management Consultants, IIMC, merged with

IMCA in 2002, to become a single organization, the Investment Management Consulting Association, IMCA. IMCA is a national nonprofit professional association for the consulting profession. They provide training and continuing education for their members and award the designation CIMA. The awarding of the designation CIMC was discontinued shortly after the merger.

Professional Designations[1]

AIMC (Accredited Investment Management Consultant): This accreditation, which was offered through the Institute for Investment Management Consultants (now merged with the Investment Management Consultant Association) is currently no longer awarded, however many consultants have achieved this designation. The AIMC was considered a level one completion to the CIMC study program. It indicates that an individual has completed a detailed course in the process of investment management consulting, including the development of investment policies, money manager analysis, asset allocation, performance monitoring and evaluation, and ERISA standards. An AIMC is a highly trained consultant.

CIMC (Certified Investment Management Consultant): This designation, which like the AIMC is no longer offered, was available only to practicing consultants. The CIMC program was the advanced training program for practicing consultants only. This designation was not awarded to money managers or marketing sales reps, as they were not practicing consultants. Those CIMCs who have shifted from consulting to other areas of financial services can maintain their CIMC however. Obtaining this designation required a background review and prescreening of the applicant to determine their professional commitment to becoming a practitioner of the investment management consulting process. The CIMC program was a private study program with monitored testing. In addition to the standards met by the AIMC, CIMC training included many of the same study materials and disciplines that were used for the CFA (Chartered Financial Analyst) program. Since the IMCA/IIMC merger, the only designation currently offered to someone focused on investment management consulting is the CIMA.

---

1. For additional designations that are used in the investment industry, however not specific to the investment management consulting process, refer to Appendix A.

CIMA (Certified Investment Management Analyst): CIMA, offered through the Investment Management Consultants Association (www.imca.org), is widely used by financial professionals to demonstrate their knowledge of the investment management consulting process. To obtain this accreditation, an individual must first complete private study materials, meet certain background questions, attend a one-week course at Wharton and pass a proficiency exam. This course of study focuses on the before mentioned areas relating to the investment management consulting process. The CIMA is available to both practicing consultants and non-practicing consultants. Examples of non-practicing consultants include inside consulting department analysts, marketing and sales reps of money management and brokerage firms.

CFA (Chartered Financial Analyst): This accreditation is awarded by the CFA Institute, Charlottesville, VA (www.cfainstitute.org). A CFA has passed tests in economics, accounting, security analysis and money management and, has three years of investments-related experience. CFAs generally utilize their analytical skills as security analysts or portfolio managers. A CFA does not have consultant-specific training; however, this designation is highly regarded in the industry. CFAs will generally be found within investment management firms, though more and more consulting practices are finding the education and training of the Chartered Financial Analyst to be a valuable asset within their practices.

Anyone seeking the skills of a consultant or financial advisor to assist with the investment management consulting process should seek out those individuals who are passionate about the real consulting process. This person can come with a variety of titles, but they must have the depth of experience and **commitment** to the investment management consulting process to effectively fulfill their role as Consultant. There are many financial advisors in the brokerage or financial services industry that sell managed money along with other products, however there is a relatively small group that has committed themselves to the consulting profession. This statement doesn't mean that someone who is not solely committed to the investment management consulting process can't pick a good money manager, although it might mean that an investor might not be receiving all of the attributes of what is available. If you are a consultant, you must stand out as a specialist to compete in today's marketplace; if you are an investor, the consultant that you select may account for the difference in meeting your objective and/or taking too much risk in the process.

INTERVIEW POTENTIAL CONSULTANTS

It is important that there is a rapport between the consultant and investor, so when beginning the interviewing process, the investor should listen for indicators of the consultant's true approach and philosophy.

- Does the consultant talk about performance before goals and objectives?
- How does the consultant develop appropriate asset allocations? Do they rely on their firm's consulting or strategy departments? If so, to what degree?
- Do you feel as though the recommendations given to you address your specific needs, or do they feel "boiler plate?"
- Does the consultant recommend static asset allocation models or does he or she use a more proactive approach? Which suits your expectations?
- Does the consultant do manager searches and due diligence or does he or she rely on their firm's consulting department?
- Money management firms are large and small and there are advantages and disadvantages to both. Is this conversation part of the selection process?

Look for a consultant who is able to articulate his or her investment philosophy and investment strategy; one who is willing to walk the client through the process; and one who has a well thought out discipline that will protect the portfolio from emotional investing. If the client has a short-term perspective for their investment portfolio, it is unlikely that they will reap the benefits that a consultant brings to the process.

In order to discover a consultants proficiencies in the skills, tools and processes described in this chapter, we have provided a list of questions that might be used in an RFP (request for proposal) or in an initial meeting. When developing an RFP, focus on the areas that are most important to you, the client.

1. **EXPERIENCE AND BACKGROUND.** The intent is to discover whether the consultant or advisor is truly focused on a consulting practice or simply "selling" managed money.

a. How long has the consultant been providing investment management consulting services?

b. What percentage of the consultant's business is dedicated to providing consulting services to clients?

c. What consulting services are provided?
- Individually tailored investment policy statements? How are they developed and maintained?
- Asset allocation studies?
- Manager search and selection?
- Objective performance monitoring and manager evaluation reports?

d. What methodology is used in capital market analysis?

e. How many assets does the consultant oversee?

f. How many consulting relationships are there and how long have they been in place? This question is interesting, because more is not necessarily better.

g. How many people are on the consulting team and what is their role in managing this account? Who are the contact people? The size of the team should align with client servicing needs.

h. Do they hold any professional credentials or designations, such as CIMC, AIMC, CFA or CIMA? Credentialing is of interest, but does not, in and of itself, determine skill.

i. Describe your investment philosophy. This is important in determining compatibility.

2. ACCOUNT INFORMATION

a. What types of accounts are consulted? Account types may provide insight into the experience of the consultant or the consultant's "preferred" client type. The key is that the client and consultant are compatible and that the consultant understands the needs of the client, i.e., fiduciaries have different requirements than high net worth individuals. It is not necessary for the account types to be the same.
- Pension plans
- Public funds
- Foundations and endowments
- Not-for-profit organizations

- Taft-Hartley
- High net worth individuals

Some investment management consultants focus primarily on servicing large, institutional investors, such as pension funds, which have $100 million or more in assets. Others specialize in "high net worth" individuals, foundations and endowments and small to medium size pension plans ($1 million to $100 million).

b. What size accounts does the consultant handle? What percentage of client relationships is above $1 million, $10 million, $25 million?

c. Account Minimums: Many consultants will not take accounts under $250,000, as it is difficult to allocate to enough managers (styles) to properly diversify the portfolio. Those consultants that deal more with institutional-types of clients may have minimums of $1 to 5 million. Neither is necessarily better; consultants generally work with clients that are a good fit for their practice.

3. **ASSET ALLOCATION.** What methodology does the consultant use to develop and maintain an appropriate asset allocation? We have discussed several approaches to asset allocation in Chapter 12, such as computer-based asset allocation models and proactive asset allocation, however some or all of the following are generally drivers of this process.

a. Investment policy, which includes periodic changes in objectives or needs
b. Macro economic conditions
c. Valuation models
d. Fundamentals
e. Technical analysis

If computer models are used:
a. What software is used? Is it purchased or developed in-house?
b. How many staff members are assigned to modeling?
c. How closely are the computer models followed?

4. **REFERENCES.** You should ask your investment management consultant for references from clients whose situations and objectives are similar

to your own. Ask your consultant how long they have been with clients and if possible, get references from clients who have worked with a consultant for at least three to five years. This time frame covers a full market cycle. Be sensitive to confidentiality constraints.

5. **MONEY MANAGERS.** What types of money managers does the consultant recommend and how are they chosen and monitored? Rather than selecting a manager who favors the latest fad or, the best return in the last quarter, the consultants should use a disciplined process in selecting money management firms. Consultants may also have a preference for the size of the money management firm or choose to use only those recommended by their brokerage firm. This topic will be covered in detail in Chapter 18.

   a. What is the search process for money managers?

   b. Does the consultant maintain a database of management firms? If so, is it compiled internally or purchased from an outside service? If purchased, what is the source?

   c. Are the managers required to pay to be included in the database?

   d. How many money managers are currently being used and tracked by the consultant?

   e. Are there any potential conflicts of interest between the manager and the consultant, such as fee arrangements?

   f. How often and where do you meet with the money managers?

   g. Do you have experience in screening and selecting managers that specialize in alternative investments?

   h. What is your internal due diligence process?

6. **MONITORING AND REVIEW PROCEDURES.** The investment management consultant updates, monitors and reviews the progress of the overall portfolio on a quarterly basis, or more often if the investor's needs change or if the markets dictate. The consultant and investor will discuss any substantive changes in market conditions, investor objectives or management firm changes, such as staffing or direction. Ask the prospective consultants how frequently they will meet with clients for this review and how accessible and responsive they will be on an ongoing basis.

Close communication increases the "comfort level" for both the client and the consultant.

a. What type of monitoring procedures does the consultant have in place, such as risk-adjusted performance measurement and adherence to the objectives set forth in the investment policy?

b. What is the source of performance monitoring data and analysis? Provide a sample report.

c. Describe the internal process for monitoring and evaluating managers.

Regardless of how often there is a personal meeting, insist on a minimum of quarterly written reports that measure actual performance against the established objectives set forth in the investment policy. The client should also receive monthly statements from the custodian that itemizes all activity within the account throughout the month.

7. **CUSTODIAN.** Who is the custodian of the assets? How will the custodian's fees be charged? Assets are generally not held by the money manager, but are held in an insured custodial account. The custodian can be the consultant's brokerage firm, or if the consultant is an independent, the designated clearing firm. The custodian can also be a bank trust department or insurance company. The custodian holds the assets and the insurance protects the investor's assets from fraud, embezzlement, and financial failure, to name a few. It does not insure against market value loss or guarantee returns. Money managers may either have an affiliate relationship with a bank or broker/dealer, in which case the custodian could be their affiliated firm. In most cases, money managers only have discretionary authority to make the buy and sell decisions within the portfolio and are bound to operating under the guidelines and custodial structure set forth in the investment policy statement. If the custodian holding the assets is (a) not the consultant's brokerage firm and (b) not part of an all-inclusive fee structure, there will be a separate fee for the custodial service or transactions, or both. Many plan sponsors and trustees opt for an all-inclusive fee structure rather than pay additional fees for custodial services. Brokerage firms hold and insure assets and provide the other required administrative services, as do banks, but rarely act as trustees under this arrangement. Some plan sponsors and trustees feel that having

an addition bank trustee adds a layer of protection; some do not. Legal counsel should be consulted to make this determination.

8. **FEES.** How is the consultant compensated, and how do they set their fees? The fees charged and the methods of payment for investment management consultants can vary greatly. Most consultants are now fee-based and charge regressive fees depending on the size of the overall portfolio, but an asset-based fee is not the only compensation structure available. There are three predominant ways in which a consultant is compensated:

   a. **Fee-Only.** Fee-only investment management consultants set fees based on a) a percentage of the value of the assets under management, b) according to a set hourly rate, or c) a flat fixed fee (hard-dollar fee). They receive no other compensation for their services, such as brokerage commissions. Determine the services that are included in the fee and if there are any incidental charges.

   - Fees based on the account value are annual fees, generally calculated quarterly. If the account value has appreciated at the end of the quarter, then the consultant's fees will show a net increase and if the account value decreases, the consultant's fees will be reduced. This fee generally includes:
     - All transaction (trading) costs
     - Establishment, review, and updates of the Investment Policy Statement
     - Asset allocation studies
     - Manager searches and recommendations
     - Performance monitoring and evaluation
     - On-going portfolio recommendation
     - Custodianship
   - Set hourly rates are the equivalent of a professional fee-for-service and are charged in the same manner as attorney's fees. These are generally used only for special projects, where there is not likely to be an ongoing relationship. These fees can range from $75 to over $300 an hour.

- Some consultants charge a fixed hard-dollar fee, also known as a flat fee, for their services. This fee structure could be an all-inclusive annual retainer or may have separate charges for each service provided. This fee structure is often used by larger plans that require ongoing monitoring and oversight by an independent professional (Prudent Expert Rule). The fees will vary depending on the complexity of the plan and the services required of the consultant. Fixed fees can range from $3,500 to $15,000 for each assignment.

b. **Commissions.** Investment management consultants, who derive any part of their income from commissions, receive this commission on the product or security transaction, regardless of the investment results. This arrangement does beg the question: "Why does my consultant want me to make this trade?" Performance results will be directly influenced by these transactions, so it is important that the consultant fully and completely disclose how he or she will be compensated, before entering into any agreement. A consultant can not "double dip," receiving both a commission and a fee on the same account.

c. **Soft dollars.** The consultant might use an "offset" fee structure, also known as "soft dollars," where the quoted or agreed upon fixed hard dollar fee is reduced by an agreed upon percentage (50% in our example) of trading commissions, which will vary with the number of trades.

> Quoted fixed hard dollar fee – 50% of Directed Brokerage = Hard dollar fee paid
> $10,000 – 0.5 x $4,500 = $7,750

Using a commission to offset a fee may be entirely appropriate, as long as the relationship between and money management firm and the investment management consultant is fully disclosed. Soft dollar payment has been around for many years and, in general has served the industry well. When the manager trades, commissions are generally generated. If the manager directs that the trades be done at the consultant's firm (directed brokerage), a portion of these commission dollars can be used to offset the hard dollar expense to the investor. This exchange can be advantageous to the investor, but it does require a certain amount of cooperation and full disclosure between the various parties, as this type of relationship between a consultant and a money manager could present a conflict of interest.

9. **CONFLICTS OF INTEREST.** How does the consultant prevent conflicts of interest? Fees and compensation agreements can cause potential conflicts of interest. These must be guarded against and all forms of compensation should be disclosed. These disclosures should include all agreements between any combinations of the consultant, custodian, money management firm/s and/or broker/dealer.

CONCLUSION

This chapter has emphasized the point that selecting an investment management consultant is not something that should be done quickly or taken lightly. There are many skills that an effective consultant should possess and it is therefore wise to review a consultant's background very carefully. Investing your time before you invest your money will allow you to be better able to select a skilled consultant and in turn, your professional money managers. The combination of these professionals is key to realizing your investment goals. The Consultant is your guide through the entire process; choose wisely.

For the financial professional who is currently providing the services of investment management consulting or wishing to become more proficient in a consulting practice, it is incumbent upon you to continually expand your knowledge and experience in order to offer exceptional value to the client and to better compete in today's marketplace. For those committed to this pursuit, a continuing process of education, on-going analysis of outside (unbiased) research data and collaboration with talented people are just a few of the essentials necessary to excel as a professional Investment Management Consultant.

7

Consulting as a Profession

BECOMING A CONSULTANT

In order to transition a practice for a transactional approach to an advisory role, there must be a desire to "partner" with the investor. You will no longer sell anything; all recommendations will be part of an overall investment plan and will contribute to the investor's objectives and goals. Become proficient at each element of the consulting process that we have provided in this book. As listed in the previous chapter, they include the ability to:

- Develop a realistic investment policy
- Design an appropriate asset allocation
- Select the appropriate money management firms and/or investment vehicles
- Effectively monitor the performance of the managers and the overall portfolio

Learn the Process

Develop a working relationship with your firm's consulting department. Get a list of the sub-advisory firms with whom your brokerage firm has contracted. Spend time with the representatives of these money management firms and understand their philosophy and style. Discuss the processes used by your firm's consulting and strategy departments to design risk appropriate asset allocations and to review money management firms. Learn everything that you can about the "processes" that are in place, what works well and what could be better. To be effective as a consultant, you will need to compare the investor's profile to that of the manager in order to create a suitable asset allocation. The more that you know about the managers, the better able you will be to substantiate your recommendations to your clients.

When communicating with managers, remember that they too rely on your ability to make an appropriate match, as compatibility is a critical element in the longevity of the client relationship. If the consultant contributes to this team effort and respects the client-consultant-manager relationship, the manager can offer many additional benefits. Managers can and do set aside time to interact directly with clients; they sponsor educational or training events that are by invitation only and, they share their research and expert opinions with the consultant who can then pass this information on to clients. Use these resources to increases the value that you add to your client relationships.

We listed six must-have traits of a consultant in the last chapter. Mastering the above information builds **Knowledge, Confidence** and is part of the **Disciplined Process.** It will not be possible to be a good **Communicator** or **Educator** if you do not have a firm grasp of all of this information. The sixth trait, **Interpreter,** requires an understanding of the capital markets, the ability to translate that information into layman's language and the capacity to listen to what an investor says and does not say. If they become stuck on something that you believe is not in their best interest, find a way to get at the cause. Determining an investor's biases does not mean that you will be able to change their mind, but you will know what you are dealing with and be able to better design a plan that is suitable for that individual investor. Consultants act in an advisory role; it is our task to convey the information necessary to make good investment decisions.

Some brokerage firms offer training programs to provide their advisors with a better understanding of the consulting process. Several offer certification programs that designate that the advisor has attained a specific level of competency in the consulting process. These firms are strongly encouraging their advisors to convert their business models to fee-based and these training programs, along with the different platforms and model portfolios (Chapter 4) provided by their strategy and/or consulting departments are there to hasten the conversion.

The Investment Management Consultants Association (IMCA) offers a certification program that provides the CIMA designation at completion. They also offer continuing education programs. The CFP and CFA programs provide valuable information, albeit not consultant specific, and the Money

Management Institute also offers educational programs. These independent associations supplement the training programs of brokerage firms. The level of professionalism however, remains in the hands of the individual consultant. Those who dedicate the time and energy into retooling their practice will be the ones who succeed in making the transition. Clearly, this change can not happen overnight; do not set unrealistic time limits on this conversion as your clients must adapt to this change in investment philosophy. It will take patience and time to prove to your clients that a fee-based arrangement will be beneficial to them.

If you are not yet proficient in the analysis of the capital markets or feel uncomfortable designing risk appropriate asset allocations, many firms are offering platforms and services, such as multiple strategy portfolios, that help to bridge the gap between a transactional business and the more complete consulting process. They provide the client profile questionnaire and risk assessments, and then make risk appropriate asset allocation recommendations. These platforms offer a temporary win-win solution. The client gets the simplicity of a single account and a higher level of advice and guidance, while the advisor's perceived value increases, as most clients respond well to this disciplined process. For those who are committed to this transition, model portfolios should be used only as a bridge to the consulting process, as they are likely to fall short of the more sophisticated investor's expectations.

Converting Your Client-Base

Evaluate your client-base and your goals. Categorize your practice using the following guidelines:

Account Size
- Set an account minimum and place clients into the two groups, one above and one below that mark.
- Review those who fall below that mark and determine whether they are likely to move into the group above that mark.
- Place those who are likely to move up in their own group.

It may be your goal to have no account below a certain level, as they can be disproportionately time consuming and/or not appropriate for the consulting process. Keep those accounts that may ultimately be candidates for managed money or who offer some other advantage to the practice that you are developing, such as those who are a center of influence.

Account Type
- Equity, balanced, fixed, other
- Focus on equity related accounts first, as the advantages of managed accounts are more readily apparent and easier to communicate for equity portfolios.

Investor Philosophy
- Begin with clients who will understand the value that the consulting process can bring to their overall portfolio, such as a more personalized approach, tax management and risk management.
- Carefully evaluate each account to determine the areas where immediate value can be shown, such as costs, diversification, transparency or professionalism. Show the investor specifically how he of she will benefit from this new concept.

Define your Investment Philosophy
- Determine your style and where managers may compliment what you have already done for your clients, e.g. add an international, value or small cap manager.
- Convince yourself that the added manager expertise and diversification is good for your practice and your clients. This step may seem obvious, but the consulting process is a conceptual change that the advisor must be committed to prior to talking with clients.
- Have a plan to phase yourself out of portfolio management and into consulting. Decide what, if any, investment disciplines that you intend to continue and work toward that goal.

Blend these components and rank your clients according to those who you believe will be the most receptive, those that have the most to gain and those who are the most valuable to you. These rankings may be due to centers of influence or monetary value. Begin speaking with those clients in the middle. You will need practice and feedback and it is best not to start with the most promising or valuable clients.

Approach the conversion from a retail practice to a consulting practice in a systematic manner. Do not talk to clients before you are intimately familiar with each element of the consulting process and do not waste time on prospects or clients who will not add value to your consulting practice. Stay focused, as it is challenging not to fall back on the familiar. The following steps will help to guide you:

Step 1 Do the work; gain the knowledge; focus on the value of the process for both you and your clients.

Step 2 Evaluate your practice; set realistic standards; be willing to "fire" those clients who are not suitable for your new focus.

Step 3 Convert your clients to the consulting process. Total conversion may take years, as client perception, market opportunity and tax consequence will all play a role in the conversion. Stay focused on those clients who will ultimately benefit from this process.

Step 4 Continue to hone your skills; the goal is to become a self-sufficient consultant; one who is skilled at all facets of the consulting process and market analysis.

TRANSITIONING TO INSTITUTIONAL ACCOUNTS

Many consultants have practices that center on high net worth individuals. These individuals often sit on boards for endowments and foundations and this involvement often generates a referral for the consultant. For those who are considering this transition, there are many differences between working with high net worth individuals and small to mid sized institutional accounts, such as foundations, endowments and retirement plans.

One of the main concerns that board members and trustees have is their fiduciary responsibility. They will be looking for someone who has the skills and knowledge to assist them in fulfilling the "expert" standard that is required of them. Fiduciaries can be subjected to considerable scrutiny, therefore the consultant must be aware of their responsibilities and provide advice accordingly. In *Fiduciary Investing* (Section V), we outline the responsibilities of fiduciaries and consultants and the higher standards that both will be held to when accounts are overseen for the benefit of others. These requirements, and the concern that board members and trustees have with complying with certain standards, will drive many of the investment decisions. A consultant must understand these constraints.

This book is dedicated to educating investment professionals as well as those who use their services, about the consulting process and the use of professional money managers. Those who wish to provide service and expertise to institutional accounts must utilize the consulting process when considering these relationships. Very few of these types of accounts have a single decision maker and the consultant must be able and willing to invest the amount of time that it may take to communicate with a board of directors or group of trustees and must have the knowledge and skills that are required to obtain a consensus among them. If you wish to make this transition, you must be proficient in the skills set forth in this book and be able to demonstrate your value as a consultant.

When being interviewed for a position as a consultant for an institutional account, there are several skill-sets that must be at your fingertips and you must have a thorough understanding of the selection process, which is likely to include:

- The consultant RFP
- An asset allocation study
- Manager searches
- Manager RFPs
- Sophisticated monitoring and evaluation tools
- Attendance and reporting at quarterly meetings

If you are unable or unwilling to fulfill these requirements for an institutional account, then transitioning your practice into this arena is unrealistic. It is imperative that a transitioning consultant understand that presentations to institutional prospects and clients are not sales presentations, showcasing a line-up of available managers, but rather a discussion of needs and process. Managers are a component of the process provided by the consultant, not the selling point. Institutional accounts are generally looking for a skilled consultant that can assist them in their duties as fiduciaries and they are far more interested in seeing a well thought out process with checks and balances than they are in unrelated performance numbers or the who's who of managers. If you do not have the skills presented in this book, it is unlikely that you will be able to make this transition. For those who seek institutional clients, we will explore some of the challenges that they may present.

The Consultant RFP

Generally speaking, the fiduciary/s will send a request for proposal (RFP) out to a number of candidates. Preparing an RFP should be the fiduciary's first step in the due diligence process of selecting a new consultant. We have outlined the various questions that should be asked in the RFP in Chapter 6. The consultant who is considering responding should ask him or herself if they are "file filler," as the fiduciary/s probably has 2 or 3 strong candidates in mind, either through personal experience and/or through a trusted referral. The other RFP candidates help to fulfill the fiduciary's obligations. These second string candidates may quickly become part of the bottom of the pile in the due diligence file. Or, the institution's policy may require a periodic review of investment professionals to determine if the services that they are providing are on par with the marketplace. In either case, consultants who receive "blind" RFPs should consider the potential of the institution becoming a client and, the consultant should only respond if he or she meets the qualifications required by the institution.

As a rule, most firms have individuals qualified to assist in the responses to RFPs. Many of the questions that will be asked are somewhat standard in content, such as "Provide information on background and experience," so these should be readily available. Do not crowd that deadline for submitting responses, as the proposal will need to be reviewed by the compliance department and revisions may be required.

Asset Allocation Study

Asset allocation is covered thoroughly in Chapter 12, but the consultant for institutional accounts will have to be aware of a different mindset that many boards may have regarding asset allocation structures and risk management, as well as generally having different cash flow considerations than most high net worth individuals. Due to the fiduciary scrutiny that board members may be subjected to, they may insist on an asset allocation that mimics their peers, not wanting to step too far out of the norm. Shifting allocations may be problematic during certain market conditions and requires that the consultant set the stage early and be very methodical about documentation. The consultant also has a fiduciary responsibility, so it is advisable to create a chronological documentation system for recommendations and subsequent actions taken by the board. There is no right or wrong here, only a clear understanding of the decision-making process. Developing and maintaining a suitable asset allocation requires the consultant to:

- Be a good communicator, providing unbiased information and advice
- Assist in the development of and ongoing compliance with the investment policy statement. Performance is a function of asset allocation and asset allocation is determined by the investment policy.
- Provide market and asset allocation recommendations.
- Maintain a performance monitoring system.
- Provide any relevant information regarding the money managers.

Manager Searches and RFPs

As we stated before, you will not win institutional accounts by presenting a bag full of managers from which to select. Managers are part of the process, but they do not win accounts for the consultant. You must first show your value, describe your philosophy and offer advice that is specific to the client's situation; do not try to sell.

As a consultant, your relationship with the managers is very important. Do not alienate the managers by asking them to participate in RFPs that there is no chance of winning. RFPs are very time consuming and these requests put managers in a difficult position. They too want to win new business, but they do not want to participate in an RFP when the consultant has not done their homework. They know that they do not win business in these situations. What often happens is that the novice institutional consultant places the cart before the horse. Consultants ask the manager to fill out an RFP before the consultant even has the client, just so the consultant can approach the prospective client with a briefcase full of paper. The consultant will not win the client with this approach and the manager knows it. Do not waste everyone's time; this approach does not work. Manager selection only becomes relevant after the consultant has a relationship with the client, an investment policy has been written and an asset allocation has been agreed upon. Following these steps is the only approach that wins institutional accounts and the board members will be insulted that you have wasted their time with anything other than a well thought out investment process.

The next step is to understand the managers and the needs of the client. Do not ask managers to participate in RFPs if you know that they do not fit the client's criteria, such as style, investment philosophy or fee structure. Your credibility with managers is precious capital in your long-term success as a consultant; don't waste it. Refer to Chapter 6 for the relationship between a consultant and money manager.

Monitoring and Evaluation Tools

When the consultant provides timely, quality performance and evaluation reports, the fiduciaries are able to more easily meet their obligations of oversight. Meeting their obligations as fiduciaries is generally the primary concern of trustees and board members, as failing to do so may result in personal, legal and/or financial consequences. The ability to deliver a sophisticated report is something that institutional clients demand.

We have provided guidance in this area in Section IV, which contains information on any number of evaluation and comparative tools of analysis. The consultant must remember that board members, top notch in their own fields, are not investment professionals and having a clear, concise, uncluttered presentation is more informative than trying to impress them with piles of data. You must control the amount of information that you present. The only thing that really matters is how the performance of the portfolio compares to the objectives and risk profile set forth in the investment policy. Understand, communicate, and report the portfolio's performance and that of each manager in that context.

The periodic board meetings are your best opportunity to show your value as a consultant. Be concise in your presentation. Discuss economic and market influences that may affect the portfolio, provide a portfolio overview, followed by the performance of each manager. This review should center on the client's investment policy and risk-adjusted returns. Discuss any client issues that may alter the objectives for the portfolio and make any allocation or manager recommendations that you feel are warranted based on these discussions. If changes are agreed upon, discuss an appropriate time frame and follow-up in writing when necessary (fiduciary documentation). This approach to meetings will demonstrate your knowledge and level of professionalism.

Attendance and Reporting

Institutional clients generally require their consultant and often their money managers to attend periodic (often quarterly) meetings. These may or may not be local and you must take travel into consideration when negotiating fees. Travel may result in a substantial time commitment as well as cost, and these concerns need to be part of the consultant's decision-making process. Many times the desire to break into the institutional marketplace clouds one's judgment in this area, but once the contractual agreement is in place, it is very difficult to change. Make sure the agreement is something that you can live with, because your credibility is at stake in a very small pond.

CONCLUSION

An individual must be committed to the time and mind-set that transitioning one's practice will require. Consultants become part of their client's vision of their future and are often consulted on matters that are outside the investment field. This relationship of trust is only achieved when the consultant provides consistent, unbiased advice that he or she believes is solely in the client's best interest. The advisor must be able to step away from the concept of a sale and focus on process.

Institutional clients need the guidance and support of a pragmatic, well-informed consultant. They have a fiduciary duty to manage funds and oversee investment professionals in a manner that is consistent with someone who is familiar with such matters (Prudent Expert Rule). This requirement is of great concern to fiduciaries and by delegating this duty to a qualified consultant, they are able to fulfill this daunting duty.

8

The Investment Policy Statement

The Investment Policy Statement (IPS) is a document or plan agreed upon by the investor and the consultant. The consultant and the investor will work together to establish a realistic, long-term investment strategy to guide the investment process. Once written, it will act as a road map for the investment portfolio. Regardless of whether the investor is an individual, corporation or retirement plan, developing a well thought out investment policy is critical in establishing an appropriate and effective investment plan. When structuring the investment plan, the investor and consultant should discuss and incorporate the following ideas and information into the investment policy statement:

- The background and financial condition of the investor
- The purpose for investing
- The goals, objectives and values of the investor
- The investment strategy and guidelines
- The process for evaluating progress

In order to obtain the information necessary to construct a realistic plan and to uncover the investor's real goals and risk tolerances, the consultant will help the investor complete a detailed questionnaire, such as the one in Appendix B, which is designed to be informative to both the consultant and the investor. In addition to the questionnaire, the consultant should ask probing questions to determine the primary concerns of the investor, which will help to develop the long-term strategic approach for the investment plan. A very telling question may be: "What does money mean to you?" or "What values or goals will money fulfill for you?" As you can see, questions structured in this manner are able to get at the heart of what is driving the investment process versus simply asking, "How much money do you think you need to retire?" It is through this process that the consultant and investor will agree upon not only the investment strategy, but also the investor's philosophy about investing. The two work hand-in-hand to create an appropriate investment plan.

The information derived from the questionnaire and the interviewing process will result in an investment policy that will paint a clear picture of the investor's tolerance to risk. The consultant and the investor must clearly understand and agree upon the investor's goals, expectations and risk tolerances in order to develop a suitable asset allocation for the portfolio and then to subsequently select the appropriate money managers and/or investment vehicles. It is an understanding of the relationship between the risk profile and the expected returns that will guide the portfolio structure. It is unrealistic for the investor to expect returns that are not consistent with the risk that they are willing to accept, i.e., 100% return and zero risk, and it is the consultant's responsibility to clearly communicate the correlation between the two. Risk tolerance and return expectations are both topics that must be constantly revisited, as neither investor circumstance nor market conditions remain static. Managing expectations and their relationship to risk may be the most challenging part of the consulting profession and therefore we have dedicated a chapter (Chapter 9) to this subject.

Each of the guidelines listed below should be considered when writing any investment policy.

Purpose and background
- Purpose of investing
- Investor's investment history
- Investor's overall financial profile and tax status
- Any legal issues affecting the structure of the account/s

Investment objectives
- Return expectations
- Risk tolerance and investor's investment philosophy

- Investment time horizons
- Assets that will be placed under management
- Income or cash flow needs
- Contributions and distributions

Investment strategy and guidelines
- Appropriate macro asset allocation (bonds, equities and cash)
- Identify duties and responsibilities
- Investment restrictions
- Asset class preferences

Investment goals, both short & long-term
- Education
- Retirement
- Second home
- Tax planning and management
- Estate planning and wealth transfer
- Charitable gifting

Performance and evaluation guidelines
- Compare overall returns to target goal
- Compare individual investment vehicles to appropriate benchmarks
- Adjust to changes in the investor's goals and objectives and/or market conditions

Once written, the consultant will use the investment policy to develop a detailed asset allocation, dividing the assets into specific styles with varying correlation to one another in an attempt to meet return expectations and to manage risk (Chapter 12). The consultant will then recommend money managers or other investment vehicles to complement these allocations. In addition to providing an investment road map, the policy also formally communicates objectives, restrictions and risk tolerances, and provides a means to reduce the possibility of a misunderstanding between the investor, consultant and/or money managers. This document also helps to keep the investor focused on long-term goals and not on temporary market extremes.

PURPOSE AND BACKGROUND

Purpose of Investing

There are inherent risks in investing and the consultant needs to understand the investor's reason for investing. Most often, investor's think only in terms of building wealth and believe that by having more money sometime in the future, they can address their other needs as they come about. This belief is only partially true and through the discovery process required to write an investment policy and an understanding of the realities of the capital markets, the investor and consultant can more effectively develop an investment strategy.

Investment History

An individual's investment history can have a substantial affect on how the investment portfolio is structured. Many people have had a bad experience in some area of the markets and have vowed to never return. Others have experience only in stocks, while still others have a broad range of investment experience. The role of the consultant is also one of educator, and as a general rule, knowledgeable, well informed investors sleep best at night and make the best investors. It is often up to the consultant to expand the investor's knowledge in order to design the most suitable portfolio.

Financial Profile and Tax Status

Before developing an investment strategy, it is important to understand the investor's financial condition. Compiling a personal balance sheet and income statement is often helpful as it will show the investor's assets, exposure to debt, cash flow and discretionary income. Combining this information with goals such as college funding, medical needs and/or retirement will help to create a realistic investment plan.

Tax considerations are almost always an important part of a portfolio's structure, unless the assets are held entirely within a retirement plan or some other tax favored structure, such as not-for-profit organizations or certain trusts. Tax concerns can affect the choice of securities, the methods used to reallocate assets and the timing choices for contributions and distributions. These should be included in the investment policy and updated as necessary.

Legal Structure

The investment policy should address the legal entity of the investor, such as a corporation, foundation, trust, personal account or irrevocable trust, and it should identify the responsible parties or fiduciary/s, such as the chairman, director, trustee or custodian. Any legal structure other than a personal account increases the level of documentation required in this area. We will discuss this further in *Fiduciary Investing* (Section V).

INVESTMENT OBJECTIVES

Return Expectations

When establishing return objectives, there should be an attempt to quantify expectations. "Aggressive growth" is open to interpretation, while "a 12% annualized return, net of fees" (nominal rate of return) is specific and measurable, as is "a return 10% greater than inflation (real rate of return)." It is important to establish a measurable return objective in order to determine the success of the overall plan and to evaluate the performance of each manager or investment vehicle.

The investor may have a specific investment goal that will require an "absolute" return. If a specific return is the only goal, the policy should differentiate between relative and absolute performance. Money manager performance is generally measured on a relative basis, which compares their results to relevant benchmarks and, they are also evaluated for their ability to control volatility and create an alpha return (Chapter 18). This relative measurement, although a valuable manager evaluation tool, may not suit the investor's needs or investment perspective if they are solely interested in a real-dollar return for a specific purpose. This distinction is important and must be clarified in the investment policy, as it may alter risk management and asset allocation decisions.

Risk Tolerance

Risk and return expectations are invariably linked and it is the responsibility of the consultant, and the goal of the investment policy, to reach a balance between the two. Risk tolerance can be both qualitative and quantitative as the investor's tolerance may be quite different from simply meeting or beating a specific index. Quantify the downside risk; can the investor tolerate a 20% loss in a year (absolute) or, in a year where the S&P 500 losses 30% (relative)?

If the investor expresses intolerance to high volatility under any circumstances, then emotions will be a more important element in risk management than a quantitative comparison. These investors will most likely provide the greater challenge to the consultant who is balancing risk with return expectations.

Investors are generally categorized in risk profiles, such as:

- **Conservative:** A low tolerance to risk and willing to limit capital appreciation opportunities in favor of preserving capital
- **Moderate:** Has the financial resources and investment experience to accept some loss of capital in order to reach his or her investment goal
- **Aggressive:** Financially able and willing to risk substantial portions of his or her investment capital in order to achieve a high investment return. This individual should have investment experience and understand various strategies that are employed to achieve high returns.
- **Growth and Income:** These investors have a desire for growth, which can be conservative to aggressive, but they also want the portfolio to generate income.

Investment Philosophy of Investor

Stating the investor's investment philosophy in the policy is valuable when trying to keep the investor on track. Investors have a tendency to change their mind, particularly regarding risk tolerance and return expectations, when their returns differ from what they believe the "market" is doing. If there is a runaway market in a high-risk sector, but the investor had expressed a conservative philosophy, it should be made clear to the investor that they may not participate in that return, as the portfolio allocations for a conservative investor would be designed to avoid exposure to high-risk areas of the market. Many investors lost their focus during the tech bubble in 2000. If the investor is unhappy with his or her returns during market extremes, it is helpful to be able to refer back to this section of the policy.

Investment Time Horizons

Communicating and developing a long-term investment strategy achieves many objectives. Time allows for a smoothing of results, as the capital markets can be volatile over short-term periods and time tends to increase the likelihood of achieving return expectations.

- This smoothing effect will reduce the overall risk of the portfolio by comparing volatility to the 3- to 5-year cycles of the markets versus quarterly fluctuations.
- A long-term investment perspective helps to reduce the investor's emotional reactions to short-term events. The emotions of fear and greed cause many investors to abandon their plan and they end up selling near the bottom (fear) and buying near the top (fear of missing out or greed).

Maintaining a long-term perspective requires a disciplined, yet proactive approach to asset allocation, which is discussed in Chapter 12. Investment strategies will differ according to time horizons. These may be dictated either by the investors needs, both short and long-term, and/or by the investor's age.

Assets

The consultant should have an understanding of all of the investor's assets and liabilities in order to determine an appropriate investment strategy for the assets that will be invested. The amount of assets that will be invested will determine the types of investments that can be made, e.g. separately managed accounts generally have a $100,000 minimum per manager (allocation style) and investments such as managed futures require the investor to have a high net worth.

Cash Flow Requirements

Portfolios that have a certain income or cash flow requirement must be structured in a manner that will accommodate that need. It may be necessary to keep cash available or to invest specifically in income producing securities.

INVESTING GUIDELINES

Macro Asset Allocation

The macro asset allocation, bonds, equities, cash, etc., is the starting point to incorporate each of the guidelines that we have covered above. The asset classes that are chosen attempt to balance risk and return in an effort to meet the investor's return expectations, risk profile and cash flow needs. The more refined style allocations are then made, with the goal of capitalizing on opportunities within the dynamic capital markets.

Identify Duties and Responsibilities

In more complex policies, it is helpful to identify the duties and responsibilities of the individuals involved in decision-making and the management of the investment portfolio. The decision makers can include corporate officers, investment committees, directors or trustees, while those involved in investment advice and portfolio management can include attorneys, CPA's, financial advisors, consultants and money managers. It is important to identify these individuals and to define their responsibilities in order to prevent misunderstandings and/or legal exposure for fiduciaries.

Investment Restrictions and Preferences

The investor may have an objection to investing in certain types of securities, such as tobacco stocks, or they may wish to limit or exclude their exposure to securities such as junk bonds. There are many types of securities that can be included or excluded and there is an extensive list of examples in the ERISA policy example in Appendix C. Depending on the investor's investment philosophy, there may be preferred asset classes or, those that are prohibited. Asset allocation guidelines can be included here, especially if there are cash flow or income needs. As an example, "the portfolio must always maintain cash or cash equivalents of 5%."

INVESTMENT GOALS

Investment goals often encompass financial goals, such as preserving and/or growing capital, generating an income stream, or meeting specific spending goals such as:

- Education
- Retirement
- Second home
- Tax planning and management
- Estate planning and wealth transfer
- Charitable gifting

Each of these goals requires a long-term perspective, with milestones set up along the way to evaluate progress. Focusing on long-term goals emphasizes the need for an investment plan and provides the structure and discipline to succeed. Build in flexibility and avoid language that implies that once the plan and asset allocation are established, there is no looking back. Investing is a dynamic process that requires flexibility and skill to capitalize on opportunities and manage risks. The investment policy is only the first step in implementing the investment management consulting process.

PERFORMANCE REVIEW AND EVALUATION GUIDELINES

There should be a structure in place to review not only the overall portfolio, but each investment option and/or manager within the portfolio. Bonds should be compared to an appropriate bond benchmark and stocks should be compared to an index that is appropriate to their market capitalization and style. Performance monitoring is covered in detail in Chapter 19 and should be an ongoing process. Performance and evaluation guidelines should be consistent with the investor's investment philosophy and the terms of the investment policy.

The investment policy should be reviewed annually for individuals and every two years for institutions or at any time there is a substantive change in the investor's financial status or requirements. This review schedule should be stated in the investment policy. Individuals may come into a large sum of money, have an addition to the family or have unexpected expenses. Institutions may have a change in funding requirements or changes in corporate structure or governance. Both may need to respond to substantial changes in the economy, requiring changes in investment guidelines.

OTHER CONSIDERATIONS

Again, depending on the complexity of the plan and the investment professionals that will be involved in the management of asset, there are other topics that can be included in the investment policy. Remember, the investment policy is a roadmap for all those associated with the management of the investment assets and the consultant and the investor should include anything that might be valuable in providing direction and methods of evaluation.

More formally constructed policies may include such sections as:

- Scope of the investment policy
- Purpose of the investment policy
- Definitions of terms used in the policy

- Assignment of responsibilities
- Specific guidelines for each money manager
- Rebalancing requirements
- Prudent expert expectations
- Criteria for terminating a manager

As we will see in *Fiduciary Investing* (Section V), ERISA plans require a great deal of documentation, so when dealing with these plans, the policy should include the required process for hiring the consultant, money managers and other relevant parties.

SIGNATURES

The Investment Policy Statement should be signed and dated by all parties, affirming that the policy has been reviewed by the decision makers and that the investment strategy and philosophy has been agreed upon by all participants, including the investor, consultant and money manager/s.

CONCLUSION

By understanding each of the elements of the investment policy, the consultant can effectively develop a plan that will meet the goals and objectives of the investor. This plan should be flexible enough to adjust to the needs of the investor and the cycles of the markets, but disciplined enough to keep the investor on course. Emotional or undisciplined investing generally creates poor results. The investment policy should outline the long-term investment goals, establishes a plan to meet those goals through appropriate asset allocation and reallocations and provide criteria to measure progress.

We have included a sample structure for an investment policy which focus on individuals and trusts in Appendix C-1. Samples for ERISA-covered plans are included in separate appendices. Depending upon the investor's objectives or the complexity of their financial profile, this sample can be expanded or condensed. There are also software programs and many publications available to assist advisors in constructing and maintaining an investment policy.

9
Understanding Risk and Risk Management

"The essence of investment management is the management of risks, not the management of returns."
                                                        - Benjamin Graham

Many who invest in the capital markets view risk as the possibility of losing money, but there is also a financial risk associated with doing nothing. When designing a suitable asset allocation for an investor, one that will meet the investor's objectives, while remaining within the investor's risk profile, the consultant must consider four elements:

1. **Investor risk tolerance:** A portfolio that falls outside of the investor's risk tolerance may be doomed to fail, regardless of its merits. If the investor is unable to tolerate market fluctuations, he or she is likely to sell at the worst time or become so uncomfortable that they opt for securities, such as CDs, that will ultimately fall short of their investment needs.

2. **Systematic risk:** After determining the investor's objectives and risk profile, the consultant will complete a capital markets analysis to determine systematic risks. This analysis, combined with the investor's profile, is used to determine a suitable macro asset allocation (percentages of equities, fixed income, cash, etc.), taking into consideration intermediate to long-term market trends, such as rising or falling interest rates.

3. **Unsystematic risk:** The consultant will then determine the unsystematic risks that may affect the types of investments, and hence managers,

that would be appropriate to meet the investor's objectives. As an example, does the investor need liquidity? If so, there are several types of managers that should not be considered. What type of fixed income manager best suits the investor's risk profile, i.e., high yield, corporate, treasuries only?

4. **Manager's risk management:** The consultant will assess how the manager manages risk (Chapter 15) through a thorough due diligence process. Unfortunately, many managers "manage risk" solely through diversification; own enough securities in a broad range of sectors to buffer both systematic and unsystematic risks. Consultants will seek out managers who are skilled in risk management, evidenced by the screening methodologies that they use for security selection and sales, such as:

- A thorough fundamental analysis, seeking companies that have strong balance sheets. This process is periodically reviewed for any signs of accounting discrepancies.
- Searching for companies that have strong leadership and management and monitoring for any changes in corporate structure
- Studying the internal metrics used by the company for growth forecasts
- Monitoring any changes in the economic landscape that may affect either the individual company or its industry

In this chapter, various types of risk are described, as well as how each can affect long-term goals. It is up to the consultant to manage a portfolio through proper asset allocation and diversification and also, to guide the investor through the emotions and challenges of investing. When investment portfolios rise over extended periods, controlling risk seems to be the last thing on many minds. Many investors become willing to take inordinate risks to chase returns and/or to keep pace with media success stories. When markets become more difficult for extended periods, many investors can become so risk-averse that they let fear guide their investment decisions and choose only "safe" investments or none at all. It is the role of the consultant or advisor to explain risk management and the relationship between risk and return to the investor, instilling realistic return expectations that are in sync with the realities of the markets and the investor's tolerance to risk. It is through this process that the investor will be able to stay focused on their long-term goals.

UNDERSTANDING RISK TOLERANCE

How does the investor define risk? Is it market volatility (standard deviation) or is it the possibility of not attaining one's goals? Proper asset allocation can only be done after conducting a thorough assessment of an investor's tolerance to risk. Discussions about risk tolerance will uncover an individual's ability to deal with fluctuations in the value of his or her portfolio and thus their ability to stay the course. It is the investor's emotions, not their intellect that will form their attitudes about safety and investment risk. The bottom line will be a much more significant talking point to an investor than asset allocation and it is therefore imperative that the investor's tolerance to risk, as well as his or her goals, be the basis of asset allocations. The consultant or advisor must communicate the concepts of risk and return, and work to manage the investor's expectations. All investors would love to have a 100% return while taking zero risk! This expectation is, of course, unrealistic and it is the consultant's job to bring the conversation back to reality.

Investors are very susceptible to two broad categories of risk: Investment risk and emotional risk. The ability of the consultant or advisor to understand and manage an investor's tolerance to these risks will be the driving force behind many of the investment decisions. This understanding, combined with realistic goals, will enable the investor to stay the course.

Investment Risk

An investor's ability to deal with market volatility and changes in their portfolio's value is a good indicator of their tolerance to the risk associated with investing. Market fluctuations and their inherent risks are a fact of life and the investor and consultant must maintain a reasoned perspective of the overall process.

Investing will expose capital to the potential of principle loss, while lack of action will result in the inevitable erosion of purchasing power over time. Unfortunately, there is no single investment strategy that entirely avoids risk, but the goal of sound investment management is to manage risk skillfully and effectively, within the parameters of the investor's goals, timeline, and risk profile. Proper asset allocation will help prevent any single investment or market condition from having an irreversibly negative effect on a portfolio and if done skillfully, it will minimize the risk of negative returns. Risk management requires a proactive approach to both the original asset allocation and subsequent portfolio reallocations. Periodic review of the allocation is an important component of managing investment risk. Being entirely risk-averse may preserve existing capital, but that capital will fall victim to the risk of inflation. Reaching for excessive returns can expose investors to precarious investment positions and the potential of severe losses. It is the role of the consultant to manage both risk and return expectations. Markets are ever-changing and an understanding of this relationship is the key to long-term investing.

Emotional Risk

Emotional risk is an intangible and sometimes costly form of risk. Investors, who misjudge their ability to handle uncertainty, often find themselves running out of patience with their investments at the worst possible times and/or they find themselves falling victim to the emotions of greed and fear. They often break from their strategy and find themselves buying at the top of markets, or selling at the bottom. Chasing the hot stock or stocks is a common, undisciplined response to the mania and greed that can be associated with investing. Investors tend to increase their holdings in these stocks by selling the "underperforming" portion of their portfolio, only to become overexposed to stocks that are trading at market highs.

These same investors often do just the opposite during panics to the downside. They liquidate stocks, generally near the bottom and are unwilling to reinvest until well after the market recovers. Those who sell during sudden market declines are acting on impulse and their investment choices are driven by fear. Mania and panic are critical times for the consultant or advisor to control the situation, as emotions can be an investor's worst enemy.

The ability to maintain one's patience during difficult times requires more than just an understanding of the markets; it also requires an understanding of the investor's emotional reactions to uncertainty. Only then can there be a working balance between the desire to achieve the highest return and the need to preserve capital.

TYPES OF INVESTMENT RISKS

A business executive in his or her mid '30s will have very different goals and risk tolerance than a business executive on the threshold of retirement. Therefore, one of the key elements in developing a sound investment policy is a clear understanding of investment risks and how they can be managed. There are two categories of investment risk to consider, systematic and unsystematic risks. Systematic risks are inherent to the markets, not the individual security. They cannot be totally eliminated through diversification, but they can be managed. Unsystematic risks are a reflection of the financial condition of individual companies and can be reduced through diversification. When combined, these risks show the degree of uncertainty that exists in markets or individual stocks.

> *Systematic risks are related to market conditions*

> *Unsystematic risks reflect the quality of the security*

Systematic Risk

There are four major types of systematic risk that must be considered when developing and maintaining the investment policy and the proper asset allocation. Adjusting for these risks is the consultant's role.

- Inflation Risk
- Reinvestment Risk
- Market Risk
- Interest Rate Risk

Inflation Risk

Investors planning for retirement often think of investing as a way to hedge inflation and indeed, inflation may be the most important risk that an individual may face when planning for retirement income. People are, with increasing frequency, retiring earlier and living longer. Most everyone fears outliving his or her money and inflation does decrease the purchasing power of a dollar. Loss of purchasing power can seriously affect the retirees' cash flow and life style. Experience tells us that periods of low inflation are followed by periods of at least moderate inflation and when planning a long-term financial strategy, it is not wise to ignore this pattern or the effect that inflation will have on the purchasing power of a person's nest egg (Illustration 9-1). As an example, the purchasing power of $50,000 in 1960, assuming 3% annual inflation, is equal to that of $163,000 in 2000. Inflation also affects the purchasing power of corporations and institutions, and should be integrated into all investment plans.

AVERAGE NATIONAL COST OF BASIC PRODUCTS BETWEEN 1950 AND 2003

Year	Gallon of milk	Tank of gas	Loaf of white bread
1950	$0.27	$2.66	$0.17
1960	$0.33	$3.27	$0.20
1970	$0.43	$4.29	$0.26
1980	$0.91	$9.11	$0.55
1990	$1.44	$14.45	$0.87
2003	$2.04	$20.45	$1.23

Source: U.S. Department of Labor, Bureau of Labor Statistics, inflation calculator

Illustration 9-1

Illustration 9-2 shows the effect inflation has had on the real return of different asset classes.

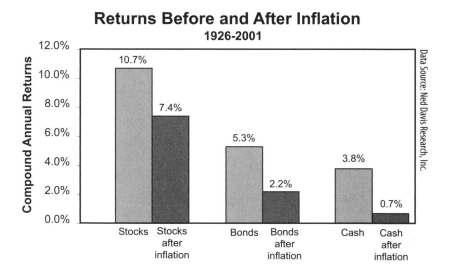

Illustration 9-2

Reinvestment Risk

Generally, an investment portfolio will include both fixed income securities and equities. This balance is designed to achieve the investment goal, while smoothing returns. In this section, we will discuss the reinvestment risk associated with fixed income securities. Reinvestment risk is related to interest rates; as interest rates increase, reinvestment risk decreases; as interest rates decrease, reinvestment risk increases.

When the investor buys Certificates of Deposit (CDs) or bonds in a stable or declining interest rate environment, the investor runs the risk of reinvesting at lower rates when these securities mature, thus the income derived from these securities will decrease. This loss of income can have a dramatic effect on retirement income when returns are solely dependent on these types of investments. Many investors feel more comfortable buying only more stable, short-term investments, however these tend to pay the lowest rates and can be a poor inflation hedge. Securities that can be "called" (redeemed by the issuing entity) prior to their maturity date (call risk) can expose the investor to reinvestment risk.

All asset classes have times when they will outperform or underperform. Fixed income securities are no exception. They can produce both volatile returns and result in loss of principal. Let us look at interest rates over the last three decades. During the early '70s, we were dealing with Vietnam, inflation, the Watergate hearings and the 1974 OPEC oil embargo. Interest rates were soaring and stock prices were plummeting. A Bear market was upon us in 1973-1974; the Dow corrected nearly 50%, while many stocks dropped over 70%. As interest rates were climbing, reinvestment risk was low, but people were reluctant to buy long maturities. Fed funds rates peaked in 1981, climbing to over 19%, thus starting the next cycle of declining rates. The '80s were marked by high inflation and declining interest rates, although rates remained historically high. People were still reluctant to buy long maturities. In the '90s, inflation moderated and by 2002, deflation had become a concern. The Federal Reserve responded to deflation concerns by consistently lowering interest rates. With the help of the Fed and war concerns, Treasuries reached 45-year lows in 2004. Reinvestment risk was high during this time period, especially for longer-term maturities (Illustration 9-3). Once the low is set, it will be the beginning of the next rising interest rate cycle, where reinvestment risk will decrease. Fear, creating the unfortunate desire by many to do nothing, caused a great deal of lost opportunity in the fixed income market in the '70s and '80s. Who wouldn't be happy with a bond that paid 15% now?

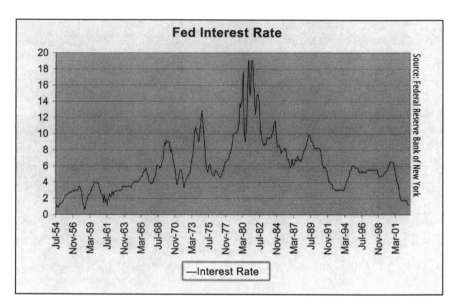

Illustration 9-3

Market Risk

Market risk is the risk associated with price level fluctuations. Most people associate price volatility with the equity market, however all investments that we have been discussing have market risk. Equities, and therefore equity mutual funds, can go up and down regardless of the condition of a particular company. We have all seen one semi-conductor company report bad news and then see the entire sector drop in price. Geopolitical events can affect the markets and individual securities, regardless of any other data.

Interest Rate Risk

The market value of bonds will move in the opposite direction of interest rates, so when interest rates are low, the prices of bonds, including treasuries, are very high. As interest rates begin to rise, the market value of bonds will decrease.

Bonds will continue to pay the coupon rate at which they were issued and they will bring par value when they mature, but if they are bought or sold in the secondary marketplace prior to maturity, their market value will fluctuate as interest rates change. An increase in interest rates may make the resultant bond yields more competitive with equity results and/or may cause corporate profits to suffer due to the increased cost of borrowing, thus having a negative affect on the stock market. It is important to remember that most bond issues can default, as corporations and municipalities can and do encounter financial difficulties or even declare bankruptcy.

Fixed income managers determine a portfolio's sensitivity to changes in interest rates by controlling the average duration of the portfolio. A rule of thumb to determine a change in rates' influence on a portfolio is to multiply the average duration of the portfolio by the percent change in interest rates.

Average duration of portfolio	Change in interest rates	Potential effect on portfolio value
7 years	+1%	7% loss
4 years	+2%	8% loss
10 years	-1%	10% gain

These elements of risk must be considered when designing an investment plan that will provide for growing income and capital for the future. No single risk is predominant at all times, therefore the advisor or consultant plays a key role in guiding the investor through various market conditions. The goal should always be to achieve the desired return with the lowest possible risk. Achieving this goal is referred to as producing a positive or high alpha return.

International Investing

There are additional risks if one invests in the international markets. These include:

- Currency risks exist when a security is bought or sold and currency must be exchanged
- Country risks due to geopolitical and economic conditions specific to a country
- Global risks can affect international trade and the companies that participate in that trade

Unsystematic Risks

Portfolio managers make the day-to-day tactical decisions when selecting securities for portfolios. Unsystematic risks, also called idiosyncratic risks, are those related to the quality of an individual security. These risks are managed by an in-depth and ongoing analysis of a company's financial condition. Diversification, spreading the risks between many companies, can reduce unsystematic risks. These risks include:

- Liquidity Risk
- Business Risk
- Default Risk

Liquidity Risk

Liquidity risk occurs when the investments that you have made are difficult or impossible to sell on short notice without accepting a reduced price or paying a penalty for an early sale or withdrawal. This lack of liquidity may be due to contractual limitations or lack of a market and can affect stocks and bonds, as well as other types of investments. Real estate is the more obvious illiquid investment however, it is important to consider liquidity needs when making other types of investments as well. CDs have early withdrawal penalties; annuities have a surrender charge if they are not held a certain number of years, as do some share classes of mutual funds, most notably B shares. Some equities have a limited number of outstanding shares and may be difficult to sell immediately. Hedge funds and partnerships often have contractual limitations for liquidations. Liquidity risks must be considered when planning for cash flow requirements, retirement income and cash emergencies.

Business and Default Risk

Business or default risks are both related to a company's income flow. If the business does not have an adequate flow of income to maintain operations and debt service, then that company is at risk to fail. The greater the volatility of income flow, the greater the business risk. The greater the debt to income ratio of the company, the greater the financial risk surrounding the company's stock and the greater the default risk for the company's corporate bonds and preferred stocks. Corporate bankruptcy affects all securities issued by a company. Two other types of risks are associated with company balance sheets: credit risk and earnings risk. General Motors bonds were downgraded to below investment grade in 2005, which is an example of credit risk and companies that report disappointing earnings, generally get a negative reaction from Wall Street (earnings risks).

HOW TO REDUCE RISK

The investment management consulting process and skillful asset allocation are great allies in the reduction of risk. Our modern, global economy can be subject to rapid changes in market conditions. Foreign competition, interest rates, trade and budget deficits, economic expansion and contraction, political uncertainty, unfunded pension liabilities, revelations of corporate malfeasance, the affects of expensing stock options on corporate profits, and unexpected corporate or municipal bankruptcies can all cause significant changes in both the general economy, and in an investment portfolio.

During 2000 and 2001, many technology stocks fell from over $100 a share to nearly nothing in a matter of months. Between March of 2000 and October of 2002, about one and one-half years, the Nasdaq dropped 78%. In 2001, Enron went from $90 per share to bankrupt in less than one year. Successful investing is a full-time job and not suitable for part-time attention. The cycles of change, driven by valuations, both global and domestic, are ever-present and anything less than the full time attention of a qualified advisor can result in unexpected and sometimes unpleasant changes in the value of the investor's portfolio. A consultant or advisor, who takes proactive steps in a timely manner, can take advantage of the opportunities that these market cycles present and significantly reduce the adverse effects that these changes can have on investment portfolios. We see examples of elevated risks and more compelling opportunities in Illustration 11-2. As we have said, no single risk is predominant at all times and it is the role of the consultant or advisor to remain proactive throughout the natural cycles of the markets. It is for these reasons and more that many careful investors look to the investment management consulting process to assist them in investing their serious money in the capital markets.

Market Cycles

There are three types of market cycles that will affect risk: Secular, cyclical and one-time events. One-time events are difficult to manage, as they are usually associated with crisis events, such as geopolitical events or the bankruptcy of Enron. Secular and cyclical cycles are relatively repetitive and can generally be anticipated.

Secular cycles refer to broad, long-term changes in stock prices that ebb and flow due to valuations or, the long-term changes in economic conditions that fluctuate within industries, or those that affect different areas of the world. Demographics can play a significant role in global secular changes. Cyclical changes follow business cycles, which may be as short as the Christmas shopping season or they may last several years. As an example, the equity markets experienced a secular bull market between 1982 and 2000, where the primary trend was up. During that time, there were several corrections, signified by sell-offs of 10% or more and two cyclical Bear markets, signified by sell-offs of 20% or more (Illustration 9-4). Both were followed by the resumption of the primary upward trend. The consultant is responsible for making strategic allocation changes, while the money managers make tactical changes in security selections. Both are attempting to capitalize on secular and cyclical changes in the markets, allocating additional funds to undervalued areas of the markets or companies at the beginning of cycles and, both are reducing risk by reducing exposure to areas of the markets that have become overvalued as their cycle has matured (Chapter 12).

Diversification of Investments

Regardless of individual objectives, there are certain principles for investing that have withstood the test of time, and have served to reduce the risks inherent to investing. Each investor has their specific needs for present or future income, and their own tolerance to risk. There is no single asset allocation that is right for everyone, but without regard to individual circumstances, the one, consistent, bedrock principle for successful investing is and always has been,

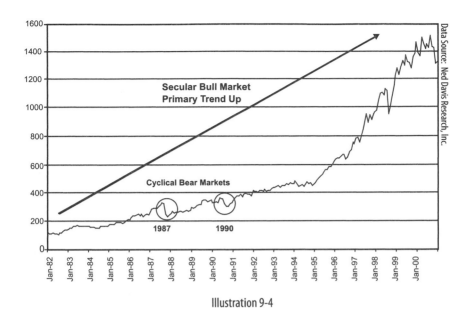

Illustration 9-4

proper and effective diversification. Harry Markowitz won the Noble Prize in 1990 for his introduction of the "Modern Portfolio Theory" in 1952. The essence of the theory is effective diversification through asset mixes with low correlation to one another. We will discuss more about the components of this theory at the end of this chapter.

Don't put all your eggs in one basket...

Putting all your assets in one market style, sector or security is a huge gamble that can put your portfolio at significant risk. When the technology bubble burst in early 2000, many investors experienced substantial losses, as the risk of being disproportionately weighted in technology stocks was realized. Each asset class and style can respond differently to changes in the economy and the capital markets, therefore diversification across asset classes and investment styles can smooth investment results and help to minimize risks due to this potential counter cyclical movement (moving in opposite directions) between different styles. A short-term decline in one style can be balanced or absorbed by an increase in another style or styles. Diversification helps to achieve this smoothing, as each class and/or style tends to follow its own pattern, resulting in an overall portfolio performance that is less volatile. The most obvious example of asset classes that often move in opposite directions is stocks and bonds. They are said to have a low correlation to one another. We will talk more about correlation later in this chapter. If stocks go down, bonds generally remain stable or go up. An investor who is properly allocated between the two should have more consistent performance than those who have limited themselves to just stocks. The trick is to be properly allocated to maximize returns while reducing risks. Analyzing markets and applying the results to asset allocations should be an ongoing and proactive process, as markets are dynamic and offer more opportunity or risk at any given point in time.

Diversification can also help with liquidity needs. Suppose all of an investor's money is invested in stocks, requiring them to sell some of their holdings for an emergency. If stocks are depressed when they need to sell, they could be forced to take a loss on their investment. Once it is sold, it is no longer a "paper loss." Owning other types of investments could give the investor greater flexibility in raising the needed cash, while allowing them to hold their stocks until prices improved. The diversified portfolio can provide both improved liquidity and comparative stability.

Types of Diversification

There are two types of diversification: Diversification among different asset classes (types of securities, such as stocks and bonds) and diversification among different companies.

1. True diversification of assets is the investment in securities that represent different investment risks. Assets are distributed among securities from different asset classes, such as stocks, bonds, and short-term or cash investments. The risks inherent to these asset classes generally show low correlation to one another and their inherent risks will fluctuate over time. Selecting among different asset classes will help to reduce the risks associated with investing in only one type of security. This type of risk is called asset class risk. The advisor or consultant should diversify investment assets into a risk-appropriate mix of asset classes and investment styles in the asset allocation and manager selection process. Various asset allocation techniques used by advisors and consultants are discussed in Chapter 12.

2. Investing in a portfolio that contains a mix of diverse companies in multiple sectors will help an investor avoid the risks that are inherent in investing in the securities of one or more companies in a single sector

(sector risk). It should go without saying that investing everything in a single security carries with it the most risk (company risk). Enron comes to mind. Company risk is present for both stocks and bonds. It is the role of each money manager to diversify within his or her investment style.

The investment management consulting process achieves both the macro diversification into various asset classes and the more tactical diversification within each investment style, striving to build a portfolio containing assets with low correlation to one another. The economy and the financial markets are global and ever changing, and spreading investments among many companies in divergent sectors and markets can significantly reduce the risk of unpleasant surprises. Diversification does not eliminate market risk, but it significantly reduces the possibility of major losses to a portfolio.

Illustration 9-5 shows the effects of different investment approaches. The all equity, somewhat diversified portfolio represented by the S&P 500, had the greatest returns and a great deal of volatility. Investing in a single security does not achieve diversification and accentuates company and sector risk. IBM, a

Illustration 9-5

DOW component, hardly outperformed the Lehman Brothers US aggregate bond index, while exhibiting significant volatility. Comparatively, we constructed a blended portfolio, made up of indexes in the follow proportions and made no reallocations for the entire time period: 30% Lehman Brothers US aggregate bond, 20% S&P 500, 25% S&P 400, 10% S&P 600, 10% EAFE (international) and 5% cash (90-day T bill). This portfolio reduces volatility, spreads risks over different asset classes and styles and has cash available if needed.

Lengthen the Time Horizon

Time is said to heal all wounds and when we take a long-term look at the markets, it certainly makes the wounds from past panic sell-offs look small. Illustration 9-5 shows that even the "crash of 87" becomes a faint memory for those who maintained their focus. The longer an investor has to achieve his or her investment goals, the greater the probability they will succeed in achieving them. The compounding effects of time, coupled with time's smoothing effects in balancing the ups and downs of the market, makes time itself a hedge against risk. The amount of risk an investor can comfortably tolerate is measured, in large part, by the amount of time the investor has to realize their goals. Once it is understood that lengthening the time horizons will help to ensure success, the investor can step off the emotional roller coaster that a short-term perspective can cause. One of the secrets to successful investing, hidden in plain sight, is the addition of time to the investment strategy.

Diversification and time are the investor's greatest allies. When these concepts are combined with the asset allocation techniques of skilled consultants who capitalize on market cycles and valuations, the investor will have a portfolio that proactively manages risks and takes advantage of opportunities or, a high alpha return.

UNDERSTANDING MODERN PORTFOLIO THEORY

The "Modern Portfolio Theory" (MPT), also referred to as mean-variance optimization (MVO), is an active, quantitative approach to asset allocation, with a focus on the technical and statistical relationship between the different types of securities within a portfolio. Using historical return and volatility data, each asset class and style exhibits a pattern of risk and return that, according to MPT, which is based on linear programming, is likely to be repeated in the future.

- The "mean" is the expected *return* of the portfolio
- Variance" it the square of the *standard deviation*
- The optimized portfolios lie on the *efficient frontier,*
  where the relationship between return and risk is displayed

This theory incorporates the standard deviation of each asset and the correlation coefficient between all of the assets within the portfolio. Practitioners of MPT work to optimize the relationship between risk and return by diversifying among asset classes and investment styles with low correlation to one another. They believe that combining assets that tend to move in the same direction (high correlation), increases the overall risk of the portfolio and conversely, that blending low correlating assets reduces the portfolio's overall risk. MPT considers each investment in context with the overall portfolio, not in isolation, thus supporting and quantifying the concept of diversification.

The relationships between return, standard deviation and correlation should be considered when constructing a portfolio designed to produce a risk appropriate return. Investors must be made to understand the risk associated with their desired return and reach a balance between risk tolerance and return expectations. Optimized portfolio analysis allows the investor to numerically see the effects of blending assets with differing correlations and, the relationship between risk and return. The optimized portfolios will display the investments that will produce the greatest expected return for each level of risk. Determining an acceptable level of risk, or "risk budget," is an important ingredient in portfolio design.

Efficient Frontier

MPT utilizes historical risk, return and correlation data to create portfolios that will produce the highest return at each level of risk. These "optimal portfolios," which are considered "efficient," lie along a line called the efficient frontier. The efficient frontier is the line that connects all optimal portfolios across all levels of risk. Illustration 9-6 displays the efficient frontier for various combinations of stocks and bonds. Viewing this illustration, one can see that a portfolio made up of 100% bonds actually exposes the investor to greater risk than one that includes stocks. The application of this Nobel Prize winning work changed the approach to portfolio risk management and asset allocation. Sophisticated computer programs have been developed to utilize the data from all asset classes and styles to create optimal portfolio models. These models are used to develop static or strategic asset allocations, but have limited value for either tactical or proactive asset allocation strategies, as the computer programs, driven by historical data, are unable to respond to current market conditions. In addition, as with the other metrics used in MPT, the efficient frontier, and therefore the optimal portfolio, can shift over time. The use of computerized modeling in the creation of risk and return appropriate asset allocations is discussed in some detail in Chapter 12.

Beta and Volatility

Volatility, or variability of returns, is generally associated with risk. Beta measures the degree of movement of an asset compared to its relative benchmark. The S&P 500 has a beta coefficient of 1.00, and is often used as a representa-

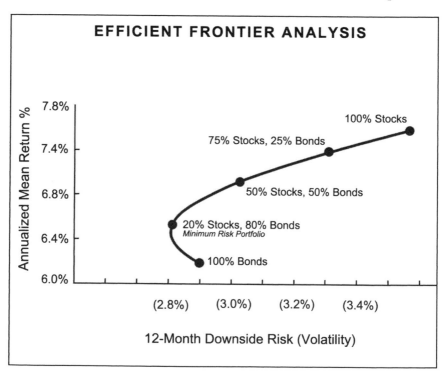

Illustration 9-6

tion of the market. If we use the S&P 500 as our relative benchmark, a security or portfolio that is more volatile than the S&P 500, where its price or value moves proportionally more than the S&P 500, will have a beta greater than 1.00. Those that move less than the S&P 500 will have a beta less than 1.00. Investors tend to prefer high-beta investments during Bull markets and low-beta investments during Bear markets. Bonds are considered low-beta investments and are generally combined with higher-beta stocks to reduce the volatility of the overall portfolio. Modern portfolio theorists believe that high-beta securities have the potential for higher returns and greater risk than low-beta securities. This relationship between risk and return is referred to as "compensated" risk, as the investor expects to be compensated with a greater return for taking the additional risk. "Uncompensated" risk is the result of too few companies in too few industries. This type of risk can be reduced through adequate diversification.

Standard Deviation

Standard deviation is another measure of volatility, which measures how much the return of a portfolio or specific investment varies from the average return of a specific benchmark or index or, a measure of relative volatility of returns. We expect investments with a high standard deviation to have less consistent returns at any given point in time, but not necessarily lower returns, than those with a low standard deviation. Securities, such as short-term Treasuries, have very consistent returns and a low standard deviation. Securities, such as small cap growth stocks, have higher volatility, producing a higher relative risk. When comparing the two, the higher volatility investment only becomes a higher risk investment for those with a short time horizon. As with high-beta securities, there is again the expectation that investments with higher standard deviations have the potential to produce higher returns. Modern portfolio theorists will endeavor to reduce the standard deviation of the total portfolio by utilizing assets that have a low correlation of volatility (standard deviation) to one another.

Another way to communicate risk is to illustrate numerically the possible outcomes of investments with differing standard deviations. In this example, the investment has an average return of 10% and a standard deviation of 15%. One-standard deviation is the range of returns that encompasses 68% of all outcomes, with the expectation that the average return will fall between -5%

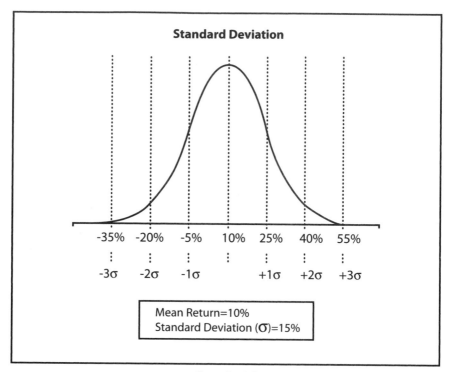

Illustration 9-7

and +25%, 68% of the time. A two-standard deviation range of returns encompasses 95% of all outcomes and falls between -20% and +40%. The flaw in using 1-standard deviation alone as a measure of risk is that it only encompasses 68% of outcomes, leaving those at either end of the range, those that are the most extreme and most volatile, out of the equation. This practice is however, standard within the industry. Additionally, standard deviation is often equated to risk regardless of whether the volatility is upside volatility or downside volatility. These relationships are further reason to dig deeper into the raw numbers. There is a long-running debate in the investment community as to how risk should be measured and many feel that standard deviation has been unfairly chosen as the predominate measure of risk.

Value investors, such as Benjamin Graham, Warren Buffett and Brandes Investment Partners, give little weight to beta-based or standard deviation-based risk assessment. They are far more interested in a company's fundamentals than measures of volatility. Brandes Investment Partners, a leading global money management firm, analyzes factors such as the company's economic characteristics, the quality of its management, and the price of the investment. They measure a stock's risk as the relationship between its value and its price and they have found that price fluctuations can create opportunity. This assessment of volatility is true for many managers, therefore volatility alone should not exclude a manager from consideration. One size never fits all, and it is up to the consultant to understand the manager's investment philosophy.

Correlation Coefficient

The correlation coefficient allows the consultant or advisor to determine if different types of investments move up or down together or, in uncorrelated movements. Correlation coefficient is measured on a scale ranging between −1.00 and +1.00. Investments that move exactly together have the highest correlation coefficient of +1.00 and those that move in completely opposite directions have the lowest correlation coefficient of −1.00. Zero or 0.0, indicates that they have no correlation or a random relationship to one another. The lower the correlation coefficient, the greater the diversification impact of mixing the assets.

Modern Portfolio Theory tells us that by mixing assets that have a low correlation to one another, one can effectively diversify a portfolio and reduce the portfolio's overall volatility. One should note that, as with standard deviation and beta, correlations do not remain constant over time and the dynamic nature of these measurement tools must be factored into asset allocation decisions. The correlation coefficient between two assets can vary substantially during different time periods and this variability of correlation must be understood when using this tool to construct or rebalance portfolios.

(See examples of the correlation coefficient between different asset classes and styles in Illustration 9-8.)

CONCLUSION

Consultants strive to design and maintain investment portfolios that will achieve long-term investment goals, while minimizing overall risk. This endeavor is a collaborative effort between the consultant and investor that can only be achieved when both the investor and the consultant have a clear understanding of risk and risk tolerance and, what this relationship will mean

ASSET CLASS NAME	T-Bill-3 Month Yield	Small Cap Stocks	Int'l Equity	Large Cap Stocks	High Yield Bonds	Mid Cap Stocks	Long Term Taxable Bonds	Int'l Fixed	REITs	Long Term Tax-free Bonds	Managed Futures
T-Bill-3 Month Yield	1										
Small Cap Stocks	0.139	1									
Int'l Equity	0.111	0.6	1								
Large Cap Stocks	0.304	0.8	0.7	1							
High Yield Bonds	0.186	0.821	0.779	0.557	1						
Mid Cap Stocks	0.218	0.92	0.65	0.875	0.774	1					
L/T Taxable Bonds*	0.55	0.25	0.155	0.35	0.385	0.376	1				
Int'l Fixed	0.303	0.35	0.37	0.376	0.669	0.404	0.913	1			
REITs	0.313	0.748	0.258	0.481	0.623	0.097	0.376	0.515	1		
L/T Tax-free Bonds*	0.55	0.25	0.155	0.325	0.385	0.202	0.92	0.9	0.39	1	
Managed Futures	-0.182	-0.121	-0.175	-0.075	-0.072	-0.098	-0.052	-0.106	-0.186	-0.07	1

Illustration 9-8

This chart shows representative correlations between selected asset classes. The values are not fixed, as they can vary somewhat over time. A correlation of "1" means that the asset classes move together and are perfectly correlated. A correlation of zero means that the two asset classes behave differently and have no correlation. A negative correlation means that asset classes move independently of one another, but when combined, can reduce overall volatility. Managed futures are one of the few asset classes that negatively correlate to other types of investments.

*(L/T = long term)

to the structure of the portfolio. Managing risk is a more significant factor in the long-term success of portfolio management than generating returns, and this skill requires a thorough understanding of not only the methods used to reduce risk, but also an understanding of the tools used in this pursuit. Investment strategies that are able to avoid large losses will ultimately produce more favorable results. The consultant must assess the emphasis that should be placed on historical returns, volatility and correlations, as well as factor in the cycles that are inherent in the capital markets, before making asset allocation decisions. This information, combined with the investor's risk profile, will affect the asset allocation and, as conditions change, the allocations within the portfolio may require adjustment. Managing risk through proper diversification, and adjusting asset allocations when warranted, should be viewed as an ongoing process. It is the adherence to this discipline that will produce more consistent results and create a much greater opportunity for the investor to achieve his or her long-term goals.

10

The Art and Science of Market Analysis

Market analysis is an integral part of a value-added asset allocation process. Many investment professionals have lived by the "buy and hold" theory, only to discover that they have missed numerous opportunities to secure exceptional profits or, they have failed to get out of the way of costly market declines. As we have discussed previously, markets move in natural 3- to 5-year cycles and signal changes in trend through both fundamental and technical indicators. Many believe there is a philosophical disconnect between fundamental analysis and technical analysis, but this chapter will attempt to bridge that gap by showing the relationship between a number of widely accepted tools used by fundamental and technical market analysts. A fundamentalist is looking at investment options to determine *what* to buy or sell, whereas the technician is looking at the trend of the stock or markets, determining *when* to buy or sell. A skilled consultant will view all analytical information in order to provide a balanced analysis of the markets, from which, he or she will make asset allocation decisions. This analysis requires not only analytical skill, but also the insight to weigh the importance or relevance of each element. The combination represents the art and science of market analysis.

The ability to analyze capital markets allows the consultant to make practical assessments of risks and opportunities when making asset allocation decisions. In this chapter, we will briefly describe several forms of analysis, many of which can be approached from either a purely fundamental perspective, or one that incorporates technical relationships. A blending of the two is likely to produce the most complete results. These include:

- Fundamental analysis
- Macro Economics
- Market trends and momentum
- Investor sentiment and behavioral finance
- Technical analysis

FUNDAMENTAL ANALYSIS

Money managers use company fundamentals when analyzing securities for purchase or sale and consultants use market fundamentals when making asset allocation decisions. Fundamentals provide "reasonable pricing" guidance that may lead to buy or sell decisions. Since individual securities make up the markets, many parallels can be drawn between the analysis of individual companies by money managers and the analysis of trends and conditions within the markets by the consultant. There are various valuation models to consider:

Price-to-earnings (P/E) ratios are reviewed for trailing earnings and projected forward earnings. Managers also review price-to-book, price-to-cash flow, free cash flow-to-total capital, return on equity, gross margins and the PEG ratio. For opportunity to exist, valuations must be compelling enough to make the manager believe that the stock will go up, because either their price looks undervalued or, their growth appears to be accelerating and/or sustainable. Different types of mangers are looking for different buy and sell indicators and therefore, they apply this information in different ways.

Consultants use similar gauges of valuations and make comparisons to the historical norms of entire asset classes and styles, as represented by indexes. The most well used measure is P/E, but consultants also use the historical comparatives of average price-to-book value and price-to-dividend ratios of indexes to determine the potential of a given asset group. Illustration 11-2 shows how comparing the average P/E of indexes to their historical norms can provide the consultant with insight into the potential opportunity or risk associated with various areas of the market. In that example, small cap value represented greater opportunity and less risk than large cap growth. This type of analysis will show maturing market cycles, as well as obvious extremes in valuations. Either can signal changes in market conditions and the need to reallocate assets. There are many elements of fundamental analysis that can be graphically displayed, such as those shown in Illustration 11-2. Technical analysts, who look for changes in trend or other indicators that may signal excess risk or increased opportunity, study these graphs. Graphs make fundamental analysis visual and often easier for many individuals to understand, while at the same time, convert data into a form that can be used by technicians.

Consultants use fundamental analysis to forecast trends in sector growth by monitoring corporate spending, capacity utilization and manufacturing output. Corporations who are willing to spend money on infrastructure believe that growth is sustainable, whereas those who feel that the economy is slowing will put off upgrading systems. Capacity utilization portends the level of manufacturing output, the need for expansion and the need to hire personnel. These ebb and flow with business cycles and economic cycles and can be early signals that an area of the markets, or the economy in general, is strengthening or weakening. Understanding these indicators allows the consultant to capitalize on opportunities and manage risk through the process of reallocation.

MACRO ECONOMICS

Both managers and consultants keep a watchful eye on the economic condition of the U.S. and that of the global economies. More and more the two are connected and events in one part of the world can quickly ripple across the globe. Interest rates play a major role in economic growth, as does the strength of the dollar compared to other major currencies. Both are linked to the U.S. current account deficit, which is a combination of the federal deficit and the federal trade deficit. When the current account deficit is high, as we have seen in the early 2000s, the value of the dollar is likely to go down. If the dollar becomes too weak, then interest rates tend to rise, making the cost of doing business and running the consumer household more expensive. A weak dollar generally causes a slowing in economic growth. The Federal Reserve plays an important role in controlling interest rates and inflation, by adjusting the Fed Funds rate. The Fed raises rates to slow the economy and slow inflation and they lower rates to stimulate growth. When the Fed is raising rates, sectors such as health care, natural resources and industrials often become the market leaders, while financials, emerging markets and small caps tend to outperform during periods of declining interest rates.

Demographics and accelerating economic growth in various parts of the world, such as China and India, affect the balance of trade and jobs. Globalization is here to stay, resulting in many changes in industry, employment and the balance of supply and demand. This trend may ultimately eliminate much of the manufacturing industry in the U.S., while providing the potential for opportunities in emerging industries and countries. Proper asset allocation can take advantage of this long-term trend.

Changes in oil prices have a global effect. Oil price shocks have historically resulted in recession and should therefore be monitored on an ongoing basis. Gone are the days of cheap oil, as the changes in the global economies will continue to strain the laws of supply and demand. Increases in the price of oil affect corporate profits and divert money from consumer spending on goods and services. The consumer, who is responsible for about two-thirds of the nations GDP, is an essential component of economic health and therefore employment data and consumer debt are monitored.

MARKET TRENDS AND MOMENTUM

Business cycles, both at the industry level and that of the economy, affect stock prices and valuations. Sometimes, when an area becomes hot, investors create excess demand for stocks in that area. This demand can result in periods of market mania, when prices are driven by momentum, despite fundamentals or valuations. This demand imbalance is also true during times of panic. During times of mania, cash levels become very low, such as those maintained at mutual fund companies. Momentum alone cannot sustain an advance, so when there is no more money available to fuel the rise in prices, prices tend to decline. Valuation models and technical support areas become very important in determining when momentum will fail. The opposite is true following panics and wholesale selling, which creates excess cash and undervalued stocks. Panics generally create great buying opportunities, but investors often allow fear to cloud their judgment.

The advance/decline line can also be insightful in determining market trends. When more stocks are declining than advancing, it is a sign that the market is losing momentum and that the overall trend may change. Trends can stay in place long after warning signs occur, so it requires the integration of many disciplines before changing allocations. Understanding the drivers of market trends and momentum is a valuable tool for consultants to possess.

INVESTOR SENTIMENT AND BEHAVIORAL FINANCE

There are many things that affect the investing inclinations of investors, not the least of which being greed and fear. Greed creates market manias, like the one that created the tech bubble in the late '90s, when price and earnings potential become irrelevant in many investors' minds. Fear can cause market panics, like the one that drove "Black Monday" in 1987. During the Bear market of 2000, there were a host of negative influences on investors' minds, such as corporate malfeasance, corporate and personal debt, a sudden rise in the cost of oil and therefore gasoline, loss of jobs, interest rates and terrorism, which no doubt affected their investment decisions. Investors' emotions, and therefore investing behavior, generally follow predictable patterns (Illustration 10-1).

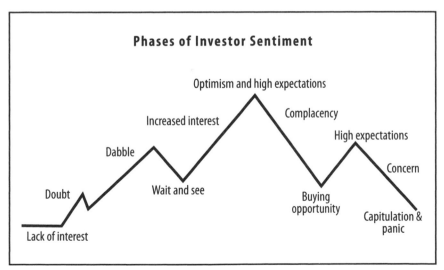

Illustration 10-1

Changes in Investor Sentiment over a Full Market Cycle (3 to 5 Years)

Investor sentiment tends to trail market activity, causing the investor to be late to invest, and late to exit (Illustration 10-1). During periods when the markets are relatively flat, investors tend to lose interest. When prices begin to increase, investors can be skeptical, doubting the validity of the move and missing the opportunity to invest in early cycle moves. This frame of mind is generally followed by dabbling, taking small positions, while waiting for the market to prove itself before becoming interested in full participation. Increased interest can lead to optimism or over-exuberance and manias, a good time to sell. While optimistic, investors begin to believe that the markets will continue to rise, despite declining prices. This optimistic bias causes investors to view declining prices as a buying opportunity (buy on dips). Expectations tend to remain high, despite weakening market internals and declining prices. Continued weakness can eventually cause the investor to become concerned, which can lead to capitulation (the investor throws in the towel), which can result in market panics. Panics generally represent buy opportunities.

These emotional patterns can be seen in bullish – bearish sentiment statistics, which are studied by market technicians (Illustration 10-2). When investors feel good about investing, bullish sentiment is high and bearish sentiment is low. This relationship may seem counter intuitive and is thus considered a "contrarian indicator" because what seems positive, widespread bullish attitudes, is actually an indication that the next market move will be to the downside. Money drives markets, so when bullish sentiment is high, available money is already in the market and valuations are most likely inflated. When investors are bullish, there is little new money to drive the market higher and new buyers are forced to buy at high prices. High bullish sentiment generally precedes some degree of market decline. The reverse is true when bearish sentiment is high.

We have described the assumptions of the Modern Portfolio Theory; markets are efficient[1] and investors make logical decisions, but psychologists who study investor behavior believe that these assumptions are not always true. There is great debate about how efficient markets can be and we know that investors often make decisions that are irrational and driven by emotion.

---

1. Efficient market theory suggests that the market is so efficient that it adjusts prices fully and instantaneously as new information becomes available and therefore, it is not possible to "beat the market." This theory disputes the assumption that technical or fundamental analysis can find opportunities in the markets. It assumes that the "correct" price for a stock is what it is trading at now.

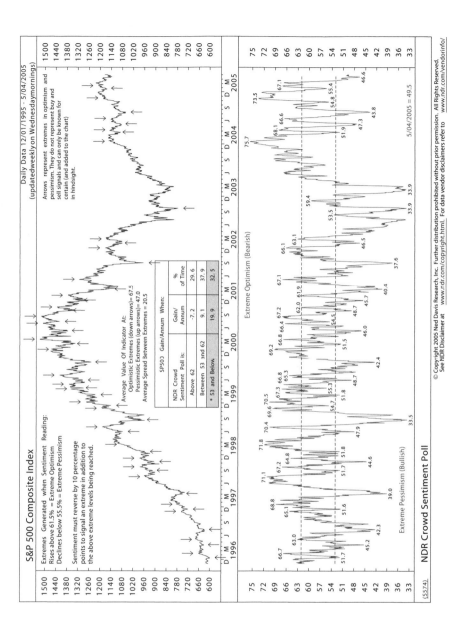

Illustration 10-2

In this illustration, the arrows on the upper chart indicate market peaks and bottoms, which correspond to high and low levels of optimism, seen in the lower chart. Markets tend to peak when bullish sentiment is at its high and bottom when bullish sentiment is at its low.

Investors are often motivated by biases and cognitive illusions, which include hindsight bias, fear of missing something, overconfidence, following the crowd (media) and others. Investors have a tendency to believe, or at least act as though, market trends will last forever and that recent returns can be extrapolated into the future. (MPT and computerized models also rely on this linear mathematical assumption.) This propensity has been seen in investment behavior since the tulip bulb craze in 17th century Holland and will no doubt continue as long as human investors are influenced by their emotions.

Studies of this concept have resulted in the field of Behavioral Finance (BF), a subject upon which books have been written. A fundamental BF principle is that investors feel losses more keenly than gains, thus driving many of their investment decisions (overreactions) in a predictable manner. Bubbles and crashes are widely attributed to this pattern of behavior. Consultants who understand the effects of investor behavior on markets can capitalize on extremes in sentiment and, prevent the investor from becoming his or her own worst enemy (buying high, motivated by greed, and/or selling low, motivated by fear). These emotions also tend to prevent investors from following the basic rule of rebalancing. Rebalancing requires that winners be sold, capturing profits and decreasing exposure to valuation risks and, that funds be allocated to underperforming areas of the market. This change is more than a little challenging for an emotional investor and thus, his or her advisor or consultant. Short-term pessimism surrounding a stock, sector or market style can create opportunities for disciplined, long-term investors and by establishing and maintaining an analytical process, the consultant can take emotion out of investment decisions.

TECHNICAL ANALYSIS

Technical analysis is based on the study of historical price movements and trends, which are based on the observation that markets move in relatively predictable and repetitive patterns. Market technicians study these patterns and incorporate this information into asset allocation decisions. These patterns are a reflection of valuations and, market and business cycles. They can give consultants and managers alike some insight on *when* to act, as technical indicators often signal trend changes prior to changes in the fundamentals. The financial services industry accepts that markets move in 3- to 5-year cycles and technical analysis graphically illustrates these cycles. The following charts illustrate several of the more common, often publicized, technical formations and terms used by market technicians. This area of expertise is part art and part mathematics. Those who are proficient in all aspects of technical analysis may receive accreditation through the Market Technicians Association as a Chartered Market Technician (CMT). These market technicians are now (2005) officially recognized by the SEC as professional analysts.

The following graphs reflect technical changes surrounding the Bear market of 2000.

- Trend Line Analysis
- Support and Resistance
- Lower Highs and Lower Lows
- Divergence
- Advance-Decline Line Analysis

Trend Line Analysis

Trend line analysis demonstrates market (or sector or stock) direction, as well as areas of resistance and support. In Illustration 9-4, we saw that the primary trend of the market remained positive or up, despite significant sell-offs, between 1982 and 2000. This knowledge allayed "Black Monday" fears for those consultants and their clients who understood that the positive, primary trend remained intact and that the sell-off would be temporary. The market direction of 2000 presented a different scenario to technicians, as the following chart patterns will illustrate. Illustration 10-3 displays five trend lines. The trends range from 20 years, represented by "Line A," to 3 years, represented by "Line E." Using multiple trend lines and time periods provides insight into long-term and short-term trends. The steeper the trend line, the less likely it will continue.

Trend line analysis is widely used when discussing how far the market may move. The move down will often stop at the trend line, which represents support or, when the market is moving up, it will often stop at the trend line that represents resistance. When a market move breaks through either support or resistance, it indicates a sustainable change of market direction. In many cases, once a trend line has been broken, the next move will be back toward the line that was just broken. If that line holds, it is verification that there is a change in market direction.

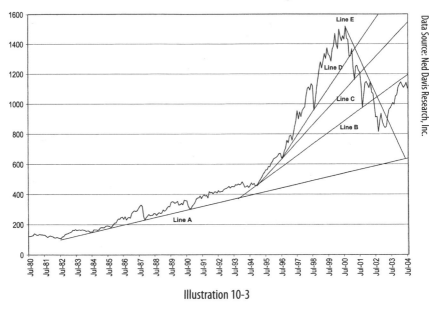

Illustration 10-3

As the market began to sell-off in 2000, Illustration 10-3 shows the market moving below Line D, Line C, and then Line B, with each attempt to rally failing to break above each successive trend line, creating lower lows and lower highs. This pattern was an indication that that each successive support line had become resistance and that the trend had turned negative, warning of lower prices to come. Had the market broken back above the trend line, it would have indicated that the upward trend was still intact. Market technicians began to report a clear reversal of trend in mid 2000, suggesting that reallocating portfolios and raising cash would be prudent.

Other measures of trends include comparisons to a moving average, the Relative Strength Indicator (RSI), which compares the magnitude of gains with those of losses, and the advance decline line.

Support and Resistance

Illustration 10-4 is a closer look at the ten-year period from 1994 to 2004, where we see that the S&P was in a primary uptrend for six years (1994 to 2000). Here it is easier to see the break down through support levels and the rallies back to resistance, which the market was unable to penetrate, creating a series of lower lows and lower highs. Areas of support and resistance are in-

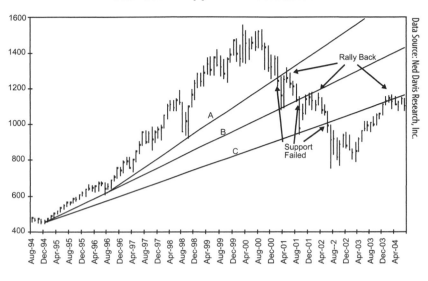

S&P 500 - Support & Resistance

Illustration 10-4

dicators of investors' moods and the technician must weigh the importance of breaks above and below these levels to determine if they may affect the overall trend. Is the break signaling a positive or negative trend that will require reallocation?

Lower Highs and Lower Lows

Illustration 10-5 is a chart of the Dow Jones Industrial Average between March 2001 and July 2004. Lower highs and lower lows is another indication of a downtrend. As long as this trend is in place, there is cause for caution. When the top line (the highs) breaks to the upside, it is an indication that the market has broken out of this trend. The final low is generally not achieved until this break-out has occurred.

Divergence

Illustration 10-6 shows the divergence between the S&P 500 with and without the technology stocks. This divergence was an early indicator of the potential weakness in the large cap weighted indices. The degree of divergence seen here will generally signal a correction, or at best a flattening in leadership. In this case, we see that the large cap stocks minus technology began their decline in early

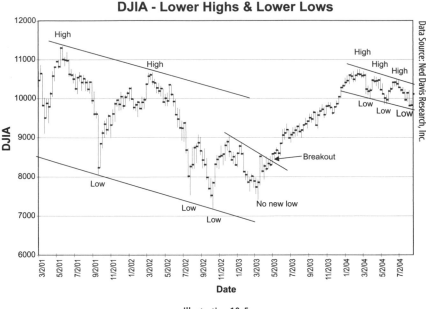

Illustration 10-5

1999, indicating a general loss of broad market momentum and the greater likelihood of a rapid contraction in the technology sector when technology followed suit. The broader market weakness was camouflaged by the strength in technology, as the S&P 500 index continued to move up, but technicians who saw this divergence had another indication for reallocating away from technology and large cap in general.

Advance-Decline Line Analysis

The advance-decline (A/D) line compares how many stocks are moving up to those that are moving down. The A/D line analysis of Illustration 10-7 indicated two things. In April of 1998, the A/D line became negative (more stocks going down than up), then later failed to reach a new high when the DOW reached its new high in January of 2000. Both were signals that the broad market was losing momentum despite the averages moving higher. This knowledge, combined with the information obtained from divergence analysis, helped to show where there was market strength and where there was weakness. In this illustration, there is also a less severe move in the A/D line in 1990 and 1994, both of which preceded difficult market conditions. In mid 2001, the advance-

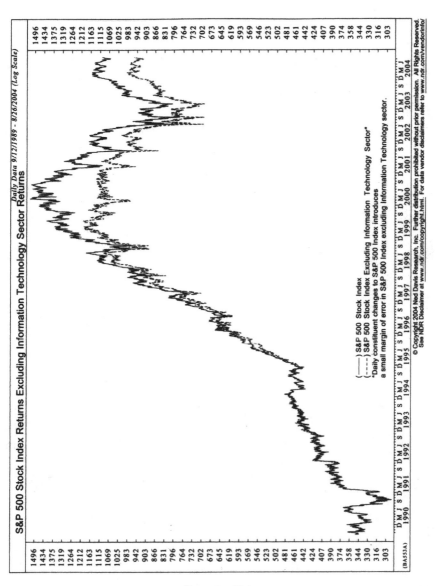

Illustration 10-6

decline line and the NYSE went to new highs, while the Dow labored. These indicators signaled that asset allocations should favor mid to small cap, which represent the broader market.

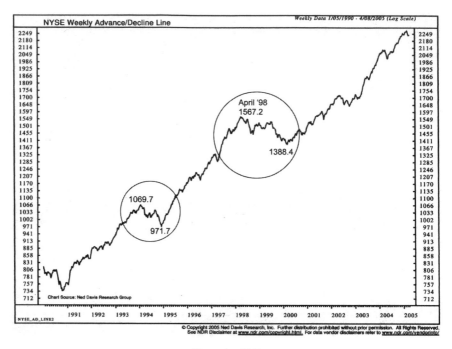

Illustration 10-7

CONCLUSION

Market analysis requires experience and special skills that consultants train and study to obtain. It involves constant attention to the markets and the global economic factors that affect them, as well as an understanding of the natural, intermediate to long-term valuation cycles of the markets. In this chapter, we have shown that there is no single indicator that tells the whole story and it is important for a consultant to use multiple tools when making asset allocation decisions. As stated throughout this book, capitalizing on market opportunities and managing risks are key to investment success. Consultants who understand the many facets of market analysis and use this knowledge to make asset allocation recommendations, add substantial value to the investment decisions of their clients.

11

Applying Market Analysis—
A Case Study

Integrating the different forms of market analysis is a skill that takes time, training and experience. Now more than ever, emerging economies and globalization play a role in the behavior of the markets. It is the consultant's role to sort through volumes of information to determine market trends, which in turn, allows him or her to seek out opportunities and to avoid excess risk. In order to accomplish these goals, the consultant must not only integrate all forms of market analysis, but he or she must have the experience to know how much weight should be given to different data at any given point in time. This is the blending of the art and science of market analysis.

The 2000 Bear market gave us the opportunity to explore an actual case study of market and investor behavior and, to apply the various forms of analysis that we discussed in the previous chapter. In April of 1998, the equity markets began a reversal of the broad based Bull market trend that began in 1982. After nearly 25 years (1974–1998) of generally positive returns, the markets were signaling a change that few had ever experienced. By the spring of 2000, several key areas of market leadership began to break down, but still, the ultimate sell-off that extended into 2003, caught many investment professionals and investors alike by surprise. We had entered a new secular Bear market and the portfolios of those who did not recognize this change, suffered significant losses.

What events collided to create such a severe Bear market and should so many investment professionals have been caught so unawares? We will dissect not only the signals that the markets were giving us, but also the behavior of investors and advisors that helped to exacerbate both the run up (irrational exuberance) and the decline. Investor behavior is a powerful driver of market extremes and during this time, we saw both sides (mania and panic) of the cause and effect relationship of such behaviors as emotional investing, momentum investing, believing in "the new paradigm" and irrational expectations. Greed, followed by panic, took the place of process, but in the end, process won the day.

So, what did the markets tell us and, as a matter of comparative interest, what recommendations did your advisor or consultant make during this time? We will describe many factors that led to both the magnitude and duration of this Bear's fall back to reality, but first we will discuss the difference between a secular Bear market and an urgent sell-off within a Bull market. There is a significant difference between the two, and therefore what investment decisions should be made, but one must first be able to recognize the difference.

Some market watchers say that any market decline greater than 20% is considered a Bear market. There have however, been many 20% declines that have occurred within two months of a recent market high, which have recovered to new highs within a year; these declines have not represented a *secular* Bear market. In 1987, the popular averages fell 29% in 13 trading days within weeks of registering a new high and these averages recovered to new highs within a year. By most measures, 1987 was an urgent sell-off within the confines of an ongoing secular Bull market. The key technical difference is that the decline occurred within two months of a recent high.

The sell-off that began in 2000 was very different. Investors and the market averages were swimming in excessive speculation and extremely high valuations. A 20% decline in the Dow and the S&P 500 did not occur for many months following their highs and therefore, a Bear market was not declared, despite the fact that the advance/decline line had been declining for 18 months. During this time, while investors were waiting for the market to rebound, as it had done each time there was an urgent sell-off in previous years, significant damage was being done to their portfolios. This is why it is important to recognize the difference between an urgent sell-off in a Bull market and the beginning of a secular Bear market. The two require a significantly different investment strategy. An urgent sell-off is a buying opportunity, brought about by panic selling and oversold conditions. A secular Bear market causes the slow degradation of stock prices. There is little or no panic selling as a Bear market begins, but hope and denial between each decline. Hope that there will be a rapid recovery following the decline, and denial that something serious is really happening. Many hung on to the belief that each successive lower low (Chapter 10) was the bottom and that a recovery was just around the corner. Investment professionals who recognized the underpinnings of a Bear market were able to proactively reallocate portfolios to preserve capital.

What did they see? We will discuss many of the events that signaled a significant market transition and demonstrate their impact on the primary trend of the markets. These warning signs were readily available and regularly reported on all the financial news networks and in financial publications. We had many sell-offs in the '90s, but the following signals marked 2000 as something different: a secular Bear market.

- Valuations as P/Es
- Advance/decline line
- Valuations outside of technology
- Rise in the value of the dollar
- Manufacturing output: ISM
- Corporate spending: Capex
- Business cycles
- Consumer debt
- Unemployment
- Corporate malfeasance
- Oil Prices
- Interest rates
- Rate cuts
- Alan Greenspan
- Technical indicators

One of the most significant causes of this secular Bear market was the total disconnect between the economy and company earnings, and stock prices. While the economy was growing at 5% during the '90s, slightly under its historical 6% growth rate, the stock market was pricing in 12 to 14% growth rates for growth stocks and 20 to 25% growth rates for technology stocks. It might be appropriate to provide a historical reference here. The annualized, inflation adjusted growth rate of the S&P 500 from 1925 through 2006 was 6.9%[1]. In

1. Ned Davis Research, Inc.

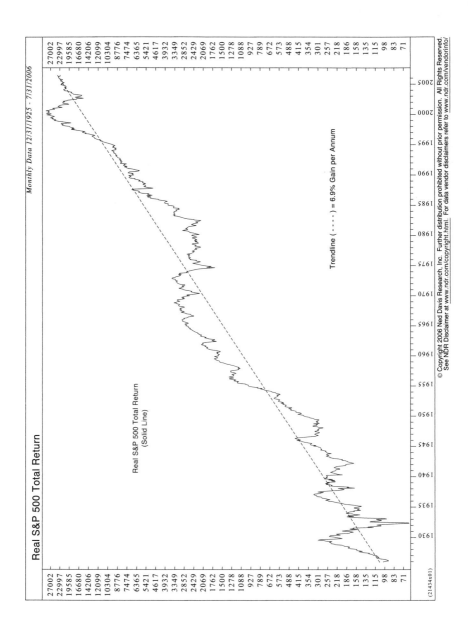

Illustration 11-1

order for companies to maintain the illusion that the prices we saw in the '90s were warranted, they had to show money on the bottom line. First, they were able to increase productivity, which increased profits. Then, they increased leverage, which caused corporate debt to soar, and finally, the accounting practices became rather aggressive. This set the stage for the heavy price that was ultimately paid.

On the surface, things looked great in the second half of the '90s. The economy was capital driven and the consumer became a spending machine. Interest rates were declining, unemployment was at record lows and salaries were rising. Companies were feverously spending on infrastructure and capacity, partially due to concerns over potential Y2K problems, inflation was under control and oil prices were declining. Oil prices went from $26.10 per barrel in late 1996 to $10.86 per barrel by the end of 1998[2]. Companies with no earnings had market capitalization's that exceeded that of General Electric. For reasons that apparently made sense to many, earnings became irrelevant. There was constant talk about a new paradigm. "It's different this time" became the mantra of the media. Investors and brokers had been trained to 'buy on dips' throughout the Bull market and buy they did, price was no object. The average monthly volume for the Dow was in the high 300 millions in 1995. By February of 2000, it had increased nearly three-fold to the high 900 millions, then over one billion as the bubble broke and the scramble began[3].

VALUATIONS

Before the technology bubble broke, the average P/E for the S&P 500 reached 29, according to several valuation models. The post World War II historical average is 14.7. The NASDAQ's average P/E reached 180, with a historical average of 46[4]. Stock prices and P/E ratios signaled unsustainable levels, especially for large cap growth, which included the big technology names, the darlings of the 90s. Companies were not able to grow at the rate necessary to support these prices. The widening gap between realistic growth capability and valuations was signaling a reversal of the primary Bull market trend. And then finally, the bubble broke. Buying on "dips" was no longer successful because

2. Cushing, OK WTI-West Texas Intermediate. www.eia.doe.gov.
3. Data Source: Ned Davis Research, Inc.
4. Data Source: Ned Davis Research, Inc.

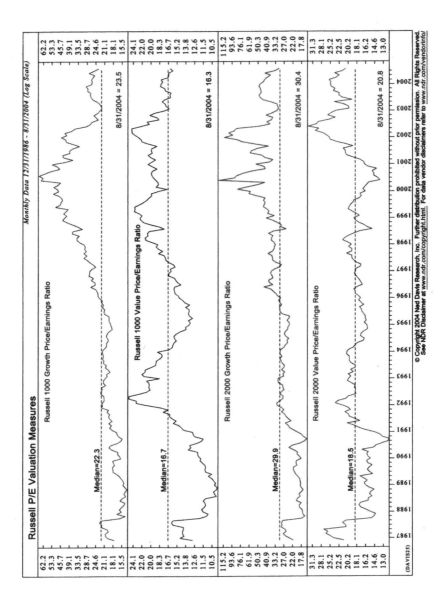

Illustration 11-2

they were no longer dips, only gasps to recover, which resulted in lower highs and lower lows. The trend was now down, not up. The signals were screaming for reallocation away from the hyper-inflated areas of the markets, but few were listening.

Illustration 11-2 shows the extremely overvalued condition of growth stocks, represented by the Russell 1000 Growth and the Russell 2000 Growth, in the first quarter of 2000, whereas value stocks, particularly the Russell 2000 Value, looked much more reasonable and represented much less market risk.

The advance-decline (A/D) line is the ratio between the number of stocks that are advancing and those that are declining (Illustration 10-7). The A/D line peaked in April of 1998 and then began to show a negative divergence, indicating limited participation in the rising value of the S&P 500 index. Eventually, very few companies were driving the index higher. The entire index continued to move higher due to the market weighting of large capitalization stocks and the huge multiples that were being applied to a few big name technology stocks. Technology reached 35% of the S&P 500 index at its peak[5]. By the end of the Bull market run, perhaps 10 technology stocks were carrying the index, some with P/Es of 150 to 200.

RELATIVE VALUES

Many investors who had not invested in technology stocks, found themselves asking, "Why are my stocks getting hit?" The over inflated values in the S&P 500 index caused a relative value problem with other stocks. When advisors and analysts talk about whether a stock is a value or not, they often compare its P/E to that of the S&P 500. If the S&P 500 has an average P/E of 25, or the 29 that we saw at the top, then other stocks that should trade at a P/E of 15, looked comparatively cheap and began to trade at higher and higher P/Es. They were considered cheap relative to the S&P 500, but neither their earnings nor expected growth could support their prices. This departure from realist pricing could not go on forever, and it didn't! It was not different this time; valuations and earnings always matter in the end. The markets will eventually correct wide variations in earnings growth to pricing, which is the answer to why so many good companies with consistent earnings had their stock price cut in half through the course of the Bear market.

5. Standard & Poor's, General Criteria for S&P U.S. Index Membership, September, 2000.

In 2000, companies significantly curtailed their spending for technology, which contributed to the collapse of the tech heavy NASDAQ. The NASDAQ dropped from 5132 to 1620 in the first 13 months of the market decline and continued down to 1109 by October of 2002. In approximately one and one-half years, the NASDAQ declined over 78%. Let's put this decline in perspective. In order to merely recoup this loss, you would have to achieve a 455% return or, a 10% annualized return for over 15 years! This reality gives a whole new meaning to "investing for the long-term."

VALUE OF THE DOLLAR

One of the factors affecting the competitiveness of U.S. companies is the strength of the dollar against foreign currencies. The stronger the dollar, the greater the cost structure for producing U.S. goods, thus a strong dollar makes it more difficult for U.S. companies to compete with the production costs of foreign goods and ultimately, the cost to consumers.

Between 1995 and 2002, the dollar appreciated approximately 45%. As we will discuss in this chapter, the consumer is a major contributor to the Gross Domestic Product (GDP) through their purchases of goods and services, however they are generally seeking the most competitive prices. As the dollar strengthened, U.S. goods became comparatively more expensive. As the U.S. economy continued to expand in the 1990s, the U.S. consumer accelerated their purchases of cheaper foreign goods, thus causing the U.S. trade deficit to grow to the record setting level of nearly $500 billion by 2002[6]. Among other things, the effects of a stronger dollar applied ever increasing pressure on U.S. companies' ability to compete and ultimately contributed to a slow down in production. There were obviously many factors at work here, but the value of the dollar compared to foreign currencies should not be ignored.

SEPTEMBER 11, 2001

We would be remiss if we did not address the market events surrounding September 11th. Many wanted to believe that 9-11 was the cause of the market declines, rather than focusing on the ongoing underlying causes of this Bear market. Prior to 9-11-2001, 56% of the market declines had already occurred

6. Department of Commerce.

and showed no signs of stopping. In the five days that followed the market reopening, the Dow completed its cycle decline to 8062. Many professionals considered the market fairly valued, not under valued, at this point.

The Federal Reserve, which had already cut rates 7 times totaling 300 basis points or 3%, accelerated these cuts to rapidly lower interest rates in an attempt to avert further economic harm, but the conditions that had created the secular Bear market were still in place and were now exacerbated. The Bear market would run its course, despite the efforts of the Federal Reserve.

MANUFACTURING AND BUSINESS

Manufacturing output is represented by the ISM, the Institute for Supply Management, formerly the NAPM, the National Association of Purchasing Managers. The ISM peaked in January 2000 at 56.80, and then began a steady decline that continued until October of 2001, when it reached 39.50[7]. Readings over 50 indicate that most companies in the survey are experiencing growth. Readings below 42.7 indicate that the economy is contracting. This data was reported monthly. Corporate capital spending was also experiencing steady declines. This data is reported quarterly and was a clear indication that manufacturing and business had significantly reduced spending and expansion. Contribution to spending by businesses, in the form of investment, was plagued by overcapacity and high inventory levels left over from the late '90s, slow sales growth and a very difficult pricing environment. Cost cutting was the only available path back to profitability and the earnings necessary to drive stock prices, however concerns about accounting issues and unfunded or under-funded pension plans kept investors nervous.

The data began to change rather quickly, indicating a shift in the business cycle. We had experienced a long and very over-extended expansion that was rapidly contracting.

BUSINESS CYCLES

Economists monitor many economic indicators to help them forecast each stage of the economic cycle. The stages are successive and repetitive in nature, however the length of each stage is difficult to anticipate. The chart below

---

7. Institute for Supply Management.

CHARACTERISTICS OF EACH STAGE OF THE BUSINESS CYCLE

<u>Characteristics*</u>	<u>Effect on Financial Assets*</u>

EXPANSION

• Low unemployment	• Prices of fixed income increase
• Business profits peak and begin to decline	• Securities decline
• Expansion and loan demand strong	• Stocks rise, but progress is more selective
• Inflation rises as demand overtakes supply and prices increase, then inflation peaks	• There are many new issues
	• Investors move from growth stocks to value
• Fed tightens money supply	stocks and quality issues with low volatility
• Interest rates increase	

CONTRACTION

• GDP slows and may decline	• Prices of fixed income decline
• Unemployment rises	• Stocks decline, build a base and move off lows
• Consumer spending declines	
• Inflation declines as demand is reduced	
• Margins narrow	
• Interest rates peak and then decline	

RECESSION

• Falling, flat, or negative GDP for 2 consecutive quarters	• Fixed income prices are low
• Deflation risk as pricing power is reduced	• Stocks rapidly lose value
• Very high unemployment	
• Consumer spending bottoms out	
• Low interest rates	

RECOVERY

• Rapid GDP increases	• Fixed income prices relatively stable
• Unemployment high, but slowly declining	• Investors buy junk bonds
• Business profits recover	• Stocks rebound from lows
• Credit demand rises	• Investors buy cyclical stocks
• Inflation is low	
• Interest rates low	

Not all of the characteristics and effects need be present at the same time to indicate a specific stage of the cycle. During this particular economic cycle, the consumer continued to spend due to the increased availability of low cost money. Low interest rates and incentive programs kept the consumer spending, which reduced the potential magnitude of the recession.

shows many of the characteristics of each stage: expansion, contraction, recession and recovery. As you will see, we have discussed many of the characteristics that indicated the transition from expansion, through contraction and into recession.

THE CONSUMER

The consumer makes up two-thirds of the U.S. GDP and consumer spending kept the economy moving in the early 2000s, but how? Interest rates, tax cuts and revolving credit, particularly credit card debt, played major roles. Spending was able to continue with help from the Federal Reserve, that continued to lower interest rates and pour easy money into the system. As interest rates went down, loans, particularly revolving loans seemed easier to handle. Mortgage refinancing soared, putting more money into the consumer's pockets, allowing the consumer to spend more and create more debt, just at lower interest rates. Cars were selling for zero percent financing, which was hard to turn down, especially if the plan was to buy in a year or two anyway. Buying products, even at delayed, low or zero percent financing, created more future debt. Taxes were reduced, including a tax rebate, again creating more available money and more spending, but little debt reduction. Personal tax payments fell by 6.3% in 2002, resulting in a real after-tax income increase of 5.0%, even though wages and salaries increased just 3.1%[8]. Since consumer spending is driven by income, most specifically disposable income, spending continued.

There were several reports that warned of an at-risk consumer, but the household liquidity numbers in the late 1990s and early 2000s were startling. The ratio of household liquid assets to total household liabilities moved from a forty-year norm of 135.5%, indicating positive liquidity, to 88.3% in first quarter of 2002. The consumer now had significantly more liabilities than assets. Revolving credit ballooned to 43% of total consumer credit, while non-revolving credit dropped to 57% of the total by 1997 and stayed near these levels into the early 2000s. These changes in consumer credit statistics indicated that credit card debt was increasing and not being paid down or off. In 1980, these percentages were approximately 18.2% and 81.8% respectively and in 1990, they were approximately 37.6% and 62.4% respectively. The consumer was using short-term credit vehicles, such as credit cards and home equity loans, to

8. Department of Treasury, Congressional Budget Office, U.S. Census Bureau.

finance their spending and these revolving credit balances continued to grow. Banks charged off an ever-increasing number of consumer loans. In 1990, the charge-off rates were 1.7%, but by the first quarter 2002, the rate was 3.6%, a 111% increase. Credit cards were responsible for the biggest portion of the write-off, going from 3.2% to 7.7%, more than double, in this same time frame[9]. Mortgage delinquencies reached a cycle high point in Q2 of 2002, and not surprisingly, personal bankruptcies nearly doubled during this time[10]. This borrowing cycle was destined to slow down due to either delinquencies or interest rate increases and indeed, there were disappointing Christmas sales in 2002.

	1980	1990	2001	2002
CONSUMER CREDIT				
Revolving	18.2%	37.6%	43%	41.4%
Non-Revolving	81.8%	62.4%	57%	58.6%
HOUSEHOLD LIQUDITY*	134%	131.5%	92%	88.75%
CHARGE-OFF RATES				
Consumer loans		1.7%	2.4%	3.59%
Credit cards		3.21%	4.9%	7.67%

* Household Liquid Assets (Cash on hand) / Total Household Liabilities= Household Liquidity

Ilustration 11-3

Layoffs and the unemployment rate began to rise steadily. By the end of 2002, the unemployment rate was 6%, the highest level since July 1994. Since the consumer had been a significant player in the Bull market, and the consumer debt data approached post World War II record levels, there should have been serious cause for concern. Consumer confidence was low due to shocking stock market losses, rising unemployment and uncertainty surrounding huge corporate accounting scandals.

9. Ned Davis Research.
10. Mortgage Bankers Association.

OIL PRICES

As an added blow to both the consumer and business, oil prices moved from their low in 1998 of $10.79 per barrel to over $35.45 per barrel in late 2000, a rather sudden 229% increase! Oil shocks and recessions generally go hand and hand. We saw this correlation in 1973, with the first OPEC shock, again in 1979, with the spike in prices associated with the Iranian Revolution and again as prices increased in 1990, preceding the Gulf War. These oil related events caused significantly higher fuel prices and created a drain on both the consumer and business, contributing to recession. In early 2003, oil prices had worked their way up to nearly $38 per barrel, preceding the war with Iraq, which contributed to prolonging this Bear market.

THE FEDERAL RESERVE

The Federal Reserve was very active in the years surrounding the year 2000 bubble, causing confusion to many and turmoil to the markets. There was, however, a story associated with their actions and very specific reasons for the interest rate changes.

It is the Federal Reserve's job to monitor the economic health of the country and to adjust interest rates to keep inflation and economic growth in balance. Their mandate is "to promote sustainable growth, high levels of employment, stability of prices to help preserve the purchasing power of the dollar and moderate long-term interest rates." It is not their job to affect the stock market. After a relatively stable Fed policy in the mid 1990s, the Fed became very active in 1998. The Long Term Capital debacle began unraveling in July of 1998. Long Term Capital was a very large hedge fund that got on the wrong side of the market. In the second quarter of 1998, they were liquidating huge blocks of securities to cover margin calls, as they reportedly lost in the neighborhood of $1 billion in 48 hours alone. Their large scale selling of equities caused a sudden and significant sell-off in the stock market, and had a significant negative effect on financial companies. The Dow fell nearly 20% from July 17th to August 31st, while interest rates moved up. In order to prevent significant damage to the U.S. economy, the Federal Reserve went to the major brokerage firms who were involved with Long Term Capital and responsible for supporting the high-risk ventures, and suggested that they get out their checkbooks to cover the losses. In trade, the Fed lowered interest rates 3 times (75 basis points) and later, after the markets and economic situation stabilized, it began raising them again to return to its normal fiscal position. From June 1999 through May 2000, interest rates were increased 6 times, totaling 175 basis points. During this time period, the stock market peaked, then experienced the first major drop in the indices.

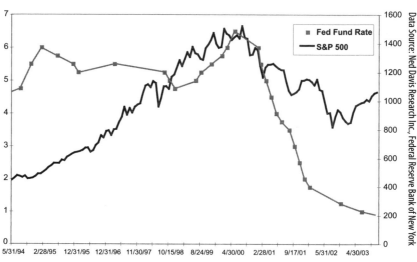

Illustration 11-4

By January of 2001, it was clear that the economy was not rebounding and the Fed stepped in and began to lower interest rates in an effort to stimulate spending. There had been so much excess built into the stock market by this time, that lowering interest rates did little to reverse the trend. Illustration 11-4 clearly shows the rapid reduction of rates, with little effect on the declining market. The famous "irrational exuberance" speech had been years before in December of 1996, but the exuberance had continued far beyond sanity and lowering interest rates could not stop the fall back to reality.

As we entered 2003, there had been 12 interest rate cuts, resulting in a stunning 525 basis point (5.25%) reduction in approximately two years, with deflation, not inflation, the fear of the Federal Reserve. The Fed Funds rate reached a 30-year low of 1.25%. In June of 2003, there was another rate cut, resulting in a Fed Funds rate of 1.00%, the lowest rate since November of 1954.

At this point, the Federal Reserve was doing everything possible to prevent deflation and to stimulate the economy.

Let's take a moment here to define terms that relate to interest rates and the Federal Reserve. The Federal funds rate is the interest rate charged between banks. The Federal Reserve has requirements which banks must meet, such as loan to cash reserve ratios. To meet these requirements, banks often loan to each other at the federal funds rate. Because the Fed funds rate is set daily, it is the most sensitive indicator of the direction of interest rates. The discount rate is the rate that the Federal Reserve charges to its member banks. The discount rate is usually lower than the fed funds rate, but the two are closely related. Prime, or the prime rate, is the rate that banks charge their best customers. Most loans are made at prime plus.

If you didn't know what was going on behind the scenes, what could you have discerned from the rate cuts? The lowering of interest rates is meant to stimulate the economy through consumer and business spending. There is more money available to purchase a product or service, as less is required to support debt service. As an example, if the consumer is able to purchase a $200,000 house at 6%, rather than 7%, there will be an extra $100 per month available to spend on other goods or services. For business, the cost of carrying inventory or buying capital equipment is reduced, which results in increased profit margins, making the company more financially secure. Strong corporate financials generally result in more favorable employment conditions. This balance is what the Fed tries to achieve.

On January 3, 2001, the Federal Reserve began lowering interest rates, as the excesses of the '90s choked business spending. There have been only two times in the last quarter century when the Fed has lowered interest rates more than 10 times in a row; once during the 1974 Bear market and again during the 1990 recession. Four cuts in a row are almost as rare. On April 18, 2001, we saw the forth rate cut and heard Alan Greenspan's comments. These were signals that the economy was in worse shape than the politicians and media had led us to believe. Each successive rate-cut reinforced the fact that we had not seen the end of economic concerns. And, let's not forget the basis of the "irrational exuberance" speech, which warned of "unduly escalated asset values." By all accounts, Alan Greenspan is a bright guy who has seen many economic cycles and is someone who has access to all the available data that might affect the economy. Why was he ignored by so many for so long? His continual concern over the prices and P/Es of the stock market should have triggered at least enough curiosity to warrant further investigation.

TECHNICAL ANALYSIS

As illustrated in the previous chapter, trend line analytics, as well as other technical indicators were showing many ominous signs. In late 1999 into the first quarter of 2000, the Dow began to exhibit several technical signs of a reversal of trend, and when the bubble broke, there were longer-term trend line failures and key support levels were violated. To a technician, these were cause for concern. To a consultant, it was time to reallocate.

MARKET FATIGUE

As the Bear market progressed into 2003, bonds had become king. Those who had finally lost confidence in equities began buying bonds, as the positive bond returns became very enticing. Chasing returns, even with bonds, can be risky. Those who had recognized this trend early had already realized two years of good returns. What could buying bonds at this point in the cycle mean? Treasury rates had not been this low since 1958 and the Treasury debt supply was destined to rise due to budget deficits. Increased bond supply and reduced demand is not a positive scenario for long or even intermediate term investments. Rushing into bonds this late in the cycle is a reactive reallocation that is likely to significantly underperform over the long-term and is not unlike buying into the NASDAQ when the index was 4500. They could go higher, but this type of reallocation must be viewed with a short-term perspective and watched closely for signs of reversal.

CONCLUSION

VALUATIONS AS P/Es	S&P 500 reached 29, Norm 14.7, tech goes to 35% of index
ADVANCE/DECLINE LINE	Negative divergence began in April, 1998
VALUATIONS OUTSIDE OF TECHNOLOGY	All stocks began to trade at higher P/Es due to rising S&P 500 average P/E
VALUE OF THE DOLLAR	Increased by nearly 45% between 1995 and 2002

MANUFACTURING OUTPUT: ISM	56.80 in January 2000, 39.50 in October 2001
CORPORATE SPENDING: CAPEX	Rapid declines in 2000, steady declines throughout 2001
BUSINESS CYCLES	Moving from expansion, through contraction, to recession
CONSUMER DEBT	Ballooned in late '90s into the '00s
UNEMPLOYMENT	Record lows of 3.8% in April '00 to 6% in December '02
CORPORATE MALFEASANCE	Enron, followed by Worldcom, etc.
OIL PRICES	Low in '96 of $10.79 to over $35 in '00
INTEREST RATES	6 increases to 6.5%, June 1999 through May 2000
RATE CUTS	13 cuts starting in January 2001, resulting in a Fed rate of 1.00%, last seen in 1958
ALAN GREENSPAN	"Irrational Exuberance"
TECHNICAL INDICATORS	Indicated a substantial reversal of trend

We have described many of the advanced signals warning of the 2000 Bear market, which collectively painted a predictable picture to the trained observer. Valuations, spending patterns, interest rate changes, oil prices and indicators of real growth were all being reported behind the hype. Those who heeded their warnings and believed that these things mattered were successful during this period. Those consultants, advisors and investors who employed a proactive, multi-style approach were able to rotate styles, capture gains and avoid the extremely overvalued areas of the markets. Those who were diversified across multiple styles, but still used a "buy and hold" strategy were not able to avoid the significant downdrafts, nor did they sell positions in order to take advantage of the extraordinary prices that the markets had offered, albeit for a limited time. Their diversification across multiple styles did however buffer their losses. Those who continued to follow the hot story of the week and were mesmerized by the hype, got killed.

12

The Art and Science
of Asset Allocation

Asset allocation is the disciplined process of combining different asset classes and styles to create a portfolio that has the potential of meeting the desired long-term investment goals, while minimizing risk and volatility. The Modern Portfolio Theory (MPT) is the current standard by which these asset allocation decisions are based, however there are limitations to the pure application of this theory, which we will discuss. MPT theorists believe that mixing different asset classes and styles that have a low correlation of movement to each other (Illustration 9-8) creates the opportunity to structure portfolios that are more likely to produce more stable returns over time than those of a single investment style or asset class (Illustration 9-6). As we saw in Illustration 6-1, it is the strategic asset allocation process, not the selection of securities, which is responsible for the majority of returns. Effective asset allocation is the cornerstone of the investment management consulting process and it is critical to the success of a long-term investment plan.

In this chapter, we will discuss different methods used to allocate assets including:

- Simple, boilerplate asset allocations
- Strategic asset allocation
- Modern Portfolio Theory and Computerized models
- Firm modeled asset allocations, *Strategic versus tactical allocations*
- Proactive asset allocation
- Indexing
- Core/Satellite strategies
- Active versus passive investing

Successful asset allocation involves more than diversifying assets, it also requires careful consideration of the investor's return expectations, tolerance to risk and volatility, cash flow requirements and time horizon. In addition, risk management techniques and market conditions can affect asset allocations. Therefore, when designing an asset allocation, the consultant will incorporate the following elements into creating a portfolio structure that is both suitable and effective:

- **Macro allocations:** Determining the degree of inclusion of various asset classes will affect the portfolio's total return. These decisions are a reflection of the investment policy guidelines.

- **Market cycles:** Is a particular asset class or investment style in or out of favor? Asset classes and styles respond differently during various economic environments and time periods. A skilled consultant can make proactive asset allocation decisions to capitalize on these variances, such as over- or underweighting certain areas of the markets depending on valuations and market cycles.

- **Risk management:** Selecting asset classes with a low correlation to one another will result in one asset class outperforming while another is lagging, thus smoothing volatility. An understanding of correlations and diversification is an important component of risk management.

- **Risk tolerance:** Understanding an investor's ability to tolerate volatility within his or her portfolio and structuring the portfolio accordingly is a critical element in asset allocation decisions. Determining the risk taken by a manager to obtain returns will tell a lot about a manager's suitability for certain investors.

In order to meet the investor's objectives, manage risks and achieve the desired return, the advisor or consultant will design a portfolio using one of the following asset allocation approaches:

- **Boilerplate** allocations are generally made according to an investor's age or the nature of the investor. As examples, if an investor is 60 years old, the investor should have 40% invested in equities and 60% invested in fixed income; one size fits all. Or, if the investor is a particular type of foundation, there should be 40% in fixed income at all times. The boilerplate approach is a limited form of asset allocation, generally employed by those individuals who have limited asset allocation skills and/or little capital market knowledge. Boilerplate allocations can provide the investor with a degree of diversification, but add little other value to portfolio management.

- **Strategic** asset allocation is a more widely used form of asset allocation. It is based on the Modern Portfolio Theory (MPT) and utilizes the most current information available in computer databases. Strategic is a static or passive type of allocation, because once the allocation is determined by the computer, no further changes are planned.

- **Firm modeled** asset allocations are generally based on MPT and can be static or dynamic in nature, depending upon the skills or orientation of the personnel at each sponsoring brokerage or financial services (bank, insurance company, etc.) firm.

- **Proactive** asset allocation incorporates market dynamics, valuations and MPT to create a portfolio that seeks to optimize both market opportunities and risk management. This strategy requires a skilled and knowledgeable market strategy group, individual or consultant to properly execute this type of asset allocation.

STRATEGIC ASSET ALLOCATION

Strategic asset allocation is both static and strategic. It is static or passive because once an allocation is determined and assets allocated to each investment style, the allocation mix is intended to remain constant; it is strategic because it utilizes the principals of MPT. Most investment policy statements provide for target ranges within each investment style to allow a degree of flexibility, but as one area of the portfolio over- or underperforms, causing a shift in the percentage allocations, the portfolio should be rebalanced to bring it back to the original allocation. Rebalancing should be done annually, however there may be a need to make these corrections as often as quarterly during periods of market extremes. Systematic rebalancing ensures that the portfolio remains within the risk tolerance stated in the policy guidelines and that those areas that have performed well do not become overweighted.

There are two general approaches used in static, strategic asset allocation:

- "Buy and Hold" and/or,
- Computerized models

Buy and Hold

"Buy and Hold" is a passive investment strategy that has been used by investors and advisors for decades. This strategy relies on the premise that markets are efficient and that no investor will be able to outperform the market. The basis for the original allocation generally has its roots in MPT, but may simply be boilerplate in nature. Those who utilize this approach should break the process into three components.

1. Design a macro asset allocation that is diversified among different asset classes that have distinct performance characteristics and react differently to changing markets. Starting the diversification process here allows the investor to take advantage of the low correlation of movement between asset classes, as well as accommodating cash flow needs and risk tolerance. Investors who require income would have a different portfolio design (such as dividend producing stocks and bonds that provide interest income) than a portfolio designed for capital appreciation.

2. Further diversify each asset class into styles that move differently during different market cycles. In doing so, consider the return expectations, volatility and risk profile of the various styles, as well as the correlation coefficient between each. Employing style diversification strategies is not for the novice, but there are standard allocations that can be used for different investor profiles, such as those seen in Chapter 4.

3. Within each style, diversify between sectors. The advisor will "hold" this allocation for the long-term. "Buy and Hold" does not utilize a rebalancing or reallocation strategy, although some advisors may readjust the allocations as the investor ages or their circumstances change. This strategy is tax-efficient due to low turnover.

The buy and hold strategy can stand alone, however if the advisor is unsure of how to structure the asset allocation (steps 1 and 2), there are many software programs available to financial industry professionals to assist in this process and thus, buy and hold can be blended with computerized models.

Computerized Models

Incorporating computerized models creates a more strategic asset allocation and it is a broadly used allocation technique. The models take advantage of the dictates of MPT and mix different asset classes and styles. This approach is an improvement over a single style approach, however it does not incorporate any of the more proactive reallocation techniques used by skilled consultants to capitalize on market opportunities. Static forms of asset allocation worked well during most of the '80s and '90s during a primary bull market, but became problematic when valuation differentials between various styles became too divergent, creating areas of excessive risk.

Over time, changing market data can cause changes in computer models based on MPT, therefore running the models more frequently will improve results, however computer models are very limited in their ability to respond to changing market conditions. The processes of rebalancing and running more frequent models improves the application of strategic asset allocation for those who do not incorporate a more proactive approach, based capital market analysis, into their recommendations.

MODERN PORTFOLIO THEORY AND COMPUTERIZED MODELS

In today's investment world, the principles of Modern Portfolio Theory dominate asset allocation decisions. Almost all allocations utilize the concept of mixing assets that have a low correlation to one another, in an effort to control risks and obtain more consistent results. Since computer programs produce the models that are used by most institutions, advisors and consultants to create asset allocations, it is valuable to know how they work in order to discern the strengths and weaknesses of models.

How Computerized Programs Work

Computerized programs typically use 20 years of historical data to create a risk appropriate blend of asset classes and styles, however consultants with capital markets experience prefer to use a 50-year database to produce results that are based on more data points. The resulting models weight each style differently according to risk and return parameters, as well as time horizons. The process within the program (mean-variance optimization using the Markowitz algorithm) will produce optimized portfolios based on the input data provided by the consultant and the market data database. The intent is to maximize expected returns while minimizing risks. The market data database includes the historical return, standard deviation and correlation data which, as we discussed in Chapter 9, can vary over periods as short as three years.

Consultants and advisors should be aware of the limitations of the models produced by unconstrained[1] Modern Portfolio Theory-based computer programs. The Markowitz algorithm is very sensitive to return data and the resulting optimized portfolios will direct allocations to those areas of the markets that have higher return forecasts. This bias is a weakness in mean-variance optimization, which can result in concentrated portfolios, a flaw made strikingly evident in Illustrations 12-1 and 12-2. In 1990, the Black-Litterman asset allocation model was published. This model is a variation on mean-variance optimization that attempts to overcome the Markowitz algorithm's tendency to over-concentrate portfolios by making changes to the way the program processes return data. The mathematics behind Black-Litterman do create more diversified portfolios, but again, the constraints provided by the consultant play a major role in producing effective models. Both programs numerically emphasize the tenets of MPT: the longer the time horizon and/or the more asset classes/styles to choose from, the more likely a less volatile, favorable outcome will result.

Computer database: Databases contain market data, including historical returns, standard deviation and the correlation coefficient from at least three different asset classes (equities, fixed income and cash), over a specified period of time. If only three asset classes are used, the indices used must be very broad, which confines output to similarly limited portfolio designs. It is preferable to use programs that have databases containing a multitude of indices, as well as those that have 50 years (versus 20 years) of data, reported monthly rather than quarterly. Studies that take full advantage of available data points will improve the ultimate output, creating more diverse and relevant portfolio mixes. The more data the program has in its database, the better the study. The program uses this data to calculate the statistical probability that a specific portfolio mix will create a certain return, with a specific level of volatility, over a specified period of time. This projection of outcomes, also known as Monte Carlo simulations, predicts the probability of achieving a desired outcome given a specified set of assumptions. In the following Illustrations (12-1 and 12-2), we have used only six indices, the S&P 500, S&P Mid Cap, Russell 2000, the international

1. No limitations are placed on the output, such as that seen in mix 4 of Illustration 12-2.

index MSCI, a bond index and a cash equivalent[2] to produce asset allocation mixes, in order to more clearly illustrate the weaknesses of unconstrained and/or limited computer modeling.

Input data: Following a determination of investor objectives and risk tolerance, the consultant will set output parameters based on the target return, time horizon, a range of tolerance to volatility, cash flow requirements and the asset classes and styles under consideration. The cash flow requirements of the investor will drive the model selection, as they will have a direct affect on the time horizon and the tolerance to volatility. As an example, if an investor needs capital within three years versus not at all, then an allocation designed to have lower volatility would be preferable. Different portfolio mixes may have the same long-term result, but a mix with short-term volatility would not suit this investor's needs. The consultant will use several variations of input data to produce multiple models in order to illustrate the degree of volatility and/or the likelihood of achieving a desired return with each asset mix and/or time period. It is up to the consultant to select the asset classes to be considered in the results. Manipulating input data requires that the consultant be well versed in working with the program, as constraining and adjusting input is generally necessary to create models that reflect the investor's objectives and, to overcome the limitations of the Markowitz algorithm. Constraining the program parameters helps to prevent the concentrated portfolios seen in Illustrations 12-1 and 12-2 and adjusting the input parameters allows the output to adhere more closely to investment goals and objectives.

Output: Of the programs used for asset allocation, Zephyr is probably one of the most widely used, and there are many others to choose from, including Effron, Frontier Analytics, Ibbotson & Mobius. The consultant provides the client-specific input data and constraints, and the program produces various asset mixes that statistically should produce the desired results. The output data can consist of 5 to 10 simulations with differing risk–return–time horizon scenarios. (Volatility represents risk and is measured as standard deviation.) The investor will see how longer time horizons produce more favorable results and see the relationship between risk and return. The result of

2. Market indices have different start dates and therefore limit how far back a study can reach, i.e., the S&P 500 originated in 1929 and the S&P Mid cap 400 originated in 1981. Studies containing both indices can only include time periods from 1981.

these simulations numerically illustrates that success (achieving one's goal) is more a result of controlling risk (low standard deviation) than producing the highest return.

Computerized models rely heavily on recent past performance and recent levels of market volatility data, then weight areas of the markets accordingly. As a result, more emphasis is placed on the areas of the markets that have performed the best most recently (blending the best returns with the least volatility), as these programs inherently assume that historical returns will continue into the future, which of course, is not the case. As an example, large caps had relatively strong, consistent performance in the late '90s, with very low volatility (50% of normal historical volatility). The computer models therefore gave large cap a high weighting, calling for them to be overweighted in portfolios; a limitation of the Markowitz algorithm. This high weighting attracted more capital to large caps very late in their Bull market cycle, as each new asset allocation study overweighted large cap in 2000. Those who exclusively followed these models, then placed even more money into large cap. It was the worst time to overweight large cap, but a good time to overweight the small to mid cap areas of the market. Computerized models overlooked small and mid cap because of the overwhelming large cap data, as neither computerized models nor a "buy and hold" strategy anticipate or recognize changes in market leadership. This weakness can be improved somewhat with more frequent modeling, but it remains very limited. The only way to overcome the limitations of computerized models is to manipulate the input data, which requires both capital markets knowledge and an understanding of the workings of the computer program. This phenomenon highlights the downside of relying solely on computerized models, as markets are more dynamic than historical data may indicate and occasionally move to unexpected extremes.

The following illustrations show the results of unconstrained studies run before the 2000 Bear market returns began to affected the databases (Illustration 12-1) and again, 6 years later (2005), after large cap had consistently underperformed small and mid caps and data reflecting this change had become entrenched (Illustration 12-2). We see that the computerized models were unable to adapt to either of these changes in an opportune manner. (Mixes 1 through 4 represent different return and risk expectations. Bonds were limited to 30% of the portfolios.)

The results:

- Large cap is overweighted at a time when their valuations were danger-ously high (1999), as large cap neared the end of its market cycle.
- Small cap is excluded during both time periods, despite performance that was on par with mid-caps, albeit with somewhat greater volatility. Small cap had experienced its cycle low in 1998 and reached all-time highs in 2006.
- The 2005 study (Illustration 12-2) is extremely concentrated in mid-caps, defying the concept of diversification. The change in the programs "attitude" about mid-cap shows how significantly recent performance data can skew the results of the output models.
- The 2005 models exclude international from most mixes, despite inter-national's strong performance following the March 2003 low, where it outperformed the S&P 500 and kept pace with mid-caps.

20 Year Historical Average (3-81 / 12-99)

PORTFOLIO STATISTICS

Target Return : 10% • 10 Year Time Horizon • 95% of Projected Return Distribution

PORTFOLIO ALLOCATIONS

Asset Allocations	Mix 1	Mix 2	Mix 3
S&P 500	40.5%	46.4%	55.8%
S&P Midcap 400	13.2%	18.4%	21.1%
Russell 2000	0.0%	0.0%	0.0%
MSCI EAFE Index	7.8%	6.0%	6.8%
Lehman Government/Credit Bonds	30.0%	29.2%	16.3%
Merrill Lynch 91-day	8.5%	0.0%	0.0%
Expected Return (annualized)			
One year	14.0%	15.0%	16.0%
Time Horizon (10 years)	13.7%	14.6%	15.4%
Expected Risk			
One year	9.2%	10.6%	12.3%
Time Horizon (10 years)	2.9%	3.3%	3.9%

Zephr Associates, Inc., Allocation Advisor

Illustration 12-1

Due to the strength of the Bull market during the 1990s, the historical return data did not allow for a return less than 14% without increasing the bond portion of the portfolio beyond the 30% constraint.

23 Year Historical Average (3-81 / 12-05)
PORTFOLIO STATISTICS
Target Return : 10% • 10 Year Time Horizon • 95% of Projected Return Distribution

PORTFOLIO ALLOCATIONS

Asset Allocations	Mix 1	Mix 2	Mix 3	Mix 4
S&P 500	0.0%	0.0%	0.0%	0.0%
S&P Midcap 400	58.8%	71.2%	84.6%	98.0%
Russell 2000	0.0%	0.0%	0.0%	0.0%
MSCI EAFE Index	3.6%	0.0%	0.0%	0.0%
Lehman Government/Credit Bonds	30.0%	28.8%	15.4%	2.0%
Merrill Lynch 91-day	7.6%	0.0%	0.0%	0.0%

PORTFOLIO STATISTICS

Expected Return (annualized)

One year	13.0%	14.0%	15.0%	16.0%
Time Horizon (10 years)	12.6%	13.4%	14.2%	15.0%

Expected Risk

One year	10.3%	12.0%	14.0%	16.1%
Time Horizon (10 years)	3.2%	3.8%	4.4%	5.0%

Zephr Associates, Inc., Allocation Advisor

Illustration 12-2

This study illustrates the extremes to which unconstrained computer models can go, recommending that nearly the entire portfolio be allocated to a single investment style.

Without manipulating the input data, it is clear that early stage opportunities would have been missed and the portfolio allocations suggested by the models would have been exposed to excess risk due to the exaggerated valuations of late-cycle assets and lack of diversification.

A consultant who analyses the capital markets and then incorporates this knowledge into the input, prior to running the optimizations, can overcome the shortcomings of this type of modeling. A thorough understanding of the inner workings of the program allows the consultant to make meaningful adjustments (i.e., no more than a 30% allocation to mid cap) that will constrain the output, thus resulting in more well-diversified portfolios. In the absence of market analysis, but still assuming some input constraints to avoid concentrated portfolios, the models can produce adequate, lower volatility results.

However, the investor will miss the opportunity to adopt an early stage asset class or style, one that is beginning its next strong market cycle and/or, avoid those that are late in their market cycle and at greater risk of decline.

FIRM MODELED ASSET ALLOCATION

Strategic versus Tactical Allocations

Most financial services firms recognize that separately managed accounts and other fee-based platforms are not only here to stay, but they will soon dominate the industry. Since the vast majority of financial advisors from traditional firms are trained and experienced in transactional, product-based businesses, not consulting or asset allocation techniques, it is incumbent upon the firms to create products and platforms that these individuals can use to convert their client base to fee-based accounts. In order to facilitate this conversion, firms have created risk-appropriate, model portfolios for their advisors to use. Consultants within the firm's consulting departments design diversified portfolios to satisfy various investor profiles. These models represent *strategic* asset allocations and reflect an intermediate to long-term (5 to 10 years) forecast of trend returns and risks within the markets. Chapter 4 describes most of the available platforms, as well as several model portfolios. The differing allocations are most likely derived using MPT and some type of computerized modeling and perhaps, made more dynamic by the consulting department's strategists. The more dynamic models are changed when there are changes in the firm's forecasts. This review is usually done annually. Some firms are proactive in their allocations, incorporating *tactical* asset allocations into their models. These decisions reflect shorter-term forecasts (1 to 2 years) and allow the firm to over- or underweight sectors of their strategic models in an attempt to add additional value.

After the asset allocations have been determined, each allocation will be implemented using style specific mutual funds or, professional money managers who act in a sub-advisory role to the brokerage firm. These managers may be independent firms or they may be employees of the sponsoring firm. Either way, it is the responsibility of the sponsoring firm to create risk appropriate allocation models and to rebalance or reallocate within the models when appropriate. Depending upon the skill of the firm's consulting department and the flexibility of the firm's investment practices, this approach can result in a range of asset allocation approaches, from static to dynamic.

The advantage to this methodology is once again, a smoothing of performance, as well as improving the chances of increasing returns while minimizing risk. If the firm's consultants are skilled at manager selection and asset allocation, the investor may expect better returns than those of static models, due to the active management of these professionals.

PROACTIVE ASSET ALLOCATION

Proactive or dynamic asset allocation is based on the idea that markets are dynamic and asset mixes may need to be adjusted in response to changing market conditions. A proactive approach is sometimes incorrectly thought of as "market timing" however, market timing plays on the short-term (week to month) momentum of the markets, whereas proactive asset allocation anticipates and responds to changes in intermediate to long-term market conditions, which includes an awareness of the markets' 3- to 5-year cycles. Proactive asset allocation incorporates both strategic and tactical approaches and utilizes both fundamental and technical analyses. A consultant, adept in capital market analysis, can take advantage of the natural cycles of the markets through a proactive reallocation strategy and can be effective, regardless of market conditions. We have discussed how market cycles are reflected in valuations and proactive reallocation, based on these cyclical changes in valuations, has shown itself to be a successful strategy.

In order to allocate and reallocate assets in a proactive manner, the consultant must be well versed in the capital markets and be proficient in the use of the analytical tools that are addressed in this book. The consultant will continually monitor the markets and make proactive asset allocation recommendations, based on the investor's objectives (the investment policy) and market conditions, when warranted. The money manager will make the day-to-day tactical decisions involving specific security selections. This approach differs from the more static approaches described previously, in that on-going, current market analysis and macroeconomic conditions play an important role in proactive allocation decisions, as does the active management of the manager (Chapter 10).

For those skilled in capital market analysis, a Dynamic Asset Reallocation Process (DARP™) is incorporated into ongoing allocation decisions. DARP™ is driven by changing market conditions, the valuations of individual styles and the overall valuations of the capital markets. It incorporates fundamental analysis, valuation models, identification of market trends and momentum, macro-economics and technical analysis. There are times when certain asset classes or styles may represent greater opportunity or risk than their historical norm and having the skills to recognize this variance and to respond accordingly, adds significant value to the investment process. We have described the results of overweighting areas of the market that are undervalued and poised for growth and, underweighting overvalued areas that represent increased risks. Understanding this process allows the consultant to take advantage of the natural cycles of the markets through the reallocation process. Reallocation differs from rebalancing in that there is no attempt to maintain a specific or static allocation. His or her reallocation decisions are based on the investor's objectives and the then current market conditions and valuations.

In March of 2000, the markets began the most sustained Bear market since the mid seventies. Consultants, who had the experience and tools to recognize that the markets were vulnerable to a significant correction and/or a change in market leadership, were able to minimize the effects of the market declines for their clients. They were able to anticipate and proactively re-allocate portfolios away from the extremely overvalued areas of the market (large cap growth, represented by the S&P 500), toward the undervalued areas of the market (small to mid cap, represented by the S&P 400). It is the consultant's role to capitalize on these changes in market valuations by reallocating the portfolio. (Individual money managers generally stay fully invested and must stay within their discipline to maintain their credibility.) Investor's who had these consultants were spared the 30 to 50% (or more) declines in their portfolios. Those who used static forms of asset allocation stayed the course, as static approaches do not consider current market conditions. The disparity between large cap and small to mid cap during the Bear market is graphically seen when comparing the performances of these two indexes. (Illustration 12-3).

The value of this methodology is again, a smoothing of performance, but it also improves the chances of increasing returns and minimizing risk or, creating a high alpha return, the hallmark of Investment Management Consulting. When using this approach, the consultant must be proactive in order to capture

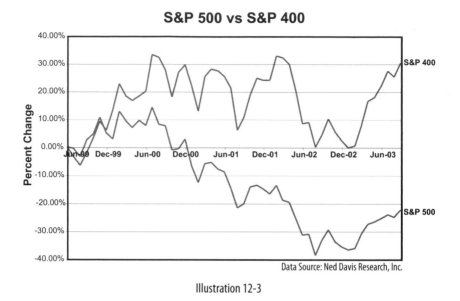

S&P 500 vs S&P 400

Data Source: Ned Davis Research, Inc.

Illustration 12-3

potential opportunities and not reactive, chasing the hot sector in hopes that the momentum will continue or, selling after it is too late. This point should be emphasized. Creating a high alpha return is the goal of consulting and, proactive asset reallocation offers opportunities to capitalize on market inefficiencies for those consultants who are proficient in capital market analysis. For those advisors or consultants who are not skilled in the types of analyses described in the last two chapters, approaches that are more static in nature will likely produce the best results.

INDEX INVESTING OR INDEXING

An index is comprised of a group of securities that represent a segment or sector of the capital markets. They cannot be purchased directly, so the financial industry has created mutual funds that mimic various indexes (index funds) and ETFs (exchange traded funds), which do the same. ETFs have become very popular with the investment industry and media and they will likely challenge mutual funds for significant market share. ETFs are gaining in popularity for a variety of reasons:

- There are an increasing number of ETFs to choose from, as Barclay Global Investors (iShares), S&P (SPDRs), Vanguard (Vipers) and others, have issued a vast number of ETFs, representing most areas of the global markets. ETFs trade like stocks and provide an easy way to buy a representation of an index.

- They are inexpensive due to their passive management and generally less expensive than index mutual funds.
- Many actively managed portfolios (mutual funds and SMAs) have underperformed their passive, less expensive cousins and investors have lost confidence.
- ETFs may be more tax-efficient, as they have internal mechanisms to control capital gains within the funds.
- Simple indexing, such as 30% in a bond index and 65% in the S&P 500 index, takes the mystery out of asset allocation. Indexing can provide broad diversification by mixing several indexes or, can allow the investor to invest in a specialized area of the market (i.e., energy or biotechnology).
- Advisors have begun to shy away from highly regulated mutual funds in favor of ETFs, which are oft times easier to explain to their clients.

The use of ETFs can be incorporated into any of the asset allocation techniques that have been discussed, as they can represent most any style or sector of the global markets. There are however, potential risks inherent in indexing that must be considered. Most indexes are capital weighted, meaning that an inordinate amount of the index may be within a limited number of sectors or stocks. As an example, the 40 largest companies of the S&P 500 index represented 50% of the index between 1998 and 2002. In the first part of 2000, the average P/E of the top ten stocks in the S&P was 55.5; by June of 2000, it was 72.2. Large technology companies, which grew to a 35% weighting in the index, were driving these changes and inherently increasing the index's level of risk. Recognizing this exposure to unintended risks, the industry has begun to issue equally weighted ETFs.

Passive management, or no management at all in the case of pure indexing, has a predetermined mix of sectors and stocks, however not all large cap growth ETFs or funds are created equal. As we describe in Chapter 14, there are multiple applications of the terms "growth" and "value," just as there are for market capitalization, consequently, the methodology used to construct and maintain an ETF or index fund must be understood to avoid unintended overlap in allocations. Additionally, due to the passive nature of these investments, if one sector becomes over-valued, then it automatically becomes a greater portion of the index. Rebalancing may occur only at pre-determined intervals, i.e., once a year. This passive form of investing offers little control over this risk exposure. It is for these reasons that the S&P 500 as a whole suffered such significant declines when the tech bubble burst.

To add an element of risk control to indexing, some fund managers have introduced **"enhanced indexing"** strategies, which add some active management to this otherwise passive approach. This form of semi-active indexing is also employed by several ETFs. The manager starts by replicating the weightings of the index and then slightly over- or underweights sectors or stocks within the index using quantitative and/or fundamental analytics as a guide. Depending on how far out of balance with the index the manager was willing to go, this strategy could have prevented a 35% weighting in technology stocks.

Many investors in the late 90s came to believe that passive management was as good as or better than active management, because some indexes had great performance numbers. But, during the S&P 500's last "run for the gold," an ever-increasing portion of the index was in ridiculously overvalued, high-risk investments that active managers would not have in their portfolios. During this time, risk management caused managers to underperform their indexes, causing many investors with short memories to abandon their investment strategy and run for the S&P 500. This move proved costly for many. Unintended consequences of indexing include:

- Capital weighting that may fall victim to momentum.
- Fundamentals take a back seat to capital weighting.
- Uncontrolled risk exposure.
- Index funds are forced to include and exclude stocks that move in or out of an index (inclusion in the S&P is determined by an S&P committee) with sometimes very unfavorable results. These companies are announced prior to inclusion and during this window, stocks tend to run up or down in anticipation of their position in an index. Telegraphing this change means that the incoming stocks generally run up prior to inclusion, thus making them expensive for the index fund to buy and outgoing stocks generally fall in value while still in the index, thus negatively affecting the index as a whole.

- The investor must understand the composition of the index, as the DIA (Dow), SPY (S&P 500) and QQQQ (largest 100 Nasdaq stocks) are all heavily weighted with the same stocks and this mix would not provide adequate diversification. In addition, the composition of ETFs that one might expect to be similar, may in fact, be quite different due to the selection methodology. As an example, the securities contained in one Basic Materials ETF may be significantly different from those of another and thus, produce significantly different results.

CORE/SATELLITE

Many advisors and consultants choose to mix indexing (core) and active management (satellite). This strategy is referred to as a core/satellite. These advisors believe that some areas of the markets, such as large caps, are more efficient than others, such as small caps or international securities. They believe that it is difficult to find managers that add value (alpha) in the more efficient areas of the markets and opt for indexing in these styles. Indexing is a low-cost, generally tax-efficient way to invest in core strategies. These advisors believe that active management is best suited to investment strategies (satellite) that are not considered market efficient, areas where active management can add alpha. Seasoned consultants may differ with this manager assessment, as they generally have access to a broad range of managers that may not be available to, or known by, those who do not specialize in a consulting practice, but they too may use ETFs to supplement the asset allocation of an overall portfolio.

Utilizing ETFs to overweight specific sectors of the markets, such as energy, or specific countries in the global markets, is an application of an ETF strategy that is becoming more popular with consultants. This targeted, more tactical approach allows the consultant to put more emphasis on certain areas of the markets than might otherwise occur when using style-specific managers that maintain generally diversified portfolios. Whatever strategy the advisor or consultant chooses, it is important to create the best asset allocation mix available, balancing risk management with return potential. A core/satellite strategy may be very efficient and cost effective at times and therefore, the value of active management should be evaluated on an investor-specific, risk-adjusted basis, where risk management or low volatility may outweigh the importance of absolute returns.

CONCLUSION

Static or passive management assumes that markets are efficient and that investors make rational decisions about investing. MPT, which guides most static asset allocations, assumes that past patterns will continue into the future. Given a long enough time horizon, this approach generally produces adequate results. Dynamic or active management on the other hand, assumes that markets are inefficient and that investors are not always rational in their decision-making processes, which sometimes drives areas of the markets to extremes. These inefficiencies create opportunities for better returns and better risk control than that which is available to the passive investor. This more dynamic approach to asset allocation recognizes the limitations of MPT and seeks to add value to the investment process with proactive decision-making.

The concepts contained in *The Art and Science of Investment Management Consulting* suggest that risk management is more critical to long-term investment success than periodically beating the market. Markets and market conditions are ever-changing and managing risk requires forward thinking, not simply the hope that things will work out in the long run. The investment management process and capital market analytical skills provide the means to capitalize on market opportunities and to avoid large losses, regardless of market conditions.

Much has been said and written about asset allocation. We have discussed the various mathematical tools used to make asset allocation decisions, such as Modern Portfolio Theory, standard deviation, correlation and market efficiencies and, have stated that they all have limitations. Some believe that they have very little value[2], whereas others believe in them implicitly. Attitudes about investing have evolved over time and are likely to continue to do so. It is often difficult to break the inertia of long held beliefs, to stand back and view all decision-making processes as dynamic. Mastering the tools is just the first step. Developing the skills to read between the lines and make decisions outside of the box is the *Art* of asset allocation. It is this ability that sets some investment professionals apart from the crowd.

2. "Radical Thoughts on Asset Allocation" by Elaine Floyd, CFP. February 17, 2005, www. horsesmouth.com.

SECTION III
Money Managers

13

Understanding Manager Styles

I n this chapter, we will describe many of the investment disciplines used by money managers and, in the following chapter, we will describe some of the elements used to evaluate these manager styles. A thorough understanding of both allows the consultant and investor to properly select investment styles and managers without falling into the trap of chasing past performance. These chapters are not intended as a discussion of asset allocation or performance analysis, as these topics are covered in later chapters. They are intended to define and differentiate investment styles, highlight factors that may influence a manager's results, and discuss the tools used to evaluate and refine the manager selection process. This process goes well beyond screening by performance and matching a style to an asset allocation model. It should include an in-depth understanding of the manager's investment philosophy, including what drives their returns, as well as how their style will match both the investor's investment profile and the current market environment. Here, we will discuss the following manager styles:

EQUITIES
- Market capitalization
- Deep or intrinsic value
- Relative value
- Growth (various types)
- Core
- Sector rotator
- Balanced or mixed
- Convertible securities
- Global, International and Emerging

FIXED INCOME
- Government securities and TIPS
- Municipal bonds
- Corporate bonds
- Mortgage-Backed Bonds
- International fixed income
- Cash reserve management
- Cash management

SPECIALTY STYLES
- Socially Responsible Investing
- REITs
- Hedge funds
- Managed futures

Those who invest in separately managed accounts, such as individuals, brokers, and pension sponsors, often focus solely on performance and chase the performance history of portfolio managers as though they were searching for a pot of gold at the end of a rainbow. But, like the rainbow myth, this approach can be merely an illusion; past performance can be very misleading.

"Rainbow chasing" describes an investor who finds a money manager (including mutual fund managers) who did exceptionally well in the past, and hires him or her on that basis alone, only to find out later that it was the manager's style that did exceptionally well, and not necessarily the manager. When large cap growth can do no wrong, a great deal of a large cap manager's performance is due to being in the right place at the right time. It is important to be able to quantify the difference in order to determine the value-added by the manager. We discuss how to make this analytical determination in Chapter 18.

Each money manager will have a specific investment style and philosophy and it is the manager's job to select those companies only within their specific style, which they believe have solid growth potential. Most managers generally remain fully invested and drifting into another area of the market (style drift) is not acceptable. Determining the overall asset allocation is the role of the consultant who must understand when a particular investment style is in favor and when it is not. This application of market analysis drives effective reallocation decisions, resulting in the over and underweighting of different styles within the capital markets as they move through their normal market cycles.

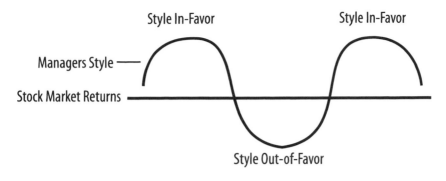

Illustration 13-1

MANAGER STYLES

The two most widely considered asset classes are equities and fixed income securities, however there are many others, some of which we will describe in this chapter. Managers will generally specialize within a single asset class and style. Equity managers will then be more specific as to market capitalization and value or growth, while fixed income managers may specialize in the sub-specialties of fixed income instruments, however many fixed income managers are generalists.

Equity managers invest in stocks and should be used by those with a long-term investment perspective, as equities are generally a more volatile asset class than fixed income. These managers typically seek long-term capital appreciation using a variety of equity investment approaches and the element of time helps to smooth the effects of the volatility. Historically, equity managers have exhibited higher variability of returns (risk), but have also achieved higher returns over the long term as compared to fixed income or balanced portfolios. Fixed income managers invest in a variety of fixed, convertible or adjustable securities. These are considered less volatile investments, however there are times when fixed income investments have considerable downside risk. Fixed income investors usually have a long-term, income-oriented objective.

After determining an appropriate macro asset allocation (equities, bonds, other, cash), the consultant will then divide the equities, fixed income securities and other potential investment classes into more specific styles.

Equities

Market Capitalization

Within the equity portion of a portfolio, investors should seek a mix of styles, differentiated by market capitalization. Market capitalization is derived by multiplying the number of outstanding shares of common stock by the share price. The dollar amounts indicating the different market capitalizations are not set in stone, but it is generally accepted that:

- A mega cap company has a market capitalization in excess of $100 billion.
- A large cap company is one with a market capitalization in excess of $10 billion.
- Mid cap companies have market caps between $1.2 and $10 billion.
- Small cap companies have market caps between $280 million and $1.2 billion.
- Microcaps have market caps under $280 million.

When a manager builds a portfolio, not all of the companies will have the same market capitalization, therefore the market cap for the overall portfolio is reported. This "averaging" can be done in different ways resulting in different values:

- **Average Capitalization:** The total capitalization of the portfolio (add the market cap of each security together) divided by the number of securities in a portfolio. This method may give too much weight to a few very large or very small securities.

EXAMPLE:	**$5,000 + $3,000 + $1,000 + $800 + $200 + $80 = $10,080** **$10,080 / 6 = $1,680** **The average capitalization is $1680**

- **Median Capitalization:** Median capitalizations are more commonly used to prevent the skewing that may occur with averaging. List the securities in the portfolio in descending order according to their market capitalization. Select the security that is halfway down the list; its market capitalization is the median capitalization of the portfolio. If the number of securities in the portfolio is an even number, 6 in this example, then add the two at the halfway point and divide by 2.

EXAMPLE:	**$5,000 + $3,000 + $1,000 + $800 + $200 + $80 = $10,080** **The 6 securities are listed in descending order: The median capitalization** **is the average of the 2 securities that are midway down the list.** **$1,000 + $800 / 2 = $900**

It is evident that these two methodologies can produce very different results, so the consultant must analyze how the manager calculates market cap to have a true understanding of the size of companies that are contained in a particular portfolio. This knowledge aids in effective diversification.

Some managers employ an all-cap or multi-cap investment strategy, which, as the names imply, does not restrict the manager to any specific market capitalization. This strategy allows the manager to seek out quality companies without regard to size. This approach can be effective in many instances, such as when market valuations are high across all market capitalizations and stock picking is at a premium. If an all-cap or multi-cap manager is part of an overall portfolio, the consultant will monitor the manager's market cap weightings so as not to allow the portfolio's mix of managers to become unexpectedly over- or underweighted in any one area of the market. After establishing market cap allocations, the consultant will further differentiate each manager's investment style by value, core or growth orientation.

Value versus Growth

Growth managers focus on companies exhibiting superior earnings growth relative to the market in general, whereas a value manager's focus is on valuation. Value managers are looking for companies whose stock is undervalued relative to traditional financial characteristics, such as price-to-earnings or price-to-book ratios. They believe that this measure provides them with an expanded "margin of safety" in their investment choices. *Margin of safety* is the difference between the intrinsic value of a company and the cost of the stock. Value managers evaluate the degree of discount that the stock is trading below its intrinsic value. A core strategy can include both value and growth, generally with a bias toward one or the other, but rarely to the extreme of either. A core approach is a middle of the road strategy. Managers will often be more specific about the type of value or growth stocks that they purchase, which we will discuss in more detail shortly. Just as the stock market may be up when the bond market is down, growth managers tend to perform well when value managers are lagging

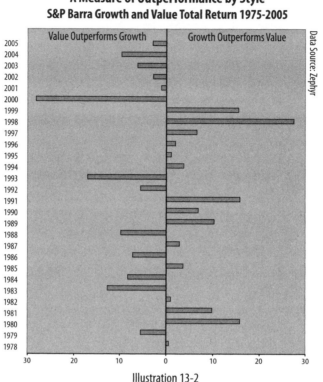

GROWTH OR VALUE?
A Measure of Outperformance by Style
S&P Barra Growth and Value Total Return 1975-2005

Illustration 13-2

and vise versa. Sometimes this divergence occurs over several consecutive years. Which style is better? Valuations and market conditions, such as momentum, help in making weighting determinations, but selecting one exclusively over the other is generally not advisable. Historically, the long-term performance of each is roughly equivalent and a value or growth manager may expose the investor to an area of the market that the other does not. As an example, the energy sector was hot in 2004 and 2005. During the same period, value managers were outperforming growth managers, but energy was not considered an intrinsic value play and was excluded from many value manager disciplines, whereas growth managers included energy in their portfolios.

Because such diversity exists among equity approaches, it is essential to understand an equity manager's philosophy before investing. To aid in this discussion, we will define some relevant terms.

The price-to-earnings ratio (P/E) compares the price of the stock to the company's after-tax, twelve-month trailing earnings. The P/E is the most commonly used assessment of how expensive a stock is. The ratio is calculated by dividing the market price (price per share) by the earnings per share, or put another way, the cost an investor must pay for each dollar of the company's earnings. High P/E ratios are generally associated with companies that have a high growth rate or, can be caused by high demand in the marketplace, which can artificially raise the price of the stock (the laws of supply and demand or market mania). The P/E ratio is sometimes reported using estimated forward earnings. This estimate cannot be thought of as an accurate gauge of value, as forward earnings may or may not materialize, but these estimates can be used when considering a stock's potential.

The price-to-book ratio is the company's market price per share divided by its book value per share. Book value is calculated using the firm's total assets minus the firm's liabilities, preferred stock value and intangible assets, such as good will, patents and franchises. A high ratio indicates the willingness of the market place to purchase a company's stock at a premium over its hard assets, whereas a low ratio would attract a value manager.

Deep or Intrinsic Value

In selecting deep or intrinsic value stocks, the manager is looking for companies that are inexpensive, but have sound fundamentals and significant upside potential. The manager will analyze each company's financial information to determine the viability of the company and its actual value, looking for such things as consistent return on equity (ROE), low debt-to-equity levels and a solid profit margin. They will then compare the price of the stock to what they believe to be the company's fair value. Fair value is a somewhat subjective measure as it includes not only the company's book value, but also its price per sales, price to cash flow, enterprise valuation and other balance sheet information. This evaluation is something of an art and requires that the manager have a depth of skill and experience to be successful. An intrinsic value manager is seeking companies whose stock is priced below the company's inherent worth (discounted), ideally buying those whose price is 30-50% less than the replacement value (true net asset value) of the company's total assets.

Value managers figure more prominently after a long market decline or at the bottom of a Bear market. They are popular during periods when market prices are low, pessimism is very high, and economic uncertainties abound. An intrinsic value manager does not focus on the economy or overall market conditions, but rather an individual company's value.

Relative Value Managers

Relative value managers select stocks that they find comparatively inexpensive. This comparison could be to the overall market, represented by the S&P 500; the benchmark that represents the specific area of the market that they are in, such as Russell 2000 value; or compared to the average P/E of the companies within a specific sector, such as biotechnology. This approach differs from that of an intrinsic value manager, because the basis for comparison is not a reflection of the tangible value of a particular company, but to a group of companies that have something in common.

At times, the value of stocks in one sector may have a much higher or lower P/E ratio than those in another sector. A relative value manager may be drawn to the sector with the lower P/Es. There are times when most areas of the market are overvalued and the challenge becomes one of finding companies that are inexpensive compared to some relevant standard. In addition to the P/E, managers will look at price to operating income, price to cash flow, and price to book value. Relative value managers, who tried to buy technology stocks in early 2000, could find stocks with P/Es that were lower than the sector average, but these companies were trading at much higher prices than their earnings could support. The same was true of many large cap stocks that were being compared to the S&P 500, which was being inflated by the large cap technology companies. We described this in more detail in Chapter 11. It was a difficult time for relative value managers, while intrinsic value managers did well.

Growth Managers

A growth manager is seeking companies whose earnings growth and market share are growing faster than others in their sector or, faster than the general economy. They look for accelerating revenue growth, return on capital and accelerating earnings growth. These companies rarely pay dividends as they use earnings for expansion. Growth managers are generally more attractive during periods when the market is doing well, however they often experience a high degree of volatility. Due to their above average growth rates, these stocks can support higher P/Es, but investors should be aware that as a rule, high P/E stocks are inherently more volatile. Some growth managers use a **GARP (growth at a reasonable price)** strategy, seeking growth companies, while maintaining a value orientation. GARP managers are cautious about how much they are willing to pay for the continued growth potential of a company, focusing on those stocks that are trading at a discounted P/E to their expected earnings growth rate. These managers often use PEG ratios to make this determination. PEG is the P/E ratio divided by the growth rate. The growth rate used is either the actual trailing 12-month growth rate or it is the forward projected growth rate. Either may be the more relevant approach, depending on the growth cycle of the company. If a company warns of lower future earnings, both the P/E and PEG, calculated using forward earnings, will be a more realistic measure of potential growth than those using trailing earnings. A PEG ratio equal to one means that the company's earnings are fully reflected in the price of the stock. Growth stocks typically have a PEG greater than one and value stocks have a PEG less than one, however growth expectations vary between sectors.

Some growth managers track growth potential by analyzing trends, while others are looking for any company within their discipline that will potentially show rapid growth. The managers who are looking at trends identify companies, both internationally and domestically, which may be part of a new emerging growth trend, such as telecommunications and technology in the 1990s or healthcare, which reflects the potential of the "graying" baby boomers. The expectation is that companies within a trend will show accelerated growth once their growth cycle begins.

Another growth strategy focuses on earnings momentum, which is often the result of a new or emerging trend. Earnings momentum of one or a few stocks will likely create momentum in an entire sector and the manager may buy most any company within his or her discipline that may benefit. **Momentum investing** often falls within the **GAAP (growth at any price)** investment philosophy. It is critical that momentum and GAAP investors know when to sell, as the ride down is often faster than the ride up. Look for managers who use their own research to make their determination of a company's potential, as Wall Street is not always the best or most unbiased source. (This cautionary note is generally true for all investment styles, however it is particularly valuable with this strategy.)

There are growth managers that specialize in each capitalization level and there are times when one style, say large cap, will outperform another, say small cap. When there is a high level of general market confidence, higher quality, better capitalized companies, such as the large cap growth stocks, will do exceptionally well. During these times, growth stocks with smaller capitalizations are often overlooked, even though they may offer the same or even better growth potential. This tendency contributes to the cycles within market capitalizations. In this example, as large cap stocks become over-loved and very overvalued, small caps companies may lag in performance. At some point, when valuation concerns arise in large caps, there will be a shift away from the overvalued stocks that now have little potential for continued appreciation, to areas of the market that represent greater potential for capital appreciation. Continuing this example, smaller capitalized companies will now become a more attractive growth alternative. These are normal market cycles that usually occur over 3- to 5-year periods.

Emerging Growth

Some people confuse growth managers with emerging growth managers. "Emerging means it is a smaller company that is emerging in size, hence the smaller capitalization, whereas growth stocks are companies which have earnings that are generally above the average for the market," says Jim Awad of Awad Asset Management. As the name suggests, these managers tend to buy stocks that have a high degree of price volatility, but also those whose growth rates are likely to be both rapid and independent of the overall stock market. Screening for emerging companies is an example of a bottom-up management style, meaning that the primary motivation for buying a particular stock is inherently found in the stock itself. Skilled managers who specialize in this style are the "stock pickers" of the profession. Some search for these companies by spending time with management and studying financials to identify a company's potential, while others buy based on price momentum. Some do both.

Quality Growth, the Classic Blue Chip Portfolio

The primary purpose of this strategy is to match or slightly exceed the performance of the S&P 500, while minimizing volatility and risk. These portfolios are made up of high quality growth companies within the S&P 500, with consistent and predictable earnings growth and dividend payments. By eliminating the smaller companies in the index, managers hope to reduce volatility for risk-averse investors who understand the advantages of equities, but have a need for consistency and/or dividend income. These managers generally screen companies for their 3- and 5-year earnings per share (EPS) growth, as well as their dividend yield, which is the current dividend per share divided by its current price per share.

Income Growth and Dividend Growth

Income and dividend growth managers are seeking securities that will produce a current yield significantly higher than that of the S&P 500. Dividend stability and the rate of growth of the dividend are of concern to the income buyer. These portfolios may own more utilities, less high-tech, and may also own convertible preferred stocks and convertible bonds, all of which pay dividends and/or interest. The income requirement is met by the dividends and/or interest paid by these securities, while the underlying equity provides the growth potential. Over time, equity growth will increase the value of the portfolio, which is an important offset to the erosive effects of inflation on yields.

Aggressive Growth

An aggressive growth manager seeks securities that have the potential to produce high capital gains, such as emerging companies, momentum plays or hot sector bets. An aggressive growth manager might buy initial public offerings (IPOs) of stock from small companies and then resell that stock very quickly in order to generate large profits. Some aggressive growth portfolios may invest in derivatives, such as options, in order to increase their gains. These portfolios are generally not appropriate for risk-averse or tax-sensitive investors. Aggressive growth managers are most suitable for investors willing to accept a high risk-return trade-off, since many of the companies that demonstrate high growth potential can also experience significant share price volatility. Aggressive growth portfolios tend to have a very high correlation to the equity markets, and therefore they often produce very good returns during economic upswings and very poor returns during economic downturns.

Core

This strategy incorporates both growth and value disciplines. Managers within this style may invest passively, with portfolios that resemble the sector weightings of their respective index, "closet indexers," while others are active managers, such as those that seek companies that are in an "out-of-favor" cycle. A core manager is able to more broadly diversify within a single portfolio, achieving a greater dispersal of risk. This style may be a wise choice for smaller investors with limited funds or useful to the institutional investor who may be slow to make portfolio adjustments due to the nature of their generally committee-driven processes. As with all-cap managers, skilled core managers can benefit from the flexibility in this investment discipline.

Sector Rotators

The main emphasis of a sector-rotating manager is to find industry sectors or specific economic sectors that they believe will outperform the market as a whole. They begin with top-down analysis, which requires them to make projections and forecasts on general economic conditions. This investment style differs from the bottom-up approach, where the greatest interest is in the company itself. This "macro" approach will then lead the manager to either over- or underweight certain sectors that are consistent with their economic assessments. Their portfolios contain individual stocks believed to be the strongest within the sector.

Some companies are cyclical by their nature and follow specific business cycles. A Sector Rotator is a manager who identifies specific sectors that are poised to move, either because they are undervalued or because the manager believes the sector will participate in a trend the market will strongly support. For example, if the manager believes that oil stocks may do well, they will become heavily invested in this sector. When they observe a trend shift, they may rotate out of the oil sector positions and move into technology, aerospace, medical, or any other sector that the manager identifies as the next emerging trend. Many of these managers are now using Exchange Traded Funds (ETFs) that represent the various indexes and sectors of the domestic and international markets.

Balanced or Mixed

Some managers specialize in balanced portfolios, which are comprised of a mixture of equity, usually large cap and fixed income securities, thus creating a more balanced risk/return environment. The mixture of equity and fixed income in a balanced portfolio is designed to achieve the investor's investment objective and the percentage of the portfolio that is allocated to each asset class may fluctuate as market conditions or investor needs dictate. Many "boutique" investment managers are balanced managers, as their flexibility allows the manager to tailor the securities in a portfolio to the specific investor's cash flow needs and objectives.

Balanced portfolios emphasize both income generation and capital appreciation. Interest payments from bonds and equity dividends generate most of the income, while the potential for capital appreciation is sought mainly through the equity holdings. Balanced portfolios have historically earned higher returns than pure fixed income investments.

Investors who are good candidates for balanced portfolio managers are relatively conservative, but are also willing to assume a moderate level of risk to seek moderately higher returns or; they are seeking growth, but require a certain amount of cash flow from the portfolio.

Convertible Securities

Convertible securities are a specific type of corporate security that pays interest like a conventional bond, but can also be converted to the issuer's common stock. These include both convertible bonds and convertible preferred stocks. Convertible securities have a place in portfolios when the investor is looking for the capital appreciation of a stock and the downside protection and income of a bond.

Convertible securities can be considered an equity/bond hybrid and they are issued by companies of all sizes. The conversion feature allows the company to issue debt securities that pay a lower interest rate than a standard corporate bond, thus making them attractive to the company. If the company does well and the stock price increases, these securities can convert to stock, thus removing the debt from the company's balance sheet. The participation in the equity upside is the investor's reward for accepting the lower coupon rate.

Convertible bonds, represented by the Merrill Lynch All Convertibles Index, have experienced about 86% of the upside of the S&P 500 and only about 61% of the downside between 1990 and 2003, both due to the stability of the fixed income component[1]. The bond component lessens the potential upside, while buffering the downside. The downside protection of a convertible securities portfolio is exactly what makes it attractive. Convertible bonds are particularly interesting to those who want small cap exposure, but are uneasy

---

1. Zephr Associates, Inc.

about small cap volatility. It is an effective way to take highly volatile stocks and reduce their volatility with the fixed income component. When the underlying stock is out of favor, the performance of convertible bonds is largely due to their return from the bond, instead of stock appreciation. When the stocks are in favor, the opposite is true.

Preferred stocks are generally purchased for the income without regard to other considerations. Preferred shareholders are senior to common shareholders. They receive dividends before those paid to common shareholders, they have a higher position in the event of a bankruptcy, but they do not have voting rights or a maturity date. Preferred stocks are most often offered by companies as a debt instrument (trust preferreds). There are two types of preferred stocks, true preferreds and trust preferreds. Approximately 84% of the preferred market is "trust preferreds" and these are structured around corporate bonds. Their dividends are treated as interest and are therefore taxed at ordinary income tax rates. As interest rates go up, trust preferreds will decrease in value because they are tied to the bond. A "true preferred" is tied to the underlying company's ability to pay the dividend and they react very little to rising interest rates. Some preferreds qualify for the new lower tax rate applied to dividends under the Jobs and Growth Tax Relief Reconciliation Act of 2004, so it is advisable to consult a tax professional when taxation is part of the decision-making process.

Convertible preferred stocks can convert to common shares at a ratio of exchange that is determined at issuance. These securities offer the investor the opportunity to participate in the price gains of the common shares, however convertible preferreds are usually callable, which allows the issuing company some control over the timing of conversion.

Global, International and Emerging Markets

Global portfolios consist of both domestic (U.S.) stocks and international stocks in any proportion that the manager deems appropriate. They can be managed as growth or value portfolios of any market capitalization. International portfolios consist of international stocks, with no U.S. exposure. These portfolios can be specific to a country or region, e.g. Japan or Asia-Pacific, or they can exclude a country, e.g. Pacific ex-Japan. International portfolios are more likely to contain multiple capitalization companies than global portfolios and are often not designated as growth or value.

Emerging markets are generally countries that are working to improve their economies to become more competitive in global markets. They have comparatively immature financial markets that are transitioning into more sophisticated systems. They are often the recipients of financial support from organizations such as the International Monetary Fund (IMF) and the World Bank and they often enjoy special trading status with more developed countries. Investment in emerging markets has the potential for high returns, however these investments also involve more volatility and risk, as these countries are in transition and may be subject to political or economic upheaval.

Fixed Income

Fixed income portfolios are frequently comprised of high quality, fixed income securities, such as U.S. government issues and/or investment grade corporate bonds, but they can include a variety of fixed income securities representing different risk/return expectations. Investors who limit themselves to fixed income portfolios are generally long-term, very risk-averse investors, who are mainly interested in capital preservation, consistency of earnings, and regular cash flow. Managers in this asset class have historically demonstrated lower variability of returns when compared to equity managers and pure fixed income portfolios have typically produced lower returns relative to equity or balanced portfolios. There are however, times when fixed income securities outperform stocks, such as in 2002. In the right environment, international and high yield bonds have generated substantial returns, but these bonds may not be appropriate for a risk-averse investor.

Fixed income securities come in many forms and are purchased for a variety of reasons. They may be purchased as an investment, anticipating growth of principal and capital gain, or they may be purchased for safety and/or income. Many investors purchase only municipal bonds specifically for tax-free income. A fixed income manager screens bonds according to call risk, credit quality, maturities, duration and coupon rates among other things. Maturities range from short-term, under one year, to long-term, over ten years and, there are bonds with 30 to 50-year maturities as well. Bonds that have different positions on the yield curve (maturity), may generate significant performance differences during different market cycles. Many do not realize the complexity of bonds and bond portfolios, and it is the consultant who can direct the investor to the most appropriate fixed income manager. Our discussion here will highlight the more common types of bonds that may be included in a fixed income portfolio.

Government Bonds and TIPS

Treasury bills, notes and bonds differ in their length of maturities, but all are direct obligations of the United States government and are considered the safest type of security. Treasury bills have maturities of one year or less, Treasury notes have maturities of two to ten years and Treasury bonds have maturities of more than ten years. Remembering that risk and return are generally related, Treasuries are generally issued with interest rates that are lower than other types of bonds.

Agency bonds, such as Ginnie Mae and SBA (Small Business Administration) are backed by the full faith and credit of the U.S. Government and interest is paid monthly. They differ from Treasuries in that they are not a direct obligation of the U.S. government and thus generally pay a slightly higher interest rate due to the slightly greater risk.

TIPS are U.S. Treasury Inflation Protected Securities, whose principal value is tied to the consumer price index (CPI). The principal value is adjusted semiannually to reflect any changes in the CPI. The fixed rate coupon is calculated on principal value, therefore, as the principal value of the bond changes, so too will the interest payments. At maturity, TIPS return the initial principal, adjusted for inflation.

Municipal Bonds

States, territories, possessions of the U.S. and public agencies all issue municipal bonds. The interest paid is federally tax-free and, if they are issued by an entity within the investor's state of residency, they are generally state tax-free. These issues have varying degrees of risk. General obligation bonds are backed by the full faith, credit and taxing authority of the issuer and are considered the safest type of municipal bond. Other types, such as revenue bonds, rely on the revenue generated by the financed project. These are less safe because if there is not enough revenue generated to meet the financial obligations of the project, the issue may default. Many of these are insured before they are issued. The insurer is then responsible for paying the interest and principal if the issuer fails to meet its obligations, which reduces the potential risk of these bonds.

Insurance is not fail proof though and a bond manager will assess the credit worthiness of each issuance.

Corporate Bonds

Corporate bonds can be backed by the assets of the issuing corporation, in which case they are considered "secured" or, they can be backed by the good faith of the issuing corporation and are then called "debentured." The credit quality of corporate issues can vary widely and should be evaluated thoroughly. Companies that may be perceived as having higher risk, such as more immature companies, issue high yield bonds that are below investment grade. These bonds are generally referred to as junk bonds. As their name would indicate, they pay a high yield and are considered the most risky of bonds. A commonly issued corporate bond is the zero-coupon bond. These are purchased at a significant discount, do not make interest payments and when they mature, they pay par value with no capital gain. The difference between the discounted price and par value is the accrued interest. Standard & Poor's, Moody's and Fitch Investors Service rate bonds for their credit worthiness. Investment grade bonds are included in the Lehman U.S. Credit Index and bonds rated below investment grade are included in the Lehman Brothers U.S. Corporate High Yield Index.

Mortgage-Backed Bonds

Mortgage-backed bonds are secured by a mortgage on property and in the event of a default, secured bondholders are paid before unsecured bondholders. They are backed by real estate or equipment that can be liquidated to meet the obligations of the bond and thus are usually considered high-grade bonds. Mortgage-backed bonds are generally backed by pools of mortgages, which add complexity to their structure, pay-outs and risks by introducing different rates of prepayments, refinancing and default risks.

International Fixed Income

Just as with U.S. fixed income instruments, international bonds rely on the creditworthiness of either the issuing country or the foreign company. Additional risks must be considered when purchasing these bonds, such as currency fluctuations or political stability. Foreign countries also have different accounting and reporting regulations that must be understood in order to properly evaluate the value of the security.

The yield curve steepens when yields of securities at the short end, e.g. 2-year notes, go down and/or those at the long end, e.g. 30-year bonds, rise. The yield curve begins to flatten as yields at short end rise and/or yields at long end decrease. A steepening yield curve can create opportunities in high yield bonds and cyclical sectors such as technology and finance, while a flattening yield curve can portend slower economic growth. Historically, small caps tend to underperform when the yield curve is flattening and a negative yield curve has preceded recessions, such as the one that we saw in 2000. Both stock and bond managers study the direction of interest rates and their effects on the yield curve.

The consultant will determine the needs of the investor and will recommend a fixed income manager with a focus that will best fulfill the investor's needs. The manager will either buy the bonds for income, wherein the portfolio will be laddered with different maturities in an attempt to minimize reinvestment risk or, the manager will populate the portfolio with securities that have the potential to produce both income and appreciation. The active management of a fixed income portfolio can take advantage of changes in interest rates and the yield curve in the mix of maturities and types of bonds. The value of a bond is inversely related to the movement of interest rates, but not all bonds respond to the same degree. Managers who specialize in fixed securities use these relationships to the investor's advantage.

Cash Reserve Management

Another investment strategy that is often used for cash reserves is the use of short duration, variable rate securities to provide both yield and principal re-payment features. Variable rate securities generally have a higher yield than similar duration fixed rate securities and automatically move when interest rates change. This feature allows them to outperform in a rising interest rate environment and makes them less vulnerable to interest rate volatility. Cash flow is provided due to monthly principal and interest payments, which can be used for cash needs or reinvested into the portfolio at then current rates.

Cash Management

Those who need to maintain a certain level of cash, yet wish to optimize their returns on this cash, will use various short-term, cash management strategies. Liquidity and principal preservation are the primary objectives in cash

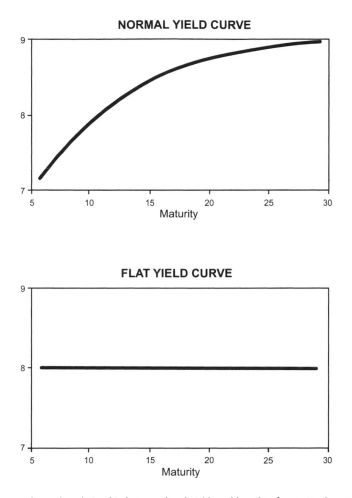

The yield curve shows the relationship between bond yields and lengths of maturity. A normal curve shows interest rates rising as maturities lengthen, whereas a flattening yield curve narrows the yield differential between short and long maturities.

management. Many use money market funds to achieve this goal, because even though these accounts have short-term (one-day) liquidity, they typically pay interest rates that are similar to 90 day to 180 day CDs, rather than passbook or one-week CD rates. These are considered cash equivalents as they are readily converted into cash. Money market funds are mutual funds that buy and sell short-term corporate paper and charge internal expenses to the fund, just as other types of mutual funds. During times when interest rates are very low, such as in 2003, this strategy may be ineffective, because the money market funds must still pay internal expenses, resulting in very low rates being paid to the investor.

Specialty Styles

There are many other types of investments that may be appropriate for certain portfolios. Some individuals require that at least some portion of their asset be invested in a socially responsible manner, and for these investors, diversification, risk or performance are not the driving forces for their choices. Other investors may be seeking high income potential, while others may want to diversify their portfolios into areas that have a low or negative correlation to stocks and bonds. Once again, investor objectives shape the portfolio design.

Socially Responsible Investing

Socially responsible investments (SRIs) are limited to companies that meet certain ethical and moral standards, which include those that are sensitive to social issues such as the environment, human rights and corporate ethics or, those that are not involved in tobacco, alcohol or gambling. The investment criteria may vary with the manager, however the primary focus is on the types of companies in the portfolio, not returns.

REITs

REITs are real estate investment trusts that use pooled capital from many investors to purchase and manage income property or finance mortgage loans. They trade like stocks and are therefore very liquid and, the investor need not be a qualified investor. These characteristics differentiate REITs from private placement real estate offerings. REITs generally have a steady cash flow that is paid to investors in the form of dividends and they are granted special tax considerations. REITs offer several benefits over actually owning properties. First, is their liquidity, unlike traditional real estate. Second, REITs enable participation in non-residential properties, such as hotels, malls, and other commercial or industrial properties. Third, there is no minimum investment for REITs. REITs do not necessarily increase and decrease in value along with the broader market (low correlation) and, they pay yields in the form of dividends, no matter how the shares perform.

Hedge Funds

Hedge funds are usually used by wealthy individuals or institutions that are looking for aggressive, high risk/reward strategies, including selling short, leverage, program trading, swaps, arbitrage, and derivatives. Hedge funds have a low correlation with the stock and bond markets and are therefore used to further diversify a portfolio and potentially reduce its overall risk. Hedge funds are exempt from many of the rules and regulations governing other investments, which allows them to utilize aggressive investing strategies. They are restricted by law to no more than 100 qualified investors per fund and as a result, most hedge funds set high investment minimums, ranging anywhere from $250,000 to over $1 million. Investors in hedge funds pay a substantial management fee, and hedge funds also charge a performance fee, calculated as a percentage (often 20%) of the returns that exceed a particular target. These targets vary and should be thoroughly understood before investing.

Hedge funds are generally partnerships with liquidity constraints and should only be purchased by sophisticated investors who have no liquidity concerns. Many hedge funds voluntarily register with the Securities and Exchange Commission, under the Investment Advisors Act of 1940, however it is currently not required. In 1990, it was estimated that there were 600 hedge funds, controlling $38 billion in assets; by 2005, the estimates had rapidly grown to 8000 hedge funds, controlling $1 trillion in assets. In response to this explosion of hedge funds, the SEC attempted to require investment advisors of hedge funds with $25 million or more in assets, to register under the Investment Advisors Act of 1940 Act by February of 2006, however this ruling was later overturned.

As with most popular investment products, the financial industry has found a way to bring both hedge funds and managed futures to a broader range of individuals through the introduction of "funds of funds." Multiple managers, usually those who employ different investment strategies, are packaged together in an offering that has low minimums, often under $5,000. The manager of these managers charges an additional layer of fees, which, along with investor suitability and a thorough due diligence of each of the individual managers, should be considered when evaluating this type of investment option.

Managed Futures

A managed futures portfolio trades in futures and forward contracts. Futures and forward contracts may represent agricultural products, bonds, cattle, currencies, financial instruments, gold, hogs, oil, silver, stock indexes and so on. They are actual contracts for the future delivery or receipt for a particular commodity, between the seller and buyer of the contracts. The investor may trade these contracts individually, assuming all of the potential risk and reward for each contract, or invest collectively with other individuals in a managed account or fund, thus sharing the risk and reward potential of many different contracts among many investors. Managed futures have a negative correlation to stock and bond markets and are also used to further diversify a portfolio and potentially reduce its overall risk. Managed futures tend to perform best during volatile market conditions, but are subject to a significant amount of risk and have significant management fees, including a percentage (often 20%) of the appreciation of the portfolio (performance fee). These investments are only appropriate for astute investors who understand the risks and advantages of volatility and, do not have liquidity concerns. Managed futures are regulated by the Commodity Futures Trading Commission and in many cases, the Securities and Exchange Commission as well.

Managed futures and hedge funds are considered "Alternate Investments," as are private placement real estate offerings, private equity investments, venture capital, timberland partnerships and others. Institutions, such as major pension plans with specific funding requirements, are feeling the pinch from years of poor to lackluster investment returns, and are allocating an ever-increasing proportion of assets to alternative investments. As the demand for these investments increases, so too will the product offerings.

CONCLUSION

In this chapter, we have described many, but not all, of the investment styles in which managers specialize. The more the investor understands about a manager's role in the portfolio design, the less likely they are to make investment decisions based on performance alone. The end-result will be an integrated, flexible asset allocation plan that will accommodate changes in the marketplace and, a combination of managers that will compliment the investor's goals, objectives and tolerance to risk. Risk tolerance and investor objectives drive the investment decisions and the asset allocation of a well-structured portfolio, not simply an attempt to achieve the highest possible returns. This distinction is a critical difference between a randomly structured portfolio and one that incorporates the skills of an experienced consultant.

14

Manager Style Analysis

Understanding manager styles, how they relate to market cycles and knowing if a manager adds value to the overall objectives of a portfolio are all part of the asset allocation and manager selection process. In this chapter, we will discuss some of the manager evaluation tools used to qualify and differentiate managers and, we will describe what constitutes benchmarks, which are used in most comparative analyses. This process will highlight the value that a manager might add to the portfolio and in doing so, help to refine the manager selection process. This evaluation includes:

- Determining the manager's true style
- Benchmarks
- What comprises an index
- Value versus growth
- Risk and volatility
- Investment philosophy and strategy
- Performance cycles

DETERMINING THE MANAGER'S TRUE STYLE

As we discussed in the last chapter, there are many variations of growth and value. In addition, a manager's preferred market cap may also vary within a range, therefore it is necessary to determine a manager's true style. Illustration 14-1 displays the standard style boxes that have been used by the industry for decades and Illustration 14-2 shows how incomplete that information can be.

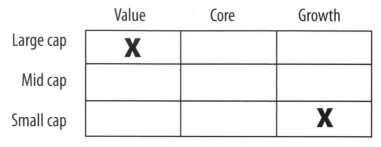

	Value	Core	Growth
Large cap	**X**		
Mid cap			
Small cap			**X**

Illustration 14-1

In the example of Illustration 14-1, we see that this portfolio is made up of Large Cap Value and Small Cap Growth, but it shows none of the fine detail that the consultant will examine prior to making manager choices.

Illustration 14-2 shows the broader range of domestic equity investment styles that are available. Utilizing this more refined assessment, a consultant can create a portfolio that is much closer to the investor's objectives and risk tolerance. Manager "A" and manager "B" would both be considered large cap value managers using the previous illustration, however their portfolios are not likely to produce the same returns or experience the same degree of volatility. The same is true of managers "C" and "D," who would both be considered small cap growth managers under the more generalized style designations used in Illustration 14-1. Managers and mutual funds will give their portfolio a name, e.g., large cap growth, but these too can be inaccurate and/or misleading, so it is up to the consultant to dig deeper.

	Deep Value	True Value	Relative Value	Core	GARP	True Growth	Aggressive Growth
Large cap	**A**						
Mid-large cap			**B**				
Mid cap							
Small-mid cap					**C**		
Small cap							**D**

Illustration 14-2

To determine a manager's style more accurately, a consultant will complete a style analysis study of each manager under consideration (Illustration 14-3). There are databases available to the financial services industry, such as Zephyr, Ibbotson and BARRA that facilitate these studies.

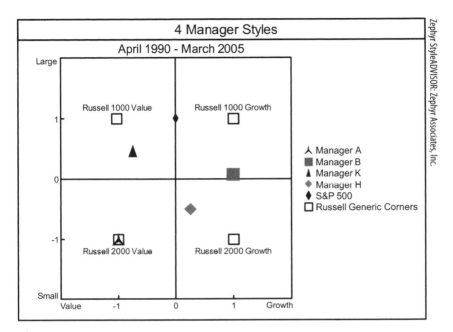

Illustration 14-3

This first step in style analysis would indicate that a consultant could begin to feel comfortable that these four managers represent styles that could be combined in a portfolio to produce a diversified style mix.

Once the style has been established, an appropriate benchmark can be selected, which then allows the consultant to properly evaluate a manager's relative performance. This selection is not an exact science, as benchmarks are rarely an exact match to a manager's style, nevertheless it is an important starting point.

UNDERSTANDING BENCHMARKS

The benchmark (index) that is used as the comparison for a manager's performance should be the one that most closely represents the makeup of the manager's portfolio and investment philosophy: Which asset class; is the manager a growth manager or value manager; aggressive or conservative; what market capitalization best describes the companies that the manager buys? It should not be the goal of an active manager to passively replicate an index, so the manager's style analysis is incorporated into the benchmark analysis. If a manager is a "closet indexer," the investor should question the value of hiring an index manager at active management prices.

The CFA Institute (formally AIMR) suggests that in order for a benchmark to be a valid tool in evaluating a manager's performance, it must be:

- Unambiguous
- Investable
- Measurable
- Appropriate
- Reflective of current investment opinions
- Specified in advance

William Sharpe, the 1990 Nobel Prize winning economist who developed the Sharpe Ratio, is credited with developing "style analysis." His work led to the concept of custom benchmarks, which combines different weightings of market indices in a like fashion to the weightings in a manager's portfolio. If a mid cap value manager has 72% mid cap value in his or her portfolio, but also has 18% small cap value and 10% large cap value, then an equivalent mix of indexes will result in a more accurate benchmark. A "style benchmark" is more reflective of the CFA Institute's suggested characteristics than a single index for most manager comparisons, however it is not readily available and therefore its use is limited. R-squared, described in Chapter 17, is one of the measurement tools used to determine how closely the manager's style matches that of the benchmark. If it is a good match, then the consultant can assume that any outperformance is a result of the manager's active management skill, not simply being in the right place (style) at the right time. The true determination of a manager's skill includes not only performance, but also risk management. This analysis is discussed in more detail in Section IV.

The value-added by active management is achieved when a seasoned manager uses his or her experience and knowledge to capitalize on opportunities, while avoiding overvalued, high-risk stocks or sectors of the markets. In the late 1990s, when large capitalization stocks were doing exceptionally well, the top 100 stocks of the S&P 500 represented approximately 80% of the index's total market capitalization. Eventually, as the tech bubble inflated, as few as 10 stocks were driving the entire S&P 500 index. Comparing active manager performance to the S&P 500 at this point was inappropriate. Very few managers were willing to take the kind of risk that these tech stocks represented and therefore, these stocks were not in most managers' portfolios. This form of risk management resulted in temporary manager underperformance. The S&P 500, carried by the large cap tech stocks, exploded to the upside, significantly outperforming many managers, but when the tech portion of the S&P 500 crashed, it dragged the entire index down with it. These events are described in more detail in Chapter 11. Meanwhile, as the S&P 500 was heading down, mainly due to the largest (by market capitalization) 100 companies, the smaller 400 companies, which represented a very small percentage of total market capitalization and exerted little to no influence on the index's returns, were actually showing significant gains (Illustration 12-3). Style analyses (and sector divergence, Illustration 10-6) would have revealed these anomalies and made comparisons more valid.

To fully understand a manager's performance, the advisor or consultant must select the appropriate comparative index and understand what is driving both the index and the manager's returns. When making a manager selection, or when considering the decision to overweight, underweight or terminate a manager, it is important to understand the relationship between a manager's investment style and philosophy and, the character of the then current market conditions. Absolute numerical comparisons do not always tell the whole story.

What Comprises a Market Index?

There are many indexes representing countries, regions, bonds, sectors and industries, but we will confine our discussion to the two major U.S. equity indexes; the S&P and the Russell. Standard & Poor's is solely responsible for the companies that it selects for its various indexes. S&P starts with a universe of over 10,000 companies and screens for five major criteria: trading analysis, liquidity, ownership, fundamental analysis, market capitalization and sector representation. The S&P indexes that get the most attention include the S&P 100, S&P 500, S&P 400 and S&P 600, and each is further divided into S&P 500/Citigroup Growth and S&P 500/Citigroup Value, defined in the next section. The S&P 500 represents 500 leading companies in leading U.S. industries. There are no market capitalization restrictions, but these are usually companies with capitalizations of $4 billion or more. The S&P 400 represents the 400 smaller capitalized companies of the S&P 500, leaving the largest 100 companies in the S&P 100. The S&P 600 represents 600 companies with market capitalizations generally between $300 million and $1 billion that meet the other S&P selection criteria.

The Russell includes the Russell 3000, Russell Mid-Cap, Russell 2000 and Russell 1000, which are each further divided into Growth and Value, also defined in the next section. The Russell 3000 represents approximately 98% of the investable U.S. Equity market and is the combination of the Russell 1000 and Russell 2000. The Russell 1000 consists of the largest 1,000 U.S. stocks ranked by market capitalization. The Russell Mid-Cap represents the 800 smallest companies within the Russell 1000 index. The Russell 2000 is comprised of the smallest 2000 companies in the Russell 3000.

Russell and S&P use different methodologies to construct their indices, including the number of companies represented, sector weightings, rebalancing strategies, how they determine value and growth and, how they determine market cap. These differences can result in significantly different returns. The S&P 600 and the Russell 2000 are the benchmarks most commonly used to evaluate small cap managers. The comparison of returns in Illustration 14-4 makes it clear that choosing the most appropriate index, the one that is most like the manager's portfolio, is critical in making relevant benchmark comparisons. Many believe that the S&P 600 and the Russell 2000 are interchangeable, which is clearly not the case.

YEAR	S&P 600 TOTAL RETURN	RUSSELL 2000 TOTAL RETURN
1997	25.58	22.58
1998	-1.31	-2.55
1999	12.40	21.26
2000	11.80	-3.02
2001	6.54	2.49
2002	-14.35	-20.48
2003	38.79	47.25
2004	22.65	18.33

Illustration 14-4

Market Capitalization

Russell and S&P separate stocks by market capitalization and their indices are cap-weighted, meaning that the larger companies have the greatest affect on the performance of the index.

Market capitalization = number of outstanding shares x share price

With this affect in mind, it is important to know how the index treats outstanding shares that are not available to the markets; is the index float-adjusted? Microsoft is included in several indices, yet a significant number of Microsoft's shares are closely held or illiquid, as they are held by Bill Gates, directors, employees, etc. In the past, Russell did not count these shares when determining market cap (float adjusted), whereas S&P did. The consultant would need to ask, "Is the large cap manager that I am evaluating more like the S&P 500 or the Russell 1000?" knowing that there were substantive differences in how returns were measured. S&P went to a float-adjusted methodology in September of 2005 and now all major U.S. indices are consistent in how they calculate market cap, however this methodology is not used globally. It should also be noted that the historical data has not been changed to reflect this change in methodology.

How Indexes Define Growth and Value Stocks

Three main index providers differentiate between growth stocks and value stocks using different criteria. Many allocation decisions are based on this information alone and, as we will see, this analysis is somewhat limited. It is therefore valuable to understand what makes up an index and how to look deeper.

- S&P/BARRA
- S&P/Citigroup
- Russell/Mellon[1]
- Dow Jones

1. Russell and Mellon Financial Corporation have formed a joint venture that services the Russell indexes.

S&P/BARRA is a collaboration between Standard & Poor's and BAR-RA. This index defines stocks as either growth or value, based solely on the price to book value of the company. Stocks in the S&P indices are ranked according to price-to-book value only and then the list is divided into two equal parts. Those stocks in the half with higher price-to-book values are considered growth stocks and those in the lower half are considered value stocks. This approach obviously has its limitations, but it is a widely used indexing method to differentiate between value and growth stocks within the S&P.

Effective December 16, 2005, S&P/BARRA changed to S&P/Citigroup. The S&P/Citigroup methodology categorizes approximately one-third of the stocks as pure growth, one-third as pure value and the remaining one-third is split between value and growth. S&P/BARRA uses the single criteria, price-to-book, to differentiate value and growth, whereas S&P/Citigroup uses several. This methodology is an improvement over the limited criteria used under the S&P/BARRA methodology, however historical S&P/BARRA performance data will not change. S&P/Citigroup indexes are reconstituted once a year on the 3rd Friday of December.

S&P/CITIGROUP GROWTH VERSUS VALUE METHODOLOGY

Growth Criteria	Value Criteria
	Price/book
5-year earnings per share growth rate	Price/cash flow
5-year sales per share growth rate	Price/sales
5-year internal growth rate	Dividend yield

Russell ranks stocks using two factors: price to book value and the consensus forecast estimating long-term earnings growth. They then combine these two factors and create a grade for each stock. This ranking is not as limiting as S&P/BARRA, however it relies on growth estimates that may not be valid. Russell then utilizes this data to create a composite that classifies 70% of the stocks as "all-growth" or "all-value" and the remaining 30% are weighted proportionately in both the growth and value indexes. This approach results in some overlap between styles. Russell ranks stocks as value or growth within the Russell 1000, Russell Midcap, Russell 2000 and Russell 3000.

Dow Jones uses six factors to rank stocks: price to book value, the consensus forecast estimating long-term earnings growth, projected price to earnings ratio, trailing price to earnings ratio, trailing earnings growth and dividend yield. This methodology is likely to produce more accurate rankings than either S&P/BARRA or Russell, but data has only been collected in this manner and rankings provided since 2000 and thus, Dow Jones rankings are not yet widely used. Dow Jones ranks stocks as "strong growth," "weak growth," "neutral," "weak value" and "strong value." Those stocks that have a neutral ranking are not included in the style indexes. Due to the change in methodology between S&P/BARRA and S&P/Citigroup, and the wide acceptance of S&P/BARRA, S&P/Citigroup is liable to remain the dominant ranking.

These are an example of the indices used for equities. There are many others, including various types and maturities of bonds, foreign securities and specialty securities, such as REITs and managed futures. Understanding and selecting the correct index for comparison is essential to a meaningful manager and portfolio evaluation.

RISK AND VOLATILITY

In addition to performance comparisons, a consultant must also be aware of the level of risk that the manager is taking in order to achieve their performance. Risk assessment is something many investors tend to overlook, however this analysis is essential to the long-term success of a portfolio, A knowledgeable consultant will focus on the advantages of selecting managers that experience lower volatility in producing returns, as the negative affects of volatility can be long lasting. Standard deviation is the numerical reflection of volatility.

It might appear that a 10% investment gain in one period, followed by a 10% loss the next period would leave you no worse off than when you started, but the math does not work out that way. If we start with an original investment of $100,000, which gains 10%, it would now be worth $110,000. If the $110,000 now experiences a 10% loss, the value of the investment is now worth $99,000, or a 1% loss. The greater the volatility a portfolio experiences, the more significant its effects can be, e.g. a 50% loss on the $100,000 investment, followed by a 50% gain, would reduce the investment to $75,000, which is a 25% loss on the original $100,000. It requires a 100% gain to get back to even following a 50% loss and, volatility diminishes the effects of long-term compounding. Remember this math when you hear, "It's up one day and down the next; I'm not losing anything."

Guide to Losses and Gains

Losses	Gains required to break even
-10%	+11%
-30%	+43%
-40%	+67%
-50%	+100%
-60%	+150%
-70%	+233%
-80%	+400%
-90%	+900%

Significant swings in returns reflect a high volatility that can seriously affect portfolio results over time, as it counteracts the advantages of compounding. Conscientious investment professionals will continuously advise their clients about the relationship between risk and return and will guard against significant volatility and the potential for large losses. A loss in just one year can affect investment results for years to come, so it is well worth reviewing volatility as closely as returns.

Consider two hypothetical $1,000,000 portfolios, each invested over the eight-year period when markets were quite volatile. Portfolio A was structured to participate in market momentum, while Portfolio B was structured to limit volatility and risk. As we can see, there is a notable relationship between returns

	PORTFOLIO A		S&P 500	PORTFOLIO B	
1996	+34%	$1,340,000	+22.96%	+26%	$1,260,000
1997	+27%	$1,701,800	+33.36%	+18%	$1,486,800
1998	+19%	$2,025,142	+28.58%	+14%	$1,694,952
1999	+31%	$2,652,936	+21.04%	+20%	$2,033,942
2000	-8%	$2,440,701	-9.11%	-1%	$2,013,602
2001	-25%	$1,830,525	-11.88%	-2%	$1,973,331
2002	-28%	$1,317,978	-22.1%	-10%	$1,775,998
2003	+20%	$1,581,736	+28.68%	+18%	$2,095,677
Standard Deviation	14.01		9.18		8.32

The same $1,000,000 invested in the S&P 500 would have had an ending value of $2,048,948. Neither portfolio was rebalanced, nor experienced any contributions or distributions.

Illustration 14-5

and volatility. In Illustration 14-5, we have included the S&P 500 as the comparative for relative returns and, compare the standard deviation (measure of risk) of all three.

Portfolio B had more muted returns during positive years, but better control of volatility. By controlling volatility, Portfolio B had better long-term results than either the S&P 500 or Portfolio A, and did so with a considerably lower standard deviation. This result is an example of adding alpha, producing a higher return while taking less risk (volatility) than the comparative benchmark. We will describe the numerical analysis of this concept in detail in Chapters 18 and 19.

INVESTMENT PHILOSOPHY AND STRATEGY

The various asset classes and styles in which manager's specialize were described in the last chapter. Since the ultimate goal is to select managers that are well suited to a specific investor profile and portfolio design, the consultant will refine the search by evaluating various manager characteristics, such as the manager's investment philosophy. Many managers passively replicate an index, while others seek to add value through active management. As consultants, we believe that managers who are successful at active management provide the investor with the most value, however many investors are uncomfortable with portfolios that differ from what they believe to be the norm. Some managers employ a sector neutral approach, where each of the benchmark's sectors is represented, but the manager makes no attempt to match the weightings.

When analyzing companies for their inclusion in a portfolio, managers may utilize either bottom-up or top-down analysis. Bottom-up analysis is an investment strategy where companies are considered based simply on their own merit, without regard to the sectors in which they are included or the current economic conditions. Managers utilizing this strategy take a fundamental approach, studying a company's management, history, business model, growth prospects and other company characteristics; he or she will not consider general industry and economic trends, as they believe that some companies are superior to their peer groups, and will therefore outperform regardless of industry and economic circumstances. Top-down analysis begins with an analysis of the overall economy, then narrows to sectors or industries and then finally to the companies that the manager expects to perform well. Many managers also use technical analysis when making investment decisions. This skill adds another dimension to their decision-making process and may provide an important element to the overall make-up of a portfolio.

Arguably, the most effective strategy is to blend all three. Begin with a top-down evaluation of macro economic, market, sector and industry trends to determine which areas of the markets offer greater risk or reward possibilities, then add a bottom-up analysis of the companies within those areas that will be considered for the portfolio. Technical analysis can then be used to confirm that the trend is favorable and/or improving and, valuations can indicate where the security is in its market cycle. In order to select the most appropriate manager for a given investor profile and portfolio design, the consultant must understand a manager's investment strategy and philosophy.

PERFORMANCE CYCLE

The consultant will have the ability to explain why a particular manager's performance is leading or lagging the market. It means very little to say that a manager had good or bad performance last year without knowing if his or her management style was in or out of favor. A manager may underperform the S&P 500, often the only measure that some advisors and investors use, but have outstanding performance compared to their relative benchmark; the index most appropriate for their style. Having this knowledge and experience is a key element in identifying trends and getting ahead of them. Do you want to put new money with the management style that is emerging as the next market leader or the one that is at the end of its cycle? Understanding this process goes far beyond merely identifying the managers who have shown exceptionally good performance in the past; it requires an understanding of the capital markets and their cycles in order to select a manager that may do well going forward.

Performance cycles are driven by valuations, among other things. As Illustration 14-6 shows, the worst performing style from one year may become the market leader the following year. This change of leadership is often caused by the investor's habit of chasing returns. As we described in Chapter 12, when a positive cycle matures, the positive performance numbers attract attention and thus more money, driving a style to become more and more over-loved and overvalued. Conversely, the lagging styles become very undervalued, thus

1991	1992	1993	1994	1995	1996	1997	1998	1999	2000	2001	2002	2003	2004	2005
Small Cap Growth 51.2%	Small Cap Value 29.1%	International 32.9%	International 8.1%	Large Cap Value 38.4%	Large Cap Growth 23.1%	Large Cap Value 35.2%	Large Cap Growth 38.7%	Mid Cap Growth 51.3%	Small Cap Value 22.8%	Small Cap Value 14.0%	Bonds 9.8%	Small Cap Growth 48.5%	Mid Cap Value 23.7%	International 14.0%
Mid Cap Value 47.0%	Mid Cap Value 21.7%	Small Cap Value 23.8%	Large Cap Growth 2.7%	S&P 500 37.6%	S&P 500 23.0%	Mid Cap Value 34.4%	S&P 500 28.6%	Small Cap Growth 43.1%	Mid Cap Value 19.2%	Bonds 9.0%	Mid Cap Value -9.7%	Small Cap Value 46.0%	Small Cap Value 22.3%	Mid Cap Value 12.7%
Small Cap Value 29.1%	Large Cap Value 13.8%	Large Cap Value 18.1%	S&P 500 1.3%	Large Cap Growth 37.2%	Large Cap Value 21.6%	S&P 500 33.4%	International 20.3%	Large Cap Growth 33.1%	Bonds 10.1%	Mid Cap Value 2.3%	Small Cap Value -11.4%	Mid Cap Growth 42.7%	International 20.7%	Mid Cap Growth 12.1%
Large Cap Growth 41.2%	Mid Cap Growth 8.7%	Mid Cap Value 15.6%	Small Cap Value -1.6%	Mid Cap Value 34.4%	Small Cap Value 21.4%	Small Cap Value 31.8%	Mid Cap Growth 17.9%	International 27.3%	Large Cap Value 7.0%	Large Cap Value -5.6%	Large Cap Value -15.5%	International 39.2%	Large Cap Value 16.5%	Large Cap Value 7.1%
Mid Cap Value 37.9%	Small Cap Growth 7.8%	Small Cap Growth 13.4%	Bonds -1.9%	Mid Cap Growth 34.0%	Mid Cap Value 20.3%	Large Cap Growth 30.5%	Large Cap Value 15.6%	S&P 500 21.0%	S&P 500 -9.1%	Small Cap Growth -9.2%	International -15.7%	Mid Cap Value 38.1%	Mid Cap Growth 15.5%	Large Cap Growth 5.3%
S&P 500 30.5%	S&P 500 7.6%	Mid Cap Growth 11.2%	Large Cap Value -2.0%	Small Cap Growth 31.0%	Mid Cap Growth 17.5%	Mid Cap Growth 22.5%	Bonds 8.4%	Large Cap Value 7.3%	Mid Cap Growth -11.8%	S&P 500 -11.9%	S&P 500 -22.1%	Large Cap Value 30.0%	Small Cap Growth 14.3%	S&P 500 4.9%
Large Cap Value 24.6%	Bonds 7.2%	S&P 500 10.1%	Mid Cap Value -2.1%	Small Cap Value 25.8%	Small Cap Growth 11.3%	Small Cap Growth 13.0%	Mid Cap Value 5.1%	Bonds 0.4%	International -14.0%	Mid Cap Growth -20.2%	Mid Cap Growth -27.4%	Large Cap Growth 29.8%	S&P 500 10.9%	Small Cap Value 4.7%
Bonds 14.6%	Large Cap Growth 5.0%	Bonds 8.8%	Mid Cap Growth -2.2%	Bonds 15.3%	International 6.3%	Bonds 7.9%	Small Cap Growth 1.2%	Mid Cap Value -0.1%	Large Cap Growth -22.4%	Large Cap Growth -20.4%	Large Cap Growth -27.9%	S&P 500 28.7%	Large Cap Growth 6.3%	Small Cap Growth 4.2%
International 12.5%	International -11.9%	Large Cap Growth 2.9%	Small Cap Growth -2.4%	International 11.6%	Bonds 4.1%	International 2.1%	Small Cap Value -6.5%	Small Cap Value -1.5%	Small Cap Growth -22.4%	International -21.2%	Small Cap Growth -30.3%	Bonds 4.3%	Bonds 4.2%	Bonds 1.6%

Data source: Zephyr Associates, Inc.

Illustration 14-6

There is no consistently "best" asset class and as Illustration 14-6 displays; one year's leader may be the next year's big loser. Strategic asset allocation and the basic tenants of diversification can help minimize this risk.

providing the better opportunity for appreciation. Valuation models are one of the tools used by consultants to anticipate periods of higher risk or greater opportunity.

CONCLUSION

It is clear there are many factors that influence a manager's performance, so it is important to understand the significance of each, as well as how the manager's investment philosophy contributes to the overall objectives of the portfolio. The most significant question that should be answered in the evaluation process is, "Does the manager add value?" As we have seen, the textbook definitions of benchmarks have considerable limitations and tell little about the securities that a manager may select for a portfolio. No benchmark will be a perfect match to an active manager's portfolio, nor should it be, so the consultant must draw from his or her knowledge of the manager to make the proper recommendations for a specific asset allocation. Looking beyond the standard comparisons will tell the consultant how the manager generates returns and therefore, how the manager's investment style will complement the portfolio design.

15

Selecting Money Managers: The Due Diligence Process

The process of selecting money managers includes identifying quality firms among the 10,000 plus firms registered with the SEC, analyzing the management firm from a qualitative and quantitative perspective and, determining their suitability for a given situation. This process is generally carried out by consultants on behalf of:

- Individuals or trustee/s, who will use a separately managed account platform through a brokerage firm to hire either independent money managers (dual contract) and/or sub-advisory managers (single contract)
- Individuals or trustee/s, who can meet the high account minimums ($1 to 5 million) imposed by money management firms that deal directly with their investors
- Brokerage firms that select managers (sub-advisors) for their separately managed account platforms

During this process, the consultant may find that a highly qualified manager (Manager A) is not acceptable in all situations. As an example, Manager A may be unable or unwilling to participate as a brokerage firm sub-advisor, but may be the right choice for a foundation or individual. To qualify as a brokerage firm sub-advisor, Manager A must have the administrative capacity to handle the unpredictable cash flows and the numbers of clients that participation with a brokerage firm is likely to produce and, they must be willing to accept reduced fees. These characteristics say nothing about the manager's skill, but are part of the selection criteria for sub-advisory managers. They will probably not play a role in the selection of Manager A if the investor is not considering a sub-advisory platform.

Corporations, foundations, retirement plans, trusts and individuals have different and specific investment concerns, which may include tax considerations, income needs, growth of capital and/or time restraints. These drive asset allocation decisions, which in turn begin the manager selection process. The most ideal investment strategy combines a knowledgeable consultant with whom the investor can build a comfortable working relationship, an appropriate asset allocation mix and, carefully selected professional money managers. This combination will provide the investor with the expertise necessary to navigate through the dynamic capital markets.

Selecting money managers was once a relatively simple process with limited options, but it is a very different environment now. Today, it is common to find quality management firms, controlling over half a billion dollars in assets, that were not even in existence just a decade ago. There are more money management firms; more brokerage firm-based, pre-packaged programs; more people calling themselves consultants; and the inevitable, more confusion. Clearly, choosing qualified, suitable managers has become a more challenging process, requiring a thoughtful, skilled screening process.

As the complexities of the investment environment expand, individuals and fiduciaries have discovered the advantages of the investment management consulting process. Fiduciaries, who may be confronted with personal liability for lapses in the trust funds under their control, are seeking a professional process to fulfill their obligations. Individuals recognize that investing for the long-term requires a well conceived, yet flexible plan to capitalize on varying market conditions. Growth in this industry has created great opportunity and along with it, the need for a qualified individual and/or process to sort through the information.

Before hiring a money management firm, the investor must know as much about the firm as possible, which includes the firm's management, investment philosophy, management structure, experience, investment process and performance in various market cycles. These criterions are often referred to as the Four "Ps": People, Philosophy, Process and Performance. A skilled consultant will be familiar with many firms and, if additional research is required, will conduct a wider screening through the RFP (request for proposal) process. All firms will be screened for their investor-specific suitability prior to making any recommendations to the investor. This process can be a lengthy procedure and generally, investors only want to interview the final cut; the most qualified, suitable firms recommended by the consultant. Individual investors may rely solely on the recommendations of the consultant, whereas plans and trusts may require an RFP prior to selecting any new managers in order to comply with their fiduciary responsibilities and guidelines.

The quest to find the most qualified and suitable money managers can begin with a questionnaire or RFP (request for proposal), but remember, the printed answers are subjective and a personal meeting and/or on-site evaluations are very valuable. There are a growing number of available manager databases, such as Mobius and PSN, that can assist in screening and compiling manager information but, it requires a skilled individual to properly evaluate the data. Many brokerage firms and seasoned consultants have gone through this on-site process and can offer this additional insight. As we have discussed in previous chapters, most brokerage firms that provide SMA platforms do a significant amount of due diligence prior to selecting money management firms as their sub-advisors, who are not only selected for their skill, but must also have the ability to meet the business needs of the sponsoring firm, such as education, sales, marketing and pricing. Advisors and consultants have varying degrees of personal knowledge about these management firms.

The manager qualifying process may vary, depending on who will be using the manager's expertise. An individual may have different requirements than a brokerage firm that is selecting firms to be sub-advisors (Chapter 4) or, than a retirement plan that will have a direct relationship with the manager. The following sample questions can be adapted to most situations and will be informative to all involved with the money management firm screening process. The questions do not have a "right" or "wrong," "good" or "bad" answer. They are designed to aid in determining the suitability of one manager for one investor, with a focus on experience, philosophy, process, execution, risk-management and risk-adjusted returns.

People
Philosophy
Process
Performance

Several of the questions on the following pages concern fee arrangements, such as soft or hard dollar arrangements, that a money management firm may have with brokerage firms and/or consultants, as this is an area of increasing concern, particularly to the institutional and/or public funds investor. Regardless of any relationships that may exist, managers must trade through a clearing firm. The clearing firm may be associated with the broker/dealer that is also the custodian of the assets or, it may be an unaffiliated firm. If the trades are part of any wrap or bundled-fee program, including the various SMA platforms that are available, the trades will go through the wrap firm's clearing firm at no additional charge. If the manager trades independently or "away," then trades can be routed through any number of clearing firms with whom the manager has a trading agreement (directed brokerage). Since away trades are commission-based, the allocation of these commission dollars should be investigated as part of the due diligence process.

1. **FIRM INFORMATION.** These questions are designed to obtain basic information about the firm, their investment philosophy, their portfolio managers and their people. Look for the qualifications and experience of key personnel. These are the individuals who control the portfolio and it is their level of experience, both in the industry and within a specific investment style, that is important. Separate the portfolio manager from the firm when gathering information, because the firm may have a long and successful track record, but the portfolio manager may not. Look for synergy and diverse skills among the key personnel. Ask questions that will allow the money management firm to distinguish itself from its competitors and those that are most important to the investor. Size need not be a limiting factor, as smaller "boutique" firms and emerging managers, who concentrate on managing money and not on marketing, may offer superior overall performance, but may not turn up on standard manager searches.

    a. Describe the firm's business structure and affiliations.

    b. Describe the firm's financial condition and capitalization.

    c. Is the firm or any of its officers, directors or investment professionals involved in any relevant litigation or enforcement actions?

    d. Describe the firm's investment style and philosophy.

    e. What year was the firm formed?

f. How many assets are under management? How many client accounts does this represent? It may be of interest to note that a firm may actually become too large to execute effectively within a given style. A value manager may find it difficult to find companies that meet their value criteria in a run-away growth market or, a small cap manager may be limited by liquidity.

g. How many years of experience do the principals have as portfolio manager/s? Please include biographies.

h. How many years has the portfolio manager of this style been in this position and is this person/s a principle in the firm? If so, what is the percentage of ownership? Is it greater than 75%, 50%, 25%?

i. In the event of the departure of the portfolio manager, what is the succession policy and will the succession have any effect on the style, discipline or philosophy of portfolio management? The investment philosophy should be well established and consistently practiced within the firm, minimizing the potential effects of the loss of a single individual.

j. Understand the history of the management team. If managers have come and gone, who were they, why did they leave and how much of the performance data was linked to their expertise? As with any organization, a management team must work well together if it is going to succeed. If there are difficulties among those making the decisions, then portfolio consistency might suffer. What are the team's strengths and weaknesses?

k. How many people are there available to provide administrative support?

l. Provide insurance policies that protect the interests of clients in the event of breach of fiduciary obligations and/or the firm's Code of Ethics.

2. **FIRM AFFILIATIONS.** Many money management firms are owned by, or have close relationships with, other financial institutions. If there are firm affiliations, it is important to uncover any areas where there may be potential conflicts of interest.

a. Are all trades done through an affiliated brokerage firm?

b. Does the manager purchase research through directed brokerage?

c. Will the money manager allow a non-affiliated brokerage firm to custodian assets?

3. **SUB-ADVISORS.** We describe the sub-advisory relationship in Chapter 4. If a manager under consideration is a sub-advisor (which is quite common), there are additional questions that should be asked.
   a. Will the investor have access to the portfolio manager? Generally, access is limited.
   b. Does the management firm "pay" to be included in a brokerage firm's sub-account database? This "payment" may take different forms:
      (1) The money management firm charges the brokerage firm a lower-than-normal fee. What is that fee and is the savings passed on to the investor? As a rule, brokerage firms do not voluntarily offer these reduced fees to clients.
      (2) In order for the money management firm to have exposure through the brokerage firm's sales force, they may be asked to contribute to various events that are sponsored by the brokerage firm.
      (3) Does the money management firm purchase research from the brokerage firm?

      (1) and (2) above are very common practices. (1) may work to the investor's advantage, but both affect the management firm's income and may limit the types of firms that choose to participate as sub-advisors.

4. **FIRM GROWTH RATE.** Growth rates can be a very telling piece of information, as growth of assets under management and account retentions will reveal a lot about the manager's philosophy and success.
   a. What are the total assets under management and how has this total changed over the last five years?
   b. How many new accounts have been acquired and lost during the past five years?
   c. If there has been substantial growth, how has staffing changed? If a firm is growing too fast, service and performance may suffer. The

faster growing manager must place additional time and attention on the administration of his or her business. If growth is not properly managed internally, it may be detriment to securities research and portfolio performance.

5. **PRIMARY STYLE.** Many firms are very large and have multiple styles. If so, it is important to understand the importance *this* (style being screened, e.g. small cap growth) style has within the firm and to have an understanding of how this *style* is managed. There must be a definable process, which supports *this* distinct investment style. This process and its execution must be consistent and disciplined.

   a. Is *this* style the firm's primary style? If not, what is?

   b. Describe *this* style: Include market cap, growth or value (intrinsic or relative)

   c. Describe the process and methodology used for security selection and monitoring.

   d. What are the major risks associated with *this* investment approach and what safeguards are in place to protect against them?

   e. How long has the firm managed *this* style?

   f. Who is responsible for the adherence to *this* management style?

   g. Discuss the systems that are in place to assure consistency within *this* style.

   h. Describe the process for adapting to changing market conditions.

   i. Describe the firm's risk-management methodology.

   j. What market environments are most and least conducive to *this* style?

   k. How many assets are currently under management within *this* style?

   l. What standard/s of investment quality does the firm have? Are there securities that are excluded from the process?

   m. How many positions are typically in a portfolio?

   n. What percentage of a company's outstanding shares will the firm purchase?

6. **OTHER STYLES.** Many believe that if a firm is large enough and has segmented staff to different disciplines, then that firm has the

potential to do a good job for all styles. Others believe that a firm that specialized in a specific style, regardless of their size, is the best choice.

a. How many other styles does the firm support?

b. If the firm supports multiple styles, what percentage of assets is managed within each style?

c. What percentage of staff is dedicated to each style?

d. How many people or what percentage of the firm supports each style?

7. **ACCOUNT OVERSIGHT.** How many people would be responsible for overseeing the management of this account? Are these people available for meetings, either by phone or in person?

8. **TRADING POLICIES.** Knowing the money management firm's trading policies will provide some insight into potential conflicts of interest or financial arrangements between the money management firm and a specific broker/dealer or advisor. These questions are more applicable to trading arrangements that are outside of wrap programs, as the "wrap" includes trades, but in all cases, the money manager should seek out the "best execution" on behalf of the client. If the manager is exchanging trades for services, "best execution" could be compromised.

a. What is the trading policy? Will the manager allow the investor to direct the brokerage? An investor may wish to direct trades in order to have an independent monitor the manager's trading activity.

b. Trades that are commission-based, generally range between $0.03 and $0.10 per share. Trades may be allocated to a specific brokerage firm:

• Under a soft dollar arrangement

• As an acknowledgement to a consultant for a large number of clients placed with that management firm. In this case, the brokerage firm will pass the commission on to the consultant as part of their payout.

c. If trades are directed to a specific trading desk under a wrap fee arrangement (which is common practice), how are issues involving "best execution" handled?

9. **PORTFOLIO RESEARCH.** Many money management firms do either most or all of their research internally. Relying on internal research helps the firm avoid being misled by analysts that may have other relationships, such as investment banking relationships, with the companies that they might recommend.

   a. Is the research derived from internal sources, external sources (please describe), or both?
   b. Does the firm buy research from other financial institutions or exchange trades at a specific firm for research? Investors should expect the brokerage commissions generated from the trades to provide additional value in the form of reduced costs.
   c. How many models are used to create the final portfolio selections?
   d. Describe your decision-making process.
   e. What percentage of buy or sell decisions are based on technical market analysis?
   f. Is the final analysis of the research and the final selection of the securities held within the portfolio committee driven or portfolio manager driven?
   g. Explain the sell discipline.

10. **PERFORMANCE.** Performance analysis, when done properly, will show the value that the manager can add to the performance and stability of a portfolio. If the management firm moves past the initial screening process and before deciding on the final candidates, the consultant will conduct a more thorough performance analysis as described in Chapter 18.

    a. What market benchmark/s are used for performance comparison?
    b. How do you measure risk?
    c. Are all reported numbers GIPS compliant?

    d. What is the upside capture ratio for the last ten (10) years, or since inception? Upside capture ratio compares the manager's percentage move to the upside to that of the appropriate benchmark.

    e. What is the downside capture ratio for the last ten (10) years, or since inception? Downside capture ratio compares the manager's percentage move to the downside to that of the appropriate benchmark.

    f. What was the performance for the last ten (10) years, or since inception? Look at each year and even each quarter.

    g. What were the risk-adjusted performance and the alpha for the last ten (10) years, or since inception?

    h. Describe the average trading activity (turnover rate) of the portfolio. A high turnover rate may have unwanted tax consequences and it may provide insight into the efficacy of the investment process.

    i. Illustrate the dispersion of returns between the model portfolio and individual portfolios.

11. **MINIMUM ACCOUNT SIZE.** What is the separate account minimum? Account minimums may be different for single contract accounts (sub-advisory), dual contract accounts (Chapter 2) or institutional accounts.

12. **REFERENCES.** Can the firm provide any part of a client list and/or references? Privacy laws have become quite strict on this issue and firms may only release specifics on those accounts that have given the management firm permission to do so.

13. **MEETINGS and COMMUNICATION.** For large individual or institutional accounts, many management firms are required to have direct contact with the client.

    a. Will the portfolio manager or senior marketing representative be able to attend meetings? How often, quarterly, annually?

    b. Is the manager ever available to meet with smaller clients?

    c. How do you monitor or measure client satisfaction?

    d. Do you provide internet-based information or reporting?

14. **FEES.** What is the fee structure and is it negotiable?

15. **ERISA.** If the manager search is being conducted for an account that falls under ERISA guidelines, there will be additional requirements.
    a. Is the firm a registered investment advisor as defined by 3(38) of the ERISA act of 1974?
    b. Is the firm bonded, as required by ERISA?
    c. Is the firm a Qualified Professional Asset Manager (QPAM), as defined in ERISA Prohibited Transaction Class Exemption 82-14? This section addresses real estate or private equity transactions and the involvement of third parties where prohibited transactions could occur.
    d. What type of professional liability insurance does the firm carry?
    e. Describe the firm's procedure for avoiding prohibited transactions.

A note to those who either issue or respond to RFPs: The SEC is taking a much greater interest in the validity of responses and it will be incumbent upon those firms that respond to these requests to ensure that the answers to questions are up to date and accurate. The SEC has levied fines for violations, such as misrepresentation of facts, misuse of soft dollars, and reporting false or misleading performance data. RFPs are most common in the institutional marketplace, where fiduciaries have a high duty to act in the best interest of those that they represent. They rely on accurate information in their decision-making processes and are likely to seek remedies when deficiencies arise.

REVIEW THE MANAGER'S ADV

Request a copy of the manager's Form ADV, Part I and Part II. Answers to many of the above questions should be included in these documents. No matter how impressive the manager's general marketing information might be, investors should keep in mind that this information is designed to serve the purposes of the manager, not the investor. Form ADV Part II should be readily available from the management firm, while Part I is quite long and not ordinarily sent to prospects and clients. Part I should be available upon request and it is on file at the Securities and Exchange Commission (SEC), the money manager's regulatory agency. In Appendix D, we have provided additional information on Form ADV, Part I and Part II.

PERFORMANCE ANALYSIS

Returns are often the first place that investors look to determine viable candidates, but do not be misled by performance numbers. They must be reviewed in the appropriate context to be valuable and by properly integrating all of the available information, the investor can develop a realistic picture of both manager performance and future expectations. Raw performance numbers often tell less about a manager than the investor assumes. Performance analysis is an important and detailed process that is covered in some detail in Chapter 18.

The Form 13F Filing

If the manager manages $100 million or more in equities, SEC regulations require the filing of a quarterly 13F. This filing states the equity positions and number of shares held by the manager. Because the manager submits his portfolio positions quarterly, some believe these reports accurately predict the manager's performance for the coming quarter. Some managers may argue that, because portfolio adjustments often occur between filings, the 13F is an inaccurate performance measure. Most managers have portfolio turnovers of about 25% a year or higher. Even at a 40% annual turnover rate, the average quarter has only a 10% change in portfolio positions, which is a relatively small amount. Using the 13F filing gives the investor another way of comparing the manager's performance.

SMA Managers Who Also Manage Mutual Funds

If a manager manages a mutual fund in addition to his or her individual accounts, then compare the performance of the manager's individual composites with that of the mutual fund. The two should be similar in performance since it is likely that they are managed simultaneously, making purchases and sales for both. Because regulations governing mutual funds are more strict and inflexible, investors may be safer using mutual fund performance rather than the manager's individual account composite, as results can vary if reporting time-periods for the SMA are shifted. If the SMA is relatively new and the management of the SMA and mutual fund are "similar in investment objective and/or strategy," managers may use results from the mutual funds to show a longer track record.

The Brokerage Network

Most full-service brokerage firms have the in-house capability of tracking the performance of managers. Upon opening a managed account, the brokerage firm begins to monitor the account's performance. Quarterly reports compare the manager's performance with those of other managers. The advisor assigned to the account often receives these reports. By tracking a large number of portfolios from a particular manager, it becomes possible to measure the performance and consistency among the manager's accounts. Consistency can give some insight into the internal operations of the manager's firm, as similar accounts should have similar performance. Some management firm's may be inconsistent in their trading activity, which might indicate an internal inefficiency.

GIPS Compliance

GIPS standards are meant to ensure consistent and ethical reporting of performance results. There are many criteria necessary to be GIPS compliant, which will be covered in some detail in Chapter 16. Inquire as to the firm's GIPS status, as compliance with these standards will create a higher degree of confidence in both the accuracy and consistency of the performance numbers. In fact, many, if not most consultants will not recommend managers who do not meet this reporting standard.

DISCRETION

Money management firms generally operate with a certain amount of discretion over investor's accounts. There are different types of discretion and the investor should be certain of what type of power that they are granting the money manager, the brokerage firm or the consultant as part of the management contract. It is generally advisable to enter into a discretionary agreement with a money management firm in order for them to execute trades efficiently within the account, as a non-discretionary manager would have to obtain authorization prior to any transaction.

A discretionary money manger can be given either limited or full power of attorney over an account. Limited power of attorney, also called limited trading authorization, enables the manager to buy and sell assets and reinvest the proceeds within the account without investor approval of specific transactions. A limited power of attorney restricts the ability of the manager to remove assets from the account, and it is the normal power granted to money managers.

A full power of attorney means that the money manager may also withdraw assets from the account. While the vast majority of money managers manage their client's accounts honestly, granting direct access to a client's assets creates an opportunity for the misuse. If a full power of attorney is granted, there should be bonding and insurance in place to cover this potential.

CONCLUSION

Regardless of the eventual purpose for the manager search, the consultant and/ or investor should know as much as possible about the management firm and its key personnel. Take the time to know the manager's investment philosophy, as this will ultimately result in selecting the manager who is most suitable for the investment objectives. Performance is not the most important selection criterion, as proper asset allocation and risk-adjusted returns are far more important to overall long-term results than an individual manager's performance. Search for the managers who will complement both the overall investment strategy and the investor's objectives. The managers that are selected will represent various components of the overall asset allocation and must be evaluated for their role in achieving the long-term goals of the investor.

16

Global Investment Performance Standards (GIPS)

I n 1990, AIMR, the Association for Investment Management and Research, was formed by a merger between the Financial Analysts Federation and the Institute of Chartered Financial Analysts. In 1993, AIMR implemented AIMR-PPS, the Association for Investment Management and Research Performance Presentation Standards, which provided the industry with ethical standards to be used primarily by money managers. These standards were developed to ensure that managers report performance results in a consistent, fully disclosed manner, so that consultants and investors can make relevant comparisons between the performance results of various money managers. In an effort to standardize guidelines for all countries, AIMR sponsored the Global Investment Performance Standards (GIPS) committee to develop one global standard for calculation and presentation of performance results. In 1999, AMIR formally endorsed GIPS, which became the only industry recognized standard on January 1, 2006. In May of 2004, AIMR's name was changed to the CFA Institute. The CFA Institute now requires that performance numbers be calculated and presented under the uniform guidelines of GIPS.

It is important to note that these are standards for calculation and presentation, not performance measurement; they are not audited or endorsed by the CFA Institute. In fact, the CFA Institute requires that a disclosure be attached to any literature that makes reference to GIPS compliance, which states that the CFA Institute was not involved with the preparation or verification of the performance report or that they have verified the firm's claim of compliance. Compliance with GIPS is voluntary, however any manager who wishes to be taken seriously, understands the importance of GIPS compliance. Those who are GIPS compliant will indicate so on their reporting materials, along with the above disclosure.

IMPROVING STANDARDS

The need for an industry reporting standard began in 1987, when a special committee of the Financial Analysts Federation delivered their report on uniform performance reporting standards. As we entered 2006, the CFA Institute adopted global standards, which reflect the industry's desire to continually raise the ethical and professional practices of the investment management industry worldwide through consistency, fair representation and full disclosure of investment results. The AIMR-PPS and now the GIPS guidelines have, and will, continue to evolve to keep pace with the needs of the industry and the investor.

In this chapter, we will provide a selection of recommended and mandatory GIPS guidelines, however for a complete set of the standards, go to the CFA Institute website at www.cfainstitute.org/centre/ips.

GIPS Standards

1. **Input Data**
   - Input data must be consistent and complete.
   - Portfolio valuations must be based on market values, not cost basis or book values.
   - Portfolios must be valued at least monthly.
   - Accrual accounting must be used for fixed income securities and all other assets that accrue interest income and must be used for dividends beginning 2005.
   - Trade date became mandatory in 2005.
   - Composites must have consistent beginning and ending annual valuation dates.

2. **Calculation Methodology**
   - Time-weighted rate of return, adjusted for cash flows, using a monthly valuation and geometric linking of period returns. Daily accounting for contributions and withdrawals became mandatory in 2005.

- Total return, including realized and unrealized gains plus income, must be used.
- Composites must be asset weighted using beginning-of-period weightings or another method that reflects both beginning market value and cash flows.
- Returns from cash and cash equivalents must be included in total-return calculations.
- Performance must be calculated after the deduction of trading costs.
- The are specific instructions for treatment of bundled fees.

3. **Composite Construction**
   - Inclusion of all actual, fee-paying, discretionary portfolios must be included in at least one composite. No models or simulated portfolios can be linked to actual performance.
   - Firm composites must be defined according to similar investment objectives and/or strategies and must not be switched.
   - New portfolios and terminated portfolios must be included in composites.
   - Convertible securities and other hybrids must be treated consistently across time and within composites.
   - Portfolios are not permitted to be switched from one composite to another unless there are documented changes in client guidelines.
   - Carve-out segments are not permitted to be used to represent a discretionary portfolio and as such, are not permitted to be included in composite returns.
   - Composites must include only assets under management and should not include portfolios that do not meet the firm's set minimum asset level for composite inclusion.

4. **Disclosures**
   - The availability of a complete list and description of all firm composites
   - Total firm assets for each period, and define the term "firm."
   - Disclose the currency used to express performance and any known inconsistencies in the exchange rates used among portfolios within a composite and, a composite and the benchmark.

- Any relevant details of the treatment of withholding tax on dividends, interest income and capital gains.
- The presence, use and extent of leverage or derivatives, including a description of the use, frequency and characteristics of the instruments sufficient to identify risks.
- Clearly label returns as net or gross of management fees, as well as other fees paid by client to firm or firm affiliates.
- Be very clear about which portfolios are included in the composites, such as any non-fee paying portfolios included in composites.
- Disclose the firm's set minimum asset level for composite inclusion.

5. **Presentation and Reporting**
   - Firms are required to present a minimum of five (5) years of annual performance history that meet the GIPS standards, including annual returns for each year. For a firm that previously claimed AIMR-PPS compliance, the firm must continue to show at least 10 years of performance results.
   - The composite creation date must be disclosed.
   - For each composite, disclosure of the number of portfolios, the amount of assets, and the percentage of managers total assets that are represented by the composite at the end of each period.
   - A measure of the dispersion of individual portfolio returns for each annual period.
   - Historical compliance is at the discretion of the manager. When the firm's historical performance record is presented, a disclosure must be made that identifies the in-compliance periods from the periods that are not in compliance. No non-compliant performance can be presented for periods after January 1, 2000. The firm must also disclose that the full historical performance record is not in compliance.
   - Performance for periods of less than one year must not be annualized.
   - There are several guidelines covering the reporting of firms that have merged, and if it applies to a firm under consideration, these guidelines should be reviewed.
   - The total return for the benchmark/s that reflect the investment strategy or mandate represented by the composite must be presented for the

same periods for which the composite return is presented. If the firm changes the benchmark that is used for a given composite in the performance presentation, the firm must disclose the reasons for change.

- Composite results may not be restated following changes in a firm's organization.

6. **Real Estate**
- Real estate investments must be valued by market value at least once every 12 months. Beginning 2008, this must be done quarterly.
- Real estate investments must be valued by an external professionally designated, certified, or licensed commercial property valuer/appraiser at least once every 36 months.
- Income and capital appreciation component returns must be presented in addition to total returns.
- Real estate has specific recommendations and required disclosures, in addition to those of the GIPS standards.

7. **Private Equity**
- Private Equity investments must be valued according to the GIPS private equity valuation principals (preferably quarterly, but at least annually).
- Firms must calculate the annualized since-inception internal rate of return (SI-IRR).
- Net-of-fees returns must be net of investment management fees, carried interest, and transaction expenses.
- All closed-end private equity investment, including, but not limited to, fund of funds, partnerships, or direct investments, must be included in a composite defined by strategy and vintage year.
- Private equity investments have many specific recommendations and disclosure requirements.

8. **Wrap-fee/SMA Accounts**
- Wrap-fee/SMA performance must be shown net of all fees charged directly or indirectly to the account, including trading costs.

- When using composites, the manager must make certain disclosures and there are specific requirements for the treatment of the composite data.
- Wrap-fee/SMA accounts have many specific recommendations and disclosure requirements.

The growth in separately managed accounts has resulted in a number of issues relating specifically to the calculation and reporting of wrap-fee and SMA performance numbers. In response, the CFA Institute issued a Guidance Statement to clarify the application of GIPS guidelines to wrap-fee and SMA accounts in 2005. These guidelines became effective January 1, 2006 and can be found at: www.cfainstitute.org/centre/ips/pdf/WrapFeeSMAGSBoard-ApprovedFINAL.pdf.

Strongly Recommended Guidelines and Disclosures

- Significant cash flows, i.e., exceeding 10% of the portfolios market value that cause distortions in performance, may require revaluation of the portfolio on the date of the cash flow. The methodology should be disclosed and be consistent. This will become mandatory in 2010.
- Present relevant risk measures, such as volatility, information ratio, Sharpe ratio, Treynor ratio, tracking error, beta and modified duration for composite and benchmark returns.
- Firms are encouraged to bring all historical performance periods into compliance with GIPS.
- Present performance of composites as gross of investment management and administrative fees.

What about when a manager uses the total return of a balanced composite to market a balanced account strategy?

- When a manager uses the total return of a balanced composite to market balanced account strategy, but wishes to present a portion (carve-out) of the balanced composite as supplemental information in presenting the balance strategy, cash must be allocated to the carve-out returns and the allocation method must be disclosed.
- When the results of the balanced segments are added to single-asset composites, a cash allocation needs to be made to each of the segments.

This adjustment prevents a manager from mixing asset-without-cash returns to asset-plus-cash returns.

Verification of Performance Data

- Verification is the thorough review of an investment management firm's performance-measurement processes and procedures by an independent third party "verifier."
- Third party verification is strongly encouraged and is expected to become mandatory at a future date (perhaps by 2010).

Many of the requirements and recommendations included in the 2006 GIPS guidelines are slated to be either updated or changed in 2010 and therefore, we should expect a noteworthy revision of GIPS at that time.

CONCLUSION

The CFA Institute has stated that its standards were developed to close the door on misrepresentation, and to reduce confusion and mistrust among clients and potential clients. They have stressed the seriousness of the need for the standards in establishing and maintaining consistent, sound, and ethical industry practices. By stating that performance reports are GIPS compliant, managers are expected to meet the "full disclosure and fair representation" intent of the guidelines. This disclosure means that those who report GIPS compliant numbers are expected to make a conscientious, good faith interpretation of the standards, consistent with its underlying ethical principals. The CFA Institute, through the use of GIPS, strives to level the playing field, making comparisons to benchmarks and between managers a valid and revealing endeavor. The CFA Institute does not audit, endorse or otherwise confirm performance data and therefore during the due diligence process, the consultant will investigate the source of data, determine how it is compiled and what makes up the composite and, examine how it is verified. Realistically, GIPS compliance has become the minimum standard that a manager must meet in order to be considered credible within the investment industry.

SECTION IV
Performance Measurement, Analysis and Evaluation

SECTION IV
Performance Measurement, Analysis and Evaluation

Performance numbers, what do they tell us? Consultants use performance data during the due diligence phase of the manager selection process and then to monitor all aspects of a portfolio's performance and adherence to policy guidelines. To maximize their value, one must know how to find and interpret the most relevant data and, how to relate that information to the client's investment goals and objectives. We have discussed the qualitative aspect of manager selection, including investment philosophy, process and the nature of the management team, all of which are important characteristics when considering the suitability of a manager for an investor. In this section, we will provide information on analyzing the quantitative data, both for the purpose of selecting managers and, to evaluate the performance of an individual portfolio. There are many influences on evaluating performance that go far beyond raw numbers, the most significant being the investor's risk profile. It is necessary to integrate many factors when determining the suitability of a manager and when evaluating the all-important "risk-adjusted" performance.

A qualified Investment Management Consultant will go through this evaluation, both during the initial screening process and repeatedly thereafter, as part of the periodic reviews with the client. When the investor understands how performance is reported and, how risk-and-return statistics are actually integrated, they will become better investors and better clients. This knowledge creates a dynamic link between the investment objectives, asset allocation and portfolio performance.

This section will provide the reader with:

- Definitions and uses of quantitative terms
- Performance Analysis–the use of perfomance data to evaluate a manager during the due diligence process.
- Performance Evaluation–the use of performance data to evaluate an investment portfolio and its managers.

17

Definitions and Uses of Quantitative Terms

Quantitative analysis incorporates both performance and risk analysis and, an analysis of the holdings' characteristics of a portfolio. The performance measurement process is mathematical; its application, a blend of skill and art. When evaluating the performance of an individual manager or investment vehicle, there can be quite a bit of confusion and, for good reason. Mutual funds, banks, brokers, insurance companies, and money managers can and do use different methods to display investment returns. They may also incorporate an element of creativity in their presentation of performance numbers in order to put the best light on the performance that they report. While these different approaches are usually legitimate, they can make fair comparisons more challenging.

In all cases, the more data points the better. More and more the industry is using monthly data instead of the old quarterly standard, as 5 years of quarterly data is only 20 data points, whereas 5 years of monthly reports have 60 data points. Regardless of the technique used, the consultant must find commonality in order to make effective comparisons. To find commonality, one must understand the meanings and uses of the various terms and calculations that are used to present data. GIPS standards strive to create consistency in reporting and the CFA Institute continues to update its guidelines and recommendations to adapt to the rapidly evolving wrap industry. The reader may access these standards through the web links included in Chapter 16. The more common terms and methods of calculation include:

Composites
- Portfolio composites
- Benchmark composites

Time periods and methods of calculation
- Trailing returns
- Rolling returns
- Average rate of return
- Compound or annualized rate of return
- Time-weighted versus Dollar-weighted returns

Rates of return
- Total rate of return
- Gross and net rate of return
- Comparative and absolute rate of return

General measurement tools
- Sharpe Ratio
- Tracking error
- Attribution analysis and others

COMPOSITES

Portfolio Composites

Before making any performance calculations, the money management firm will first determine the "universe" of client data that is used in calculations. The data chosen is referred to as the composite and the rules governing its composition are defined by GIPS. The universe defines the criteria used by the management firm to determine which accounts are included or excluded in the performance numbers that they report. As an example, a firm may elect to exclude all personal accounts of firm members or, they may include or exclude portfolios that are underinvested (i.e., 30% invested and 70% cash) compared to their investment norm (i.e., 90% invested) or, portfolios that have significant restrictions, such as those required in socially responsible investing.

Managers may also include performance data from other sources, such as the data from a mutual fund that the firm manages in a like manner to that of their separate accounts. The firm may choose to include their mutual fund data to show longer performance history if the SMA has a relatively short track record and the like mutual fund has a long record of performance data. The firm may also "adjust" the time-period that is included by altering the inception date. They may choose to do this if say, the first year under management was poorly executed and performance was sub standard. In this example, including a bad, and perhaps non-representative first year, would be reflected in performance data for years to come. There are many ways to manipulate the composite, so in order to make representative comparisons, the source of the data must be known. This disclosure is required of those investment firms who state that they are GIPS compliant.

Benchmark Composites

When making comparisons to a benchmark or "the market," a consultant must determine if the comparison will be made to a single benchmark, such as the S&P 500, a custom style benchmark (Chapter 14), a pre-determined split benchmark, such as 60% S&P 500, 35% Lehman Brothers Aggregate Bond and 5% cash or, an asset weighted blend, which better matches the asset allocation of a portfolio (described later in this chapter).

TIME PERIODS AND METHODS OF CALCULATION

Another creative way that some firms (brokerage, money management or mutual fund) enhance the perception of their returns is to "sell" or report returns from a specific time-period, which can be differentiated by the day! It is amazing how many "number one" firms that there are at any one time. Marketing is designed to attract positive attention. A management firm may have a great quarter or year and focus only on that time-period. If you do not look behind the numbers, there may be an unpleasant surprise awaiting you.

It is very common for a manager to report 1-year, 3-year and 5-year returns, as well as longer time-periods, including "from inception." The more data points that are available, the more likely one can extrapolate reasonable long-term expectations. When comparing two investment options, use exactly the same time periods and methods of calculation.

Time Periods

Time periods can include any dates, such as the headline "Fund X up 51% for the period October 9, 2002 through June 30, 2004." Choosing specific dates, as well as calculating returns in different ways, is all part of "creative presentation."

Time periods are generally reported as either trailing returns over fixed time periods or, progressive time periods represented by rolling returns.

- **Trailing returns** represent the return measured backwards (trailing) from a specific date. Trailing returns are generally annualized, but can represent any stated calculation. If the date represented is "ending 12-31-2003," then the trailing 3-year returns include the 3 years ending 12-31-2003. By selecting and/or excluding a particular time period, such as selecting a 1-year or 5-year period instead of a 3-year period, the impression that the returns give about overall performance can be quite different.

In the following illustration, we use returns of the S&P 500 for the period ending 12-31-2003. The 1-year return is +28.68%, however the 3-year annualized return is -0.57% (or a -1.71% cumulative return over the entire 3-year period) and the 5-year annualized return is -4.05% (or a negative cumulative return of -20.25% over the entire 5-year period). Clearly, the 1-year return gives a better impression than either the 3-year or 5-year returns.

QUARTERLY RETURN FOR THE S&P 500, 1996 THROUGH 2003

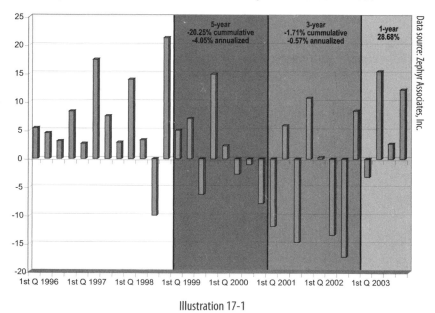

Illustration 17-1

- **Rolling periods:** Comparisons can be more representative when viewing *rolling periods,* which can be either cumulative or annualized returns grouped by a specific time period. We will use a rolling 3-year period in this illustration. The rolling 3-year period will continually drop the oldest quarter while adding the most recent as it "rolls" forward in time. Three-year returns may change considerably as the time period rolls forward and, the selection of a specific ending point (terminal point), can significantly alter the perceived performance. The influence of changing end-points is called *terminal point bias.*

In Illustration (17-2), we again use the returns of the S&P 500, but this time look at 3-year rolling periods ending in successive quarters. Note the rather significant change in returns between 3-31-02 and 6-30-02, where positive quarters begin to be excluded from the 3-year window and negative quarters are added. The reverse is true between 3-30-03 and 6-30-03. These differences clearly demonstrate the effects of terminal point bias and the need to study performance data thoroughly. Viewing rolling returns smoothes results, which reduces the effects of extremes, such as an exceptionally good or bad quarter. This type of reporting helps the consultant determine a manager's true, long-term ability to add value to a portfolio.

S&P 500 returns for rolling 3-year periods, beginning with a terminal point of 12-31-2001								
12-31-01	3-31-02	6-30-02	9-30-02	12-31-02	3-30-03	6-30-03	9-30-03	12-31-03
-1.02	-2.53	-9.17	-12.89	-14.55	-16.09	-11.20	-10.13	-4.05

Data source: Zephyr Associates, Inc.

Illustration 17-2

As we see in Illustration 17-1, very good periods, such as the late 1990s, are often followed by underperforming periods, as segments of the markets have a tendency to return to their long-term average return. This return is called *reversion to the mean.* Reversion is, in part, what is occurring when the worst performing style of one year may become the best performing style the next, as styles go through their natural market valuation cycles (Illustration 13-1). Analyzing rolling periods allows the consultant to determine when a style may be at or near the bottom or the top of a market cycle and, whether or not it is a good time to buy or to sell.

Methods of Calculation

Reporting returns for a specific time-period, such as 1, 3 or 5 years, only tells us that over that specific period, the manager produced a particular return. It does not tell us what happened each year, whether the entire return was due to a spectacular quarter, or if the returns were consistent year over year. Nor does it tell us how the rate of return was calculated. If a manager shows a 3-year return totaling 33%, did the investment earn 10%, 11% or 12% a year? All answers and others can be correct.

There are several ways to calculate rates of return, which is the percentage change in market value over a specified period of time, including dividends and income. We will begin by looking at the two most basic methods of calculating returns, average returns and compound annualized returns. As the following illustrations show, they can produce very different results.

- **Average (or arithmetic) rate of return:** The returns for any number of past periods are added together and divided by the total number of periods to determine the average or mean return. Averaging is the simplest method of calculating returns and in the following example, the average 3-year return would be 21.6% per year. This methodology, although not as accurate as a compound annualized return, will show the smoothing effect of time and can be used when assessing long-term risk.

	RETURN
YEAR 1	100%
YEAR 2	-50%
YEAR 3	15%
TOTAL RETURN/3 YEARS	$65/3 = 21.6\%$

- **Compound annualized rate of return:** This calculation, also referred to as geometric return, is a more informative measure of the change in wealth over time and is more widely used by the investment community. Unlike the average return, the compound annualized return takes into account the sequence of earnings or losses. A gain or a loss in any one period directly affects the amount of money left to build upon in the next and subsequent periods. In addition, the bigger the swings in the returns from one period to the next, the lower the returns will be when compared to the average rate of return calculations. (We have used return extremes to accentuate this point.) Using this method of calculation, volatility becomes more evident, which helps the consultant determine whether the investment is appropriate for the investor's risk tolerance.

	RETURN
YEAR 1	100%
YEAR 2	-50%
YEAR 3	15%
COMPOUND ANNUALIZED RETURN	4.7%

In addition to calculations that focus on yearly returns, the cumulative return shows the entire return over a specified period.

- **Compound cumulative return:** This calculation includes the compounding of the previous example and is additive over the specified time-period. A cumulative return calculation answers the question, "how much gain has the portfolio experienced since inception?" Using the previous example, the cumulative return over the 3-year period is 15%.

Each of these return calculations can be useful in reviewing an investment's track record. The average rate of return will provide information about what will most likely happen over time and when used in conjunction with the compound rate of return, volatility becomes more evident. Both can play a role in determining suitability. Cumulative returns provide results over the specified period of time, which may be helpful in making absolute (dollar for dollar) comparisons, but may also mask volatility.

While average and compound calculations can produce different returns over several periods, time-weighted and dollar-weighted calculations can produce different return results within the same time-period.

- **Time-weighted versus dollar-weighted rates of return:** The dollar-weighted rate of return is calculated using the average dollars invested during a specified period, including cash added to, or withdrawn from the portfolio by the investor. The result shows the change in the value of a portfolio. Dollar-weighted returns provide an overall picture of a portfolio's progress (how is my money doing?), but cash flows, both in timing and magnitude, can distort the true performance of a money manager.

  Time-weighted returns are used to effectively evaluate the managers. Because the manager cannot control the size or timing of money flowing in and out of an account, a time-weighted calculation is used to calculate the value of one dollar invested for the entire period, eliminating distortions from cash flows. Time-weighting factors out the effects of cash flows and more accurately reflect the manager's ability to manage their portfolio. Since a performance report should provide a means to evaluate both the individual managers' performance and the portfolio's performance as compared to investment objectives, there is value in reporting both time-weighted and dollar-weighted results. If the portfolio experiences no cash flows, then there will be no difference between the two calculations, whereas changes in cash flow, either contributions or withdrawals, will affect only dollar-weighted returns.

The following table is an example of how these two calculations differ. Assume two portfolios, Portfolio A and Portfolio B, each with a beginning value of $100,000. Each portfolio experiences a 10% return in year 1. Investor A then adds an additional $100,000, while investor B does nothing. In year 2, both portfolios lose 10%.

	Portfolio A	Portfolio B
Starting Value	$100,000	$100,000
Year 1, both portfolios gain 10%	$110,000	$110,000
A adds $100,000	$210,000	$110,000
Year 2, both portfolios lose 10%	$189,000	$99,000
Dollar-weighted rate of return*	-2.71%	-0.50%
Time-weighted rate of return*	-0.50%	-0.50%

*Calculations are annualized over 2 years

On a time-weighted basis, at the end on the second year, the returns for Portfolio A and B are the same, -0.50%. On a dollar-weighted basis, investor A's account shows a negative return of -2.71%, as the effects of cash flow show the impact of a loss on the greater dollar amount. Investor B, with no cash flows, reports equivalent time- and dollar-weighted returns.

Over short time periods of, say a month, the differences between time-weighted and dollar-weighted calculations on portfolios that have experienced cash flows are usually insignificant. But, as time and/or cash flows increase, the difference can become statistically significant. Other examples of time and dollar-weighted returns include per-share values of mutual funds, which are calculated on a time-weighted basis and savings accounts, which can be calculated as time-weighted or dollar-weighted because they pay a constant rate of return.

RATES OF RETURN

- **Total rate of return,** generally referred to as total return, assumes that all dividend and interest income are reinvested when paid and are included in any calculation of capital appreciation or loss. This calculation can be done on a gross or net basis.

- **Gross rate of return** equals the total rate of return with no deductions, such as fees. This calculation is used to compare manager performance to their respective benchmarks. Benchmarks have no deductions, therefore comparing gross returns to a benchmark is the most informative and accepted comparison.

- **Net rate of return** is the gross return minus all applicable fees. It would seem as though all returns should be reported as "net" since net more accurately reflects returns from the investor's perspective, however comparative indices have no fees and therefore benchmark comparisons would be inaccurate.

- **After-tax returns** are net returns that also exclude taxes paid. After-tax returns are not generally part of a performance report, however some mutual funds do include them in their reporting.

Gross rate of return and net rate of return are often both reported, as both have their place in performance monitoring. When reviewing standardized performance reports, such as those used in marketing pieces, remember that the fee that is applied in calculating the net returns may be different from the actual negotiated fee of an individual client, making customized reporting a more accurate and necessary comparison.

- **Comparative or relative rate of return:** Relative returns are a raw-number comparison between the manager or portfolio's return and that of a specific benchmark. It is the same as "relative return." The manager's relative return is a measure of how well the manager is performing compared to the market benchmark that most closely replicates their style, i.e., large cap growth managers will be compared to the S&P 500, whereas small cap growth managers may be compared to the Russell 2000 growth or the S&P 600 growth. The portfolio's relative return measures returns compared to an asset weighted blend. The return should be stated as gross when compared to a specific benchmark and net when compared to an absolute return expectation.

- **Absolute return:** Absolute returns compare the manager or portfolio's return to that of a specific return expectation. The investment policy may state that the portfolio is expected to have a net return of 8% per year or, produce a net return equal to 5% above the rate of inflation.

GENERAL MEASUREMENT TOOLS

- **Alpha (α):** Alpha measures the risk-adjusted performance of a portfolio. Compare what the portfolio earned to what it would be expected to earn, given the amount of risk that exists in the portfolio. Positive alpha can result from the portfolio producing a lower standard deviation and/or excess returns when compared to those of the benchmark and reflects the value of the selection process. In Illustration 17-3, there is a positive alpha, as the manager has produced both a higher relative return and has done so at a lower relative standard deviation.

- **Asset weighted blend:** A blend of the portfolio's comparative benchmarks (indexes) in ratios equal to that of their representative individual investment styles. As an example, a portfolio made up of 30% large cap managers, 40% mid cap managers and 30% international managers would have an asset weighted blend comprised of a 30% weighting of the S&P 500, a 40% weighting of the S&P 400 and a 30% weighting of the MSCI-EAFE.

- **Attribution analysis:** This analysis shows which segment of the portfolio (individual stocks, sectors, market cap, etc.) is responsible for performance, good or bad and, how it relates to the benchmark. This analysis tells the consultant if the manager is making good sector calls and/or security selections and thus, adding value. The manager may choose to over- or underweight a sector compared to their benchmark. The attribution analysis will tell how much of the portfolio's performance can be attributed to that asset allocation decision. Stock selection is another area where management decisions can add value. If an individual security within a given sector is up 25%, while the sector is up only 10%, then the manager is adding value through their security selection.

- **Batting average:** Batting average is a measure of a manager's ability to consistently beat their benchmark. Divide the number of quarters that the manager beat the benchmark by the total number of quarters in a given period.

- **Beta (β):** Beta is the relative volatility of a portfolio (or stock) compared to its benchmark. A beta greater than "1" means that the portfolio is more volatile than its comparative benchmark, whereas a beta of less than "1" means it is less volatile. Beta represents the measure of systematic risk.

- **Correlation coefficient:** Correlation coefficient is the statistical measure of the relationship between two variables. When applied to performance analysis, we are referring to different asset classes and styles. A negative correlation means that two asset groupings are moving in an unrelated manner to one another. A positive correlation indicates that they are moving in a similar fashion to one another. The range is between −1.00 and +1.00. Investments that move exactly together have the highest correlation coefficient, +1.00 and those that move in completely opposite directions to one another have the lowest correlation coefficient, −1.00. Zero or 0.0, indicates that they have no correlation or a random relationship to one another (Illustration 9-8). The lower the correlation coefficient, the greater the diversification impact of mixing the assets.

- **Dispersion:** Dispersion measures the consistency of performance results between accounts at the management firm. Do accounts of like objectives and time of investment have the same or similar performance? When performance numbers are reported, do they reflect all assets under management or only a select group of clients? This information will clarify the source and quality of the performance data, as well as reveal possible operational inconsistencies within the management firm's trading or account tracking disciplines. Managers with high levels of dispersion can produce performance results that are not reflective of all assets under management if all like-accounts are not performing in a similar manner.

- **Downside capture ratio:** The downside capture ratio reports how much of the benchmark's negative returns the manager captured during a down-market. A down-market is one in which the benchmark's return for a quarter is negative. All down-markets are compared over a specific time period, i.e., 3 years, 5 years, 10 years, etc. A number less than 100%, means that the manager is adding risk management value, not losing as much as the relative benchmark. A number greater than 100% would indicate that the manager lost more than the benchmark. Aggressive growth managers, who tend to be quite volatile, may have upside and downside capture ratios that exceed that of their benchmark, but they may still have a positive alpha.

- **Information Ratio:** Information Ratio, also referred to as the selection Sharpe ratio, is a gauge of the value added by the manager and, it is an excellent risk-adjusted measure of performance, measuring the alpha per unit of active risk. It measures a manager's consistency in beating their benchmark. Divide excess manager returns (as compared to the benchmark) by the tracking error. The information ratio compares returns, relative to the risk taken, and is therefore a useful tool to differentiate managers. A higher ratio usually indicates better active management skills. Ratios from 0.50 to 0.75 are considered good, with 1.0 being exceptional. The information ratio for the benchmark is always 0.

- **Risk/return quadrant:** Quadrants describe the area of a graph that plots risk (measured as standard deviation) on the "x" axis and return on the "y" axis. A manager or portfolio with risk/return plot points in the northwest quadrant indicates that there has been a better return with less risk exposure than that of the comparative benchmark.

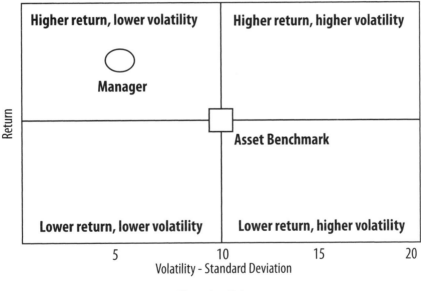

Illustration 17-3

- **Risk/return ratio:** A risk/return comparison is the measure of the return achieved per unit of risk (standard deviation) over a specific period of time. It is another measure of risk-adjusted return.

- **R-squared:** R-squared measures the correlation between a portfolio and a benchmark and aids in predicting or analyzing the behavior of a portfolio. The range is between 0, where there is no correlation to the benchmark and +1, which indicates that the two are perfectly correlated. An R-squared of +1 would indicate that the manager is indexing. The closer this relationship is to +1, the more the portfolio will behave like the benchmark. If there is a low correlation between the two, then the benchmark is not a good comparison when considering relative performance. R-squared can assist in determining how much of the manager's performance can be attributed to the performance of the benchmark and, help to determine how much risk a manager is taking to achieve his or her returns. R-squared greater than 0.8 is considered acceptable when determining if a benchmark is appropriate for comparisons.

- **Security overlap:** When combining multiple managers, the consultant should determine the degree of duplication that might exist among the securities held by each manager. Some overlap (less than 15%) is acceptable, however it should be limited to provide for maximum diversification.

- **Sharpe ratio:** The Sharpe ratio is a risk-adjusted measure of performance used to quantify the reward per unit of risk. It is calculated using excess return (manager's returns greater than that of the benchmark) and total risk (standard deviation); the higher the Sharpe ratio, the better the portfolio's risk-adjusted performance. The Sharpe ratio has an advantage over alpha, because in order for alpha to be meaningful, the R-squared must be high, whereas the Sharpe ratio is meaningful all of the time. If the Sharpe ratio of a manager is above that of the comparative benchmark, the manager's investment strategy resulted in excess return per unit of risk. The Sharpe ratio is a good predictor of consistency of returns and, differentiates one manager's risk-return to another. The Sharpe ratio can be one of the most important elements in choosing managers or constructing portfolios. The Sharpe ratio can also be used to compare the returns of a manager to that of a proposed comparative benchmark to determine their degree of correlation.

- **Standard deviation:** Standard deviation is a measure of volatility, seen as variability of returns. Standard deviation compares the measured return to that of the mean return for a specific period. If the mean return of an investment or a manager is 10%, and the standard deviation is 15, then the mathematical expectation of returns, by definition, would be between -5% and +25%, two-thirds of the time. (Illustration 9-7).

- **Style drift:** Style drift occurs when a manager places securities into a portfolio that are inconsistent with their stated investment philosophy and discipline. This practice is not acceptable to the consulting process, as asset allocation decisions are dependent upon style consistency within management firms. Manager portfolios should be reviewed for style drift as part of the due diligence process to ensure that they remain true to their stated discipline.

- **Tracking error:** Tracking error is the percentage difference in total return between an index fund and the benchmark the fund is designed to replicate. Tracking error is most relevant when used to evaluate a passive manager or index fund. When used with active managers, who generally do not intend to replicate a benchmark, it provides insight into the amount of risk the manager is taking to produce a return, as it measures the difference in the standard deviation of excess returns between the manager and the benchmark. Tracking error may be the result of sector bets within a particular style, or style bets within a particular portfolio. The comparative index must be a good fit for the tracking error to be valuable. A low tracking error to the benchmark, e.g. 2, would indicate that the portfolio may outperform the benchmark by 2% and will not underperform the benchmark by more than 2%. A higher tracking error, e.g. 5, would indicate that the portfolio may outperform the benchmark by 5% and will not underperform the benchmark by more than 5%. A tracking error of 0 indicates that the manager tracks the benchmark perfectly; 10 or less is considered acceptable.

- **Treynor ratio (T):** The Treynor ratio is similar to the Sharpe ratio in that it too relates excess return to risk, however the Treynor ratio considers only systematic risk, whereas the Sharpe ratio is calculated using total risk (standard deviation). The higher the Treynor ratio, the better the performance.

- **Universe inclusion:** The "universe" not only defines the criteria used by the management firm to determine which accounts are included or excluded in the performance numbers that they report, but it is also used to identify the group of like-style managers that the consultant may use as a comparative during the manager screening process. The universe can vary depending on the selection criteria. Is the universe all (possibly dependent on size of firm) large cap managers (value, growth and core) or only large cap growth managers? Does it include all historical data or, are terminated accounts excluded, presumably due to poor performance (survivorship bias)? Are the portfolios concentrated or more broad-based? The universe in which a manager is included must be relevant in order for comparisons to be meaningful.

- **Upside capture ratio:** The upside capture ratio measures how much of the benchmark's positive returns the manager "captured" during an up-market. A number greater than 100% indicates that the manager's returns exceeded those of the benchmark during up-markets. Conversely, a number less than 100% indicates that the manager underperformed the benchmark in up-markets. An up-market is one in which the benchmark's return for a quarter is positive.

CONCLUSION

Quantitative analysis depends on the accuracy of the data and the number of time periods being evaluated. Remember the adage: "Garbage in, garbage out." Most comparative analyses make use of benchmarks and therefore, one must begin the process by determining the most relevant index for comparison. There should be at least three years of reliable quarterly numbers available, however longer time periods and more frequent data points (monthly) allow for more accurate and relevant comparisons. Many consultants are moving from the use of quarterly data to monthly data to increase the statistical significance of their analysis. As a rule, consultants are looking for managers that exhibit top quartile Sharpe ratios, performance and alpha and bottom quartile Beta and standard deviation. Nevertheless, quantitative analysis is but one piece of the puzzle when evaluating the suitability or performance of a manager and its role must be clearly understood for the decision-making process to be effective.

18

An Introduction to
Performance Analysis

In addition to the qualitative criteria that go into determining a manager's suitability, the consultant must also analyze the manager's performance. The consultant is rarely seeking the manager with the highest returns, rather one who achieves his or her returns in a consistent, risk-managed manner and of course, one whos investment style is compatible with that of the investor and the overall portfolio design. This quantitative analysis tells the consultant if the manager adds value (alpha) on a consistent basis and, illustrates the degree of risk and volatility that the manager experiences in generating returns. Each individual manager plays a role in diversification and risk management and should therefore not be evaluated in isolation or over a short-term time frame. Effective analysis compares the investor's risk profile with the degree of risk assumed by each manager and that of the total portfolio, as well as the performance of each, compared to relevant benchmarks. This analysis will reveal the value-added by the managers, as well as the asset allocation.

As we have seen, there are many factors that can affect performance, such as the manager's style and/or the investment cycle. Diversification means that the portfolio is made up of assets with low correlation to one another and at any given time, some managers will outperform while others lag. Short-term underperformance and/or viewing performance without context, ignores the principals of the investment management consulting process. Understanding the character of performance results is an integral part of the consultant - investor educational process.

Quantitative analysis examines returns in relationship to appropriate benchmarks, as the consultant is generally more interested in risk-adjusted returns than absolute returns. From this comparative data, many conclusions can be drawn about *how* the manager generates returns. Performance analysis is used as part of the due diligence process in manager searches and in ongoing performance monitoring and evaluation, therefore a consultant should be skilled in the following types of analysis:

- Benchmark analysis
- Analysis of risk and volatility
- Holdings-based analysis
- Attribution analysis
- Consistency and stability
- Operational consistency and style adherence
- Universe rankings
- PODs
- Performance-based analysis

BENCHMARK ANALYSIS

In order to evaluate a manager's performance, there must be a standard for comparison. The standard most often used is the benchmark that most closely reflects the manager's investment style. We therefore begin with a benchmark analysis, which will tell the consultant how closely the manager's style matches that of the benchmark used for comparisons. In Chapter 14, we described how Russell and S&P differentiate styles, as well as the composition of their respective indices. Consultants understand that benchmark analysis is not an exact science, nonetheless, benchmark comparisons are universally used to evaluate performance and risk management, so it is incumbent upon the consultant to pick the best match available and to understand the variances.

Begin the process by asking the manager what benchmark he or she feels most closely represents their style and then, complete a style analysis (Illustration 18-1) to verify the validity of the comparison. Asking the manager is helpful because it should expedite the process, as well as tell the consultant which benchmark the manager uses when reporting comparative data. If the benchmark is a poor match, the reported comparisons have limited value. As we have discussed in previous chapters, active managers should not be a perfect match to a benchmark, but the closest match produces the most relevant performance analysis. R-squared and tracking error (Illustration 18-3) are used in this portion of the analysis. If R-squared is high and the tracking error is low, the benchmark is probably a good comparative match.

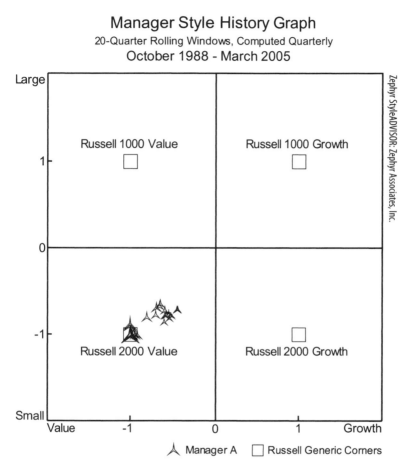

Illustration 18-1

This illustration maps how closely Manager A's style matches the Russell 2000 Value. The Russell 2000 Value would appear to be a good comparative benchmark for Manager A.

R-squared also measures the degree to which a manager's performance can be explained by the index and thus provides insight into performance that may be the result of the manager's style being in-favor or out-of-favor. Is the manager just in the right place (style) at the right time, or does the manager add real value? Or, put another way, is the manager lucky or good? (Illustration 18-2)

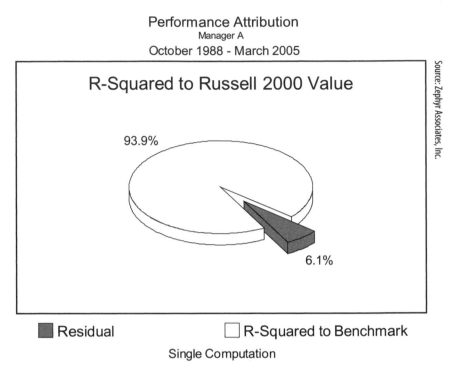

Performance Attribution
Manager A
October 1988 - March 2005

Source: Zephyr Associates, Inc.

R-Squared to Russell 2000 Value

93.9%

6.1%

■ Residual   ☐ R-Squared to Benchmark

Single Computation

Illustration 18-2

In this illustration, Manager A adds a limited amount of performance value in excess of that which can be attributed to the benchmark.

ANALYSIS OF RISK AND VOLATILITY

The next step is to analyze the risk taken by the manager to produce returns. This analysis is done by reviewing the portfolio's overall volatility utilizing beta comparisons, standard deviation, tracking error, information ratio and the Sharpe ratio. Returns and standard deviation for the manager, and those of the benchmark, are compared on a year-by-year basis. This comparison will show both volatility and relative risk. A standard deviation that is less than that of the benchmark is generally preferable, however volatility associated with up-side capture is of less concern when considering risk management than volatility associated with downside capture. The two should be evaluated separately. Beta and tracking error illustrate how closely the manager and benchmark correlate to one another, and therefore provide some insight into comparative performance expectations. Low beta and tracking error would indicate that the manager's portfolio experiences less volatility (takes less risk) in achieving returns than the benchmark. A high information ratio (excess return to tracking error) is generally preferable, as it measures the return per given level of risk. A lower number however, may not necessarily be bad as it depicts the manager's variance from the benchmark and indicates how well a manager takes advantage of available opportunities, taking into consideration variances in investor risk aversion and objective.

Standard deviation is the mathematical standard by which risk is measured, however it is actually a measure of the variability of returns. A portfolio with a high standard deviation is generally considered to be a higher risk portfolio, but this assessment may not be the case in actual fact, as volatility may create opportunity for certain investment styles. Nonetheless, it is the conceptual standard used by the financial industry and one that must be understood to properly evaluate risk.

Risk/Return Table

October 1988 - March 2005: Annualized Summary Statistics

	Standard Deviation	Sharpe Ratio	Tracking Error	Information Ratio	Alpha	Beta	R-Squared
Manager A	19.69%	0.52	4.94%	0.33	1.25%	1.05	94.01%
Russell 2000 Value	18.12%	0.47	0.00%	0.00	0.00%	1.00	100.00%

Zephyr StyleADVISOR: Zephyr Associates, Inc.

Illustration 18-3

In this analysis, R-squared and Tracking Error indicate that the Russell 2000 Value is a good comparative benchmark for this manager. Standard deviation and Beta are slightly higher than those of the benchmark, indicating that the manager's portfolio is more volatile than the Russell 2000 Value. The Sharpe Ratio and alpha are positive, indicating that the manager is providing greater returns per unit of risk taken or, a solid risk-adjusted return. The Information ratio, another risk-adjusted measurement, is average.

HOLDINGS-BASED ANALYSIS

The consultant will carry out a holdings-based analysis to determine the types of securities that the manager holds, as well as to determine where and how the manager achieves results. A holdings-based analysis reveals characteristics such as the P/E, growth rate and dividend yield of the stocks in the manager's portfolio. Looking at the types of stocks that a manager holds can give the consultant insight into the manager's investment philosophy. Investors that are more conservative often require a portfolio that provides stable returns and/or income generation, thus the consultant may select managers primarily for this characteristic. Relatively stable, blue chip, dividend-paying portfolios may be the only suitable equity style for some investors, whereas aggressive portfolios may be appropriate for others. A holdings-based analysis will help make these determinations. In addition to determining the type of securities that a manager buys, the consultant can compare the holdings of all the investor's managers to ensure that there are a limited number of securities that overlap within the total portfolio. Duplication can occur when, as an example, a small cap stock grows to be a mid cap stock that may be held by both the small and mid cap manager. Or, a high level of overlap can indicate either a poor manager mix or style drift by one or more of the managers. Both situations are generally unacceptable and warrant action on the part of the consultant.

ATTRIBUTION ANALYSIS

Where and how is the manager adding value? By combining the holdings-based analysis with an attribution analysis the consultant can determine if the manager is skilled at selecting the best performing areas within their style and/or selecting outperforming securities within a sector. As an example, if a specific sector is underperforming in general, but the manager has selected "winners" from that sector, then the manager is adding value or, if the manager has underweighted an underperforming sector, this action also adds value. The attribution analysis will compare the composition of the manager's portfolio to that of its comparative benchmark and will show where there are differences. This analysis is also used on an ongoing basis to determine why a manager may be outperforming or underperforming their benchmark. When making this comparison, one must go back to the benchmark analysis to determine more precisely the relevance of the comparison. In 2005, energy became richly valued and more heavily weighted within the value indices than the norm. Many intrinsic value managers began to underperform their value benchmarks because their style discipline would not allow them to hold the benchmark's level of richly valued energy stocks. Through proper analysis, the consultant understood the reasons for this temporary underperformance and was likely unconcerned. It is more important for the manager to maintain their discipline than track a benchmark or add unanticipated risk to the portfolio.

The following illustration is a very abbreviated example of a attribution analysis, comparing a manager's portfolio to its applicable market benchmark. We have limited the data from the report to that information which demonstrates the value added by the manager's stock selections and sector weightings. This manager has over- and underweighted sectors compared to the benchmark and, has chosen stocks within each sector that have either improved or hurt performance. In this example, the technology sector is over-weighted compared to the benchmark and stock selection added significant value to the portfolio, whereas the health care sector weighting and stock selections detracted from performance. Overall, during the time period represented in the report, the manager significantly outperformed the benchmark.

A full attribution analysis makes many other comparisons between the benchmark and the manager's portfolio, such as performance by P/E quartile,

ATTRIBUTION DETAIL BY SECTOR

SECTOR	Portfolio		Market Benchmark	
	WEIGHTING	RETURN	WEIGHTING	RETURN
Technology	19.0	17.9	12.8	-15.5
Health Care	17.9	-6.3	12.5	-3.4
Consumer Discretionary	17.7	-2.8	18.3	6.0
Consumer Staples	2.1	23.7	1.7	8.1
Integrated Oils	-0-	-0-	0.1	39.3
Other Energy	3.5	72.9	4.7	51.8
Materials & Processing	4.5	-6.5	9.7	23.5
Producer Durables	4.4	15.0	7.9	5.1
Autos & Transportation	5.1	55.2	4.4	9.6
Financial Services	24.6	4.2	23.1	3.6
Utilities	1.2	-0-	4.2	15.1
Other	-0-	-0-	0.4	32.0
TOTAL	100	8.3	100	5.4

Source: Oak Ridge Investments
Annualized 1 year returns ending March 31, 2005

Ilustration 18-4

market cap, quality, or stock price to name a few. As an example, in 2003, the highest P/E, lower quality stocks outperformed the more reasonably priced, higher quality stocks within the benchmark. Managers with higher quality stock portfolios tended to underperform, which again, was not a cause for concern.

Holdings-based and attribution analyses help to paint a more complete picture of risk and return, skill and consistency. These analyses help the consultant determine the manager's overall active management skills. Active management is not intended to replicate a benchmark, so the combination of an attribution analysis, information ratio and tracking error may help to uncover "closet indexers."

CONSISTENCY AND STABILITY

The consultant is very interested in the manager's consistency in risk management and generation of returns. The upside capture ratio and downside capture ratio numerically illustrate how the manager performs during up and down markets and, each should be analyzed separately. The upside capture ratio illustrates a manager's performance compared to that of the benchmark during up markets (measured by quarters) and the downside capture ratio gives the consultant some insight into how well the manager manages the incidence or degree of loss during difficult market periods or, when the manager's style is out-of-favor. Controlling risk during difficult markets is a key element in risk management. Selecting managers with low downside capture ratios helps to preserve capital and reduce portfolio volatility.

The analysis in Illustration 18-5 compares 3 managers to each other and to the S&P 500 (market). Manager C outperforms managers D and E, not only because of a high upside capture ratio, but more importantly, because of a low downside capture ratio. We have repeatedly emphasized the long-term value of managing risk and controlling losses and this illustration numerically demonstrates this fact. Outperforming in a bull market is fun, but retaining one's gains is how success is ultimately measured.

Other measures of consistency include consistent annual returns and low relative standard deviation. A manager with a high batting average will have produced excess returns, but for how long? Consistency of returns and low volatility should be achieved over long periods of time for the manager to be

Upside/Downside Graph

January 1993 - March 2005: Annualized Summary Statistics

	Return	Standard Deviation	# of Up Periods	# of Down Periods	Average Up Return	Average Down Return	Best Period Return	Worst Period Return	Up Capture vs. Market	Down Capture vs. Market
Manager C	15.85%	23.12%	32	17	10.65%	-7.44%	40.52%	-18.75%	117.82%	79.90%
Manager D	10.79%	18.96%	34	15	7.80%	-7.78%	26.90%	-17.71%	108.57%	111.62%
Manager E	4.64%	22.25%	27	22	9.58%	-7.85%	24.87%	-23.31%	91.84%	140.05%
S&P 500	10.54%	16.28%	35	14	6.74%	-6.84%	21.30%	-17.28%	100.00%	100.00%

Zephyr StyleADVISOR: Zephyr Associates, Inc.

Illustration 18-5

considered skillful and all measures of manager performance are better viewed with this perspective in mind.

The manager's turnover ratio provides the consultant with information about the possible tax consequences of the manager's investment style and insight into the effectiveness of the manager's discipline and process. High turnover ratios are likely to generate higher capital gains, which should be considered when selecting managers for a tax sensitive portfolio. Also, if a manager has a disciplined process in place for the selection of securities, one would generally not expect a high turnover ratio; unless something unforeseen happens with the company, one would anticipate that the security would be held for an extended period of time.

OPERATIONAL CONSISTENCY AND STYLE ADHERENCE

Consultants compare the performance of portfolios within money management firms to determine the manager's consistency in portfolio management (dispersion) and performance reporting. GIPS compliance is intended to create consistency in reporting, but only audits, preferably on-site, will uncover management inconsistencies. Managers must also be consistent in their investment style (style drift) in order for consultants to make appropriate asset allocation decisions. In the following illustration, we see quite a bit of style drift in Manager A and almost no drift in Manager B. Both require further investigation, as Manager A, with a stated discipline of large cap value, appears to drift in an unacceptable manner across several different styles, while Manager B, with a stated discipline of large cap core, appears to be a closet indexer. The graphic alone does not reveal the investment practices of the managers and constitutes only one part of the analysis.

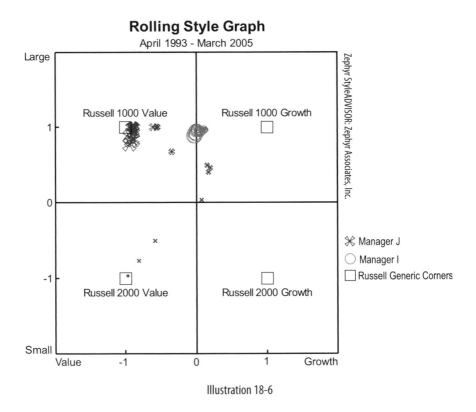

Illustration 18-6

UNIVERSE RANKINGS

Universe rankings (peer group analyses) compare managers of a like-style to their peers (Illustration 18-7). Comparing a specific manager to a group of managers with a similar style can be tricky because managers with poor performance records tend not to report data for inclusion in these databases. This anomaly is called "survivorship bias" and can be significant. Managers are not required to report performance data and therefore universe rankings can be suspect and should be viewed with this bias in mind. In addition, managers within a universe tend to have varying degrees of correlation to the benchmark, which will also affect performance data and hence, universe rankings. Different databases have differing criteria for inclusion, which has created material differences in performance rankings. These are examples of classification and composition biases. For these reasons, manager universes do not make good benchmarks. And, they are not "unambiguous, investable, appropriate, or specified in advance," as called for by GIPS (Chapter 16).

The universe is segmented into four quartiles. The top quartile includes managers in the top 5th to 25th percentiles, followed in ranking by the 26th to 50th percentile, then the 51st to 75th and finally the 76th to 95th percentile. The top and bottom 5% are excluded. These comparisons can include returns, standard deviation, alpha, upside and downside capture ratios, etc. and generally reflect cumulative data representing specified time periods. This data can be skewed by short-term success or failure, just as 1-yr returns can mask 3- and 5-year volatility and therefore longer time periods are preferable.

PODS

Universe rankings, and benchmark (index) analysis for that matter, do not necessarily tell us if a manager's performance is good. A manager can be at the top of their universe while still underperforming their benchmark or, be at the top of one universe and mediocre in another. To overcome the limitations of these comparisons, PODs were developed by Ronald Surz in 1986. PODs, or Portfolio Opportunity Distributions, use Monte Carlo type portfolio simulations as the comparison. These portfolio simulations create random portfolios that conform to the individual manager's approach. The manager's actual results are compared to all possible results within a given criteria (benchmark), thus customizing performance evaluation to each manager and alleviating the ambiguity of traditional universe rankings. (Refer to http://www.ppca-inc. com/intro_PODs.html for a detailed description of PODs.)

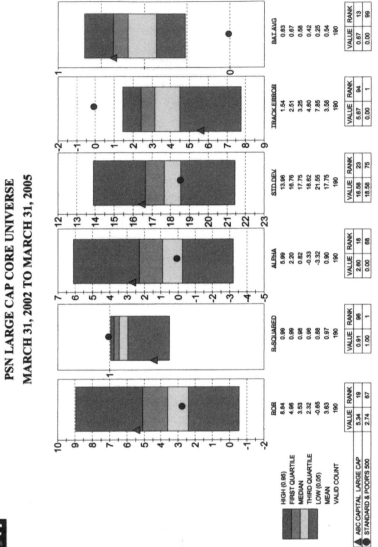

Illustration 18-7

PODs offer two important benefits: timeliness and accuracy. PODs are timely, as they are available days after each quarter's end, whereas traditional peer group reporting takes weeks to assemble. POD universes are accurate and unbiased, as they eliminate the biases of traditional universe rankings that were discussed in the previous section. PODs are new* and therefore not widely accepted or understood in performance evaluation, however they offer solutions to the widely known weaknesses of traditional universe rankings.

PERFORMANCE-BASED ANALYSIS

Performance or returns-based analysis includes both actual returns and risk characteristics of the portfolio. These can be measured using the Sharpe ratio, information ratio, upside and downside capture ratios, alpha, excess return and batting average. The focus should not be solely on returns, but of course, return data is the first place most people go to see if they might be interested in examining a manager further. Managers and consultants alike understand that risk management is important, but investors demand performance. Even the most risk-averse investor must reach a balance between performance and risk management. Illustration 18-8 is a risk/return analysis that compares three different managers to their respective benchmarks and to each other. This analysis can be used in the manager selection process, as well as portfolio monitoring and evaluation. This graphic integrates many of the performance measurement tools used by consultants to determine the suitability and effectiveness of managers.

DOES THE MANAGER ADD VALUE?

We have looked at several of the comparisons that are made when evaluating managers and each tell their own story. Managing risk is a key element of the consulting process, thus selecting managers that add value to risk management, as well as total returns, is the best of both worlds. Illustration 18-9 demonstrates "value-added" by looking at both performance and incidence of loss. The graphic shows consistent returns with a low incidence of quarters that result in a loss, illustrating that this investment style has significantly reduced the

* Modern Portfolio Theory (MPT) took 30 years to become established.

Risk Return Table

	Return (%)	Std Dev (%)	Downside Risk (%)	Beta vs. Benchmark	Alpha vs. Benchmark	R-Squared vs. Benchmark	Sharpe Ratio	Tracking Error vs. Benchmark
Manager H	14.38	20.57	14.63	0.9013	3.83	79.09	0.5104	9.6061
Russell 2000	11.25	20.20	14.68	1.0000	0.00	100.00	0.3647	0.0000
Manager G	11.29	20.73	14.94	0.9776	-1.61	82.81	0.3573	8.5903
S&P SmallCap 600	13.65	19.22	14.09	1.0000	0.00	100.00	0.5084	0.0000
Manager D	13.92	13.70	10.33	0.7106	4.88	68.63	0.7330	8.9208
S&P 500	10.80	15.96	11.79	1.0000	0.00	100.00	0.4333	0.0000

Zephyr StyleADVISOR: Zephyr Associates, Inc.

Illustration 18-8

In this illustration, each manager is compared to their benchmark and to each other, even though they have different styles. Manager D produces the highest alpha and Sharpe ratio due to their outperformance, low volatility and downside risk, whereas Manager G has a negative alpha compared to its benchmark and the lowest Sharpe ratio, due to underperformance and higher volatility. Manager D has the highest alpha, but lowest R-squared, limiting the comparative value of alpha in this case, however Manager D's Sharpe ratio is also the highest, indicating that its return was achieved with less risk than that of the other managers.

volatility of the overall portfolio, while also contributing to returns. The concepts of margin of safety and preservation of principal should not be forgotten in the performance debris that dominates headlines and manager searches. One must seek out managers that are as good at managing risk as they are at generating returns to achieve long-term investment success.

CONCLUSION

Historical returns are just that, in the past. A consultant must determine whether the manager is skilled, which would result in the expectation of continued

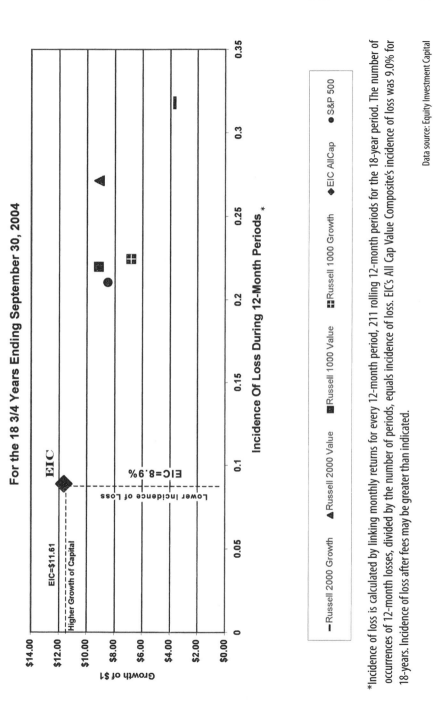

Data source: Equity Investment Capital

Illustration 18-9

success or, just lucky, in the right place, at the right time. When looking at returns alone, most large cap growth managers looked very good in 1999 and many looked very bad in 2002. The consultant must understand the art of quantitative analysis in order to separate skill from luck. We have suggested at many points throughout this book that the tools used to numerically evaluate managers and their performance are not perfect. Each form of analysis has its strengths and weaknesses and it is up to the consultant to integrate as much information as possible into making manager recommendations. Quantitative analysis must be used in conjunction with qualitative analysis, as numbers alone do not make a manager an appropriate choice for an investor. There are many criteria that must be met for the manager to be the right choice. This blend of qualitative and quantitative analysis represents a major component of the investment management consulting process.

19

Performance Evaluation

Performance evaluation is the process of determining how well the portfolio and its individual managers are performing when compared to stated investment objectives and appropriate benchmarks. When the consultant and investor meet for this review, they will revisit the objectives of the investment policy statement, where return expectations, risk tolerance and time horizons have been established. It cannot be overemphasized that asset allocations and hence, portfolio and manager returns are dependant on the risk and return criteria established in the policy. It perhaps seems obvious to state that an aggressive investor is likely to have different results than a conservative investor, but the investor does not always make that distinction if they do not think that they are "beating the market." An investor's perception of "the market" is likely to change along with media coverage, therefore consultants should use investor meetings to not only review performance, but also to keep the investor focused.

Periodic performance evaluations are a good time for the advisor or consultant to remind the investor of the relationship between risk and return. Few serious investment policies are designed to maximize returns with no regard to risk, so comparing portfolio or manager returns to the ever-changing hot stock or sector of the market, is irrelevant and nonproductive. The performance evaluation should tie performance to the guidelines in the investment policy by numerically illustrating the risk-adjusted returns of the individual managers as well as those of the total portfolio and, it should provide a means to evaluate the portfolio's adherence to the policy guidelines. These assessments are done using a variety of performance measurement tools, such as those in the last chapter, all of which are designed to uncover the true value of the portfolio design. Throughout this chapter, we will refer to components of a comprehensive performance evaluation report, which will illustrate how these comparisons can be displayed.

REPORTING

Performance monitoring is broken into two distinct categories, that of the total portfolio and that attributed to its individual managers. Clearly, the performance of each manager or investment vehicle will affect the performance of the total portfolio and therefore each should be analyzed separately to evaluate its contribution to the portfolio as a whole. The report should include a means to evaluate both the contribution to performance, *"Return %,"* and to risk management, displayed as *"Standard Deviation."* Returns are reported gross of fees in order to make meaningful comparisons to benchmarks, which do not have fees or other deductions.

Total Portfolio Evaluation

The following illustrations from the sample report provide actual and relative performance information for the portfolio. When reviewing the data, direct your attention to three risk-return comparisons.

1. **Returns by time periods:**
   Compare the *"Your Portfolio"* return to that of the *"Asset Weighted Blend,"* and then to the other major indices (Illustration 19-1). These comparisons allow the consultant to make a relative return comparison to that of the expected return for a like portfolio made up of indexes. If the portfolio's returns exceed that of the asset weighted blend, the combination of managers is adding performance value. This display also allows for the comparison of the portfolio's return to that of other major indices in absolute terms. This comparison is often of interest when evaluating the portfolio's design and it is generally something that investors like to see.

	Last 3 Months Oct 05-Dec 05 Return%	YTD Jan 05-Dec 05 Return%	1 Year Jan 05-Dec 05 Return%	3 Year Jan 03-Dec 05 Return%	5 Year Jan 01-Dec 05 Return%	Total Period Apr 90-Dec 05 Return%
■ Your Portfolio	1.16	5.96	5.96	10.30	2.38	11.06
■ Asset Weighted Blend	3.06	8.14	8.14	12.93	1.29	9.94
▨ Dow Jones Industrial Avg	2.04	1.65	1.65	11.12	1.98	10.79
■ S&P 500 Composite	2.05	4.83	4.83	14.38	0.54	11.04
▨ NASDAQ Composite	2.61	1.71	1.71	18.70	-1.66	12.51
■ Russell 2000	1.14	4.52	4.52	22.16	8.24	11.15
■ MSCI World	3.14	10.03	10.03	19.28	2.65	8.49
☐ Wilshire REIT	2.40	13.88	13.88	30.97	21.20	10.83

Illustration 19-1

2. Numerical Risk/Return comparison since inception:

Next, compare the standard deviation of *"Your Portfolio"* to that of the *"Asset Weighted Blend"* (Illustration 19-2). This comparison provides the information necessary to determine if the portfolio design is lowering the risk exposure of the portfolio compared to the indexed blend. If so, the combination of managers is adding risk management value to the portfolio. This sample portfolio has a long-term growth risk profile, which would generally have a standard deviation between 12 and 15. If the risk profile were aggressive, indicating that the investor has a higher tolerance to risk, we would expect the standard deviation to be much higher, say 20, while that of a conservative portfolio would be much lower, perhaps 10.

	Return%	Standard Deviation
▲ Your Portfolio	11.06	12.50
● Asset Weighted Blend	9.94	12.82
○ Dow Jones Industrial	10.79	14.52
● S&P 500 Composite	11.04	14.27
◔ NASDAQ Composite	12.51	31.17
● Russell 2000	11.15	18.56
● MSCI World	8.49	14.18
○ Wilshire REIT	10.83	12.06
● 90-day T-Bills	4.10	0.51

Illustration 19-2

Note that the standard deviation of this all equity *"Your Portfolio"* is less than that of the asset weighted blend and those of the major indices, with the exception of bonds and T-Bills. Standard deviation quantifies the risk management value of the portfolio design and validates the concept that blending assets of varying correlation to one another reduces volatility.

3. **Graphical Risk/Return comparison since inception:**
Illustration 19-3 is a scattergram of risk/return quadrants, which graphically displays the numeric points of the comparisons above. It is the goal of the consultant to have the *"Your Portfolio"* data points (return and standard deviation) intersect in the upper left-hand or northwest quadrant of the scattergram, meaning that the investment returns of the entire portfolio produced a higher return, while taking less risk, than the *"Asset Weighted Blend."* In this example, both criteria are met resulting in a high alpha return. Portfolio structure and investment choices, including manager selection, begin with the investor's risk profile, therefore risk management, not returns, may be the most important outcome. This form of evaluation allows the consultant to make these determinations.

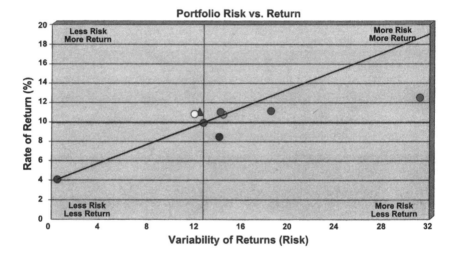

	Return%	Standard Deviation
▲ Your Portfolio	11.06	12.50
● Asset Weighted Blend	9.94	12.82
◉ Dow Jones Industrial	10.79	14.52
● S&P 500 Composite	11.04	14.27
● NASDAQ Composite	12.51	31.17
● Russell 2000	11.15	18.56
● MSCI World	8.49	14.18
○ Wilshire REIT	10.83	12.06
● 90-day T-Bills	4.10	0.51

Illustration 19-3

Individual Manager Evaluation

Having reviewed the portfolio as a whole, the next step is to analyze the risk management and return contributions to the portfolio by each of the managers. Illustration 19-4 provides the return by time periods and 19-5 details the risk and return since inception by manager (versus the portfolio as a whole), allowing the consultant to compare managers to each other, as well as to their relative benchmarks.

	Last 3 Months[1] Oct 05-Dec 05	YTD Jan 05-Dec 05	Last 12 Months[1] Jan 05-Dec 05	Last 3 Years[1] Jan 03-Dec 05	Last 5 Years[1] Jan 01-Dec 05	Total Period Apr 90-Dec 05
	Return %	Return %	Return %	Return %	Return %	Return %
■ Manager A (11/91)	1.71	-0.45	-0.45	9.88	2.90	10.24
■ Manager B (5/92)	-1.05	4.34	4.34	23.28	9.23	15.74
▢ Manager C (10/96	-1.04	3.99	3.99	31.94	9.86	9.57
■ Manager D (4/90)	3.66	6.48	6.48	10.96	-1.48	10.70
■ Manager E (9/96)	-	-	-	-	-5.78	-4.49
■ Manager F (4/90)	1.78	4.14	4.14	8.59	0.50	7.94
■ Manager G (12/00)	0.11	6.01	6.01	11.74	1.45	1.20
▢ Manager H (4/02)	2.73	7.15	7.15	13.18	-	9.32
■ Manager I (6/01)	0.83	2.59	2.59	2.21	-	2.70
■ Manager J (2/04)	3.82	10.95	10.95	-	-	3.52
▢ Manager K (11/05)	4.02	4.02	4.02	-	-	4.02
▢ Portfolio Totals	1.16	5.96	5.96	10.30	2.38	11.06

1. For accounts with lifetimes shorter than these periods, the returns displayed reflect unannualized performance since inception.

Illustration 19-4

Variability of Returns (Risk)

	Return%	Standard Deviation
▲ Manager A (11/91)	10.24	28.82
▲ Manager B (5/92)	15.74	15.50
△ Manager C (10/96	9.57	21.24
▲ Manager D (4/90)	10.70	15.57
▲ Manager E (9/96)	-4.49	30.01
▲ Manager F (4/90)	7.94	12.11
▲ Manager G (12/00)	1.20	12.46
△ Manager H (4/02)	9.32	8.36
▲ Manager I (6/01)	2.70	1.45
▲ Manager J (2/04)	3.52	11.73
▲ Manager K (11/05)	4.02	2.85
● Portfolio Totals	11.06	12.50
● Asset Weighted Blend	9.94	12.82
○ 90-day T-Bills	4.10	0.51

Illustration 19-5

The scattergram in Illustration 19-6 shows that the managers in this sample have varying risk and return profiles (their correlation to one another), yet blend together to create a portfolio that exceeds the return expectation of the asset weighted blend and maintains the risk profile outlined in the investment policy. The risk-return expectations are represented by the dot in the center of the cross-hairs. The goal is again, to have the *"Portfolio Total"* in the northwest quadrant of the graph, which is achieved by this portfolio. This blend of managers resulted in excess comparative returns and reduced volatility. A positive alpha is achieved utilizing strategic diversification among different investment styles.

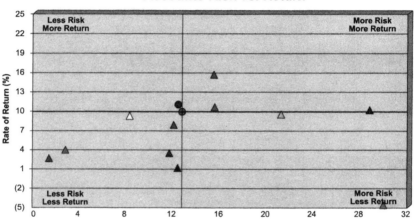

Accounts Risk vs. Return

	Return%	Standard Deviation
▲ Manager A (11/91)	10.24	28.82
▲ Manager B (5/92)	15.74	15.50
△ Manager C (10/96	9.57	21.24
▲ Manager D (4/90)	10.70	15.57
▲ Manager E (9/96)	-4.49	30.01
▲ Manager F (4/90)	7.94	12.11
▲ Manager G (12/00)	1.20	12.46
△ Manager H (4/02)	9.32	8.36
▲ Manager I (6/01)	2.70	1.45
▲ Manager J (2/04)	3.52	11.73
▲ Manager K (11/05)	4.02	2.85
● Portfolio Totals	11.06	12.50
● Asset Weighted Blend	9.94	12.82
○ 90-day T-Bills	4.10	0.51

Illustration 19-6

Absolute return versus Relative return: Many evaluate a manager's performance solely on the basis of his or her "absolute return;" how much money did the manager make (or lose) this month, quarter or year. This limited assessment does not do justice to style diversification or the manager's role in meeting the investor's objectives and risk profile, but it does aid in manager evaluation. To more effectively evaluate the contribution that a manager makes to the overall process, performance should be evaluated on a relative basis; comparing the manager to their benchmark (Illustration 19-7). The "relative return" will tell the consultant and investor if the manager is adding performance value when compared to their representative benchmark (index).

	Return %	Index	Index Return%
Manager A (11/91)	10.24	Russell 2000	11.09
Manager B (5/92)	15.74	MSCI World	9.17
Manager C (10/96)	9.57	MSCI EAFE	6.21
Manager D (4/90)	10.70	S&P Composite	11.04
Manager E (9/96)	-4.49	Russell 3000	16.03
Manager F (4/90)	7.94	Russell 1000 Value	12.31
Manager G (12/00)	1.20	Russell 2000 Growth	3.44
Manager H (4/02)	9.32	Russell MidCap Value	13.60
Manager I (6/01)	2.70	90-day T-Bills	1.94
Manager J (2/04)	3.52	Barclay CTA	2.19
Manager K (11/05)	4.02	MSCI EMer Mkts	14.69
Your Portfolio	11.06	Asset Weighted Blend	9.94

Illustration 19-7

We again see the pros and cons of two different approaches to reporting returns, absolute versus relative. Seek reporting software that gives both, as a manager's style will not always be in the strongest area of the market in absolute terms, but he or she may be achieving excellent relative performance and adding value to the objectives of the overall portfolio.

RISK-ADJUSTED PERFORMANCE

The analysis illustrated in the sample report shows the **risk-adjusted performance** of individual managers as well as that of the total portfolio. This analysis is a powerful tool for the consultant and investor. It shows both the true value of the manager selection and that of the portfolio design, as well as their adherence to the investment policy. It provides comparative data to help answer the due diligence question, "Does the portfolio as a whole, and

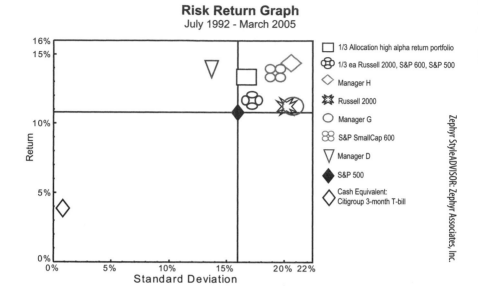

Risk Return Graph
July 1992 - March 2005

Risk Return Table

	Return (%)	Std Dev (%)	Downside Risk (%)	Beta vs. Benchmark	Alpha vs. Benchmark	R-Squared vs. Benchmark	Sharpe Ratio	Tracking Error vs. Benchmark
1/3 Allocation high alpha return portfolio	13.29	16.68	12.42	0.9227	2.08	90.77	0.5640	5.2307
1/3 ea Russell 2000, S&P 600, S&P 500	11.69	17.17	12.63	1.0000	0.00	100.00	0.4547	0.0000
Manager H	14.38	20.57	14.63	0.9013	3.83	79.09	0.5104	9.6061
Russell 2000	11.25	20.20	14.68	1.0000	0.00	100.00	0.3647	0.0000
Manager G	11.29	20.73	14.94	0.9776	-1.61	82.81	0.3573	8.5903
S&P SmallCap 600	13.65	19.22	14.09	1.0000	0.00	100.00	0.5084	0.0000
Manager D	13.92	13.70	10.33	0.7106	4.88	68.63	0.7330	8.9208
S&P 500	10.80	15.96	11.79	1.0000	0.00	100.00	0.4333	0.0000

Ilustration 19-8

the managers individually, produce a comparative return that both meets or exceeds the investment objectives and, reduces the risk of the portfolio?" In other words, "Did the manager and consultant (portfolio design and manager selection) earn their keep?"

Some institutions and manager selection searches use data provided by a few industry-based databases that offer performance analysis and/or performance evaluations. Illustration 19-8 is an example of one such analysis. It provides the risk and return information that have been discussed in chapters 18 and 19, including individual and blended benchmarks and individual and blended managers. Consultants are able to access the databases and performance monitoring software that is commercially available, but these sources are very pricey and thus not readily available to most individuals.

Illustration 19-8 builds on 18-6, and shows the effects of blending three manager styles and their respective benchmarks. There is a smoothing effect on overall volatility and performance when the blend is compared to each individual manager and, the blended portfolio produces a positive alpha when compared to the blend of benchmarks, improving on both performance and volatility.

EVALUATING A LAGGING MANAGER

When looking at the results of a lagging manager, representing a specific investment style, how do you effectively evaluate their results? The performance evaluation process will determine the nature of the manager's underperformance and therefore alert the consultant if there is cause for concern. A manager's performance may lag:

- An absolute number or,
- A relative comparison

When striving to achieve a risk-adjusted return, **absolute** comparisons are not a primary concern. It is however, human nature to make this mental comparison and investors can become concerned if a manager's returns are different than those of some standard, e.g. the Dow. Limiting one's analysis to this single comparison is a very common trap for those who are not well versed in performance evaluation and it is the consultant's role to keep all numbers in their proper perspective. We have discussed in detail throughout this book the virtues of diversification and its role in realizing investment goals and managing risk. Diversification requires the mixing of asset classes and/or styles and at times, one will outperform, while another will lag. These differences are inherent when portfolios are diversified among styles that have a "low correlation" to one another and expected in risk managed portfolio designs. The consultant must ask, "Is the portfolio meeting or exceeding the return expectations, reducing volatility and minimizing risk?" Moreover, "What role is the manager playing in meeting the investment objective?" There are certainly times when areas of the market represent either more opportunity or more risk, and it is the role of the consultant to reallocate by over- and/or underweighting different investment styles when appropriate. We have described how a manager's style may simply be out of favor; this alone is not reason for concern unless the investor's only objective is to meet or exceed a specific (absolute) return, but this expectation is rare.

When a manager's **relative** return is lagging, the consultant must first look at the benchmark. A benchmark analysis may reveal that the benchmark has varied from its norm, such as the S&P 500 in the late 1990s, when technology exposure and overall valuations were significantly higher than the norm and the index was being driven by a very few, very risky stocks or, in 2003, when low quality stocks significantly outperformed. In both cases, there were very valid reasons for many managers to underperform their benchmarks. As we have seen, indexes are rarely a perfect fit for active managers and there are times when benchmark analysis is necessary. The Sharpe ratio, information ratio, R-squared and tracking error are all useful in making this analysis.

A manager may lag his or her relative benchmark by design. Capital preservation and low volatility may be the manager's primary investment style and in these cases, the consultant will focus the manager's standard deviation, expecting it to be low relative to other standards. If this manager was selected for this investment style, then somewhat lower returns may not be cause for concern. Again, the manager's value-added performance, both quantitatively and qualitatively, is the criteria on which the consultant will focus.

The consultant must be able to explain why lagging returns for a money manager do not necessarily indicate that a change is in order, as long as the manager's risk-adjusted performance is on track. Proper due diligence in the selection process will generally alleviate short-term concerns. Making changes too often or too quickly is ill-advised and can lead to poor long-term results, so do your homework early and often. Performance evaluation is one of the value-added services the consultant provides to the investor, as ongoing monitoring is essential to all successful investing. It is through this analysis that the investment management process comes full circle.

MANAGER TERMINATION

There are many factors that will go into the decision to terminate a manager. We will list a number of possible reasons to terminate, which may include the consultant's "gut" feelings. If information about the manager or the management firm becomes unsettling, it is generally unwise to take a "wait and see" posture. A great deal of financial damage can be done in a short period of time. When reviewing managers, consider the following quantitative and qualitative factors:

1. Key changes within the money management firm may negate many of the reasons for originally hiring the manager. Evaluate the following on that basis:
   - Investment philosophy or style.
   - Significant changes in the investment process.
   - Style drift.
   - Personnel changes: Did the portfolio manager leave or is their conflict within the firm?
   - Ownership changes: When a money management firm is purchased by a larger entity, such as a bank or brokerage firm, decision-making and investment philosophy most often change.
   - Other significant organizational changes.
   - Performance lags.
2. Changes in the investor's financial situation, goals or risk tolerance may make a manager no longer suitable.
3. Substantial changes in the market environment may increase the risk of a management style to an unacceptable level or, the cyclical underperformance of a style may make other styles more suitable to the investor. As an example, in 1999 and 2000, large cap growth became extremely overvalued on a historical basis, while the small and mid cap areas of the markets offered more opportunity with less risk.

Reasons for a change must be communicated to the investor and the consultant and the investor should discuss the tax consequences of termination. If the reasons for terminating a manager are compelling, tax consequences should not prevent a manager change. During 2000 to 2003, a 20% capital gains tax was much more palatable than the 30%, 50%, or even 80% loses realized by some investors.

CONCLUSION

We have described many tools that consultants use to evaluate returns, but we cannot over-emphasize the need to relate all data to the investor's goals and objectives. The consultant must make all asset allocation and manager recommendations in accordance with the investor's objectives and risk tolerance. Raw rates of return, examined in isolation, can often create a very incomplete picture of the manager's performance and do not express their contribution to risk management and portfolio design. Good returns do not indicate the type of risk the manager is taking to produce that rate of return, nor does it offer any other insight into how the manager might do going forward. To accurately evaluate a manager's performance, the consultant must integrate risk management, standard deviation and investor goals, all of which are important drivers of portfolio design and manager selection. Comprehensive performance analysis and evaluations allow the consultant to make the comparisons necessary to select and effectively monitor managers.

SECTION V

Fiduciary Investing: An Essential Guide
for Trustees, Plan Sponsors
and Investment Professionals

SECTION V
Fiduciary Investing: An Essential Guide for Trustees, Plan Sponsors and Investment Professionals

In this section, we will discuss a variety of trusts and plans that require individuals to assume fiduciary responsibilities and how the Investment Management Consulting Process can assist these individuals in properly fulfilling these duties. We will cover the following topics:

Standards for Fiduciaries
- Prudent Man Rule
- Prudent Expert Rule
- Prudent Investor Rule
- Uniform Prudent Investor Act (UPIA)
- ERISA and the Department of Labor (DOL)
- Uniform Management of Public Employees Retirement Systems Act (1997) (UMPERS)

Investment Professionals and the Delegation of Fiduciary Duties
- Non- ERISA plans and trusts
- ERISA plans
- 401(k) plans

Foundations, Endowments and Other Trusts

ERISA and Fiduciary Liability
- General plans such as Define Benefit or profit-sharing
- 401(k) plans

Questionnaires and Sample Policy Statements *(see Appendices B and C)*

20

Standards for Fiduciaries (Prudent Investing Rules and Regulations)

In this chapter, we will begin to describe the duties and expectations of fiduciaries, as it is essential that trustees and plan sponsors focus on these requirements. Fiduciaries are those individuals who exercise any authority or control over assets that are entrusted to them for the benefit of others. Most are specifically named, however it is important to note, that being considered a fiduciary is determined by the role played by the individual, not necessarily the title. Naming an individual in documents may or may not make them a fiduciary and conversely, an individual may be a fiduciary without having been named as such. We will continue to emphasize this point throughout this section, as there are many individuals who are unaware of their responsibilities and their exposure to liability.

Fiduciaries are guided by the standards of care set forth by the following:

- Prudent Man Rule
- Prudent Expert Rule
- Prudent Investor Rule
- Uniform Prudent Investor Act (UPIA)
- ERISA and the Department of Labor (DOL)
- Uniform Management of Public Employees Retirement Systems Act (1997) (UMPERS)

TYPES OF FIDUCIARY REGULATIONS AND APPLICABLE FUNDS

	Corporate Retirement	Public Retirement	Taft-Hartley	Foundation Endowment	Private Trusts
Legislation	ERISA	UMPERS	ERISA	UPIA	UPIA
Oversight	DOL, IRS, PBGC	State Attorney General	DOL, IRS	State Attorney General	State Attorney General

We will quote from several sections of the Prudent Investor Rule and the Uniform Prudent Investor Act and include other rules and processes that should guide a fiduciary's actions. These investment standards must be met in order for trustees and plan sponsors to properly fulfill their responsibilities and duties. It is our opinion that the investment management consulting process can assist fiduciaries in understanding their duties and provide them with a disciplined process to comply with the required standards of care.

Looking at the more recent prudent investing criteria, combined with the other standards of the "Prudent Man Rule," the "Prudent Expert Rule" and the "Modern Portfolio Theory," it is clear that the standards for fiduciaries have been intensified. Plans governed by ERISA require the even higher standard of Prudent Expert.

THE PRUDENT MAN RULE

"All that is required of a trustee to invest is that he shall conduct himself faithfully and exercise sound discretion. He is to observe how men of prudence, discretion and intelligence manage their own affairs, not in regard to speculation, but in regard to the permanent disposition of their funds, considering the probable income, as well as the probable safety of the capital to be invested."

Some states allow the fiduciary to invest in securities that a prudent man of discretion and intelligence would select with regard to a reasonable income and preservation of capital. Other states require that the fiduciary only invest in a list of securities designated by the state (legal list), while others require fiduciaries to uphold the Prudent Investor Act.

PRUDENT EXPERT RULE

ERISA applies a revised version of the Prudent Man Rule to pension and profit sharing portfolios. The main addition that they made is that the fiduciary must act as someone with familiarity with matters relating to the management of money, not just prudence. A fiduciary must manage a portfolio *"with the care, skill, prudence and diligence, under the circumstances then prevailing, that a prudent man acting in a like capacity and **familiar with such matters** would use in the conduct of an enterprise of a like character and with like aims..."*

Complying with this level of oversight requires that the fiduciary be both prudent and experienced.

PRUDENT INVESTOR RULE

The Prudent Investor Rule, as stated in the *Restatement of the Law Third, Trusts: Prudent Investor Rule,* 1992, was established to provide investment standards for trusts and is the current standard by which most fiduciaries must act.

§ 227. General Standard of Prudent Investment

The trustee is under a duty to the beneficiaries to invest and manage the funds of the trust as a prudent investor would, in light of the purposes, terms, distribution requirements, and other circumstances of the trust.

a. This standard requires the exercise of reasonable care, skill and caution, and is to be applied to investments not in isolation but in the context of the trust portfolio and as a part of an overall investment strategy, which should incorporate risk and return objectives reasonably suitable to the trust.

b. In making and implementing investment decisions, the trustee has a duty to diversify the investments of the trust unless, under the circumstances, it is prudent not to do so.

c. In addition, the trustee must:

1. conform to fundamental fiduciary duties of loyalty (§ 170) and impartiality (§ 183);

2. act with prudence in deciding whether and how to delegate authority and in the selection and supervision of agents (§ 171); and

3. incur only costs that are reasonable in amount and appropriate to the investment responsibilities of the trusteeship (§ 188).

d. The trustee's duties under this section are subject to the rule of § 228, dealing primarily with contrary investment provisions of a trust or statute.

Fiduciaries now have specific standards to meet and must be more deliberate in investment decisions, well beyond the older standard of "prudent man." As the General Standard of Prudent Investment states and later as we discuss the UPIA, fiduciaries must attend to the following:

- **Diversification:** Sound diversification is fundamental to risk management and is therefore ordinarily required of trustees.
- **Risk and return:** These two inseparable elements of asset allocation decisions must be analyzed in relationship to objectives, risk tolerance, liquidity requirements and other circumstances that may affect the trust. Investment risk should be measured and taken only when it is judged likely to contribute to desirable investment performance for the portfolio as a whole.
- **Fees and expense:** Trustees have a duty to contain costs and must be able to justify expenses to the trust.
- **Impartiality:** The fiduciary duty of impartiality requires a balance between the elements of production of income and the protection of purchasing power. Strategies designed only to generate current income and preserve principal are likely to be inadequate due to the effects of inflation. It is often more prudent to invest both for income and capital appreciation.
- **Delegation:** Trustees may have a duty as well as having the authority to delegate as prudent investors would.

UNIFORM PRUDENT INVESTOR ACT

The Uniform Prudent Investor Act (UPIA) was approved by the American Bar Association in 1995 and draws upon the *Restatement of the Law Third, Trusts: Prudent Investor Rule,* 1992. The UPIA applies to "trustees" of private gratuitous trusts and some believe the language is less stringent than that of ERISA. It has been adopted by most states and it is rapidly becoming the accepted standard for trustees of non-qualified trust assets. This revision of trust investment law is in recognition of the changes that have occurred in the practice of investment management and, most significantly, the acceptance of the "Modern Portfolio Theory" (Chapter 9). The Modern Portfolio Theory entails a methodology and process designed to manage risk while striving to achieve a reasonable return. It is the relationship between risk and return that is the key driving element of the UPIA. A trustee, who invests and manages trust assets, owes a duty to the beneficiaries of the trust to comply with the Prudent Investor Rule set forth in this Act.

The UPIA makes five fundamental changes to the criteria for prudent investing, which we list here to emphasis how the standards of prudent practices are becoming more demanding.

1. Balancing risk and return is identified as the fiduciary's central consideration.
2. The standard of prudence is applied to the entire portfolio, rather than individual investments.
3. Categoric restrictions on types of investments have been dropped (legal list), however investments must play a role in achieving the risk/return objectives.
4. Fiduciaries must diversify their investments.
5. Delegation of investment and management functions is now permitted.

What is proper diversification and how are risk and return evaluated and managed? These decisions must be made prudently and must adhere to the overall objectives for the assets. Most individuals who are not investment professionals may have difficulty with these and other allocation questions, yet it is by these standards that fiduciaries will be measured.

In outlining the Uniform Prudent Investor Act (UPIA), we will make several comparisons to ERISA standards that will appear in italics. UPIA and ERISA are the two modern statutory models that govern the actions of fiduciaries and they are used by many states as the standard for fiduciary regulation. We believe that it is therefore helpful to compare and differentiate the two. The Uniform Prudent Investor Act is a model for the oversight of investing trust assets. This act, in conjunction with ERISA standards, provides a structure from which fiduciaries can act and, these are the standards that courts use to adjudicate the cases that come before them. Each model has different requirements, as well as strengths and weaknesses, so it is incumbent upon those who have a fiduciary role to clearly understand their responsibilities in order to properly perform their duties. ERISA standards will be described in more detail in the following chapters.

The Uniform Prudent Investor Act provides the following investment standards for fiduciaries of trusts:

Section 1. PRUDENT INVESTOR RULE states that a trustee who invests and manages trust assets owes a duty to the beneficiaries of the trust to comply with the Prudent Investor Rule, however this can be varied by the settler or grantor of the trust. *ERISA standards apply to all fiduciaries regardless of their "title."*

Section 2. STANDARD OF CARE; PORTFOLIO STRATEGY; RISK AND RETURN OBJECTIVES

(a) A trustee shall invest and manage trust assets as a prudent investor would, by considering the purposes, terms, distribution requirements, and other circumstances of the trust. In satisfying this standard, the trustee shall exercise reasonable care, skill and caution. *ERISA has similar language.*

(b) A trustee's investment and management decisions respecting individual assets must be evaluated, not in isolation, but in the context of the trust portfolio as a whole and as a part of an overall investment strategy having risk and return objectives reasonably suited to the trust. *ERISA is silent on this important point, however the DOL has issued regulations under Section 404 of ERISA to suggest how fiduciaries should satisfy their investment duties. These include viewing each investment as part of the portfolio and its contribution to further the purposes of the plan, while considering the risk of loss and the opportunity for gain.*

(c) Among circumstances that a trustee shall consider in investing and managing trust assets are such of the following as are relevant to the trust or its beneficiaries:

(1) General economic conditions;

(2) The possible effect of inflation or deflation;

(3) The expected tax consequences of investment decisions or strategies;

(4) The role that each investment or course of action play within the overall trust portfolio, which may include financial assets, interests in closely held enterprises, tangible and intangible personal property, and real property;

(5) The expected total return from income and the appreciation of capital;

(6) Other resources of the beneficiaries;

(7) Needs for liquidity, regularity of income and preservation or appreciation of capital; and

(8) An asset's special relationship or special value, if any, to the purposes of the trust or to one or more of the beneficiaries.

ERISA offers little guidance in making investment decisions, however the DOL regulations under Section 404 of ERISA suggest that the liquidity and current return of the portfolio, achieved through proper diversification, be related to the anticipated cash flow requirements and funding objectives of the plan.

(d) The trustee shall make a reasonable effort to verify facts relevant to the investment and management of trust assets. *ERISA has this same requirement.*

(e) A trustee may invest in any kind of property or type of investment consistent with the standards of this Act. This language is a significant expansion of old trust law. *ERISA has no comparable provision.*

(f) A trustee who has special skills or expertise, or is named trustee in reliance upon the trustee's representation that the trustee has special skills or expertise, has a duty to use those special skills and expertise. *This subsection applies a higher standard to professional versus non-professional fiduciaries. There is no differentiation under ERISA.*

Again we see the need to balance risk and return with risk tolerance and investor circumstances. Allocations must be made to accommodate both concerns, as well as tax considerations in some instances. The portfolio must be monitored and evaluated on a regular basis, specifically as it relates to the investment policy. Specific investments or techniques are not prudent or imprudent per se, but must be evaluated as part of the overall portfolio and risk/return expectations. It is the trustee's task to invest at a risk level that is suitable to the purposes of the trust. There must be no self-dealing in any decisions that are made regarding these assets.

Section 3. DIVERSIFICATION states that "a trustee shall diversify the investment of the trust unless...the trust is better served without diversifying." This Act treats diversification as one of the fundamental elements of prudent investing. *ERISA also addresses the issue of diversification, using somewhat different language.*

Section 4. DUTIES AT INCEPTION OF TRUSTEESHIP deals with a new trusteeship and requires the trustee to dispose of unsuitable assets within a reasonable time. This requirement extends to investments that were proper when purchased, but are no longer proper. *ERISA does not address this topic.*

Section 5. LOYALTY, states that a trustee shall invest and manage the trust assets solely in the interest of the beneficiaries. *ERISA has a sole purpose and benefit standard.*

Section 6. IMPARTIALITY, states that the trustee must exercise prudence and impartiality if there is more than one beneficiary. *ERISA's "sole purpose and benefit" standard has a similar application.*

Section 7. INVESTMENT COSTS, states: "In investing and managing trust assets, a trustee may only incur costs that are appropriate and reasonable in relation to the assets, the purposes of the trust, and the skills of the trustee." Wasting money is imprudent and trustees are obligated to minimize costs. *ERISA has a similar standard.*

Section 8. REVIEWING COMPLIANCE, states that compliance with the Prudent Investor Rule is to be judged in light of the facts and circumstances that existed at the time the decision was made, not in hind-sight. *ERISA requires prudence in all decisions that affect the plan and implies a Prudent Expert standard.*

Section 9. DELEGATION OF INVESTMENT AND MANAGEMENT FUNCTIONS

    (a)   A trustee may delegate investment and management functions that a prudent trustee of comparable skill could properly delegate them under the circumstances. The trustee shall exercise reasonable care, skill and caution in:

        1)   Selecting an agent

2) Establishing the scope and terms of the delegation, consistent with the purposes and terms of the trust; and

3) Periodically reviewing the agent's actions in order to monitor the agent's performance and compliance with the terms of the delegation

(b) In performing a delegated function, an agent owes a duty to the trust to exercise reasonable care to comply with the terms of the delegation.

(c) A trustee who complies with the requirements of subsection (a) is not liable to the beneficiaries or to the trust for the decision or actions of the agent to whom the function was delegated.

(d) By accepting the delegation of a trust function from the trustee of a trust that is subject to the law of a state, an agent submits to the jurisdiction of the courts of that state.

The beneficiaries of the trust rely on the trustee to enforce these terms in the delegation of responsibilities and therefore it is wise to have a procedure in place that can be documented. *ERISA permits delegation under similar standards, however ERISA does not fully relieve a fiduciary from responsibility [Section 405(c)]. Under the ERISA standard, it is a violation not to seek assistance when it is prudent to do so.*

Although old law (1950s) had a non-delegation rule, newer law encourages delegation for most trustee or trustee-like fiduciaries. This newer position reflects a realization of the complexity of modern investing and the application of the Modern Portfolio Theory.

- The Uniform Trustee Powers Act (1964) authorizes trustees "to employ such persons, including attorneys, auditors, investment advisors, or agents...to advise and assist the trustee in the performance of his duties...."

- The Uniform Management of Institutional Funds Act (1972) (UMIFA) authorized the governing boards to delegate investment matters to outside investment advisors, investment counsel, managers, banks or trust companies.

- Employee Retirement Income Security Act of 1974 (ERISA): "...a fiduciary shall discharge his duties with respect to a plan solely in the interest of the beneficiaries and...with care, skill, and diligence under the circumstances then prevailing that a prudent man acting in a like capacity and familiar with such matters would use in the conduct of a enterprise of like character and with like aims...."

- Uniform Management of Public Employees Retirement Systems Act (1997) (UMPERS): UMPERS, which is specific to state, county and municipal retirement plans, and ERISA have very similar language and standards.
- Prudent Investor Rule (1992) provides that:
  - Delegation: "the trustee must...act with prudence in deciding whether and how to delegate to others...."
  - Charitable trusts: "In making investments of trust funds the trustee of a charitable trust is under a duty similar to that of the trustee of a private trust."
  - Charitable corporations: "The duties of the members of the governing board of a charitable corporation are generally similar to the duties of the trustee of a charitable trust."

The Department of Labor and the federal courts involved in DOL-initiated litigation have clearly indicated that they favor a well diversified portfolio approach to investment decisions and that they consider the use of independent investment professionals prudent. A review of case law reveals that fiduciaries whose investment strategies fail, may be protected from liability if they have prudently selected and delegated investment management to a consultant, while those who develop their own prudent strategy, without the assistance of a consultant, may be subject to the risk of being second-guessed should their strategy fail.

As we have seen, there are many duties for which the fiduciary will be held accountable and therefore a fiduciary will be well served to maintain a "fiduciary file." A fiduciary has a "duty to know" and a "duty to investigate" all matters that involve the assets for which they are responsible and maintaining a well documented file provides evidence of the steps taken to fulfill their obligations. This file should include documentation attesting to all of the fiduciary's actions, such as:

- An outline of the processes in place to carry out each of the fiduciary's duties

- The procedures followed by the fiduciary in making each decision regarding the assets entrusted to them
- An investment policy statement
- Procedures followed to assign responsibilities or delegate fiduciary duties to others

CONCLUSION

In this chapter we have begun to define and describe the responsibilities of a fiduciary. They boil down to seven standards of care of which every fiduciary should be aware.

1. Know the standards and who may have fiduciary liability; ignorance of one's duties is not a defense
2. Prepare an investment policy statement to act as a road map for all those involved with the management of the funds
3. Diversify assets in a manner consistent with the guidelines of the investment policy
4. Delegate to prudent experts following a documented, due diligence selection process
5. Control, monitor and document costs in a manner consistent with the services provided
6. Have a monitoring process in place that includes documentation for all those who have been delegated duties
7. Avoid conflicts of interest and prohibited transactions

Understanding these steps prepares fiduciaries to carry out their duties in the most effective manner possible, while complying with the governing laws. As we have seen, the combination of the Prudent Man Rule, the Prudent Expert Rule, the Prudent Investor Rule and the Modern Portfolio Theory, make the role of "fiduciary" more challenging than ever before. In the following chapters, we will describe the responsibilities and potential liabilities of fiduciaries, and outline duties and processes that will help the fiduciary achieve the standard of "prudent investing."

21

Investment Professionals and the Delegation of Fiduciary Duties

A consultant plays a vital role in the investment process, while money managers make the day-to-day investment choices. Throughout this book, we have discussed various elements that are required to properly structure and manage portfolios. These skills are now expected and/or mandated for fiduciaries. Portfolio management has become increasingly more complex, requiring a sophisticated approach to asset allocation and risk management through the incorporation of the Modern Portfolio Theory (MPT). We have seen that small lapses in due diligence can result in large losses in portfolios and although no process can control the markets, a properly designed and managed portfolio can reduce and manage risk. A qualified consultant can provide the level of expertise that ERISA mandates and that trusts require, thus reducing the personal liability exposure of fiduciaries.

In this chapter, we will discuss the role of investment consultants in the management of assets entrusted to fiduciaries in the following types of trusts and plans:

- Non- ERISA trusts and plans
- General ERISA plans
- 401(k) plans

As we discussed in the previous chapter, trustees have an obligation to comply with the standards of the Prudent Investor Rule when investing assets for the benefit of others. In the following chapters, we will discuss how this duty is elevated to that of Prudent Expert when investing assets for plans governed by ERISA. If the trustees and fiduciaries are not qualified to effectively fulfill these duties, they are encouraged by these standards to delegate this responsibility to investment professionals. If they do not, this failure alone is considered a violation of ERISA standards and can result in personal liability for the fiduciary. Prudence dictates that fiduciaries seek the advice of individuals who possess the knowledge and skills to properly construct and manage an investment plan.

Four (4) basic elements are always prudent to employ when investing in the capital markets and these should be considered mandatory duties for fiduciaries.

1. Develop a well thought out investment policy or investment plan, which includes the standards by which performance can be judged. Review the policy annually.
2. Design an asset allocation that conforms to the goals and objectives of the investment policy, including risk tolerance and return expectations and, one that is properly diversified to enable risk management strategies.
3. Select appropriate investment vehicles, which can include individual securities, mutual funds and/or money managers.
4. Have an objective process in place to monitor and evaluate results.

Depending upon who is investing, and for what purpose, these four elements can be simple or quite complex. Unfortunately, many sponsors and trustees have not developed a written statement of investment objectives, nor do they have systems in place for defining or selecting investment vehicles and money managers, or reporting overall portfolio performance. Regardless of the size or type of plan or trust for which an individual or company has a fiduciary obligation, a qualified Investment Management Consultant can assist with the development of a sound investment plan including:

- The development of realistic, comprehensive investment policies (Chapter 8)
- An understanding of the complexities of risk and risk management (Chapter 9)
- Translating investment objectives and risk management into an appropriate asset allocation (Chapter 12)
- Analysis of investment options, which can include screening and recommending money managers (Section III) or other investment vehicles

- An ongoing monitoring and evaluation (Chapter 19) system

Successful investment management depends, now more than ever, on the disciplined processes found in the investment management consulting process. Consultants and money managers can provide assistance in delivering an effective investment strategy through the use of this process and significantly reduce the liability exposure for fiduciaries. If a fiduciary appoints investment advisors in accordance with the Prudent Investor Rule, the fiduciary is not held liable for the investment decisions made by these professionals.

When choosing a consultant, look for someone who has processes in place to aid the fiduciary in meeting the standards of care (Chapter 20) required of them. The consultant should be able to deliver independent, objective, unbiased advice. They should do so in an environment that is free of conflicts and results in a cost effective structure. (Refer to Chapter 6 for a sample of questions that can be used when selecting a consultant.)

NON- ERISA PLANS AND TRUSTS

Smaller trusts or plans, such as family trusts or small endowments, may only need an appointed co-trustee, such as a consultant, to assist in investment decisions and to help establish and implement an appropriate investment plan. Depending on its complexity, the consultant can meet with the trustees on an annual or semi-annual basis for review. This level of involvement is generally provided on a fee-for-service basis or an asset-based fee.

Trustees of larger trusts will be wise to have a consultant continuously monitor the trust. The consultant can be compensated with either an annual fee or an asset-based fee. Since no fiduciary should spend money unwisely, there should be a cost analysis done prior to choosing a compensation structure. Although there may seem to be an inherent conflict of interest, the consultant has the skills to assist in this analysis. Remember to include all fees or charges that the trust might incur, including custodial fees and transaction costs. If the trust is large enough to diversify through individual money managers, the process expands to manager searches and the proper monitoring and evaluation of the overall portfolio. These trusts should most likely have a "full time" consultant compensated with an asset-based fee.

Regardless of the size of the trust or plan, or the complexity of the process, this duty is time consuming and requires specific investment skills. Trustees should evaluate the time commitment and their comfort level with the complexity of the process that will be required for their situation. As we will see in Chapter 22, trustees of non-ERISA plans can be subject to monetary damages and personal liability if they fail to meet the standards of the Prudent Investor Rule and UPIA.

GENERAL ERISA PLANS

Delegation to Investment Professionals

As we will see in Chapter 23, the typical fiduciary will likely be unable to meet many of ERISA's requirements without professional assistance. The Prudent Expert Rule alone is a sobering mandate for investing, but the writing of investment objectives, creating and maintaining a risk appropriate asset allocation, selecting managers and establishing monitoring criteria for the plan's assets are also key areas requiring compliance. Under ERISA, it is considered prudent to seek out expert advice when the fiduciary lacks the experience or knowledge to properly evaluate investments or carry out his or her fiduciary duties. Due to the complexities of investment management, it is therefore prudent to seek the assistance of investment professionals.

The delegation of plan asset management provides two specific benefits to the plan and fiduciary. First, it fulfills the obligation under the Prudent Expert Rule, and secondly, the trustee is not liable as a co-fiduciary for any acts or omissions of a discretionary money manager.

ERISA encourages fiduciaries to use financial professionals, especially money managers. By stressing the use of professional money managers, the Department of Labor is giving tacit recognition to the fact that most fiduciaries do not possess the necessary skills to adequately discharge their duties; therefore, working with a consultant and money manager/s is often the only prudent course of action. Only a named fiduciary can delegate responsibility for the management of plan assets, and delegation is permitted only if the plan instrument expressly provides procedures for such delegation or designation and, it is carried out in accordance with such procedures. Once the investment professional accepts this position, he or she then has a fiduciary responsibility to the plan.

A fiduciary who delegates responsibility for management or control of plan assets, to any person other than a professional investment advisor (consultant and/or money manager) as defined by ERISA, remains liable for that person's acts and omissions. Conversely, if done properly, much of the fiduciary's liability can be avoided if a consultant and money managers are appointed. A trustee of a plan whose assets are managed by a money manager will not be responsible for the manager's investment choices, any acts, or an omission of the manager unless the trustee knowingly takes part in, or conceals a breach of fiduciary responsibility by the manager. Nonetheless, the trustee will retain "oversight" responsibility for the acts of the consultant and money manager/s, and must have a reporting, monitoring and evaluation procedure in place.

The delegation of investment duties should start with the selection of a qualified consultant, who will then assist the plan sponsors with the entire investment process. The steps that plan sponsors should consider are:

- The prudent selection of a qualified consultant. The selection process can be done through the use of a Request for Proposal (RFP), as we illustrated in Chapter 6.
- The consultant selected should have the skills to:
  - (a) write an investment policy containing specific investment objectives and guidelines, and
  - (b) determine a risk appropriate asset allocation
- The consultant will then screen and recommend appropriate investment vehicles (money managers, mutual funds, etc.). This process may include manager RFPs (Chapter 15).
- The consultant should be well versed in performance analysis and have a performance monitoring system in place.

The Department of Labor gives little guidance in this area, but strongly urges fiduciaries to improve the odds of providing better results by selecting investment professionals. They do state that monitoring the prudence of the investment is a two-step process:

1. *Funding and investment policies should be determined and should be set down in writing as a written investment policy.* This language suggests, but does not mandate a written investment policy statement.
2. *Managers doing the investing must be found capable and appropriate.* The plan sponsor should be aware that suitable money managers:

- Must be registered with the SEC under the Investment Advisors Act of 1940 (unless exempt, as are most banks and insurance companies). Request the managers ADV Part I & II (Appendix D) to verify this information.
- Must acknowledge their fiduciary status in writing.

Any professional providing advice must do so pursuant to a written agreement between themselves and the plan and they must have an understanding of their role in the management of the plan. This requirement includes the consultant and money managers, who must adhere to the investment plan as it is set forth in the Investment Policy Statement and all professionals must be prudently monitored in order for the fiduciaries to reduce their liability.

Although ERISA does not specifically address guidelines for the delegation process, Section 9 of the Uniform Prudent Investor Act (Chapter 20) does, and the language of this act provides a reasonable approach.

(a) A trustee may delegate investment and management functions that a prudent trustee of comparable skill could properly delegate under the circumstances. The trustee shall exercise reasonable care, skill and caution in:

1) Selecting an agent
2) Establishing the scope and terms of the delegation, consistent with the purposes and terms of the trust
3) Periodically reviewing the agent's actions in order to monitor the agent's performance and compliance with the terms of the delegation

For those plan sponsors that delegate any part of their fiduciary duties, following the recommendations of Section 9 is likely to be considered "best practices."

In plans governed by ERISA, which we will cover in the following chapters, the fiduciary is held to the standards of the Prudent Expert Rule and subject to penalties and personal liability, as well as potentially affecting the tax-exempt status of the plan. This exposure obviously sets the compliance bar much higher and generally necessitates at least some involvement from an investment professional, such as a consultant and/or money manager/s.

Engaging a consultant to assist in compliance with ERISA will assist in meeting the requirements of Section 404(c) of the ERISA code, which if done properly, can create a "safe harbor" for 401(k) fiduciaries. We will cover Section 404(c) in detail in Chapter 24. It is important to remember that ERISA standards must be met, regardless of the size of the plan.

When considering the delegation of investment portfolio duties, two basic structures are used. The first, shown in Illustration 21-1, shows the separation of each of the major service areas (each charging a separate fee, Chapter 5), with the consultant acting solely in a third-party oversight capacity. He or she will advise on market conditions, money manager performance and asset allocations, but has no control over any element of the plan; each element reports back to the plan sponsor. This structure is often inefficient in making portfolio adjustments and places more responsibility on the plan sponsor in the coordination and implementation of decisions.

In Illustration 21-2, the consultant acts as a conduit for investment management, reporting to and advising the investment committee. The consultant executes decisions that are made with the committee, either directly with the

MAJOR SERVICE AREAS

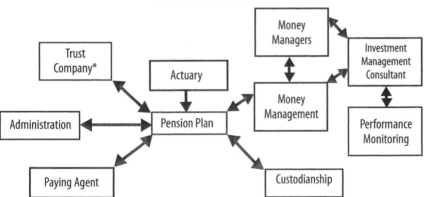

* Assets must be held in trust and the trust company provides an audit service verifying the securities in the portfolio.

Illustration 21-1

In this example, each of the service areas are separate, with the consultant producing the portfolio performance report, with information provided by the pension's money management (investment committee) and directly from the money managers. Consultants will generally report to a group of trustees who are elected or appointed to the position of oversight and who may receive data either by way of plan management or directly from the custodian.

money managers or through plan administration. In this case, the consultant, who is usually better able to manage the investment process, has more responsibility. This structure is a more efficient and less expensive way for investment management and information to flow, however it does eliminate some of the checks and balances that multiple parties may offer, placing more dependence on the service provided by the consultant.

INVESTMENT MANAGEMENT CONSULTING

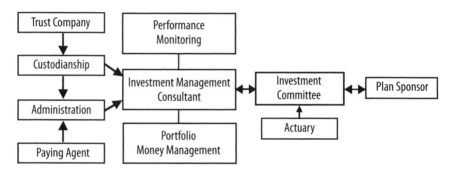

Illustration 21-2

In this example, the consultant gathers data from the custodian and/or plan administrator, then prepares the performance report, before reporting to the trustees of the investment committee. Any changes in asset allocation are carried out by the consultant.

When establishing the needs, safety and liquidity requirements of a pension plan, the fiduciary must consider many things, such as the balance between safety and growth and their tolerance to risk and volatility. Consultants have the skills required to make appropriate asset allocation decisions that balance risk and return.

Safety versus Growth

Fiduciaries must make investment decisions that balance the desire for safety with the need for growth. Many fiduciaries believe that the best method of operating conservatively (and not risking fiduciary liability exposure) is by investing in short-term CDs (certificates of deposit) or other passive money market instruments that produce income, but no growth. This example describes saving, not investing. As we have seen in our discussions of risk, by accepting the security of short-term passive investments, growth potential is lost and inflation can wipe out the minimal growth that interest earnings provide. Many studies have shown that over time, equities (common stocks) outperform fixed income securities and have produced returns that offset inflation and provide real growth in principal. Through the implementation of the Modern Portfolio Theory, growth can be achieved and risk managed. This growth can sometimes be sufficient to allow a plan to be perpetual.

Risk and Volatility

The "prudent man" knows higher returns sometimes require the assumption of higher risks, but how much risk is acceptable? Measuring the level of risk to be taken by a retirement plan is a matter of great concern. A consultant will develop a set of standards and an investment plan to mitigate the risks of investment, while striving to achieve a realistic return. The portfolio must also be designed in a manner that achieves a tolerable level of volatility, as some plans are subject to regular distributions and must have more predictability.

ERISA Standards

ERISA standards require that investment decisions be made with the skill and care of a prudent expert (Prudent Expert Rule). Prudent Expert is a high standard for corporate officers or investment committees to meet. ERISA also provides for a "safe harbor" against liability claims if, among other things, investment decisions have been made by properly appointed investment professionals. However, these appointments must be made prudently and all appointees must be monitored regularly. An Investment Management Consultant can play an invaluable role in helping plan sponsors satisfy these requirements and meet their responsibilities to the plan's participants.

If the plan sponsors decide to appoint a consultant, there must be a process in place for the selection, as this appointment must also be done with the "care, skill, prudence and diligence...that a prudent man in like capacity...would use...." The plan sponsors should endeavor to select an experienced, qualified Investment Management Consultant, seeking the same qualifications that were described in Chapter 6.

The consultant should have no financial link to the money management firms that the consultant recommends and his or her only compensation should come from the plan. Establishing this requirement will help to avoid conflicts of interest. If money management firms are used, the consultant must have a large number of money management firms about which he or she is knowledgeable and preferably has some working experience with them as well. This knowledge will enable the consultant to give unbiased opinions about appropriate money managers to the plan sponsors or trustees. If mutual funds are used, the consultant should have comprehensive analytical tools available to effectively evaluate the funds. The following are many of the duties required by ERISA that a qualified Investment Management Consultant can fulfill. Each is covered in detail in the following chapters.

1. **Develop an investment policy**—Policies for ERISA plans should lay out responsibilities, allocation parameters, and standards for measuring performance and plan procedures, in addition to the more standard elements of investment policies. The policy provides written guidelines for all to follow and by which fiduciaries will be evaluated.

2. **Create an asset allocation**—An appropriate asset allocation must be developed to meet the objectives and cash flow requirements of the plan. The allocation should consider return expectations, risk tolerance, time horizons and distribution schedules.

3. **Due diligence in the manager search**—Investment Management Consultants can offer plan sponsors access to a variety of professional money managers, and assist them in evaluating each firm's historical performance, philosophy, investment style and suitability to the plan (Chapter 15). This process can also be applied to mutual fund companies.

4. **The Manager Selection**—The plan sponsor is the ultimate decision-maker when hiring a money management firm or selecting mutual funds, however the consultant can be very helpful in this process. The professional money manager selection, which includes mutual funds, should be based on comprehensive criteria such as risk versus return, total years of management experience, dollars under management, staff size, level of communications, etc. The manager being considered must be a good fit on all levels, especially the relationship between the manager's philosophy and plan's risk tolerance, to be eligible to work with the plan sponsor. A good consultant will bring objectivity to the

selection process and will make it easier for the plan sponsor to understand the differences between the money managers or mutual funds being considered, and enable the plan sponsor to confidently make an informed decision.

5. **Ongoing monitoring and evaluation**—A qualified consultant will have reliable monitoring capabilities and processes in place. Monitoring criteria should be consistent with the plan's investment objectives, while allowing enough flexibility for the manager to practice their specialty. Establishing reasonable criteria is important, especially with respect to time frames, as most managers need at least three to five years to prove themselves. Three to five years can seem too long for many plan sponsors, therefore it is the consultant's role to communicate the relationship between the manager's style, market cycles and risk management. It is imperative for the plan sponsor to understand and feel comfortable with the money manager's investment style and philosophy, otherwise, the investor will not have the patience to allow the manager's discipline to produce the desired results (Chapter 19).

401(K) PLANS

401(k) plans are no different than any other plan or trust that is operated for the benefit of others. All individuals who exercise any control over the administration of the plan, including the selection and monitoring of the plan's investment options, have a fiduciary responsibility to the participants and under ERISA, can be held personally liable. 401(k) plans are generally the responsibility of the human resources department, as opposed to the treasury or finance department where other investments are generally administered, and the investment skills required to properly administer a 401(k) plan are generally outside the area of expertise of most human resource professionals.

More plan sponsors than ever before are utilizing the skills of investment consultants, as they realize the importance of unbiased, professional input to assure that the plans investment options are both appropriate for the workforce and in compliance with ERISA standards. Plan sponsors are realizing that they should not delegate this fiduciary function to their vendors or service providers, as their advice may be biased resulting in the potential for conflicts of interest.

401(k) plans are "self-directed", and because of this, many plan sponsors feel that their job is complete once the plan is set up and operating through a plan administrator and/or service provider. Unfortunately, it is not true and many unsuspecting human resource people and plan sponsors are finding themselves in the middle of lawsuits, brought on by the strikingly poor performance of some mutual funds and plans throughout the Bear market that began in 2000. 401(k) plans are only self-directed after a policy has been established and after all investment options have been selected by fiduciaries. These fiduciaries have the responsibility and control over the selection and monitoring of the investment options that are made available to the participants, and it is these individuals that often misunderstand their fiduciary role and potential exposure to liability.

Many plan sponsors have an adequate understanding of required 401(k) plan documentation, but few are qualified, or understand the necessity of, meeting the "Prudent Expert" standards of ERISA when applied to the selection and monitoring of investment options. Well-intentioned investment committees rarely rise to the level of "expert." Selecting and monitoring investment options is an area where the assistance of an investment professional can significantly reduce the liability exposure of fiduciaries, as few people outside of the investment industry understand how to properly analyze and select mutual funds for 401(k) plans.

- How are investment options (mutual funds) selected?
- Is there an adequate and appropriate mix of styles to enable the participant to properly diversify?
- How are the funds monitored in order to assure the participants that the funds that they have to choose from continue to be diverse (style drift analysis) and perform at least on par with their peers? (performance analysis)
- Are the funds' expense ratios reasonable? (cost analysis)
- Are all of the fees charged to the participants reasonable?

We will discuss the requirements of establishing and maintaining a 401(k) plan in Chapter 24, which, as with all investments, should start with a well thought out investment policy, provide for adequate diversification and risk management, and have a monitoring and evaluation process in place.

CONCLUSION

Consultants and money managers provide the levels of expertise that UPIA and ERISA require and allow trustees to focus on the many other requirements of properly administering trusts and plans. The consultant will design an investment plan that fulfills the purposes of the trust or plan in a way that will be most beneficial to its beneficiaries, while reducing the fiduciary's exposure to potential liability.

22

Foundations, Endowments and Other Trusts

In this chapter, we will describe the duties and responsibilities of those individuals entrusted with the management of investment assets for foundations, endowments, not-for-profit organizations and a myriad of other types of trusts. The topics we will cover include:

- The role of the fiduciary
- Basic investment principals
- Trustee responsibilities

These types of plans and trusts, which for the sake of consistency we will call "trusts" in this chapter, are governed by the standards of the Prudent Investor Rule and the Uniform Prudent Investor Act (UPIA). Anyone who acts as a trustee, or otherwise exercises any authority or control over any type of trust, has a "fiduciary" responsibility. Fiduciaries are expected to adhere to these standards and may be liable for damages assessed by the courts for breaches of this duty.

Interpreting the Prudent Man Rule of old, many trustees felt that an all bond portfolio or CDs (certificate of deposit) were the best way to avoid risk and minimize the potential for a loss of capital, whereas now, a well constructed portfolio utilizing multiple asset classes and styles is considered the standard for prudent investing. This modern asset management practice is a result of the general acceptance of the Modern Portfolio Theory, which clearly shows that diversification through asset allocation, can result in a portfolio with lower risk and better performance than one that it made up solely of bonds (Illustration 9-6).

This more active form of portfolio management requires the market knowledge and investment skills that we will discuss in this chapter and in the balance of this section. In support of this concept, Commonfund, which was founded in 1971 to improve investment management practices of nonprofit institutions, believes that "a portfolio that is based upon active investment choices, made by means of a well-articulated, repeatable investment process that takes risks commensurate with desired returns, should over the long term outperform a passive one. All sectors of the capital markets are dynamic. Therefore, we believe that active management includes strategically underweighting (relative to the investor's long-term equilibrium policy portfolio) those asset classes and sectors where capital is plentiful, prices are rich and the expected return is not commensurate with the risk and similarly, overweighting those assets where capital is scarce, prices are cheap and there is less risk relative to the expected return."

ROLE OF THE FIDUCIARY

Most foundations and endowments have the goals of self-sustainable growth and gifting. Fiduciaries are expected to invest trust assets in a prudent manner that will accommodate the spending policy, manage risk and sustain the trust. To fulfill these goals, the following steps should be taken:

- Develop an investment policy (refer to a sample questionnaire in Appendix B).
- Determine an effective risk management strategy.
- Develop an asset allocation mix to compliment spending goals and the risk management strategy.
- Select investment vehicles, which can include individual securities, mutual funds or professional money managers.
- Create and implement a system to continuously monitor and evaluate the portfolio. The evaluation should include the portfolio's compliance with the trust's goals of sustainability and gifting when applicable.

In addition to investment related duties, fiduciaries will be expected to maintain certain records, which include:

- A written investment policy and any documentation about decisions that are made regarding trust assets.
- Any statements, journals, appraisals, certificates or other documents.
- All reports involving the consultant, money managers, performance, annual copies of Form ADV for each money manager and any significant litigation against the money manager or key personnel.
- All documents involving other types of investment options considered, such as individual securities, mutual funds or alternative investments.
- All fees and expenses.
- All appropriate reporting, filing and disclosure requirements must be completed for the trust in a timely manner.

BASIC INVESTMENT PRINCIPLES

The following outline covers five broad areas, which set the standards for fiduciary conduct in administering a trust. These principles, which are embodied in the Prudent Investor Rules, instruct trustees and courts that:

1. Sound diversification is fundamental to risk management and is therefore ordinarily required of trustees.

2. Risk and returns are so directly related that trustees have a duty to analyze and make conscious decisions concerning the level of risk appropriate to the purposes, requirements and circumstances of the trust.

   The first two of these principles are fundamental to risk management. The duty to diversify has been incorporated into the Prudent Investor Rule and is also a basic tenant of the duty to exercise care and skill in investing.

3. Trustees have a duty to avoid fees, transaction costs, and other expenses that are not justified by the needs and realistic objectives of the trust's investment program.

   A trustee also has a duty to be cost sensitive and monitor such matters as the costs of commissions, agent fees, and management charges. In addition, the costs of active management strategies must be evaluated on a "value added" basis. Is an active management strategy likely to improve returns beyond its costs?

4. Fiduciary duty of impartiality requires a balance between return expectations, current income and the protection of purchasing power.

There must be sensitivity in investment management between the desire for returns and the need for income in a trust, or more broadly stated, the needs of tomorrow versus those of today.

5. Trustees may have the duty, as well as having the authority, to delegate as prudent investors would do in a similar circumstance.

Prudent investing may require or benefit from expert assistance in investment matters. There is authority under Probate Code §16006 to hold a trustee liable if they fail to seek advice in matters where they lack the skill or knowledge to make prudent investment decisions.

TRUSTEE RESPONSIBILITIES

The scope of trustee responsibility is much wider than generally recognized, mainly because the definition of "trustee" is very broad. To be thought of as a trustee there must be an element of authority or control over the trust, including trust management and administration or disposition of assets. "Named" trustees are those listed in the trust documents as having responsibility for the management of trust assets, but remember, an individual does not have to be named to be considered a fiduciary. It is an individual's role that will ultimately determine whether or not they are a fiduciary.

Investment professionals and trustees are fiduciaries if they provide advice on the value and advisability of owning investments, or have discretionary authority to purchase or sell investments with trust assets. It is important to note that if trustees properly select and appoint an investment professional, such as a qualified consultant and/or money manager, they will not have a co-fiduciary responsibility for acts and omissions of these professionals, unless they knowingly participate or try to conceal any such acts or omissions.

If the trustee feels that he or she needs help in fulfilling their duties and decides to appoint another trustee to assist in the process of properly administering the trust and/or investing the assets, then the two will be co-trustees, as a fiduciary can never fully discharge his or her total responsibility. Before appointing a co-trustee, the trustee must consider the cost. Is it cost effective and reasonable to hire a co-trustee? Many of the required duties are often performed by others, such as the custodian, consultant and/or money manager and therefore a co-trustee might be redundant and an unnecessary expense.

Delegation

Delegation of duties by fiduciaries is encouraged under the Prudent Investor Rule and UPIA, as it is recognized that properly fulfilling these standards will most likely require the use of investment professionals. This process should be clearly outlined in the investment policy and should include:

- Describe the selection process and the standards by which each will be evaluated
- Establish a monitoring procedure
- Establish performance standards for both the consultant and money managers
- Define reporting expectations; frequency and location

Although delegation is encouraged, the trustee/s must maintain their role of oversight. They should meet regularly with those to whom they have delegated duties and have a system in place to evaluate their performance and contribution to the management of trust assets.

Investment Policy

Trusts have the same need for an investment policy as do other plans and individuals, and the same criteria apply (Chapter 8). We will reiterate these here and include specific points that trustees should consider.

- Determine investment goals and objectives; what is the role of these funds in supporting the trust's mission?
- Establish reporting criteria, i.e., real returns (after taxes and/or inflation) versus nominal rates of return.
- Determine the criteria for selecting benchmarks and measuring performance. We have discussed many of the strengths and weaknesses of comparative benchmarks in this book, so it is important to establish how benchmarks will be used.

How will the performance of the portfolio and the managers be measured? Is there an expected rate of return and how will it be measured? Will it be compared to a benchmark in relative terms or in absolute percentages? State a realistic objective, as courts may focus on the return objective when determining a fiduciary's liability and limit exposure to any comparative shortfall. In contrast, if there is no objective stated, the calculation of damages is open to the court.

- Define risk and determine how it will apply to this portfolio
- Determine risk tolerance
- Establish a time period for review, evaluation and rebalancing
- Establish parameters for allowable investments and quality standards
- Determine liquidity requirements
- Establish policy asset allocation and re-allocation (rebalancing) guidelines; this will show an optimum balance between risk and return and ranges that will allow for changes in market conditions.
- Develop a procedure for selecting and/or terminating money managers and other investment options
- Project cash flow of the trust (both in and out). Foundations and Endowments often have a mandate to fund various endeavors, therefore a spending policy should be included providing guidelines for:
  - Determining a balance between funding the institution, meeting distribution obligations and paying operating expenses
  - How the institution will deal with a negative return from investments
- Define roles and responsibilities

Risk Management

All investments involve some risks; risk management assesses the potential for loss in making investment decisions. The duty of a trustee does not call for the avoidance of risk, but rather for the prudent management of risk. The management approach that is undertaken requires that careful attention be given to the trust's tolerance for risk and volatility.

Trustees have a duty to diversify, and asset allocation decisions are a fundamental aspect of a sound investment strategy. These decisions are also fundamental in the management of risk, which is an ongoing process of evaluation and asset re-allocation.

The degree of risk permitted for a particular trust is ultimately a matter for interpretation and judgment. It is important that trustees make a reasonable effort to understand the levels of risk and the types of investments that are suitable for the trust's assets.

An Evaluation of Risk versus Return

The concept of risk versus return is as important in trust portfolios as any other portfolio that we discuss in this book. A fiduciary must make every effort to minimize the risk of large losses. Importantly, this responsibility applies to the portfolio as a whole, thus adequate diversification will help to reduce losses due to concentrated holdings. When considering individual investments, each should be reviewed as to its impact on the total portfolio and its appropriateness for the trust's goals and objectives. This prudent investment strategy assures beneficiaries that trustees are following a reasonable process in the investment of assets.

Four criteria should be used to evaluate the risk and return characteristics of investment alternatives, namely:

1. In terms of liquidity, diversification, return and safety, each individual investment should be appropriate to the total portfolio.
2. Once the asset classes are selected (stock, bond, etc.), the fiduciary is required to find the prevailing rate of return for that asset class, given the appropriate levels of risk. In other words, the investment choice should represent the "fair" return, not necessarily the "highest," and the choice must be made in the context of the overall risk profile that has been established in the investment policy.
3. A fiduciary faced with investments of equal risk should not choose the one with the lower return if a higher return is available.
4. In order to evaluate alternatives, objective standards must be set forth in the investment policy against which to measure them.

Diversification of Assets

Diversification is fundamental to risk management and is a key element in reaching long-term goals, yet this concept is often overlooked or simply not understood by fiduciaries. Diversification among asset classes and styles is the most prudent action a fiduciary can take to protect the long-term health of the trust (Chapter 12). Determine the optimum relationship between investment choices, return expectations and risk tolerance.

In addition to risk management strategies, the following should be considered when evaluating an appropriate diversification model for the trust's portfolio:

- The amount of trust assets to be invested or otherwise considered
- Types of investments (stocks, bonds, real estate, etc.)
- Projected portfolio returns versus funding objectives. Are the return assumptions in balance with the funding capabilities and objectives? Will there be enough money to fulfill cash flow requirements if the return assumptions fall short?
- Volatility of investment returns
- Liquidity and future cash flows
- Funding or spending requirements and time lines
- Tax consequences
- Other resources available to the beneficiary
- The beneficiary's need for income, liquidity, preservation of capital or long-term appreciation needs
- An asset's special relationship or special value, if any, to the purposes of beneficiaries

Monitoring and Evaluation

Establishing a quarterly review of investment returns is vital. Trustees should review the performance of the investments in the account in relation to their appropriate benchmark, as well as understand any potential changes in the economy that may impact the portfolio (Chapter 19). This quarterly review should also provide a forum for open discussion with other trustees regarding all aspects of the trust's operation.

The following minimum standards should be considered when designing a monitoring process:

- Establish a time frame and frequency for review.
- Establish benchmarks (or indices) against which the investments will be judged.
- Review real returns versus nominal rates of return.
- Review risk and return objectives.
- Analyze investment performance on a risk-adjusted basis, relative to established benchmarks and trust objectives.

- Review any changes regarding investment professionals, such as the consultant and/or the money manager/s. Qualitative aspects, such as change of philosophy or management should be considered.
- If the trust has engaged other professionals to assist in the management of the trust's assets, these individuals must be monitored and evaluated as well.
- Discuss any changes in the trust's objectives.
- Discuss changes in market conditions that may affect the allocation of trust assets and any other issues that may materially affect the management of trust assets.

Evaluating performance, service and risk is an effective way to determine if the assets are being appropriately managed and it is this information that will allow the trustees to facilitate future changes when needed. The Investment Policy Statement should be reviewed annually to ensure that the contents remain valid.

CONCLUSION

Trustees are now held to the standards of the Prudent Investor Rule and the Uniform Prudent Investor Act (UPIA) and can be subject to monetary liability for failure to act prudently and in compliance with the UPIA. Many of these standards require the skills of individuals who are proficient in investment management and therefore, trustees rely on Investment Management Consultants, who are expert in fulfilling the requirements of the Act. Many trustees are unaware of their exposure, as the UPIA was first approved in 1995 and must be accepted on a state-by-state basis. Trustees should familiarize themselves with the UPIA, as courts are utilizing these standards to adjudicate trustee—beneficiary disputes. Trustees who institute the processes contained in *Fiduciary Investing* and *The Art and Science of Investment Management Consulting* will have taken the prudent steps necessary to comply with the Act, thus enabling them to successfully defend their actions.

23

ERISA and Fiduciary Responsibility

"Fiduciaries must act with the care, skill, prudence, and diligence under the circumstances then prevailing that a prudent man acting in a like capacity and familiar with such matters would use in the conduct of an enterprise of a like character and with like aims."

ERISA 404(a)(1)(B)

Prior to 1974, bank trust departments and large insurance companies managed most corporate and public funds. There was little accountability and no performance monitoring standards. In 1974, the Employee Retirement Income Security Act (ERISA) was enacted to protect the beneficiaries of private-sector retirement and welfare plans, and radically altered how employee benefit plans were to be managed. The magnitude and complexity of ERISA has led to a widespread lack of understanding of its basic implementation principles and a commensurate lack of understanding of the fiduciary liabilities that these create. We tend to think of employee retirement plans as profit-sharing plans, pension plans and 401(k) plans. However, any plan maintained by an employer for the benefit of employees is covered by ERISA, including stock bonus plans, insurance plans (life, health, and disability), welfare plans and vacation and scholarship funds. (Public-sector plans and plans sponsored by churches are not covered by ERISA.)

As a rule, only the more egregious violations have made their way to the courts, but this is likely to change. Employee benefit plans have grown steadily and now constitute a major source of private investment capital. By 2004, these plans held in the neighborhood of $3 trillion in assets[1]. Perhaps in response to the capital that is now part of these plans, or in responds to the damage done to employee benefit plans during the Bear market that began in 2000, the Department of Labor (DOL) has dramatically increased its audit force and its scrutiny of these plans. Expect a much greater focus on participant issues, including diversification, investment options, education and risk management by the DOL. Plan sponsors and fiduciaries will be well advised to thoroughly understand ERISA standards and the "safe harbor" provisions of Section 404(c) of the ERISA code (described later in this chapter).

Under Section 404(a)(1)(B) of the ERISA code, employee benefit plans must be "managed... with the care, skill, prudence and diligence, under the circumstances then prevailing, that a prudent man acting in a like capacity and **familiar with such matters** would use in the conduct of an enterprise of a like character and with like aims...." This language implies that fiduciaries must be both prudent and experienced in the management of investments in order to meet the mandated level of skill now required for ERISA plans. Fiduciaries of ERISA plans are now expected to meet the standards of the Prudent Expert Rule, not solely those of the Prudent Man Rule and they will be measured against those individuals who are knowledgeable in retirement plan investing. These plans are "qualified plans," meaning that they are given favorable tax treatment, but in order for the plan to maintain its tax-exempt status, it must stay in compliance with ERISA under the Internal Revenue Code. To meet this standard and to prevent personal liability exposure for the fiduciaries, all areas of management and administration of the plan must comply with ERISA standards.

This chapter is designed to assist plan sponsors in becoming aware of the responsibilities they have as fiduciaries and the penalties that could be imposed if they do not comply with ERISA standards. The investment management consulting process will provide plan sponsors of pension and profit sharing plans with many of the processes required to effectively comply with ERISA and the plan's investment objectives. 401(k) plans are also regulated by ERISA, and have some inherent differences which we will cover separately in Chapter 24. Both chapters provide a framework that allows plan sponsors to develop a system of compliance to properly fulfill their fiduciary obligations. It is in the

---

1. Handbook on ERISA Litigation, second edition, James F. Jorden, Waldemar J. Pflepsen, Jr., and Stephen H. Goldberg, Aspen Law & Business.

implementation and maintenance of the ERISA standards that plan sponsors can protect themselves from personal liability. And, we should add, scrupulous documentation every step of the way.

We will describe many of the standards required by ERISA in an attempt to bring some procedural clarity to these regulations. We will include information regarding:

- Plan documents
- Service providers
- Identifying fiduciaries and their responsibilities
- The basic principals of ERISA compliance
- Developing an Investment Plan
  - Investment Policy Statement (refer to sample questionnaire in Appendix B and sample policies in Appendix C)
  - Diversification of assets
  - Evaluating risk and return
  - Expense control
  - Prohibited transactions
  - Monitoring and evaluation of performance
- Monitoring and evaluation of appointed fiduciaries
- Documentation
- Liabilities and penalties for breach of compliance
- Limiting personal liability
- Corporate governance and proxy voting
- Correcting errors

PLAN DOCUMENTS

Prior to implementing a qualified plan, the plan sponsors, who are generally the company's board of directors or other officers, must create the plan documents. These documents are generally produced with the assistance of actuaries, accountants and attorneys who are well versed in ERISA regulations, as the "expert" standard applies to all areas of plan administration and management, not just investments. Once written, all fiduciaries must understand and act in accordance with these documents to the extent the documents are consistent with Titles I and IV of the ERISA code.

The plan document describes the benefit structure and guides day-to-day operations. It must include the following information:

- Identity of the fiduciaries
- A procedure for establishing and carrying out a funding policy
- A description of plan procedure for allocating responsibilities for the operation and administration of the plan
- A procedure for amending the plan and identifying persons with authority to do so
- A description of the basis on which payments are made to and from the plan

It is also advisable, but optional to include:

- The named fiduciaries, or the fiduciaries designated by them, who may employ persons to render advice with regard to any responsibility such fiduciaries have under the plan
- The named fiduciaries who will provide control or management of plan assets and/or those who may appoint investment professionals to manage plan assets

The plan sponsors will generally appoint a plan administrator who may be an employee or an outside entity. Outside entities, including plan administrators, are often called third-party service providers. The plan administrator is responsible for managing the plan, however the plan sponsor must continue to monitor the activities of all appointees (duty to monitor). The plan administrator is then required to prepare a summary plan description (SPD) for distribution to the plan participants and beneficiaries. The SPD is a description of the plan's provisions, benefits and participant's rights and obligations, written in simple language. Eligibility, vesting periods, claim procedures and sources of contributions are to be included in the SPD. As of 2003, plans are also required to include their intentions to comply with Section 404(c) of the ERISA code. The SPD must be given to all active participants, retirees, or beneficiaries of deceased participants receiving benefits or, terminated participants with vested rights, and it must be filed with the Department of Labor. If there are any material modifications to the plan, participants and beneficiaries must be notified and the modifications must be filed with the DOL.

Many plan sponsors feel that carefully structured plan documents are the key to ERISA compliance and subsequently, their potential liability to the plan. Do not make this mistake. The plan documents are only the first step in establishing an ERISA compliant plan, as administration and management thereafter are being held to an ever-increasing level of scrutiny by the DOL. Fiduciaries must stay current with governing regulations and continually comply with all areas of the ERISA code, as well as maintain documentation regarding all actions taken on behalf of the plan, its participants and beneficiaries.

SERVICE PROVIDERS

Service providers may be desirable for the complex functions of retirement plans, including 401(k) plans. Hiring any service provider is a responsibility of the fiduciary and therefore should be carried out with a well-documented, deliberate process. The selection process should include obtaining information from potential providers, such as:

- The financial condition of their firm
- A description of the firms business practices
  - How will the plan assets be invested
  - How are participant directions handled
  - Detailed fee structure, including all fees associated with investment options and possible "kick-backs" from investment providers (see the "pay-to-play" discussion in Chapter 24)
  - Fidelity bonding
- The service provider's experience in providing services to retirement plans of similar size and complexity as the plan under consideration
- The experience of those who will handle the plan's account
- Any recent litigation or enforcement action
- The firm's experience or performance record

As with all fiduciary appointees, there must be an on-going review process in place to evaluate the provider's adherence to the plan's intentions. These will vary, depending on the type of service provider and plan, but will include adherence to all contractual obligations and expectations of the fiduciary.

FIDUCIARIES

It is important for fiduciaries to understand who they are. If an individual exercises any authority, control or influence over "plan assets" (funds that are set aside for the benefit of employees), they are probably a fiduciary. Persons are deemed fiduciaries by the virtue of the type of work and services they perform on behalf of the plan, regardless of their "title." ERISA takes the view that "if it walks like a duck...." If you behave like a fiduciary, you will probably be considered a fiduciary. Plan sponsors and plan trustees are always fiduciaries, as well as those individuals who are involved with:

- Discretionary oversight of plan administration, such as:
  - Those who appoint other plan fiduciaries
  - Those select and monitor third party service providers
  - Those who exercise discretion in denying or approving benefit claims
  - Those who perform a purely ministerial function are excluded
- Plan management
- Selecting investment professionals
- Providing investment advice for a fee
- Asset management
- Selecting and monitoring plan investment options

ERISA requires each plan to have one or more "named fiduciaries" who are either identified in plan documents or appointed pursuant to a formal procedure outlined in the plan, such as the plan administrator, asset trustee (as assets must be held in trust) and ERISA-qualified money manager/s. A named fiduciary is a person who has the authority to control and manage the operation and administration of a plan. Named or not, if you meet the control standard, either by appointment in the plan documents or by delegation, you have a fiduciary responsibility to the plan.

Plan administrators are generally responsible for administrative functions, including recordkeeping (service records, benefit records, vesting records, participant information); directing distribution of benefits; determining eligibility for plan participation, vesting and accrual of benefits; providing individual statements to employees regarding vesting benefits; hiring outside experts; and, advising participants or beneficiaries of their rights and options. It is also their responsibility to see that the plan provisions are kept current with the law and that all documents are properly maintained and filed in a timely manner. If no one is named or designated "plan administrator," this responsibility becomes that of the employer.

Money managers, advisors and Investment Management Consultants are considered professional advisors and are therefore considered fiduciaries. They are providing advice on the value and advisability of owning investments and/ or have the discretionary authority to purchase or sell investments with plan assets. There was a time, pre-Enron, when only those investment professionals who had *discretion* were considered fiduciaries, but now the courts consider any investment professional who is in a position to *influence* investment choices, a fiduciary. It is important to note that if trustees or named fiduciaries properly select and appoint qualified advisors, they will not have a co-fiduciary responsibility for acts and omissions of these advisors, unless they knowingly participate in, or try to conceal any such acts or omissions. The appointment of investment professionals is an element of the fiduciary's "safe harbor," however fiduciaries must still supervise these professionals (duty to monitor).

Due to the importance of this often-misunderstood point, we will re-emphasize those who fall under the purview of "fiduciary." These persons all have a responsibility to the plan and are potentially liable for its mismanagement, regardless of any delegation of authority.

- Employers who have the power to appoint fiduciaries
- Corporate officers, directors and board members
- Trustees
- Plan officers and directors
- Plan sponsors
- Union sponsors
- Named fiduciaries within the plan documents
- Plan committee members who select and monitor investments
- Those with discretionary authority over plan administration
- Consultants or other investment advisors
- Money managers
- Outside consultants such as attorneys, accountants, actuaries, insurers and banks who perform fiduciary functions or who can reasonably be alleged to exercise control over the performance of such functions

The Pension Protection Act of 2006 (PPA) provides additional rules and guidelines for ERISA-covered plans. Under Title VI: Investment advice, prohibited transactions, and fiduciary rules, the debate surrounding investment advice and fiduciary responsibility is addressed as follows:

- For ERISA-covered plans, a fiduciary that is a registered investment company, bank, insurance company, or registered broker/dealer will be allowed to give investment advice to participants without engaging in a prohibited transaction if either (1) its fee does not vary depending on the investment choices that the participants make, or (2) its recommendations are based on a computer model certified by an independent third party. This applies to advice provided after Dec. 31, 2006.
- Fiduciary advisors must provide a disclosure statement that includes: fees and other compensation; any potential conflicts, past performance of the plan's investment options, available services, a statement that the advisor is acting as a fiduciary of the plan, a statement that the recipient of the advice may arrange for advice from an unaffiliated advisor, and how participant information will be used.
- Investment funds (e.g., hedge funds) and limited partnerships will not be treated as ERISA fiduciaries if investment by ERISA-covered plans account for less than 25% of assets. (Under prior law, the investments of non-ERISA governmental and foreign plans were also taken into account.)

There has been a significant amount of concern over the issue of advice, as plan sponsors, particularly of 401(k) plans, are required to educate their participants, however providing investment advice has been either prohibited by ERISA or severely restricted due to liability concerns. The 2006 PPA provides guidelines and clarity to this issue for plan sponsors and advisors alike.

Fiduciary Responsibility and Liability

A fiduciary, who does not act in accordance with ERISA standards, is subject to personal liability, and any breach could also cause a plan to lose its tax-exempt status. ERISA does not differentiate between large and small plans. All plans must be ERISA compliant and all fiduciaries must meet the same performance standards and will bear the same level of fiduciary liability. Meeting this standard is why small plans are often more costly to participants than large plans, as ERISA makes no provisions or exceptions due to the size of the plan. The cost of compliance is spread over fewer participants, therefore each must pay a higher per rata share, unless the plan sponsor is willing to absorb more of the expenses.

It is extremely important for all plan fiduciaries to understand the gravity of their responsibilities and the potential penalties. Fiduciaries can be held personally liable for the breach or violation of these responsibilities, even to the extent of restoring lost profits to the plan. Fiduciaries CANNOT completely discharge their duties, but they can appoint professionals who can help to minimize their liability. It is considered prudent to consult with experts in matters where the fiduciary lacks adequate knowledge or skill.

THE BASIC PRINCIPALS OF ERISA COMPLIANCE

Fiduciaries, under Section 404 of the ERISA code, have a duty to "discharge the duties with respect to a plan solely in the interest of the participants and beneficiaries and...for the exclusive purpose of...providing benefits to participants and beneficiaries and...defraying reasonable expenses of administering the plan." This standard applies to the administration of the plan as well as the management and investment of plan assets. The fiduciary must act in accordance with the plan documents and follow a course of procedural prudence. To do so, certain prudent measures must be implemented in order to meet the standards of fiduciary conduct required in plan administration. These include:

Sole Purpose
All fiduciary duties must be discharged solely in the interest of plan participants and their beneficiaries and, for the exclusive purpose of providing benefits to participants and their beneficiaries.

Prudent Expert Rule
The Prudent Expert Rule defines the standard of competence to which a fiduciary will be held responsible for all aspects of administering the plan's management and its investment decisions. ERISA states that a fiduciary must discharge his or her duties "with the care, skill, prudence and diligence under the circumstances then prevailing that a prudent person acting in a like capacity and *familiar with such matters* would use in the conduct of an enterprise of a like character with like aims." From an investment perspective, fiduciaries

can be held to the same level of skill as that of a professional consultant or money manager in making investment decisions. It is important to remember that pension dollars belong to employees and beneficiaries, not the sponsoring company.

Note: The courts have thus far, generally rejected the Prudent Expert standard. The standard of "prudence" has focused on the *process* that the fiduciary undertakes in reaching a decision. That is, prudence is a test of conduct and procedure, not results. If the fiduciary lacks the experience or knowledge to investigate a matter, prudence dictates that he or she seek outside expert advice when appropriate to arrive at a reasonable decision. It is this lack of procedural prudence that is at the heart of most fiduciary litigation.

Adherence to Plan Documents

An employee benefit plan must be formalized in writing (plan document) and should have written investment objectives (investment policy statement). Fiduciaries must discharge their duties in accordance with the plan documents and instruments insofar as such documents and instruments are consistent with Title I and IV of the ERISA code. Fiduciaries may rely upon professional assistance to meet this obligation. (Refer to the sample guidelines at the end of this chapter.)

Duty to Diversify Assets

A fiduciary must diversify the investments of a plan so as to minimize the risk of large losses, unless it is clearly not prudent to do so. A consultant is qualified to make these recommendations, whereas an investment committee may not have adequate investment expertise.

Duty to Monitor

Plan sponsors must monitor the performance of all appointed fiduciaries, as well as the investment performance of the overall portfolio and each investment option. Investment comparisons should be made on the risk-adjusted basis called for in the investment policy and plan documents. Underperforming funds or investments should be discontinued and replaced.

Fiduciary duties do not end once the fiduciary has prudently selected and delegated duties to others. A fiduciary has an ongoing duty to monitor the actions of those individuals to whom fiduciary responsibilities have been delegated. Those who have been delegated duties should be reviewed and evaluated for their performance and their contribution to the plan at reasonable intervals and in a manner that may be reasonably expected to ensure that the performance of the delegate fiduciary complies with the terms of the plan and all statutory standards. Breach of these duties can include a failure to train and supervise.

Duty to Control Expenses

All expenses must be evaluated and controlled. Reasonable expenses may be paid to a fiduciary if his or her duties are discharged for the exclusive purpose of providing benefits to participants and their beneficiaries. Transactions for the benefit of any other entity are prohibited.

Avoid Prohibited Transactions

Prohibited transactions (Section 406) must be understood and avoided.

Documentation

Fiduciaries should maintain a due diligence file to document all decisions made on behalf of the plan, including selecting and appointing fiduciaries, the investment process, and monitoring and evaluation. This file should also include the basis for decisions.

Assets Must Be Held in Trust

Employee benefit plan assets are to be held in trust, and such assets are not to inure to the benefit of the employer.

If fiduciaries do not properly fulfill their duties as a fiduciary, they may be:

- Subject to a civil action brought by a participant or beneficiary
- Personally liable for losses incurred due to mismanagement
- Subject to a jail sentence
- Subject to fines

Plan sponsors must always maintain the duty of oversight, but depending upon the size and type of the plan, there may be several areas of responsibility that may be delegated to independent providers.

DEVELOPING AN INVESTMENT PLAN

Following the development and execution of plan documents and, the assignment of fiduciary responsibilities in accordance with the plan documents, an investment plan is designed. There are several basic steps required to meet ERISA's standards of fiduciary responsibility for the investment of plan assets. Fiduciaries involved in the investment management of the plan's assets will begin, as all investment plans do, with the structuring of an investment policy.

The Investment Policy Statement

ERISA does not specifically require a written investment policy, however it is considered part of "best practices" for fiduciaries and, there is legal precedent that lack of a policy statement does not meet ERISA's Prudent Expert standard. All employee benefit plans should establish and maintain a written policy statement, specifying the objectives and purposes of the plan. The policy statement establishes the guidelines by which fiduciaries will be measured and provides comparative standards for reviewing investment options. A written policy statement will also provide a legal defense for investment decisions. We have provided a sample format in Appendix C-2.

The Investment Policy Statement is the foundation upon which investment goals, asset allocation, investment option evaluation and monitoring will be based. It must be clear and specific enough to be a working document, as broad-based generalities do not allow for sustentative comparisons. As an example, "long-term appreciation" is a nebulous goal; a better standard would be "returns that meet or exceed the average growth of inflation, plus 6%, over a three year period." Qualitative aspects are also important; therefore, at a minimum, the following items should be covered when designing an investment policy statement:

- Plan objectives and purpose.
- Return expectations—These must be realistic in order to avoid future under-funded pension liabilities.
- Nominal return benchmarks and "real" rate of return. How will the performance of the portfolio and the investments be measured? Is there an expected rate of return and will it be compared to a benchmark or measured in absolute percentages?
- Definition of risk and how it applies to this plan.

- Risk tolerance (refer to sample questionnaire, Appendix B).
- Time horizon for investment.
- Time period for portfolio review and evaluation.
- Allowable investments and quality standards.
- Liquidity requirements.
- Policy asset allocation guidelines.
- Procedure for selecting and terminating investment options, which may include mutual funds and/or money managers.
- Cash flow expectations for the plan (both contributions and distributions). Obtain actuarial projections if possible.
- Company finances.
    - Is the company strong enough to make future contributions in order to stay fully funded?
    - Are there any accrued or projected liabilities that may effect the management of the plan, such as under-funded (or over-funded) pension liabilities?

The written plan of investment objectives does not have to be overly complex as long as the objectives are specific enough to meet the needs and goals of the plan participants. Some very comprehensive Investment Policy Statements have been contained within three pages. Written objectives are as integral a part to a three-person pension plan as they are to massive plans. Fiduciaries in both cases are held to standards defined by ERISA and must act in accordance with the plan documents. All parties should sign this written policy to confirm their agreement to the terms of the plan.

Diversification of Plan Assets

Adequate diversification is essential to risk management and it is the key to reaching long-term goals. Nonetheless, this standard is often violated by pension plans. The initial asset allocation should be a reflection of the investment policy guidelines, and the portfolio should be monitored and rebalanced to stay within these parameters, market conditions permitting. Many benefit plans end up with too many eggs in one basket in an effort to seek maximum return, or perhaps, due to lack of timely review and/or rebalancing on the part of the fiduciary. If a particular asset class or style of the portfolio has had exceptional (or dismal) returns for a time, and the portfolio is not rebalanced in a timely manner, the portfolio will be over- or underweighted in that style. It will no longer have the asset allocation that was developed to reduce volatility and the plan will have a higher risk profile than that which was established in the investment policy. Quarterly reviews and annual rebalancing are reasonable time frames for maintaining a proper balance. Do not overlook this responsibility. Inadequate diversification is an easy target for litigation.

ERISA does not specify recommended percentages among asset classes, nor does it suggest a specific minimum or maximum for each asset class. ERISA does state that a fiduciary should not invest an unreasonably large percentage of the plan's assets in any single investment type, and it is understood that diversification is the only prudent action a fiduciary can take to protect the long-term health of the plan.

If the plan intends to offer employer stock, there are several specific rules that apply. It is the fiduciary's responsibility to understand and comply with these rules. Traditional defined benefit plans have limits on the amount of employer stock that can be held, whereas there are no limits in 401(k) plans, profit-sharing plans and employee stock ownership plans. If employer stock is an option, the employer must ensure that those responsible for making the investment decision (investment manager or participant) have critical information about the company's financial condition, to ensure that their investment decision is properly informed.

There are several approaches to creating and maintaining a diversified portfolio (Chapter 12), but regardless of which approach is used, the following should be considered when evaluating diversification for the plan's portfolio:

- The amount of plan assets to be invested or otherwise considered.
- Time horizons.
- Types of investments (stocks, bonds, real estate, etc.).
- Asset allocation to different styles with low correlation to one another
- Projected portfolio returns versus funding objectives. Are the return assumptions in balance with the funding capabilities and return objectives? A defined benefit plan has a required benefit distribution schedule and therefore a required minimum return to fulfill that obligation. Will there be enough money to meet the distribution requirements if the return assumptions fall short and are there alternative funding sources available?
- Volatility of investment returns and risk tolerance.

- Liquidity and future cash flow requirements.
- Aligning maturity dates in the fixed income portfolio with retiree pension distributions.
- Economic conditions affecting the company and plan investments.
- Company and industry condition.
- Geographic distribution of assets.

A corollary to diversification is whether the fiduciary has considered enough comparable investments to ensure that the best alternative for each asset class or style was chosen for the plan. This process may involve a formal search for money managers or a thorough analysis of mutual funds in order to make these comparisons. The plan's investment committee should review and consider an adequate mix of investment alternatives to make the most suitable choices for the plan. The fiduciary should consider comparable yields, risk versus return, and consider bond maturities that correspond to future benefit payments. This entire procedure should be well documented.

An Evaluation of Risk versus Return

The concept of risk versus return is pervasive in the investment business, and nowhere is it more important than in the management of employee benefit plans. Specifically, the fiduciary must "minimize the risk of large losses, unless it is clearly not prudent to do so." Opting to take large losses would be a rare phenomenon indeed, and the Department of Labor has yet to decide a case where it was not prudent to minimize losses. Importantly, this responsibility applies to the entire portfolio, not each single investment, so adequate diversification will help to reduce losses due to concentrated holdings.

ERISA specifies four criteria to use in evaluating the risk and return characteristics of investment alternatives:

1. In terms of liquidity, diversification, return and safety, each individual investment should be appropriate to the total portfolio.
2. Once the asset class is selected (stock, bond, etc.), the fiduciary is required to find the prevailing rate of return of that market, given the appropriate levels of risk. In other words, the choice must be made in the context of overall risk; and the investment choice should represent the "fair" return, not necessarily the "highest."

3. A fiduciary faced with investments of equal risk should not choose the one with the lower return if a higher return is available.
4. In order to evaluate alternatives, some objective standards must be established against which to measure them.

Expense Control

Plan sponsors are responsible for insuring that the fees paid by the plan and the expenses charged by the investment options are reasonable (Chapter 5). Know the method by which all investment professionals are paid by the plan or in association with plan assets. These costs should be reviewed twice a year and can include such things as:

- Trading costs or brokerage fees: Fees or commissions paid to execute trades. These typically range between 2.5 to 10 cents per share for institutional level trades and can be billed separately or included in an all-inclusive wrap fee.
- Money manager fees: The fee is generally billed as a percentage of the assets under management, broken into quarters. This treatment applies to both single and dual contract arrangements (Chapter 2). Other fee arrangements may apply.
- Mutual fund expense ratios and other related costs. Is the consultant receiving a fee from the plan as well as a "trail" (12b-1) from the mutual fund company?
- Incentive fees or performance-based compensation. Some investments, such as hedge funds and managed futures, collect both an asset based fee and an additional performance-based fee (Chapter 13).
- Soft dollar fees for directed brokerage (the advisor or consultant receives commissions generated from trades made by the money manager).
  - Account for all commission dollars spent.
  - Ensure that the costs are reasonable.
  - Verify that the manager has fully disclosed the use of all commission dollars.
- Custodial fees are sometimes charged if the management of the assets is completely unbundled and the assets are custodianed by a firm that holds the assets, but does not execute the trades.

- Investment Management Consultant fees: This fee is generally charged as a flat fee, fee for service or an asset-based fee, however offset arrangements or wrap fees may apply.

A reasonable fee for an all-inclusive account that is managed in the manner described in this book should not be more than 2%, with a regression to 1.5% at $10 million under management. The fee regression should continue as the assets under management increases. Remember that fees are negotiable.

A fiduciary has the duty to know and investigate all relevant facts, particularly the reasonableness and consistency of fees and any potential conflicts surrounding fee structures. As a part of best practices, seasoned consultants will generally fully disclose and explain all relevant fees for both themselves and the managers or investments that they recommend.

Prohibited Transactions (ERISA Section 406)

Fiduciaries must act in the sole interest of plan participants and beneficiaries and basically, any action that is contrary to this requirement is considered a prohibited transaction. ERISA's prohibited transaction rules state that a fiduciary may not self-deal, utilizing plan assets in his or her own interest or, act in a manner that may adversely affect plan participants. Prohibited transactions must be avoided and plan assets must be regularly monitored to assure that the portfolio remains free of these investments. If a prohibited transaction is identified, it must be eliminated and disclosed to ensure the plan's compliance.

The following are examples of prohibited transactions, but it is not intended to be a complete list. If a fiduciary has any question about the legitimacy of a specific transaction, legal counsel should be consulted.

- Sale, lease or exchange of property between the plan and a party-in-interest (those individuals who are in a position to exercise undue or improper influence over the plan, such as an employer).
- Lending of money between the plan and a party-in-interest.
- Transferring any plan assets to or, the use of plan assets by, a party-in-interest.
- A fiduciary who is self-dealing.
- Compensation paid to a fiduciary by a party involved in a transaction with plan assets.

- Transactions "tainted by a conflict of interest" and thus highly susceptible to self-dealing.
- Compensation that varies depending on the investments selected.
- As a general rule, ERISA Section 407(a) prohibits a plan from acquiring any "employer security" or "employer real property" unless such
  asset is a "qualifying employer security" or "qualifying employer real
  property." A plan's purchase of these qualifying assets is limited to
  10% of the value of plan assets. This restriction may not include savings plans, profit-sharing plans and ESOP's, including employee stock
  bonus plans.
- Investing in assets that are outside the jurisdiction of the U.S. courts
  therefore, foreign stocks must be held in a mutual fund or as ADRs.
- ERISA Section 408 provides a list of exemptions from Section 406.

A party-in-interest who participates in a prohibited transaction is personally liable to the plan for any losses incurred as a result of his or her actions.
If there was a profit made, that too must be returned to the plan. Those who
participate in prohibited transactions may be subject to civil penalties under
ERISA or excise taxes under the Internal Revenue Code. Breach of the ERISA
code may result in fines and/or imprisonment, so a thorough understanding of
this regulation is advisable.

When selecting a money manager, the plan may wish to require that the
manager qualify under the Prohibited Transaction Class Exemption 84-14,
commonly referred to as the Qualified Professional Asset Manager (QPAM)
Exemption. Transactions subject to this requirement include those related to
parties-in-interest or real estate transactions. Qualifying under the QPAM Exemption requires that the manager have a minimum of $85 million in assets
under management and that the shareholders or partners of the management
firm have a minimum of $1 million in equity (effective August 23, 2005)[2]. This
standard is meant to provide added protection to the ERISA plan in the event
of a breach or violation of ERISA Sections 404 and 406 by the manager. This
protection may or may not be relevant to the plan and/or the types of investments made by the manager, particularly if these types of transactions are prohibited under the investment policy statement and/or the manager's ADV.

---

2. QPAM requirements, which are more extensive than those listed here, are regulated by the
DOL.

Potential Conflicts of Interest

The most common areas where conflicts may arise are directed brokerage and soft dollar payments. When the money manager directs that transactions be done at a specific broker/dealer firm, that firm benefits from the trading commissions. If these commission dollars are then paid to the advisor or consultant, then there is the potential for conflict. This payment would be considered a soft dollar payment for services rendered by the consultant and it could appear as though the money manager is paying the consultant to recommend placing assets with their firm. While not in and of itself a violation, directed brokerage concerns revolve around two issues:

1. Is the brokerage cost reasonable in light of the services provided?
2. Has the manager fulfilled his fiduciary obligation to obtain the best execution for the transaction?

"Best execution" is not necessarily the lowest price, but price must be considered along with the quality of execution. The ability of a firm to execute transactions where others may be unable should be part of the evaluation of the total costs of execution. The quality of execution can be affected by liquidity, spreads, market making, capacity and timeliness.

Other potential conflicts may arise when the relationship between the money management firm and the consultant and/or his or her firm, is not kept independent from one another, such as in the buying and selling of research materials (Chapter 15). In general, all investment decisions must be made in the best interest of the beneficiaries and participants and every effort must be made to avoid any conflicts of interest.

Monitoring and Evaluation

The Investment Policy Statement will establish the criteria by which performance of both the total portfolio and, the individual money managers and/or other investment options will be evaluated. It is rarely the goal of a plan to maximize returns without regard to risk or cash flow and therefore the risk-adjusted performance of the portfolio should to be evaluated in relationship to the goals and objectives set forth in the policy. This evaluation should be done on a regular basis, generally during quarterly meetings and should include any substantive changes in the management and operations of the money management firms, changes in plan objectives, changes in market conditions that may affect the allocation of plan assets and, any other issues that may materially affect the management of plan assets. Annually, the Investment Policy Statement should be reviewed to ensure that the contents remain relevant to the plan. Costs should be periodically reviewed and any unusual transactions should be evaluated for their compliance with Sections 406, 407 and 408 of the ERISA code.

In addition to matters that involve the investment management of the portfolio, fiduciary performance should also be evaluated. It is critical to bear in mind that the fiduciary's responsibilities are ongoing, and liability still exists even when other fiduciaries are appointed and investment professionals are hired. It remains the responsibility of the plan sponsor to monitor the performance of all other fiduciaries, plan procedures and performance. Any breach of these duties, either in the breach and/or the duty to monitor, can result in personal liability to all involved. *Delegation alone will not protect a fiduciary; a system of delegation and oversight can.*

DOCUMENTATION

ERISA plans have significant compliance requirements for documentation. A trustee or plan sponsor must maintain certain documents and will often appoint a co-trustee who is proficient in plan administration and the maintenance of the required documents to assist in this process. ERISA requires the reporting and disclosure of certain information regarding employee benefit plan provisions and individual benefits, as well as the notification of changes or amendments to that information. There are expressed penalties for the violation of reporting, disclosure and notification requirements.

These documents are required to satisfy plan participants and regulatory authorities that plan assets are being properly administered and prudently invested. The following is a list of many of the documents that should be maintained by the plan administrator:

- A written investment policy and documentation regarding any decisions that are made regarding plan assets.
- Any statements, journals, appraisals, certificates or other documents.
- All reports involving the consultant, money managers and performance.

- Annual copies of Form ADV for each money manager and any significant litigation against the money manager or key personnel.
- Proof of ERISA bonding.
- A record of all fees and expenses, including a cost analysis of hiring appointees.
- All appropriate reporting, filing and disclosure requirements. These must be completed for the plan on an annual basis.
- Published annual report, Form 5500, including the summary annual report (SAR) which outlines the information in the Form 5500 and is furnished to the participants annually.
- A summary plan description (SPD) must be written in understandable language, given to all participants and updated when appropriate.

BONDS AND INSURANCE

Federal law requires that each fiduciary (such as directors and officers of the employer) and every other individual who "handles" plan assets (such as individuals who transmit contributions to the trustee), be bonded. Other individuals, who have exposure to penalties due to their fiduciary status, may wish to be insured.

- **ERISA Bond:** ERISA Section 412 requires that fiduciaries of plans be bonded. The bond is to protect the plan and money from losses due to fraud and dishonesty on the part of those covered by this fidelity bond. The bond required is an amount equal to 10% of the plans assets or $1000, whichever is greater.
- **Errors and Omissions:** E&O insurance protects the fiduciary from liability in the case of administrative errors.
- **Director and Officer Insurance:** D&O insurance is designed to cover the company's directors and officers from liability associated with fiduciary breaches.

LIABILITIES AND PENALTIES

ERISA Section 409 (a) states *"Any person who is a fiduciary with respect to a plan who breaches any of the responsibilities, obligations, or duties imposed upon by this title shall be personally liable to make good to such plan any profits of such fiduciary which have been made through use of assets of the plan by the fiduciary, and shall be subject to such other equitable or remedial relief as the court may deem appropriate, including the removal of such fiduciary."*

Any fiduciary who breaches a fiduciary obligation under ERISA will be held personally liable for losses caused by the breach of duty, even if they were unaware of the duty. In addition, a fiduciary can be held liable for the breach of another if they knew or should have known of the breach. ERISA does not consider ignorance a defense. The fiduciary has a duty to monitor the activities of co-fiduciaries, co-trustees and those who have been delegated fiduciary responsibility, and he or she has a duty to remedy or prevent any breach or potential breach for which they become aware. The fiduciary has a duty to disclose anything that may threaten the plan. He or she must not mislead, lie or act to conceal any of this information. Even those who are not fiduciaries, but have knowledge of a fiduciary's breach, or participate in a breach of duty, can be subject to a DOL civil penalty of up to 20% of any judgment.

Penalties may be imposed for up to six years after the fiduciary violation, or three years after the party bringing the suit had knowledge of the breach. A willful violation of the reporting or disclosure provision in Title I carries personal criminal penalties of up to $5,000 ($100,000 for corporations) and/or up to one year in prison. Losses to the plan, as well as profits made from the improper use of plan assets, must be restored to the plan by the fiduciary. An intentional violation of the prohibition against service as a fiduciary to an employee benefit plan by any person convicted of any offence specified in ERISA Section 411(a) is punishable by a fine of $10,000 and/or imprisonment of five years. Accepting kickbacks carries a fine of $10,000, and/or imprisonment of five years.

Plan participants, beneficiaries, other fiduciaries and the Department of Labor can initiate civil actions for appropriate equitable relief. The DOL may also impose civil monetary penalties in connection with breaches of fiduciary duty or knowing participation by any other person, even those who are not fiduciaries, equal to 20% of the applicable recovered amount.

Failure to respond to plan participants in a timely manner (30 days) can result in a daily civil penalty of $110. The Department of Labor can assess a civil penalty of $1000 per day for failure to file a completed Form 5500 and the IRS can assess a late fee of $25 per day, up to $15,000, for failure to file the

Form 5500 in a timely manner. The Department of Labor can also remove the fiduciary and take control of plan assets.

To summarize, a breach of fiduciary obligation or duty can result in:

- The fiduciary becoming personally liable for losses to the plan.
- The fiduciary becoming personally liable to return any gains obtained that were not for the sole benefit of the participants and beneficiaries, such as those obtained through party-of-interest transitions.
- Fines and/or imprisonment of fiduciary.
- Monetary damages that may be recovered by the plan only. Only equitable relief, such as injunctions or the removal of the fiduciary, is available for injuries to individual participants or beneficiaries, which may include equitable monetary relief in certain circumstances. No punitive damages are imposed.
- Loss of tax favored status for the plan.

This chapter provides an incomplete listing of violations and the penalties that can be imposed for breaches of fiduciary duties, however we believe that it makes the point: Take your fiduciary responsibility seriously.

Keys to Limiting Personal Liability

Court records show many cases where a fiduciary became personally liable, perhaps for acts for which he or she was unaware, or in areas where they did not realize their responsibility. Again, ignorance is no defense, and the cost of defending oneself will probably be borne personally, not by either the Plan or plan sponsor. This liability can be relatively easy to avoid if the fiduciary maintains a good system of documentation and acts prudently and defensively. The following is a list of the prudent steps that should be taken.

1. Delegation: The most effective way to meet the standard of Prudent Expert is to appoint experts to assist in areas of administration and investment, such as plan administrators, service providers and investment professionals, including a consultant and/or independent money managers. Remember, ERISA considers consultation with experts prudent if a fiduciary:

   (1) Lacks the necessary expertise to make a decision

(2) Hires and consults an expert responsibly, and

(3) Continues to monitor the expert's performance

By delegating in this manner, the fiduciary can reduce, not eliminate, the risk of fiduciary liability. In evaluating candidates for delegation, the DOL provides screening guidelines that state that the process must be designed to produce "...a range of candidates whose expertise is consistent with the proposed investment guidelines established and/or investment style identified for the Investment Manager position in question," that "the process by which such candidates are identified shall be documented," and that "investment guidelines shall be established for any Investment Manager ultimately hired."

2. Plan documents: Be well versed in the provisions and requirements stated in the plan documents. ERISA requires that the plan remain in compliance with current law and that all actions taken on behalf of the plan adhere to the terms set forth in these documents.

3. Understand and comply with the ERISA mandated fiduciary requirements described in this chapter.

4. Keep plan participants fully informed as to:
   a. Their account balances, or accrued benefits
   b The investment options available to the plan
   c. Any changes in the plan's provisions, either by receipt of a modified summary plan description or a summary of material modification (SMM) within 210 days after the end of the plan year in which the change was adopted.
   d. Any other features of their employee benefit package that may require disclosure to the plan participants

5. Documentation: There should be a clear paper trail of all decisions made regarding the plan. This documentation can be maintained in a fiduciary or due diligence file and should include the procedures and qualifications used to select outside experts and, the selection and

monitoring processes used regarding investment options. Maintain records and minutes to reduce the risk of fiduciary liability. Documenting procedural prudence can be reviewed in court.

6. Provide the annual report, plan description, summary plan description and individual benefit statements, as well as all other required information, to the participants in a timely manner.

7. File Form 5500 with the federal government in a timely manner.

8. When dealing more specifically with the investment portfolio, develop a good safe harbor-type system. "Safe harbor" is a term associated with ERISA Section 404(c) for 401(k) plans and covered in the Chapter 24, but its fundamental mandate of prudence is applicable to all investments made by fiduciaries:
   a. Select investment professionals, such as a consultant and money manager/s.
   b. Establish the time frame and frequency of review.
   c. Define risk and return objectives in the investment policy.
   d. Measure return in relationship to plan objectives.
   e. Have a performance monitoring process in place (Chapter 19):
      • Establish benchmarks (or indices) against which the money manager's performance will be judged.
      • Review real versus nominal rates of return.
      • Evaluate the manager's performance relative to its peers.
   f. Consider the degree of personal attention the plan will require from investment professionals.
   g. Qualitative aspects, such as change of philosophy or personnel turnover should be monitored, evaluated and documented.
   h. Establish a process to monitor and evaluate the activities and performance of all appointed fiduciaries, such as plan administrators and investment professionals.
   i. Document all activities associated with the plan.

CORRECTIVE MEASURES

In the event that the fiduciary violates certain ERISA standards, there is a DOL sponsored program in place to assist in correcting these mistakes. The Department of Labor's Voluntary Fiduciary Correction Program (VFCP) encourages employers to voluntarily correct any of 15 different violations. The program provides a description of how to apply and methods for correcting violations. In addition, the Department's Delinquent Filer Voluntary Compliance Program (DFVCP) assists filers of Form 5500 who have filed either late or not at all. To access either program, refer to www.dol.gov/ebsa.

CORPORATE GOVERNANCE AND PROXY VOTING

Proxy voting, shareholder rights and the role the plan takes as "part owner" of a public corporation are matters of corporate governance and the plan documents should include how these matters will be addressed. The major administrative concern is the voting of stock held by the plan, which can sometimes be rife with conflicts of interest. The best way to eliminate conflicts is to ensure that the fiduciary with voting responsibility is totally independent of the plan sponsor.

Fiduciaries have a legal obligation to carefully evaluate all sides of governance issues which may affect the value of plan assets and shareholder rights. Stock should be voted in the best interests of plan participants, therefore a system of voting oversight and policies is the best way to ensure compliance with ERISA. The money manager/s is both independent and in a position to make an informed decision regarding company stock owned in their portfolio, thus making them a good candidate to assign this obligation. This provision can be part of the money management agreement.

CONCLUSION

ERISA is extensive and complex. We have only scratched the surface of its regulations, exclusions and exemptions. It is our purpose here to provide the reader with the basic requirements placed on ERISA plans, as well as provide an understanding of the extent to which fiduciary responsibility and liability exists. Our best advice to the reader is to remain ever vigilant, document all actions that are taken on behalf of the plan and utilize professionals who specialize in the application of the ERISA code, as surveillance and audits by the DOL for plans of all sizes is rapidly accelerating and plan sponsors must be more observant than ever before.

There has been much discussion of late regarding unfunded pension liability and the ability of the PBGC to meet this ever increasing financial burden. The Pension Benefit Guarantee Corporation (PBGC) was established by the U.S. Government in 1974 and provides protection for employee pension assets. When plan sponsors are unable to meet pension obligations, PBGC steps in. In 2005, the PBGC guaranteed pension benefits to approximately 44.1 million workers[3]. As a result of the 2000 Bear market, as well as corporate governance issues, many companies have significant unfunded pension liability. A major portion of the Pension Protection Act of 2006 is focused on measures to remedy this threat to the nation's pension system. PBGC's solvency depends on both a manageable payout rate, which the new Act is designed to address, and the collection of premiums. PBGC may choose to increase insurance premiums for its insureds, but they are also increasing their monitoring efforts to uncover and perhaps terminate plans that may not be able meet their future obligations. This scrutiny adds additional pressure on private pensions to meet ERISA's standards.

Congress passed the massive, 900 plus page Pension Protection Act of 2006 (PPA) to address pension funding requirements, as well as many other issues that affect pension plans. It was signed into law August 17, 2006. This new piece of legislation will soon become required reading for all those who advise plan sponsors and participants, as well as other individuals who are planning for retirement. This new law, combined with the many other layers of duties and increased regulatory scrutiny, reinforces the need for fiduciaries to seek out the advice of qualified professionals.

---

3. PBGC website, 2005 Annual Report.

TIPS FOR MEETING YOUR FIDUCIARY RESPONSIBILITIES[4]
Guidelines provided by the U.S. Department of Labor,
Employee Benefits Security Administration

Understanding fiduciary responsibilities is important for the security of a retirement plan and compliance with the law. The following tips may be a helpful starting point:

- Have you identified your plan fiduciaries, and are they clear about the extent of their fiduciary responsibility?
- If participants make their own investment decisions, have you provided sufficient information for them to exercise control in making those decisions?
- Are you aware of the schedule to deposit participants' contributions in the plan, and have you made sure it complies with the law?
- If you are hiring third-party service providers, have you looked at a number of providers, given each potential provider the same information, and considered whether the fees are reasonable for the services provided?
- Have you documented the hiring process?
- Are you prepared to monitor your plan's service providers?
- Have you identified parties-in-interest to the plan and taken steps to monitor transactions with them?
- Are you aware of the major exemptions under ERISA that permit transactions with parties-in-interest, especially those key for plan operations (such as hiring service providers and making loans to participants)?
- Have you reviewed your plan document in light of current plan operations and made necessary updates? After amending the plan, have you provided participants with an updated SPD of SMM?
- Do those individuals handling plan funds or other plan property have a fidelity bond?

None of the information contained in this chapter should be construed as legal advice, nor should it be considered a complete accounting of ERISA standards and requirements. An attorney who specializes in ERISA law should review employee benefit plan documents and provide oversight and guidelines for the implementation and management of the plan.

4. U.S. Department of Labor and Employee Benefits Security Admin. publication, May 2004.

24

401(k) Plans

A 401 (k) plan, also known as a defined contribution plan, is a qualified retirement plan, governed by ERISA, but with a few twists. In this chapter we will discuss what is unique to these plans and how fiduciaries can avoid liability issues.

401(k) Plans	Other Qualified Retirement Plans
Employees can make pre-tax contributions	Employer contributions only
Employers must provide investment education	Employee education not required
Investments are participant directed	Investments are made by fiduciaries
Fiduciary protection under Section 404(c)	No such protection

401(k) plans are a version of a Profit Sharing Plan, with an additional feature called CODA or "Cash or Deferred Arrangement." CODA allows both the employee and the employer to contribute pre-tax dollars to the plan, whereas in non-CODA profit sharing plans, contributions are made solely by the employer and at the employer's discretion. 401(k) plans can be used in conjunction with other retirement plans, subject to total annual funding limitations. 401(k) plans have given the employer a way to provide a retirement plan for employees, even if the employer is unable or unwilling to fund one from company profits. 401(k) plans allow employees to contribute to a tax deferred plan with their own pre-tax dollars, while allowing the employer the option to contribute. This type of plan assures the motivated employee a retirement plan through self-funding, without regard to the employer's financial condition.

Many employers see 401(k) plans as a necessary benefit, both to attract qualified applicants and to retain experienced employees. In order to enhance this benefit, the employer will make matching contributions to the plan. Employer contributions (profit sharing) must only be made in equal percentages to all eligible employees; even so, participation by the more highly compensated employees, who are often the owners, can create a very top-heavy disbursement of funds. In order to keep plans more balanced, ERISA imposes top-heavy limits. Non-highly compensated employees who benefit from the plan must equal at least 70% of the total funding of the plan. Funding from highly compensated employees that benefit from the plan cannot dominate. In other words, for the highly compensated employees to maximize the potential benefit of the plan for themselves, they must achieve a substantial level of employee participation. Matching is an excellent incentive to encourage employees to participate in the plan.

401(k) plans are referred to as "self-directed" or "participant directed" retirement plans, and are still subject to all ERISA standards. They differ from the other retirement plans that we have discussed in that the participants not only make contributions to the plan, but they also make their own investment decisions. This structure however, does not eliminate fiduciary responsibilities. So, we again ask, "Who are the fiduciaries and what role will they play?" All individuals who act with any control or authority over the plan have fiduciary responsibilities. In Chapter 23, we provided both a list of responsibilities that would make one a fiduciary, as well as a list of individuals who are considered fiduciaries. These are the same for 401(k) plans, with the addition of investment committee members, who are often appointed to select and monitor investment options, and other providers to the plan. These may include a plan administrator, a benefits services provider, an investment provider and/or an investment consultant.

Investment committees are not exclusive to, or required by 401(k) plans, but are most often used by these plans. Plan sponsors should be aware of their duty to educate investment committee members of their roles and responsibilities. The DOL has issued a brochure, "Meeting your Fiduciary Responsibility," to provide new committee members with this basic information. It can be found on their website at www.dol.gov/ebsa.

THE 401(K) PROCESS

All fiduciaries of 401(k) plans have a duty to act with procedural prudence, as with all ERISA plans. In order to comply with ERISA standards and the "safe harbor" conditions of Section 404(c) of the ERISA code, plan sponsors should have a process in place for every stage of the plan's administration and each step should be thoroughly documented. The first step that most 401(k) plan sponsors take is to appoint an internal investment committee or, name one or more people to be responsible for the management of the plan—the named fiduciary/s. ERISA requires each plan to have at least one named fiduciary. Document this process, including the qualifications required for each position. The plan sponsor must act prudently in all selection processes, must monitor all fiduciaries' performance on a regular basis and document all activities that are carried out on the plan's behalf.

Once these individuals have been selected, they can assist in designing and implementing the plan. There are many components that must be in place prior to enrolling participants and the plan sponsor may wish to use actuaries, CPAs, attorneys who specialize in ERISA compliance and investment professionals to create the plan documents and assure the proper structure and operation of their 401(k) plan. 401(k) plans are subject to the same ERISA standards of duties and obligations, as well as the mandates of the Pension Protection Act of 2006 (PPA) that were described in the last chapter:

- Identify fiduciaries and their responsibilities.
- Understand the basis principals of ERISA compliance.
- Write an Investment Policy Statement (IPS), which includes performance monitoring guidelines (We have provided a sample IPS in Appendix C-3).
- Provide for adequate diversification for participant's assets.
- Evaluate the risk and return characteristics of the investment options, selecting those that are compatible with plan objectives. This selection is subject to the standards of care of a Prudent Expert.
- Monitor and evaluate the performance of the investment options.
- Monitor and evaluate the performance of appointed fiduciaries.
- Conduct a cost analysis of the investment options, including management fees, trading costs and 12b-1 fees (Chapter 5).

- Conduct a cost analysis of the plan's total expenses. These include recordkeeping, total investment management and trusteeship. Surveys indicate that a surprising number of plan sponsors are not fully aware of what they are paying for each of the services provided to the plan. These costs may be paid from the participants' plan assets and/or paid directly by the plan sponsor. Fees must be reasonable for the level of services provided, but not necessarily the least expensive.
- Document all processes that involve the plan or its participants.
- Understand what constitutes a prohibited transaction.
- Assure that all documentation and filings are made in a timely manner.

In addition to these standard ERISA requirements, 401(k) plans have other characteristics and requirements that we will address in this chapter, including:

- Investment providers
- Investment options
  - Roth 401(k) plan versus Traditional 401(k) plan
  - Mutual funds
  - Company stock
  - Self-directed brokerage accounts
- Recordkeeping
- Self-directed investing
- Monitoring
- Education
- Compliance with 404(c)
  - Diversification
  - Selection of investment options
  - Monitoring of investment options
  - Participant control
  - Participant notifications
  - Blackout periods
  - Informational requests
  - Due diligence file

If an investment committee has been charged with complying with all of these requirements, and does not have the expertise to effectively discharge this duty, they should consult with outside experts.

INVESTMENT PROVIDERS

Investment providers provide investment vehicles for the plan. These providers are usually a mutual fund company, bank or insurance company and they provide an array of mutual funds from which the final investment options that will be offered to the participants will be chosen. Seek an investment provider that offers a broad range of fund families from which to choose and one that does not emphasis their proprietary funds.

INVESTMENT OPTIONS

Roth 401(k) versus Traditional 401(k): In 2006, the Roth 401(k) became available under the Economic Growth and Tax Relief Reconciliation Act (EGRRA) of 2001. Plan sponsors now have the option of offering this savings strategy to their participants as part of their Defined Contribution plans. The rationales for contributing to a Roth versus a Traditional 401(k) are similar to those used when selecting between a Roth and Traditional IRA. Factors that influence the choice are the participant's age, time horizon, and current and anticipated retirement tax brackets. Those who contribute to a Roth 401(k) make *after-tax* contributions. After-tax contributions do not reduce taxable income, but the participant will benefit from tax-deferred growth and *tax-free* distributions when the funds are withdrawn, which tends to favor younger employees with lower salaries. There are no income limitations on participation in a Roth 401(k), as there are with Roth IRAs. There are currently no minimum distribution requirements at age $70\frac{1}{2}$ when a Roth 401(k) is rolled into a Roth IRA, potentially enhancing the tax-free transfer of assets to one's heirs. These variances may make Roth 401(k) plans appealing to high-income earners, despite giving up the benefits of pre-tax contributions. If the employer matches contributions, the employer contributions and associated earnings benefit from tax-deferred growth, however they are taxable when withdrawn. A participant may elect to split their contribution between a Roth and Traditional 401(k) as a hedge against potential future tax rates, as we neither know what tax policy will be in place in the future, nor do most people know what their income will be at a future date.

From an employer's perspective, Roth 401(k) plans present administrative challenges. As one can surmise from the discussion above, integrating this option into a company's Define Contribution plan requires additional recordkeeping, and therefore administrative costs and, additional education. Many employers are not prepared to offer the additional education necessary to describe the pros and cons of opting for a Roth versus a Traditional 401(k). In addition, the Roth 401(k) provision of EGRRA had been scheduled to expire (sunset) in 2011, making employers reluctant to pursue this option, however the PPA removed that objection by making this provision permanent. It will be interesting to monitor the success of Roth 401(k) plans, as employer's try to balance their concerns with potential employee demand for this savings option.

Mutual funds: The investment options offered to the participants will generally be limited to a list of mutual funds, whereas with other pension plans, most individual securities, mutual funds or independent money managers can be combined. The diversification and risk management is up to the participant, but there should be enough fund diversity for the participant to achieve some risk and return management. ERISA only requires that 3 funds of sufficient diversity in risk and return expectation be included, but most plans include a wider range of options, optimally from more than one fund family. Most fund families have many funds, but there is often considerable overlap in the securities which make up each fund portfolio. This concern is often lessened by having multiple fund families from which to choose, which also provides for greater choice if it becomes necessary to replace one of the funds. These issues should be addressed in the due diligence process used to select the funds. In the sample policy provided in Appendix C-3, a list of selection criteria is included. We will discuss the selection process in more detail below, as it is an often-misunderstood point for fiduciaries and it is essential for ERISA compliance.

Model portfolios, made up of a diversified selection of mutual funds and constructed by investment professionals, provide participants with risk appropriate portfolio choices. These funds are referred to as life-cycle funds and are generally grouped as either target-date or target-risk funds. Target-date funds ask, "When will you retire?" and then match that time horizon to a model portfolio. Managers of these funds gradually adjust risk, and therefore allocations, according to the participant's age and time to retirement. Age and time to retirement are the only criteria used for asset allocation. Target-risk funds, also referred to as lifestyle funds, focus on investment objectives and risk tolerance (conservative, moderate, aggressive) and provide greater flexibility and individuality to the investor. When using model portfolios, the asset allocation and rebalancing decisions are left to professionals. Models liberate the participant from the task of creating an appropriate portfolio asset allocation, which, for the most part, they are unqualified to do. Employers may find inclusion of these options of great benefit to the participants and by extension, themselves.

Model portfolios do not relieve the plan sponsor (employer) of their duties under ERISA. Employers must still analyze the funds within the models for their appropriateness (including fees) and establish a means by which to monitor and evaluate performance. Questions that must be answered include, "Is this model truly appropriate for an individual who plans to retire in a certain number of years?" and "What is an appropriate benchmark for evaluating performance?" Models provide simplicity for the participant, however the underlying due diligence may create unexpected challenges for the plan sponsor.

Employer stock: Employer stock can be offered, but cannot be considered one of the core options. If employer stock is part of the plan, there are additional 404(c) compliance rules:

- The participant must control voting and tender rights
- Information about participants holding employer stock must be kept confidential and participants must know who is in charge of this information
- Participants must understand the procedures relating to owning company stock
- Participants and beneficiaries must be allowed to divest employer stock (conditions specified in the PPA)

Self-directed brokerage accounts: The plan can offer self-directed brokerage accounts, either as the only option or as one of the options available to the participants. Self-directed brokerage accounts have become a popular option of late, as plan sponsors are looking for ways to reduce or eliminate the liability associated with selecting and monitoring mutual funds. However, plan sponsors should consider the greater risks of loss that can be associated with these accounts. If offered, they must be offered to everyone and there may be only a few employees with the experience needed to fully self-manage a portfolio. There is no portfolio management oversight of the investments, nor does the employer monitor investment choices, which may be problematic for the plan sponsor. If self-directed brokerage accounts are not suitable for the pool of participants, and there is no investment supervision, the plan sponsor may be held liable. This option is not free of oversight responsibility, as the plan sponsor is still liable for monitoring the appropriateness of fees, commissions and expenses, trade execution and other services, and potentially the ultimate choices that the participant makes.

RECORDKEEPING

Recordkeeping is a critical function for all plans and trusts, but it is far more labor intensive for 401(k) plans. These plans generally select a plan administrator and service provider to handle the daunting task of recordkeeping, which includes allocating each participant's monthly or bi-monthly contributions to the appropriate funds in a timely manner, maintaining a system for the participants to make trades and to access information, such as daily account balances and, process distributions. As you might imagine, recordkeeping is a critical function and the selection and monitoring of the plan administrator and service providers is a responsibility of the fiduciary.

Common operational pitfalls:

- If deferrals are not made in a timely manner, which the Department of Labor concludes is within one week of the pay date, it is considered both a breach of fiduciary duty and a prohibited transaction.
- If participants fail to direct their plan, the plan fiduciary must prudently invest the funds. A default account must be set up and may be used for a short term however, favorite default options, such as money market or stable value funds are not considered prudent for long-term investing. This requirement also applies to participants who have passed away.
- If providers need to make corrections to individual contributions or deferrals, calculations of earnings should be done using money market rates, rather than the rate of return for the participant's account.
- Improperly classifying individuals as independent contractors, thus improperly excluding them from participation in the plan

- Other eligibility issues. All employees must be allowed to participate in the plan as soon as they become eligible. All too often, recordkeeping is inadequate and some employees are overlooked.
- Conversion from temporary to regular employment must be handled properly. The IRS requires that employees be given credit for periods of service that they performed for the plan sponsor as a leased or "temp" employee. The IRS only classifies workers as employees, non-employees and leased employees. Failure to properly include individuals in the retirement plan can have serious consequences, including plan disqualification.
- Properly defining and accounting for participant compensation.
- Inappropriate fees or expenses charged to the plan. Maintain good records to justify all charges to the plan.

PARTICIPANT OR SELF-DIRECTED INVESTING

401(k) plans are participant or self-directed. The participant is responsible for making investment decisions from the available options. The plan fiduciaries are not liable for investment decisions as long as they comply with the requirements of Section 404(c), which include providing adequate diversification choices and the monitoring of each fund's performance. There is however, precedent for fiduciary liability if the participant consistently makes inappropriate choices with no fiduciary oversight. And, as previously mentioned, if the participant fails to direct their plan, the plan fiduciary must prudently invest the funds. The funds cannot sit idle for the long-term. Fortunately, the PPA now provides relief for plan sponsors who designate default investment options.

This potential for fiduciary liability exposure due to poor participant decisions is an area of increasing concern for plan sponsors. There are 20 to 25 conditions that must be met to be in full compliance with 404(c) and very few plans meet this standard. This gap in compliance makes fiduciaries personally responsible for the imprudent investment decisions of participants, which was made clear in decisions made by the Enron court on September 30, 2003. Even if the plan is in full compliance with 404(c), there are issues surrounding the suitability of investment decisions by participants who lack the skills to make informed, prudent choices, despite educational efforts. Thus far, there has been no guidance offered by the DOL or the courts, so a conservative approach for fiduciaries may be to accept greater responsibility in participant investment decisions. They can do so by including a statement in the summary plan description stating, "Those participants who feel unqualified in making investment decisions may elect to appoint the fiduciary as the responsible party for the management their account." The fiduciary, not wanting to take on any additional liability, can provide account management through an investment advisory firm that offers this service. Another option is the use of pre-determined asset allocation models, such as age-based or life-style funds. These funds shift allocations as the participant gets closer to retirement and, professionals make all of the investment decisions, allocations and re-allocations within each model. Offering these options fulfills ERISA's ultimate objective for fiduciary responsibility, which is to see that the participant's funds are well-invested.

A fiduciary remains responsible for selecting and monitoring investment options, regardless of any intent to comply with Section 404(c). This duty may be delegated to investment providers, or preferably, an independent consultant, however the duty of oversight remains constant.

MONITORING MUTUAL FUNDS AND INVESTMENTS

Participants must choose from the list of funds chosen by the plan sponsor, therefore these funds must be monitored for performance and expenses, and those that underperform or have expenses that are not competitive, should be removed and replaced by more appropriate funds. This requirement is discussed in much more detail later in this chapter when we discuss 404(c) compliance and, in the sample IPS in Appendix C-3.

If the participant selects the self-directed brokerage account option, the fiduciary must monitor the account to the degree that the participant is capable of making prudent investment choices and that the investments are suitable for the investor. The fiduciary maintains the duty to monitor in all cases.

EDUCATION

ERISA Section 404(c) imposes the duty of educating participants upon the plan sponsor. The plan sponsor must provide participants with enough education on the fundamentals of investing to make informed investment decisions. Adequate education is intended to enable the participant to select a combination of funds that will meet their individual risk tolerances, goals and time horizons. The plan sponsor does not have to provide this information in the form of lectures or written materials.

What is appropriate investment education? Plan sponsors should provide access to information on investment concepts, such as diversification, risk management, characteristics of the different asset classes, market volatility, time horizons, the advantages of a long-term perspective, realistic expectations, the effects of rebalancing, the power of compounding, things to look for when reviewing investment options and how to review performance information. There are publications designed to provide these basic principles to participants[1]. Pre-determined asset allocation models can provide insight into portfolio design, as investment professionals incorporate these concepts into the model's allocation. Those who provide general financial and investment education are not considered fiduciaries. Many investment providers and service providers have websites that provide a great deal of educational material and offer these sites to participants as part of the services that they provide to the plan sponsor. Unfortunately, despite these services, participants in self-directed plans are making investment decisions that they are often ill-equipped to make.

How does education differ from investment advice? Education provides individuals with general information, such as the value of diversification and the differences between different asset classes. Investment advice is the process of reviewing investment goals and making specific investment recommendations, e.g., buy this, sell that. Providing this advice is something that most companies avoid, due to liability concerns. Some employers do see the benefit of providing this guidance to their participants, but offering advice should only be done by an investment professional and preferably, by one that is not associated with the investment provider. As an example, if the investment provider is a major mutual fund company and the mix of investment options includes eight (8) funds from their company and two (2) from other mutual fund companies, then it calls into question bias and conflict of interest in their recommendations. If the advisor is not affiliated with the investment provider, there will be no reason to question the recommendations that are made. As described in the

1. An example would be "Lessons for a Lifetime of Investing; Your guide to disciplined, productive investing," distributed by Mulberry Communications.

previous chapter, the Pension Protection Act of 2006 provides new guidelines for providing advice to workplace savings plans and their participants.

Some plan sponsors, who understand the pitfalls of trying to effectively educate participants with no experience in investment matters, are offering the services of independent investment professionals as part of their flexible benefits programs. The employee may talk with an advisor, who will then customize a financial plan and make investment suggestions.

ERISA SECTION 404(C), A FIDUCIARY "SAFE HARBOR"

ERISA provides a "safe harbor" for fiduciaries of defined contribution plans under Section 404(c) and the Pension Protection Act of 2006 adds to these provisions. Compliance within these standards reduces, but does not eliminate a fiduciary's liability exposure. To comply with Section 404(c), fiduciaries must first maintain proper records, properly supervise all appointed fiduciaries, such as plan administrators, investment providers, service providers and investment professionals and, have procedures in place for prudently reviewing, selecting and monitoring investment options. In addition to these basic requirements, Section 404(c) more specifically requires that the plan:

- Offer at least 3 investment options, each of which is in itself diversified and each has materially different risks and return characteristics than the other.
- Give participants the ability to transfer funds between investment options at least quarterly.
- Automatically provide participants with "sufficient information," including certain investment information and also make additional information available on request.

We will discuss each of these in more detail and remind fiduciaries that many of these often slip through the cracks, resulting in liability exposure. This list is incomplete, as the DOL lists approximately twenty (20) to twenty-five (25) requirements for shifting legal liability.

The 404(c) provision does not provide protection when the participant does not exercise an investment choice, but the Pension Protection Act of

2006 now provides 404(c) protection when plan sponsors designate default investment options and, the PPA allows for automatic enrollment.

Diversification: There must be at least three investment options, providing materially different levels of risk and return expectations, however a broad range of investment alternatives representing many investment styles is much more preferable. ERISA 404(c) states "a broad range of options where a participant has a reasonable opportunity to materially affect the potential risk and return...at any point within the range normally appropriate for the participant." In other words, the investment options must be diverse and appropriate for the workforce. It is appropriate for a risk-averse workforce to have more conservative investment choices than aggressive choices. Many companies form an internal investment committee to assess the needs of the workforce and to research funds; however consulting with an investment professional is the best way to meet the standards of the Prudent Expert Act.

Selecting investment options: Selecting and monitoring investment options are arguably the most important and least addressed ways to avoid liability. The best-case scenario for properly discharging this duty would include the following steps:

1. Conduct a prudent due diligence search for a consultant or advisor.
2. Appoint an internal investment committee to monitor all aspects of the plan.
3. Conduct a prudent search for an investment provider. Look for one that offers several fund families in their plan. The goal is to select funds that are the best within a style, regardless of the fund family, not to have all choices from the same fund family. Many fund families have significant overlap in the stocks that are held in each fund, which can effect actual diversification. Have criteria in place for replacing funds if need be.
4. The investment provider and/or the investment committee and/or consultant will determine how many funds the plan will offer to the participants. The funds should represent a broad range of asset classes and styles, and it may be advisable to include models in the mix. Some plan sponsors may think that the more funds offered to participants, the better, however this assumption is not the case. Too many choices

can lead to confusion. The DOL has stated that the investment menu should take into account the characteristics (sophistication and risk tolerance) of the workforce.

5. Establish a set of criteria to initially screen each fund, i.e., style, consistency of management, size of the fund and marketing practices.

6. Break the available funds into styles for a comparative analysis. Funds should be analyzed for their:

- Size: Small funds may have liquidity issues.
- Portfolio manager information, including tenure and turnover.
- Style consistency (style drift analysis).
- Comparative performance versus peers and appropriate benchmarks.
- Risk-adjusted performance.
- Upside capture ratio.
- Downside capture ratio.
- Turnover rate.
- Security overlap between funds: When selecting several funds, every attempt should be made to minimize the duplication of securities to ensure diversification.
- Diversification within the fund: Fund options should not have concentrated holdings in any one stock or sector, unless the fund is specifically a sector fund.

7. Conduct a cost analysis. In addition to reviewing the mutual fund expenses discussed in Chapter 5, 12b-1 fees must be tracked. Mutual fund companies benefit from their inclusion in 401(k) plans by investment providers and therefore, 12b-1 fees may be directed to the provider in exchange for the opportunity. This exchange is often referred to as "pay to play." Funds that return the 12b-1 fees to the investor are preferable, because it lowers the cost to the participants and it eliminates this potential conflict of interest. 12b-1 fees may also be directed to the advisor or consultant, potentially influencing his or her advice, thus resulting in a potential conflict of interest.

8. Choose the best relative performers for each style that also meet the other selection criteria. Choose funds from the upper quintile.

9. The use of pre-determined asset allocation models, such as those designed for a conservative or aggressive risk profile or, life-cycle funds. It is helpful to include these for those participants whose knowledge, education or attention to detail may not result in appropriate asset allocation choices for their portfolios. These funds are allocated and rebalanced by the fund company's portfolio manager. Again, fiduciaries have an investment oversight obligation, even though 401(k) plans are self-directed. Participants should not be allowed to commit financial suicide.

Monitoring investment options: After the selection of the investment options, there must be an ongoing process in place to monitor and evaluate the funds, at least annually, to fully comply with Section 404(c). Funds should be re-evaluated using the same criteria used in the original selection process. Funds that no longer measure up should be replaced with more appropriate funds.

Failure to prudently carry out the duties of selection and monitoring can result in loss of participant benefits and personal liability for the plan sponsor and/ or investment committee.

Participant control: The participants must have control over their investments and be able to transfer funds between these options at least quarterly, however most plans now have systems in place that allow for daily access. The plan can however, set reasonable trading guidelines or restrictions on the frequency in which participants can make investment changes. The service provider generally facilitates these restrictions, but compliance remains the responsibility of the plan sponsor.

Participant notifications: Participants must be notified of a variety of plan elements, which is usually done in the plan's Summary Plan Description (SPD), or notification can be by letter. Compliance with this requirement usually falls upon the plan administrator. Participants must be made aware of the following items and those points in italics are the *most common reasons that 401(k) plans are out of 404(c) compliance.*

- Participants will be able to direct the investments within the plan, so there is a clear understanding that the plan is "self directed." They must have clear instructions regarding how and how often they can make investment changes to their portfolio or account.

- Participants have the right to receive written confirmations of any investment instructions.
- *The participants must be told that the plan intends to comply with Section 404(c), thus potentially relieving the fiduciaries of their liability for any losses and, the individual responsible for assuring this compliance must be provided to the participants. This statement must be included in the plan's SPD.*
- The participants must be told that they can request information about the plan or the investment options at any time and the appropriate fiduciary must respond in a timely manner.
- *The identity and contact information for the 401(k) fiduciary must be provided.*
- A description of each of the investment options must be provided, including the risk and return characteristics of each. This information must include any changes that are made to the list of options.
- All charges to the plan and fees to the participant accounts must be provided.
- Educational access information and/or any educational programs
- All investment managers and /or investment advisors should be disclosed.
- *A copy of all fund prospectuses must be made available and delivered to the participant either immediately before or after the participant initially purchases a fund.*
- If company stock is to be part of the plan, all procedural information must be made available regarding the purchase and sale of the stock, including any restrictions.
- Participants must be informed as to all distribution options.
- *A list of the additional information that the participant can request (a sampling listed below) must be provided.*

Blackout periods: As of January of 2003, the Employee Benefits Security Administration, EBSA, previously the Pension Benefit Guaranty Corporation, in compliance with the Sarbanes-Oxley act, adopted final rules regarding upcoming "blackouts." A blackout period is a period of time when the participants or beneficiaries are unable to direct, transfer or withdraw monies in their retirement accounts. Companies must notify, in writing, their participants and beneficiaries at least 30 days, but no more than 60 days prior to the blackout period. The notice must include:

- Reasons for the blackout
- A description of the right's that will be suspended
- The dates of the blackout period
- Which investments will be subject to the blackout
- A statement to the participants and beneficiaries advising them to evaluate their current investment positions in light of their inability to make changes during the blackout period

Should this requirement be breached, there are civil penalties of up to $100 per day per affected participant or beneficiary that will result in personal liability to the person against whom the penalty is assessed. These penalties are not a liability of the plan.

Informational requests: Participants should understand that they may request information about the plan and that it must be provided to them in a timely manner. This information may include:

- Annual operating expenses of each investment option
- Fund performance information
- Copies of any prospectuses, financial statements and reports regarding the funds that are provided to the plan
- A list of the investment portfolio holdings
- Confirmations of investment instructions, if requested
- The name of the insurance company issuing group annuity contracts, if applicable
- Information concerning the value of shares or units in designated investment options

Due diligence file: 401(k) plan sponsors should maintain a due diligence file for all activities associated with the plan, including the selection process for appointees and any contracts entered into with these individuals or firms.

- *Plan Documents (Originals, Updates and Amendments)*
  - All plan and trust documents
  - Summary Plan Description
  - IRS Determination Letter and all associated application documents
  - All employee related communications, such as enrollment and 404(c) intensions
  - Annual reports, including SAR (Summary Annual Report) and Form 5500

- *Plan Structure and Providers*
  - Investment policy statement
  - Documentation of the process used to select the investment options offered within the plan
  - Process used to select service providers: RFP, cost analysis, any consultant recommendations or referrals
  - Proof of insurance for service provider and fidelity bond to comply with Section 412 of ERISA
  - Any agreements with the service provider, investment professionals, plan administrators or others. There should be a formal agreement on file for all outside appointees
  - Process to provide education to plan participants
  - Annual plan design review

- *Plan Monitoring*
  - Performance reports: Investments are monitored in compliance with the review criteria established in the investment policy or any updates to investment policy. Fund performance and expense information are to be reviewed within the time frame designated in the investment policy.
  - Notices to participants of any plan changes.
  - Information provided to participants concerning plan administrators, i.e., proof of insurance.
  - Document proper orientation of each new employee.
  - Establish a meeting schedule for plan fiduciary meetings.
  - Maintain the minutes of plan fiduciary meetings.

- Document the review of service provider's performance.
- Maintenance of fiduciary liability insurance, ERISA fidelity bond and D&O insurance (director and officer).
- Filings, including Form 5500.

CONCLUSION

401(k) plans require a great deal of documentation and recordkeeping, but they have nonetheless become a force in retirement plan offerings. Employers see them as a necessary benefit to attract and retain qualified employees and, employees have an opportunity to save for retirement with pre-tax dollars, regardless of their employer's ability or willingness to contribute to their retirement planning. Both see 401(k) plans as a winning strategy, but unfortunately, plan sponsors have allowed their 401(k) plans to be administered by third parties, without realizing their responsibilities and liability. These plans generally have many layers of third party providers who fulfill many of the administrative and management requirements, distancing the plan sponsor from the operation of the plan. This "transfer of responsibility" has lead to widespread neglect by plan sponsors, who do not understand that their duties and obligations under ERISA cannot be fully eliminated by delegating duties to these providers. This lack of oversight resulted in inappropriate and unsuitable investments going unchecked, as participants of all ages attempted to maximize their returns in the late '90s. When the tech bubble broke, many who were near retirement, found that their savings had lost 50% of their value and they were looking for someone to blame. The lawsuits that have followed have alerted plan sponsors to their risk of liability and have made the value of an investment consultant more pronounced. Plan sponsors are realizing that it is essential to make effective oversight of their plans a priority going forward.

None of the information contained in this chapter should be construed as legal advice, nor should it be considered a complete accounting of ERISA standards and requirements for 401(k) plans. An attorney who specializes in ERISA law should review employee benefit plan documents and provide oversight and guidelines for the implementation and management of the plan.

APPENDICES

Appendix A
Professional Designations

There are many designations associated in some fashion with the investment industry, however only the AIMC, CIMC and CIMA are specific to consulting and the investment management consulting process. We have listed additional designations here for informational purposes, although this should not be considered a complete listing.

Accredited Asset Management Specialist (AAMS)
Sponsored by the College for Financial Planning and awarded to individuals who have completed testing covering a broad range of investment applications including retirement, tax and estate planning and insurance.

Chartered Portfolio Manager (CPM)
Sponsored by the American Academy of Financial Management, this individual has completed coursework in both portfolio design and technical analysis, has at least three years of experience in active portfolio management and has an accredited college degree.

Certified Divorce Financial Analyst (CDFA)
Sponsored by The Institute for Divorce Financial Analysts and awarded to individuals seeking to provide financial planning for divorcing couples. Most CDFAs tend to be Certified Financial Planners or attorneys.

Certified Fund Specialist (CFS)

Sponsored by the Institute of Business & Finance and awarded to individuals after completing testing on fund related subjects including fixed income funds, open and closed-end funds, diversification, asset allocation, retirement strategies, global investing and risk.

Certified Retirement Counselor (CRC)

Sponsored by the International Foundation for Retirement Education and awarded to individuals who complete course work and testing covering the fundamentals of retirement planning, investments, plan design and counseling, communication and ethics.

Certified Senior Advisor (CSA)

Sponsored by the Society of Certified Senior Advisors and awarded to individuals tested on a wide range of senior concerns including Social Security, long-term care, housing, and even spirituality.

Chartered Advisor for Senior Living (CASL)

Sponsored by the American College and awarded to those who have completed a curriculum covering retirement and estate planning, understanding the older client, investments, health and long-term care financing.

Chartered Advisor in Philanthropy (CAP)

Sponsored by the American College, and awarded to those who have completed courses designed to supplement the knowledge of those professionals who work with non-profit organizations and philanthropically inclined individuals.

Certified Financial Planner (CFP)

The College for Financial Planning awards the CFP designation. These individuals must pass a test indicating their proficiency in financial planning techniques, such as tax preparation, insurance, investing and estate planning. CFPs are "generalists" who can provide a valuable service to investors, however their course of study does not include the consulting or managed money process.

Chartered Financial Consultant (ChFC)

This designation is an extension of the CFP, including the same courses, plus three additional electives. Courses are offered from the American College and satellite schools.

Chartered Mutual Fund Counselor (CMFC)

Sponsored by the College for Financial Planning and designed to broaden advisor's knowledge of various types of mutual funds and the ways they can be utilized to meet clients' needs.

Chartered Retirement Planning Counselor (CRPC)
Chartered Retirement Plans Specialist (CRPS)

Sponsored by the College for Financial Planning, these designations are awarded following studies and examinations, which are focused on pre- and post retirement concerns, including estate planning and asset management.

Long-Term Care Professional (LDCP)

Sponsored by the American Association for Long-Term Care Insurance and the Health Insurance Association of America, this designation is awarded to individuals who have completed studies related to long-term care.

Certified for Long-Term Care (CLTC)

The Corporation for Long-Term Care Certification designates individuals who have completed course work and examinations relating to long-term care.

Chartered Market Technicians (CMT)

Accreditation is received from the Market Technicians Association by those individuals who are proficient in all aspects of technical analysis and, have completed a three-part examination process.

Appendix B

Profiling Questionnaire for Individuals

Profiling Questionnaire for Trustees

Profiling Questionnaire for Establishing a Written Investment Policy Statement

INDIVIDUAL ASSETS

Including Personal Accounts, IRAs, Rollovers and Personal Trusts

Establishing investment goals, objectives and cash requirements for individuals is extremely important, as is understanding the investor's investment philosophy and perspective on financial matters. The answers to the following questions will assist the consultant in assessing the investor's expectations of returns, risk tolerance in different market cycles, investment goals, as well as the investor's vision of his or her financial future. This will help the consultant design an investment plan, establish a framework for communications and create a mutual understanding in the client-consultant-money manager relationship.

Name_____Contact Number _____

CURRENT STATUS

1. What is your current source of income?
    - ☐ Employment
    - ☐ Prior business success (Savings)
    - ☐ Inheritance
    - ☐ Pension or other retirement money
    - ☐ Income or payments form divorce decrees, alimony, child support, prenuptials

    (If you answered anything other than employment, skip to question 7.)

2. What is your current employment status?
    - ☐ Working full-time
    - ☐ Working part-time
    - ☐ In transition

    What type of work do you do?

3. Are you part of a two-income household?
    - ☐ Yes
    - ☐ No

    If so, what type of work does your spouse/life partner do?

4. How many years have you been with your current employer or in your current position? _____years   Your spouse/life partner?_____years

5. How stable is your income?
    - ☐ Very Stable (salaried)
    - ☐ Stable Base (salary + bonus)
    - ☐ Volatile (commission or seasonally based)

6. How stable is your spouse's/life partner's income?
    - ☐ Very Stable (salaried)
    - ☐ Stable Base (salary + bonus)
    - ☐ Volatile (commission or seasonally based)

ECONOMY

7. How do you feel about the short-term outlook for the U.S. economy (12-24 months)?
    - ☐ I feel the outlook is good.
    - ☐ I'm neutral; there are opportunities and problems.
    - ☐ I'm quite concerned; the outlook is poor.

8. How do you feel about the inflation outlook over the long-term (5-10 years)?
    - ☐ It will be a problem for a long time and may get worse.
    - ☐ The rate of inflation will probably remain at about current levels.
    - ☐ Inflation is only a temporary problem; the rate will back down.

9. How would you describe your outlook on the U.S. economy over the next five years?
    - ☐ Positive
    - ☐ Negative
    - ☐ Undecided

INCOME AND RETURN EXPECTATIONS

10. Total return for the entire portfolio consists of both income return (i.e., dividends from stocks and interest from bonds) and capital appreciation. In general, the securities that produce higher income return have lower capital appreciation. Do you have a yield expectation from your portfolio, which would be derived from dividends of stocks, and interest of bonds?

   ☐ No

   ☐ Yes. Please indicate the appropriate income yield range you expect the total portfolio to generate (dividends and interest income).

   ☐ 8-12%

   ☐ 4-8%

   ☐ 2-4%

11. Do you have any requirements for immediate and ongoing income cash flow from your portfolio?

   ☐ No

   ☐ Yes Please, specify annual dollar amount. $_____

12. If you have an income requirement, do you expect it to increase in the next 5 years?

   ☐ No

   ☐ Yes (by how much?)

13. Generally, the higher the anticipated growth or capital appreciation of securities, the smaller the dividend yield. If you would like or require dividend yield from your portfolio, what dividend yield range would you target?

   ☐ I feel capital appreciation is more desirable than dividend yield.

   I would like the dividend yielding **stocks** in my portfolio to have an average dividend yield of:

   ☐ 0-4%

   ☐ 4-6%

   ☐ 6-8%

   ☐ Over 8%

14. In general, the higher the return goal, the greater the risk the manager must take. What average annual rate of return (as opposed to a "relative" rate of return which is compared solely to a market index) do you consider to be the investment objective for the portfolio on a long-term basis? The average total return for the past 70 years (from 1926 to 1996) has been 10% for stocks and 5.2% for corporate bonds[1].

    Total Return Expectation
    ☐ Over 12% per year
    ☐ 10-12% per year
    ☐ 8-10% per year
    ☐ Below 8% per year
    ☐ Exceeds inflation (CPI) by_____%

CASH NEEDS

15. If a circumstance were to arise that caused you to be unable to work, how would you supplement your income to maintain your lifestyle?
    ☐ Disability Insurance
    ☐ Income from your portfolio
    ☐ Other (please specify)

16. If not currently retired, at what age do you plan to retire?_____Age
    In approximately:
    ☐ Less than 5 years
    ☐ 5-10 years
    ☐ 10-15 years
    ☐ 20-25 years
    ☐ More than 25 years

17. If your spouse/life partner is currently working and not retired, at what age do they plan to retire? _____Age
    In approximately:
    ☐ Less than 5 years
    ☐ 5-10 years
    ☐ 10-15 years
    ☐ 20-25 years
    ☐ More than 25 years

1. Ned Davis Research, Inc.

18. Once retired, anticipate your net (after tax) annual spending needs?
    $_____

19. Do you anticipate needing access to significant amounts of your invested money?
    ☐ Yes
    ☐ No
    ☐ If so, when?

20. Do you require regular draws from your account?
    ☐ Yes
    ☐ No

ASSET ALLOCATION/DIVERSIFICATION

21. Do you think common stocks are a good inflation hedge?
    ☐ Yes
    ☐ No

22. How do you feel about investing in common stocks in general?
    ☐ I feel stocks are very attractive and should occupy a dominant role in a portfolio.
    ☐ Common stocks should have a place in an investment portfolio.
    ☐ I have no opinion.
    ☐ I feel stocks are relatively risky and their use should be limited.
    ☐ I feel stocks should be used sparingly, if at all.

23. Do you believe it is necessary that the portfolio always contain bonds if it is to be adequately diversified?
    ☐ Yes
    ☐ No

24. Do you think that the stock market is currently offering enough potential return over the next year to assume the potentially greater risk associated with stocks as opposed to fixed income instruments?
    ☐ Yes
    ☐ No

25. What is your attitude about owning stocks at various points in a market cycle?

  ☐ I believe the percentage of stocks in the portfolio should be based on the potential value in each stock held, regardless of the economic or overall market environment.

  OR

  ☐ I believe the economic and market outlook should be evaluated first and the percentage of stocks should reflect that outlook.

26. Bonds too have market cycles, what is your attitude toward owning bonds in the various points in a market cycle?

  ☐ I believe bonds are always a good investment regardless of the outlook for bond prices.

  OR

  ☐ I think the economic and market outlook should be considered in making bond investments and the percentage in bonds should vary with this outlook.

27. The quality of bonds and their length of maturity have an effect on risk. Generally bonds pay a higher interest when there is a greater risk. What bond quality and maturity length do you feel is most appropriate for your portfolio?

  QUALITY

  ☐ All AAA rated highest possible

  ☐ None lower than AA

  ☐ None lower than A

  ☐ None lower than BAA

  ☐ Speculative bonds for high return and capital gains

  MATURITY

  ☐ Under 5 years (short-term)

  ☐ 1-10 years (intermediate)

  ☐ 10+ years (long-term)

28. In regards to your ongoing objectives, you may have an established opinion on how your portfolio should be balanced among stocks, bonds, other fixed income investments and cash. Please indicate your preferred maximum/minimum mixes for the following asset classes.

	Maximum	**Minimum**	**Target**
Domestic Equities (stocks)			
International Equities (stocks)[1]			
Fixed Income (bonds)			
Cash (money market)			

FUTURE PLANNING

29. Do you have, or plan to have, children, grandchildren, or any other individuals that will require funds for schooling?
    ☐ Yes
    ☐ No

30. When and for what level of schooling will these funds be required?

Name	Relationship	Years to Save	Type of School

Relationship	**Type of School**
Child	1. Private Pre-College School
Grandchild	2. Private College
Other (specify)	3. In State College
	4. Out of State College
	5. Ivy League

1. Global/International investing involves risks not typically associated with US investing, including currency fluctuations, political instability, uncertain economic conditions and differing accounting standards.

31. Do you or any of your dependents or family members have medical problems that will require financial consideration?

    ☐ Yes
    ☐ No

Please specify:

32. Do you foresee a need to provide your parent(s) with financial help in the future?

    ☐ Yes
    ☐ No

33. If so, what type of help do you anticipate?

    ☐ Medical
    ☐ Housing
    ☐ Other (please explain):

34. How much financial help do you anticipate they will need?

    ☐ Extensive
    ☐ Moderate
    ☐ Little

RETIREMENT PLANNING

35. Do you have an IRA?

    ☐ Yes
    ☐ No

If so, what is the current value?

36. Do you contribute to a 401(k) and/or deferred compensation plan?

    ☐ Yes
    ☐ No

If so, what is their current value?

37. Do you or your employer contribute to any other employer sponsored retirement plans, including stock options?
    - ☐ Yes (type of plan): _____
    - ☐ No

    If so, what is the current value?

38. When will you be eligible to receive the funds?

39. How do you plan to receive the funds?
    - ☐ Lump sum
    - ☐ Monthly Income
    - ☐ To be determined

INVESTMENT PHILOSOPHY

40. What is your opinion on investing in the international securities markets (excluding money market) for this portfolio?
    - ☐ This portfolio is to be invested solely in international securities.
    - ☐ This portfolio is to be invested in international and domestic securities (global).
    - ☐ The majority of the portfolio is to be invested in domestic securities and may own international securities as determined by the manager.
    - ☐ This portfolio is to have no international securities.

41. For each group, indicate the attitude that most closely resembles your own expectations regarding the policies of the money manager.
    (Choose One)
    - ☐ Invest in established companies.
                    OR
    - ☐ Invest in new companies, which are considered to have a good growth potential.
                    OR
    - ☐ Both of the above.

(Choose One)
- ☐ Generally sells individual stocks when the stock price is higher in value than the financial value of comparable companies in the market.

OR

- ☐ Generally sells stocks when indicated by technical market analysis. This approach relies on trend analysis, not the fundamentals of the individual stocks.

42. Overall, how would you generally categorize your investment objectives? **(Choose One)**
- ☐ Growth – maximum growth of capital with little or no income considerations.
- ☐ Growth plus Income – primary emphasis on capital growth with focus on income.
- ☐ Balanced – a balanced portfolio with equal emphasis on capital growth and income.
- ☐ Income Oriented – income as a primary emphasis.
- ☐ Other – please explain:

43. It is important to understand your goals and risk tolerance for your investment portfolio. Please rank the following 1 through 5, with 1 being the most important.

_____ Maximum capital appreciation
_____ Preservation of capital
_____ High current income
_____ Inflation hedge
_____ Consistent returns, low volatility

44. The investment process requires various tradeoffs in the quest for positive results. Deciding what tradeoffs an investor is willing to accept in order to achieve a competitive total return constitutes an ongoing challenge. In evaluating your own attitudes, please check one item for each where you feel most uncomfortable.

(Choose One)

☐ Holding large cash reserves during a strong market environment.

OR

☐ Being fully invested during a weak market environment.

(Choose One)

☐ Selling an investment and seeing it immediately rise.

OR

☐ Buying an investment and watching it immediately decline.

45. What is the most attractive alternative?

☐ Being invested in both up and down phases of a full market cycle.

OR

☐ Trying to time the market's direction of movement.

46. The potential for an increase in return is usually associated with an increase in market volatility. What is most **attractive** to you?

☐ Accepting a wider possible range of market volatility in an attempt to achieve a higher return.

☐ Consistent returns with lower market volatility.

47. How much downside market volatility can you tolerate in an attempt at potentially higher returns?

☐ Can tolerate more than one year of negative absolute returns through difficult phases in a market cycle.

☐ Can tolerate 2 to 3 quarters of negative absolute returns through difficult phases in a market cycle.

☐ Can tolerate only infrequent, very moderate losses through a market cycle.

48. Are there any securities that you would prefer to exclude from your portfolio?

☐ No

☐ Yes (i.e., Tobacco stocks; please explain)

MEASUREMENT

49. When examining the investment performance for this account I would base it upon:
    - ☐ The "absolute" comparison. Looking at the net return.
    - ☐ The "relative" comparison. Looking at return as it relates to a specific benchmark (i.e., S&P 500).
    - ☐ Using both methods above.
    - ☐ I have no real preference.

50. The time period used in evaluating an investment performance has a significant impact on the probability of realizing a stated return objective. The longer the period used the better the chance that up and down market cycles will average out to a "normal" or "expected" return. What investment time horizon seems most appropriate for the account?
    - ☐ Ten years or more
    - ☐ Five to ten years
    - ☐ A complete market cycle (3-5years)

51. Relative to popular stock market indices, such as the S&P500, which of the following is your goal for equity performances?
    - ☐ Generally beat the market index in each UP market year.
    - ☐ Generally beat the market index in each DOWN market year.
    - ☐ Surpass the market index, on average, over an extended period of time (without regard to each individual year).
    - ☐ Do as well as the market over an extended period of time.
    - ☐ I consider the performance relative to a market index to be irrelevant. I prefer to specify our objective in another way.

52. What time periods would be preferred for performance reporting and analysis of the money manager(s) and the portfolio?

Reports	Evaluation Meetings
___ Annually	___ Annually
___ Semiannually	___ Semiannually
___ Quarterly	___ Quarterly
___ When deemed necessary	___ When deemed necessary

INSURANCE

53. Do you or any member of your family have any of the following policies or coverage
    - ☐ Disability
    - ☐ Short term
    - ☐ Long term
    - ☐ Long Term Care
    - ☐ Critical Illness
    - ☐ Chronic Illness
    - ☐ Death of a family member

54. What type of Life insurance policy(s) do you have? Mark all that are applicable.
    - ☐ Term (T)
    - ☐ Universal Life (UL)
    - ☐ Variable Universal Life (VUL)
    - ☐ Whole (WL)

ANNUITIES

Please list any annuities that you have.

ESTATE PLANNING

55. Do you have any of the following in place?
    - ☐ Last Will & Testament
    - ☐ Living Trust
    - ☐ Revocable
    - ☐ Irrevocable
    - ☐ Durable Power of attorney
    - ☐ Medical Power of attorney
    - ☐ Living Will
    - ☐ Irrevocable Life Insurance Trust

56. When was the last time these were reviewed?

57. If it is your goal to leave an estate, how large of an estate would you like to be able to leave? $_____

58. Do you have an interest in charitable gifting?
    - ☐ Yes
    - ☐ No

GENERAL INFORMATION

59. Do you have Power of Attorney for any other individual's accounts?
    - ☐ Yes
        - ☐ Limited
        - ☐ Full
    - ☐ No

60. Are you a trustee for any accounts related or unrelated?
    (i.e., Family Living Trust, other peoples children, etc.)
    - ☐ Yes
    - ☐ No

    If yes, please provide the: Name of Trust, Tax ID, Date of Trust, Trustee(s) & Mailing address.

61. Are you a member of, or on the board of, any of the following?
    - ☐ Partnership
    - ☐ LLC
    - ☐ Not for Profit
    - ☐ Foundation
    - ☐ Corporations
        - ☐ Sub-chapter S
        - ☐ C corporation

    If so, please provide the: Name of Foundation, Partnership, LLC and/or Corporation, Tax ID, General Partner(s), Trustee/s or Managing Member and Mailing Address.

62. Is someone other than you or your spouse a trustee for related trust accounts, such as trusts for your children?

    ☐ Yes

    ☐ No

If yes please complete the Trust section on the profile sheet.

OTHER ASSETS & LIABILITIES

63. Please list your homes, rental property, and any other significant assets that may be held at other financial institutions. How are they titled? (Sole and Separate; Joint tenant with right of survivorship; Tenants in common)

Asset	Approximate Value	Liability	Titling
_____	_____	_____	_____
_____	_____	_____	_____

COMMUNICATION

64. What regularity of direct contact with your financial consultant is preferred?

Meetings	**Phone or Letter**
___ Annually	___ Annually
___ Semiannually	___ Semiannually
___ Quarterly	___ Quarterly
___ When deemed necessary	___ When deemed necessary

65. Is geographic location of your portfolio manager important to you?

    ☐ No

    ☐ Yes (please explain)

Profiling Questionnaire for Establishing a Written Investment Policy Statement

TRUSTEE/COMMITTEE DIRECTED ASSETS

Including Profit Sharing Plans, Retirement Plans, Foundations and Endowments, Not-For-Profit and Taft-Hartley Funds

The Employee Retirement Income Security Act of 1974 (ERISA) and the Uniform Prudent Investor Act (UPIA) have mandated the need for prudence and structure in investing assets for the benefit of others. To fullfill this requirement, fiduciaries must formalized investment objectives in writing. This questionnaire has been created to assist plan sponsors, investment committees, trustees and others in determining specific investment objectives, within established guidelines. The answers to the following questions will assist in this process and, at the same time, establish a framework for communications and mutual understanding in the client-consultant-money manager relationship.

ECONOMY

1. How do the trustees feel about the short-term outlook for the U.S. economy (12-24 months)?
   - ☐ I feel the outlook is good.
   - ☐ I'm neutral; there are opportunities and problems.
   - ☐ I'm quite concerned; the outlook is poor.

2. How do the trustees feel about the inflation outlook over the long-term (5-10 years)?
   - ☐ It will be a problem for a long time and may get worse.
   - ☐ The rate of inflation will probably remain at about current levels.
   - ☐ Inflation is only a temporary problem; the rate will back down.

3. How would the trustees describe their outlook on the U.S. economy over the next five years?
   - ☐ Positive
   - ☐ Negative
   - ☐ Undecided

ASSET ALLOCATION/DIVERSIFICATION

4. Do the trustees think common stocks are a good inflation hedge?
   - ☐ Yes
   - ☐ No

5. How do the trustees feel about investing in common stocks in general?
   - ☐ I feel stocks are very attractive and should occupy a dominant role in a portfolio.
   - ☐ Common stocks should have a place in an investment portfolio.
   - ☐ I have no opinion.
   - ☐ I feel stocks are relatively risky and their use should be limited.
   - ☐ I feel stocks should be used very sparingly, if at all.

6. Do the trustees believe it is necessary that the portfolio always contain bonds to be adequately diversified?
   - ☐ Yes
   - ☐ No

7. Do the trustees think that the stock market is currently offering enough potential over the next year to compensate for its increased price fluctuation versus the bond market?
   - ☐ Yes
   - ☐ No

8. What is the trustee's attitude about owning stocks and bonds at various points in a market cycle?
   - ☐ I believe the percentage of stocks in the portfolio should be based on the intrinsic values available in each stock, regardless of the economic or overall market environment.

   OR
   - ☐ I believe the economic and market outlook should be evaluated first and the percentage in stocks should reflect that outlook.

   - ☐ I believe bonds are always a good investment regardless of the outlook for bond prices.

   OR

☐ I think the economic and market outlook should be considered in making bond investments and the percentage in bonds should vary with this outlook.

9. Bond interest rates generally vary inversely with the quality and maturity length of the bond. What bond quality and maturity length do the trustees feel is most appropriate for the portfolio?

Quality
☐ All AAA rated highest possible.
☐ None lower than AA.
☐ None lower than A.
☐ None lower than BAA.
☐ Speculative bonds for high return and capital gains.

Maturity
☐ Under 5 years (short-term)
☐ 5-10 years (intermediate)
☐ 10+ years (long-term)

10. How do the trustees believe the portfolio should be balanced among stocks bonds, other fixed income investments and cash? Please indicate preferred ranges for the following asset classes.

	Maximum	Minimum	Target
Equities (stocks)	_____	_____	_____
Fixed Income (bonds)	_____	_____	_____
Cash (money market)	_____	_____	_____

11. How do the trustees believe the equity portfolio should be diversified?
☐ Each equity position in the portfolio should represent no more than 5% of the total portfolio value.

OR

☐ Any one equity position can represent as much as_____% of the total portfolio value.

___

☐ No combined equity positions should represent more than 15% of any one industry group and/or 30% of any industry sector.

OR

☐ Combined equity positions can represent as much as _____% of an industry group and/or _____% of any industry sector.

INVESTMENT PHILOSOPHY

12. Choose the investment philosophy that most closely reflects the needs of the trustees.

☐ Invest in established companies.

OR

☐ Invest in new companies which are considered to have good growth potential.

OR

☐ Both

☐ Generally sells individual stocks when the stock price is higher in value than the financial value of comparable companies.

OR

☐ Generally sell stocks when technical market analysis indicates by exercising a high degree of stock market timing judgment, regardless of the financial value of the individual stocks.

13. Overall, how would the trustees categorize the investment objectives for these funds? (choose one)

☐ Growth: Maximum growth of capital with little or no income considerations.

☐ Growth with Income: Primary emphasis on capital growth with some focus on income.

☐ Balanced: A balanced portfolio with equal emphasis on capital growth and income.

☐ Income: The primary emphasis of the portfolio design should be income.

☐ Other. Please describe.

14. Please rank the following in order of priority (1 being most important):
    ___ Maximum capital appreciation
    ___ Preservation of capital
    ___ High current income
    ___ Inflation hedge
    ___ Consistent returns, low volatility

15. The investment process requires various tradeoffs in the quest for superior results. Quantifying the risk an investor is willing to accept in order to achieve a superior total return constitutes an ongoing challenge. In evaluating investing attitudes, please check one item from each group that best describes the most uncomfortable situation for the trustees.
    ☐ Holding large cash reserves during a strong market environment.

    OR

    ☐ Being fully invested during a weak market environment.

    ☐ Selling an investment and seeing it immediately rise.

    OR

    ☐ Buying an investment and watching it immediately decline.

16. Which is the most attractive alternative?
    ☐ No down years.

    OR

    ☐ Outperform the market over a full market cycle (3-5 years).

    ☐ Being invested in both up and down phases of a full market cycle.

    OR

    ☐ Trying to anticipate and time the market's direction of movement.

17. An increase in capital return is usually associated with an increase in the volatility of the portfolio's value. Which is most attractive to the trustees:
    ☐ Accepting a wider possible range of volatility in an attempt to achieve a higher return.
    ☐ Consistent returns with lower volatility.

18. How much downside market volatility can the trustees tolerate in an attempt to achieve higher returns?
    - ☐ Can tolerate more than one year of negative absolute returns through difficult phases in a market cycle.
    - ☐ Can tolerate 2 to 3 quarters of negative absolute returns through difficult phases in a market cycle.
    - ☐ Can tolerate only infrequent, very moderate losses through a market cycle.

19. Are there any securities that the trustees would prefer not to own, i.e., potential conflicts of interest?
    - ☐ No
    - ☐ Yes – Please explain.

INCOME AND RETURN EXPECTATIONS

20. A portfolio's total return includes income return (i.e., stock dividends and bond interest) and capital appreciation. As a general rule, the securities that have a higher income expectation, have lower capital return expectations. Do the trustees have an absolute income requirement from this portfolio?
    - ☐ No
    - ☐ Yes – please indicate the appropriate income yield range the trustees expect the total portfolio to generate.
    - ☐ 8-12%
    - ☐ 4-8%
    - ☐ 2-4%
    - ☐ Other – please specify annual dollar amount _____.

21. Do the trustees see a need for growth in the income produced by the portfolio within the next five years?
    - ☐ Yes
    - ☐ No

22. Seeking securities that have dividend yield may be suitable for the portfolio. As a rule, the higher the anticipated growth or capital appreciation, the smaller the dividend yield. Do the trustees require stocks in the portfolio to have a specific dividend yield?
    - ☐ No. I feel capital appreciation is more desirable.
    - ☐ I would like the equities in the portfolio to yield an average of 0-4%.

☐ I would like the equities in the portfolio to yield an average of 4-6%.

☐ I would like the equities in the portfolio to yield an average of 6-8%.

☐ I would like the equities in the portfolio to yield an average of greater than 8%.

23. What is the average, annualized, total net return expectation for this portfolio on a long-term basis? In general, the higher the goal the greater the risk the manager must take. The average total return for the past 70 years (1926 to 1996) has been 10% for stocks and 5.2% for corporate bonds[2].

☐ over 12% per year

☐ 10-12% per year

☐ 8-10% per year

☐ below 8% per year

☐ exceeds inflation (CPI) by_____%

☐ exceed our spending goal/distribution requirements of $_____

24. The primary emphasis in examining the investment performance of this portfolio should be based upon:

☐ "Absolute" comparison. That is, comparing the actual portfolio net returns to an absolute (target) rate of return.

☐ "Relative" comparison. That is, comparing the actual portfolio net returns to various market indices.

☐ Reporting the "real" return (net return minus inflation) and comparing this to a specific number, such as funding or distribution requirements.

☐ Using "target" and "relative" rates of return comparisons.

☐ I have no real preferences.

25. The time period used in evaluating an investment has a significant impact on the probability of realizing a stated return objective. The longer the time period, the better the chance that up and down market cycles will average out to a "normal" or "expected" return. What investment time horizon seems most appropriate for this portfolio?

☐ Ten years or more

☐ Five to ten years

☐ A complete market cycle (3-5 years)

2. Ned Davis Research.

26. Relative to popular stock market indices (S&P 500), rank your preference for equity performances, 1 being the most important and 4 the least important:

    □ Generally beat the market index in each UP market year.
    □ Generally beat the market index in each DOWN market year.
    □ Surpass the market index, on average, over an extended period of time (without regard to each individual year).
    □ Do as well as the market over an extended period of time.
    □ I consider performance relative to a market index to be irrelevant. I prefer to specify our objective in other way. (Please specify).

27. Does the trust have a specific funding mandate?

    □ Yes
    □ No
    If yes, please specify

COMMUNICATION

28. How often will the trustees require performance reporting and analysis of the money manager(s) and the portfolio?

	Reports	Evaluation Meetings
Annually	□	□
Semiannually	□	□
Quarterly	□	□
When deemed necessary	□	□

29. How often do the trustees expect to have direct contact with the money manager/s?

	Meetings	Phone or Letter
Annually	□	□
Semiannually	□	□
Quarterly	□	□
When deemed necessary	□	□

30. Is the geographical location of the consultant or money management firm important to the trustees?

    □ No
    □ Yes – please explain.

NOTE: This questionnaire does not purport to represent the design, administration or any other aspect of a formal retirement plan. It is only to be used as a general guideline to help trustees and/or plan sponsors and consultants in the preparation of an investment policy statement.

Appendix C

Appendix C-1

Investment Policy Statement for Individuals or Trusts

I n this appendix, we will provide a sample of an Investment Policy Statement. It can be used as a guide to establish an investment policy that is client specific. We have included a broad range of headings, some of which may or may not be applicable for the reader's purposes. Many individual policies may simply require a statement of goals and objectives, with specific attention to investment philosophy, risk tolerance and return expectations, as well as reporting standards. More complex estates and trusts will require a more detailed investment policy, such as the one included here. This is especially important when there is a fiduciary relationship.

CLIENT NAME
Statement of Investment Policy, Objectives, and Guidelines

SCOPE OF THIS INVESTMENT POLICY STATEMENT
This investment policy statement reflects the investment policy, goals, objectives, and constraints of *Client* as it applies to *specify assets*.

PURPOSE OF THIS INVESTMENT POLICY STATEMENT
This is an outline of the possible areas to be covered in the policy statement. This is generally adaptable to most types of clients.

1. Define and assign the responsibilities of all involved parties, such as the consultant, money managers, committees, trustees and governing boards if applicable.
2. Establish a clear understanding for all involved parties of the investment goals and objectives for the investment portfolio.
3. Offer guidance and limitations for all money managers regarding the investment of assets. If other investment vehicles are used, provide similar guidance for their use in the portfolio.
4. Establish a basis and timetable for evaluating investment results.
5. Manage assets according to prudent standards as established in common trust law (Chapter 20).
6. Establish the relevant time horizon for which the assets will be managed.

In general, the purpose of this statement is to outline a philosophy and attitude that will guide the management of the investment assets toward the desired results. It is intended to be sufficiently specific to be meaningful, yet flexible enough to be practical.

DEFINITIONS

It is often helpful to define certain terms that may be used in the policy, both to clarify their usage and to avoid potential misunderstandings. Commonly used terms could include:

1. "Client" – define the legal entity that is the client. This should be done if the client is any legal entity other than an individual.
2. "Portfolio" shall mean the total portfolio of securities that will be invested on behalf of client.
3. "Money Manager" shall mean any individual or group of individuals, employed to manage the investments of all or part of the portfolio's assets.
4. "Investment Management Consultant" (Consultant) shall mean any individual or group of individuals employed to provide consulting services, including advice on investment objectives and/or asset allocation, manager searches, and performance monitoring and reports. Some or all of these services may be included in the fee agreement

between the Consultant and the client and therefore should be clearly stated.

5. "Securities" shall refer to marketable investment securities, which are not prohibited within this statement.

6. "Time Horizon" shall be the time period over which the investment objectives, as set forth within this policy, are expected to be met.

7. Trusts often assign responsibilities to individuals and it is helpful to indicate any special roles, such as who may make up any committees or who may be a trustee. Define the authority that each may have regarding portfolio management and state any qualifications required to hold these positions.

ASSIGNMENT OF RESPONSIBILITY

Responsibility of the Money Manager(s)

Each Money Manager should have *full discretion* to make all investment decisions for the assets placed under its jurisdiction, while observing and operating within all policies, guidelines, constraints, and philosophies as outlined in this investment policy statement. Indicate specific responsibilities of the money manager(s) which may include:

1. Discretionary investment management includes decisions to buy, sell, or hold individual securities, and to alter asset allocations within the guidelines established in this statement. It is wise to define and limit discretion. Managers should be free to invest the assets entrusted to them within the limits of the policy, however caution should be used in expanding this authority.

2. Communicating any major changes to the economic outlook, investment strategy, or any other factors that may affect the implementation of the investment plan, or the achievement of the investment objective.

3. Informing the Consultant and/or client of any qualitative change to the firm's organization, such as changes in portfolio management personnel, ownership structure, investment philosophy, etc.

4. Voting proxies.

Responsibility of the Investment Management Consultant

The Investment Management Consultant is a non-discretionary advisor to *client*. Investment advice concerning the use of money managers and other investment options will be offered by the Consultant, and will be consistent with the investment objectives, policies, guidelines and constraints as established in this statement. Indicate specific responsibilities of the Investment Management Consultant, which may include:

1. Assisting in the development and periodic review of the investment policy.
2. Developing an asset allocation or providing asset allocation studies.
3. Conducting money manager searches.
4. Providing "due diligence" and/or research on money manager(s).
5. Monitoring the performance and providing performance reports on both the portfolio as a whole and on the individual investment options and money manager(s).
6. Communicating matters of policy, manager research, and manager performance to *client*.

Responsibility of Other Professionals or Individuals

Include any information that is relevant. This could include the responsibilities of a committee, trustees, legal council or accounting professionals if they have a role in managing the investment portfolio.

INVESTMENT MANAGEMENT POLICY

There are several common expectations of consultants and money managers that can be included in the policy, as they are consistent with the Prudent Expert Rule.

1. Preservation of Capital–Consistent with their respective investment styles and philosophies, money managers should make reasonable efforts to preserve capital, understanding that losses may occur in individual securities.

2. Risk Aversion–Understanding that risk is present in all types of securities and investment styles, *client* recognizes that some risk is necessary to produce long-term investment results that are sufficient to meet the policy objectives. However, the money managers are to make reasonable efforts to control risk, and will be evaluated regularly to ensure that the risk assumed is commensurate with the given investment style and objectives.

3. Risk Management–State the strategy, or exit strategy that the consultant may utilize to manage risk during times of extreme market turmoil. This may be a passive approach or one that is more proactive (Chapter 12).

4. Adherence to Investment Discipline–Money managers are expected to adhere to the investment styles for which they were hired. Managers will be evaluated regularly for adherence to their investment discipline.

INVESTMENT OBJECTIVES

State the investment objectives, using those listed in Chapter 8 as a guide.

- Return expectations, including performance measurement standards, i.e., absolute versus relative returns (Chapter 17).
- Risk tolerance and client's investment philosophy.
- Describe the client's attitudes about investing, such as the use of international securities; risk tolerance (conservative, aggressive); what is most important to the client (maximize returns, income, low volatility); or the use of fixed income securities. As market conditions change and portfolio returns don't follow those of the "hot stock" of the day, the client may have to be reminded of the philosophy that guided the structure of their portfolio.
- Investment time horizons.
- Assets that will be placed under management as a percentage of overall assets.
- Income or cash flow needs.
- Expected contributions or required distributions.
- In the case of trusts, establish a funding policy.

INVESTING GUIDELINES

Indicate specific investment guidelines or criteria, which may include:

- Any preferred or prohibited securities or types of securities.
- Attempt to quantify the client's tolerance to risk and volatility, i.e., *Client* could tolerate a maximum loss of 5-10% over any one-year period.
- Guidelines that would limit the percentage of the portfolio that can be invested in any one security or any one sector.
- Cash flow requirements.

Asset Allocation Guidelines: Indicate a preliminary asset allocation, ranges and optimal targets of each asset class. If appropriate, indicate the money management firms hired for each allocation style. Note that this can be subject to change, either due to a change in client objectives or market conditions. Indicate those individuals who are authorized to make changes, and/or the process required to change managers or invest outside of these guidelines.

ASSET CLASS/ STYLE	RANGE	TARGET
Large Cap	10 - 50%	20%
Mid Cap	10 - 30%	15%
Small Cap	5 - 30%	10%
International	0 - 20%	10%
Fixed Income	30 - 60%	30%
Other*	0 – 20%	10%
Cash	0 - 30%	5%

Other may include any type of security discussed in Chapter 13 or any other investment that the policy authorizes. These guidelines are for illustration purposes only and are not intended to suggest any specific allocations.

PERFORMANCE REVIEW AND EVALUATION

Reporting guidelines should be stated for both the Investment Management Consultant and the money managers or other investment vehicles. A reasonable reporting period is quarterly. The reports should include each manager and/or investment option's performance, acceptable benchmarks and total return. These should be compared to the investment objectives, goals, and guidelines set forth in this policy. The client should have the right to terminate a manager for any reason, at any time with written notice, and termination should become effective upon receipt of such notice. The criteria for manager termination may include any of the following:

1. Investment performance that is significantly less than anticipated given the discipline employed and the risk parameters established, and/or the manager provided unacceptable justification of poor results.
2. Failure to adhere to any aspect of this investment policy statement, including communication and reporting requirements.
3. Significant qualitative changes to the investment management organization.
4. Failure to adhere to the manager's stated style and/or philosophy.

Money managers shall be reviewed regularly regarding performance, personnel, strategy, research capabilities, organizational and business matters, and other qualitative factors that may impact their ability to achieve the desired investment results. These general criteria should also apply to other types of investment options selected for the portfolio, as applicable. Adapt the policy language to the investment vehicles that will be considered for the portfolio.

Depending upon the complexity of the investment policy, the policy may contain guidelines for hiring money managers or selecting other investment vehicles. This process is usually carried out by the Consultant.

INVESTMENT POLICY REVIEW

Set guidelines as to how often the policy should be reviewed. This "tune up" should be done a least every two years, as client's goals and objectives can, and most often do, change over time.

DATE AND APPROPRIATE SIGNATURES

It is important that all involved parties acknowledge the terms set forth in this policy and therefore, it is advisable to secure all relevant signatures.

Appendix C-2
Investment Policy Statement for an ERISA plan

In this appendix, we will provide the elements of an Investment Policy Statement that are relevant for an ERISA plan. They include investment objectives, guidelines, restrictions and responsibilities, as well as other elements that may be included. Once completed by the plan sponsor, the investment policy statement will provide the guidelines necessary to create a clear understanding of the overall direction and goals of the plan between the interested parties. Each plan will have its own requirements, which may result in a far more complex or simple policy statement, depending on the company. Plan sponsors and trustees should seek the help of a qualified consultant to develop an appropriate policy.

CLIENT NAME
Statement of Investment Policy, Objectives and Guidelines

SCOPE OF THIS INVESTMENT POLICY
Indicate the purpose and scope of the policy, such as "This statement of investment policy reflects the investment policy, objectives, and constraints of the *Client*."

PLAN BACKGROUND
Include any pertinent information about the plan, such as size, number of participants or annual contributions, as well as naming those involved in its management or parties of interest.

PURPOSE OF THIS INVESTMENT POLICY STATEMENT

State the purpose of investing, including who is making this statement, such as trustees. Include the following areas within the investment policy.

- Define and assign the responsibilities of all parties.
- Establish a clear understanding for the Consultant, money managers and/or Investment Monitor of the investment goals and objectives for the investment of the funds.
- Offer guidance and limitations for all money managers regarding the investment of the assets.
- Establish a basis and timetable for evaluating investment results, including benchmark criteria.
- Establish a basis for evaluating, hiring and terminating managers.
- Manage assets according to prudent standards as required by ERISA law.

In general, the purpose of this statement is to outline clearly a philosophy and attitude that will guide the investment management of the assets toward the desired results.

DELEGATION OF AUTHORITY

Define the duties that will be delegated to each professional involved in the management and operation of the plan's assets. These include, but are not limited to:

1. **Investment Management Consultant.** The consultant assists the Trustees in: Establishing the investment policy, objectives and guidelines; asset allocation studies; selecting money managers; reviewing such managers over time; measuring and evaluating investment performance; and other tasks as deemed appropriate.

2. **Money Manager.** The trustees may wish to specifically delegate the management of the plan's assets to the money manager/s, giving them full discretion to purchase, sell, or hold the specific securities that will be used to meet the investment objectives. They may also state that the manager must adhere to the Prudent Investor Rule.

3. **Custodian.** The custodian will physically maintain possession of securities owned by the plan, collect dividend and interest payments, redeem maturing securities, and effect receipt and delivery following purchases and sales. The custodian also performs regular accounting of all assets owned, purchased, or sold, as well as movement of assets into and out of the accounts.

4. **Trustees.** Take this opportunity to specify delegation of investment decisions and discretion. Example: TRUSTEE RESPONSIBILITY: The trustees are required by law to oversee the investment of the assets of the plan. The trustees shall discharge their duties solely in the interest of the participants and their beneficiaries. They shall "discharge their duties with the care, skill, prudence and diligence, under the circumstances then prevailing, that a prudent man acting in a like capacity and familiar with such matters would use in the conduct of an enterprise of a like character and with like aims."

DEFINITIONS

Define who or what is meant by such terms as "assets," "Trustees," "money manager," "Investment Management Consultant," "Investment Monitor" or others that are used in the policy.

ASSIGNMENT OF RESPONSIBILITY

Define the responsibilities of each of the parties involved with the management and/or investment of the assets. Responsibilities can vary widely, depending on a plan's structure:

- Money manager(s), including such things as discretion, reporting, communication, voting proxies and transactions
- Investment Management Consultant, including such things as development and periodic review of the investment policy, market analysis and asset allocation recommendations, manager searches, money manager monitoring, including their adherence to the policy guidelines and, performance monitoring
- Any other individuals involved with the management of the assets

MONEY MANAGER SELECTION

If the plan sponsors do not appoint a consultant, then there must be a section in the investment policy that addresses the due diligence process that the plan will employee to select and terminate managers. This should include those who will be responsible for this process. If the plan does appoint a consultant, the consultant should provide the plan with its process for inclusion in the plan's fiduciary file.

GENERAL INVESTMENT PRINCIPLES

Outline the standards of conduct, such as investing with skill within the meaning of the Prudent Investor Rule, including diversification, risk assessment, use of cash and other tools used to meet the objectives set forth by the trustees.

INVESTMENT MANAGEMENT POLICY

Describe key points that the money managers should adhere to, such as preservation of capital, risk aversion and adherence to their investment discipline.

INVESTMENT OBJECTIVES

Establish the investment objectives for the assets and emphasize total return; that is, the aggregate return from capital appreciation and dividend and interest income. Focus on describing reasons for investing and underlying objectives for the assets. Include preservation of purchasing power and preservation of capital. Focus on the long-term growth, expected return for the portfolio, and control of risk and volatility. Include a reference to actuarial assumptions that will affect cash flow requirements, if applicable. There should be a time frame established for investing and for the review of the policy, such as annually. Basic investment objectives include:

- Return expectations
- Risk tolerance and client's investment philosophy
- Investment time horizons
- Assets that will be placed under management
- Income or cash flow needs
- Contributions and distributions

SPECIFIC INVESTMENT GOALS

State the long-term investment goals, e.g. the primary investment goal of the Trustees is to achieve a desired return (specify, as stated in Chapter 8), while controlling risk and volatility, in order to provide a level of liquidity sufficient to meet the need for timely distributions to the participants. In keeping with the basic plan objectives, the money managers should strive for a positive total rate of return in each fiscal year. Total return is defined as dividend and interest income, plus capital appreciation, minus capital losses, net of all related management fees.

DEFINITION OF RISK

Define risk as the trustees see it, such as the possibility of losing money over the investment horizon, the possibility of not maintaining purchasing power over the investment horizon, the possibility of not meeting distribution requirements, and include the plans tolerance to volatility (fluctuation) of investment returns, i.e., provide a range of returns within a specified period of time, such as a loss of 15% over a one-year period of time.

VOLATILITY OF RETURNS

Proper diversification will help to reduce volatility and it should be stated that the individual money managers are required to minimize losses of individual investments whenever possible and, taking the portfolio as a whole, the portfolio must be structured in such a way as to agree with the trustee's objectives, such as minimize loss or protect against erosion of capital, etc. Discuss the trustees' tolerance to loss and volatility.

MARKETABILITY OF ASSETS

Liquidity needs should be described here. There are many illiquid investments available and there should be a clear understanding regarding their potential use.

INVESTMENT GUIDELINES

List allowable and prohibited assets, as well as grade or rating limitations on fixed securities. Allowable assets and limitations can include:

1. Cash Equivalents
   - Treasury Bills
   - Money Market Funds/Common Trust Cash Equivalent Funds
   - STIF Funds
   - Commercial Paper with A1 or P1 Ratings
   - Banker's Acceptances
   - Certificates of Deposit
   - Savings Accounts

2. Fixed Income Securities
   - U.S. Government and Agency Securities
   - Investment Grade Corporate Notes and Bonds
   - Mortgage or Other Backed Bonds
   - Preferred Stock

3. Equity Securities
   - Common Stocks, e.g. OTC not to exceed 20% of each advisors total investable funds)
   - Convertible Notes and Bonds
   - Convertible Preferred Stocks
   - American Depository Receipts (ADRs) of Non-U.S. Companies
   - Stocks of Non-U.S. Companies, e.g. Ordinary shares, not to exceed 20% of each advisors total investable funds, as long as they are traded on a stock exchange within the United States

Prohibited investments can include:

1. Private Placement Investments
2. Venture-Capital Investments
3. Real Estate Properties
4. Interest-Only (IO), Principal-Only (PO), and Residual Tranche CMOs
5. GICs

6. Repurchase Agreements
7. Floaters/Inverse Floaters
8. "Junk" debt

Stock Exchanges

To order to address an issue of marketability and liquidity, acceptable exchanges should be listed, such as the New York Stock Exchange, American Stock Exchange and NASDAQ market, however there may be other considerations that should be listed here.

Prohibited Transactions

Prohibited transactions can include:

1. Short Selling
2. Margin Transactions

Asset Allocation Guidelines

The Trustees will agree to a macro asset allocation guideline, as well as target allocations and ranges for style diversification. The guidelines and ranges are usually based on the asset allocation studies and recommendations of the Consultant. The most common macro breakdown would be between equities, fixed income and cash, but can include other asset classes, such as REITs, private equity or managed futures. Style diversification can be quite broad.

Investment management of the assets should follow asset allocation guidelines, calculated at market value at specific intervals. These intervals will represent points where the portfolio may require rebalancing to stay within the guidelines. State the interval, who will be responsible for maintaining compliance with the guidelines and how compliance will be maintained (i.e., rebalance annually).

Diversification for Money Managers

State a preference for the number of managers and who will dictate the composition of the manager portfolios. This statement may be "no preference" and/or "at the discretion of the managers," however it should be stated that the money managers will adhere to the style for which each is contracted. An asset allocation breakdown between specific managers can be included.

MONEY MANAGER PERFORMANCE REVIEW AND EVALUATION

The monitoring and evaluation process is important in maintaining a "safe harbor," so describe the process, including comparative criteria that will be used and who will be responsible for this duty. The investment results should be compared to the investment objectives, goals and guidelines set forth in this statement. This review should compare the performance of the overall portfolio and that of the individual managers to appropriate benchmarks, such as:

- A composite of the representative benchmarks in ratios equal to that of the individual investment styles in the portfolio
- Specific indexes which compare most closely to the manager's style
- The Consumer Price Index
- A comparable universe of money managers who experience similar levels of risk
- Risk-adjusted performance analysis

This analysis and evaluation is covered in detail in Chapters 18 and 19. Establish a frequency for review, as well as rebalancing or reallocation criteria.

PROCEDURES FOR TERMINATING A MANAGER

In the event that a manager is to be terminated, the policy should dictate the procedure. Chapter 19 discusses reasons why a manager might be terminated and the IPS should describe the notification, termination, liquidation and transfer procedures.

SIGNATURES

Include the signatures of the trustees, consultant, money manager/s and any other relevant parties involved with the management of plan assets. This assures that all parties agree to the guidelines set forth in the policy.

Disclaimer: The preceding policy is a specimen policy and should not be construed as being appropriate for every situation. Investors should seek help from a qualified consultant and legal council when formulating specific investment policies for their companies.

Appendix C-3

Investment Policy Statement
for Retirement Plans
(401(k) Profit Sharing and Savings Plan Policy)

This appendix provides a sample Investment Policy Statement, which has been prepared by Nationwide Financial for use with 401(k) plans and/or profit sharing plans in which they are the investment provider. This is a comprehensive policy statement, including the various non-designated investment alternatives available to plan sponsors and we believe a helpful, complete example of what plan sponsors should consider when writing an investment policy. The reader will note that Nationwide has included optional language for employer contributions (profit sharing) and a Money Purchase Pension Plan. In addition to the investment options described in Chapter 24, this sample policy includes a mutual fund window, which is a non-designated investment alternative that has not been prudently selected, nor is it monitored, but it is something the plan sponsor may choose to make available to those with greater investment expertise.

As with all of the sample formats presented in this book, the terms of this investment policy may not be appropriate for all plans, but it does offer structure and ideas for plan sponsors to review.

401(k) Profit Sharing and Savings Plan Investment Policy Statement

The Model Investment Policy Statement should be completed with the assistance of a competent investment professional. The model is designed to reflect the investments and services offered by Nationwide Financial through The BEST of AMERICA® Group Retirement Series and, thus, is not drafted for the specific needs or fiduciary decisions of any plan or plan sponsor. As a result, this is only a sample, and it is the responsibility of the plan fiduciary to adopt a policy that meets the needs of the plan and its participants. This Model should be customized (including the selection or deletion of optional provisions) by the responsible plan fiduciaries to reflect the decisions made by the fiduciaries concerning the investment structure and the investment options for the plan and its participants.

Publication of this work has been made possible by Nationwide Financial and is under copyright protection. This information is general in nature and is not intended to constitute legal or investment advice on any particular matter. This handbook and accompanying tools do not create an attorney-client relationship. These materials are designed exclusively for use with a Nationwide retirement plan product or program. Not for participant use.

Table of Contents

[OPTION IA(1)—401(a)/401(k) Plans]

401(k) Profit Sharing and Savings Plan
Investment Policy Statement

I. OVERVIEW AND PURPOSE

A. Overview of Investment Policy

The_____401(k) Profit Sharing and Savings Plan ("401(k)
Plan" or "Plan") is a retirement plan established by_____("Plan
Sponsor") for the benefit of the participating employees and their beneficia-
ries. The Plan is a profit sharing plan qualified under Section 401(a) of the
Internal Revenue Code ("IRC"). The Plan is also a 401(k) plan, which permits
voluntary pre-tax deferrals by participants from their pay.

The Plan offers eligible employees a convenient, tax-deferred and flexible
method to save for retirement.

[Option IA(1)-1A for Plan Sponsor matching and profit sharing contributions]	At the Plan Sponsor's discretion, employer matching contributions and/or profit sharing contributions may be made.
[Option IA(1)-1B Employer Matching Contributions Only]	At the Plan Sponsor's discretion, employer-matching contributions may be made.
	The Plan permits participants to direct the investment of their accounts.
	The responsibility for the amount of retirement benefits belongs in part to each participant. Eligible employees are responsible for:

- determining how much to contribute as a deferral of their pay, up to the allowable limit each year;
- deciding whether to use the Plan's withdrawal and loan provisions; and
- allocating their monies among the investment alternatives offered by the Plan.

The provisions of the Plan document govern the investment structure of the Plan, the identification of the Plan fiduciaries and the authority and responsibilities of those fiduciaries. The Federal law governing the operation of retirement plans—the "Employee Retirement Income Security Act" or "ERISA"—requires that fiduciaries follow the terms of the Plan (unless the Plan's provisions conflict with ERISA). Accordingly, the provisions of the Plan document govern the selection of Plan fiduciaries and the allocation and delegation of duties among the fiduciaries.

The ultimate authority to establish the investment structure, to prepare and amend this Investment Policy Statement and to select and review the investment alternatives resides with the Plan Sponsor. The Plan Sponsor may retain those functions, or if authorized by the Plan document, may appoint specific officers or a committee to fulfill those functions. The Plan Sponsor, the designated officers or the committee, as the case may be, is designated as the Investment Fiduciary for the plan and shall have the responsibilities and authority provided in this Investment Policy Statement.

[OPTION IA(2)—401(k)/MPP Plans]

401(k) Profit Sharing and Savings Plan
and Money Purchase Pension Plan
Investment Policy Statement

I. OVERVIEW AND PURPOSE

A. Overview of Investment Policy

The_____401(k) Profit Sharing and Savings Plan ("401(k) Plan" or "Plan") is a retirement plan established by_____("Plan Sponsor") for the benefit of the participating employees and their beneficiaries. The Plan is a profit sharing plan qualified under Section 401(a) of the Internal Revenue Code ("IRC"). The Plan is also a 401(k) plan, which permits voluntary pre-tax deferrals by participants from their pay.

The Plan offers eligible employees a convenient, tax-deferred and flexible method to save for retirement.

[Option IA(2)-1A for Plan Sponsor matching and profit sharing contributions]	At the Plan Sponsor's discretion, employer matching contributions and/or profit sharing contributions may be made.
[Option IA(2)-1B Employer Matching Contributions Only]	At the Plan Sponsor's discretion, employer matching contributions may be made.
[Option IA(2)-1C 401(k)/MPP Combination]	The Plan Sponsor also maintains the XYZ Money Purchase Pension Plan ("Pension Plan") for the benefit of its participating employees and their beneficiaries. The Pension Plan is a defined contribution plan qualified under IRC Section 401(a). The 401(k) Plan and the Pension Plan are collectively referred to as the "Plan" in this document

The Plan permits participants to direct the investment of their accounts.

The responsibility for the amount of retirement benefits belongs in part to each participant. Eligible employees are responsible for:

- determining how much to contribute as a deferral of their pay, up to the allowable limit each year;
- deciding whether to use the Plan's withdrawal and loan provisions; and
- allocating their monies among the investment alternatives offered by the Plan.

The provisions of the Plan document govern the investment structure of the Plan, the identification of the Plan fiduciaries and the authority and responsibilities of those fiduciaries. The Federal law governing the operation of retirement plans—the "Employee Retirement Income Security Act" or "ERISA"—requires that fiduciaries follow the terms of the Plan (unless the Plan's provisions conflict with ERISA). Accordingly, the provisions of the Plan document govern the selection of Plan fiduciaries and the allocation and delegation of duties among the fiduciaries.

The ultimate authority to establish the investment structure, to prepare and amend this Investment Policy Statement and to select and review the investment alternatives resides with the Plan Sponsor. The Plan Sponsor may retain those functions, or if authorized by the Plan document, may appoint specific officers or a committee to fulfill those functions. The Plan Sponsor, the designated officers or the committee, as the case may be, is designated as the Investment Fiduciary for the plan and shall have the responsibilities and authority provided in this Investment Policy Statement.

[OPTION IA(3)—401(a) Plan]

Profit Sharing Plan
Investment Policy Statement

I. OVERVIEW AND PURPOSE

A. **Overview of Investment Policy**

The_____Profit Sharing Plan ("Plan") is a retirement plan established by ("Plan Sponsor") for the benefit of the participating employees and their beneficiaries. The Plan is a profit sharing plan qualified under Section 401(a) of the Internal Revenue Code ("IRC").

[Option IA(3)-1A for Plan Sponsor profit sharing contributions]

At the Plan Sponsor's discretion, profit sharing contributions may be made from time to time and in varying amounts.

The Plan permits participants to direct the investment of their accounts.

The responsibility for the amount of retirement benefits belongs in part to each participant. Eligible employees are responsible for:

- allocating their monies among the investment alternatives offered by the Plan; and
- deciding whether to use the Plan's withdrawal and loan provisions

The provisions of the Plan document govern the investment structure of the Plan, the identification of the Plan fiduciaries and the authority and responsibilities of those fiduciaries. The Federal law governing the operation of retirement plans—the "Employee Retirement Income Security Act" or "ERISA"—requires that fiduciaries follow the terms of the Plan (unless the

Plan's provisions conflict with ERISA). Accordingly, the provisions of the Plan document govern the selection of Plan fiduciaries and the allocation and delegation of duties among the fiduciaries.

The ultimate authority to establish the investment structure, to prepare and amend this Investment Policy Statement and to select and review the investment alternatives resides with the Plan Sponsor. The Plan Sponsor may retain those functions, or if authorized by the Plan document, may appoint specific officers or a committee to fulfill those functions. The Plan Sponsor, the designated officers or the committee, as the case may be, is designated as the Investment Fiduciary for the plan and shall have the responsibilities and authority provided in this Investment Policy Statement.

B. **Purpose of Investment Policy**

The purpose of this Investment Policy Statement ("IPS") is to establish the investment structure for the Plan and to adopt a set of guidelines for the selection of the Plan's investment alternatives and for the periodic evaluation, or monitoring, of the investment alternatives. These guidelines do not constitute a contract or a statement of mandatory requirements, but are instead an explanation of the general principles established for the selection and retention of the investment alternatives. The Investment Fiduciary will determine the weighting to be given to each of these principles and may consider factors in addition to those described in these guidelines.

This IPS explains how the Investment Fiduciary will discharge its obligations to:

- prudently select investment alternatives;
- periodically monitor and evaluate those alternatives; and
- based on such periodic evaluations, determine whether or not the alternatives will continue to be made available to the participants.

These guidelines will be reviewed informally at appropriate intervals and will be reviewed on a formal basis as circumstances warrant. The alternatives, along with their benchmarks, descriptions and performance evaluation measures, may be changed from time to time; so this information, and other decisions that may be periodically reviewed and changed are attached as exhibits, which can be amended without modifying the principles of the IPS.

[Option IB-1 for 404(c) ERISA Plans]

This IPS is intended to be consistent with the criteria for an "ERISA Section 404(c) Plan" as described in Section 404(c) of the Employee Retirement Income Security Act of 1974, as amended ("ERISA"), and the regulations thereunder. If the plan intends to obtain the fiduciary protections of ERISA Section 404(c), the Plan must satisfy the conditions in the regulations under ERISA Section 404(c), including the designation of a broad range of investment alternatives, which permit participants to make independent choices regarding the manner in which the assets in their individual accounts are invested and which afford the participants the opportunity to materially affect the potential returns on their accounts and the degree of risk involved.

[Option IB-2 for Governmental 401(a) Plans]

While this is a governmental plan as defined in Section 3(32) of Title I of the Employee Retirement Income Security Act of 1974, as amended ("ERISA"), and is therefore not subject to the provisions of that title, including the fiduciary requirements, the Plan Sponsor intends to generally follow the fiduciary best practices of ERISA, including the information and disclosure standards of ERISA Section 404(c). As a result, this IPS is intended to be consistent with the criteria for an "ERISA §404(c) Plan" and the regulations thereunder. Accordingly, the Plan will designate a broad range of investment alternatives, which permit participants to make independent choices regarding the manner in which their individual accounts are invested and which afford the participant the opportunity to materially affect the potential returns on their accounts and the degree of risk involved.

II. INVESTMENT STRUCTURE

A. Overview of Structure

The investment structure of the Plan will allow participants to create investment portfolios by allocating their accounts among a group of prudently selected and monitored investment alternatives that together constitute a broad range of asset classes and investment styles. From time to time the Plan's investment structure will be reviewed by the Investment Fiduciary. The Plan's designated investment alternatives shall be look-through investment vehicles as that term is defined in the regulations under ERISA Section 404(c) (the "Funds"), although other types of investment alternatives may also be offered.

[Option II-A1 Asset Allocation Funds Note: If you elect this option, you should also select Option II-E, Option IV-C and the asset allocation fund option section on Exhibit B.]

In addition, the structure will include asset allocation funds, which will enable participants to direct the investment of their accounts into a single diversified vehicle designed to be consistent with their time horizons and risk tolerances.

[Option II-A2 Brokerage Account Note: If you elect this option, you should also select Option II-F, Option III-D Option IV-D and Exhibit F.]

The investment structure will allow participants to invest, through a brokerage account, in nondesignated alternatives such as individual stocks and/or mutual funds. These nondesignated alternatives will not be individually selected or monitored by the Investment Fiduciary.

[Option II-A3 Mutual Fund Window. Note: If you elect this option, you should also select Option II-G., Option III-E., and Option IV-E. *This option is not yet available but will be offered in the future.*]

The investment structure will offer participants the opportunity to select among a large number of mutual funds and similar vehicles (the "mutual fund window") in addition to the Designated Funds. The investment options in the mutual fund window will constitute all of the investment alternatives that it is administratively feasible for the Plan to hold and, as such, will not be designated by the Plan and are not selected and monitored subject to ERISA's fiduciary standard of prudence.

[Option II-A4 Employer Stock. Note: If you elect this option you should also select Option II-H, Option IV-F and Option V-C]

The structure includes the opportunity for participants to invest in Employer Stock.

[Option II-A5 RIA Managed Account Services. Note: If you elect this option you should also select Option II-I, Option, Option III-F, and Option IV-G]

The Plan will allow participants to obtain investment advice and/or investment management services for the allocation of their accounts utilizing the Designated Funds in the Plan. To assist in the implementation of that decision, the Investment Fiduciary will select an investment adviser (the "RIA Management Firm") and offer its services to the participants. The participants may elect to use the services of the RIA Management Firm or may select an investment adviser of their choice. Any investment adviser for participants must qualify as an "investment manager" under ERISA Section 3(38). The cost of the investment adviser will be borne by the participant.

B. **Designated Funds for Broad Range**

In order to offer a broad range of investment alternatives so that each participant and beneficiary has a reasonable opportunity to:

- materially affect both the potential return and degree of risk relating to his or her accounts,
- choose from diversified investment alternatives, and
- diversify his or her investment to minimize the risk of large losses,

the Plan will offer a selection of open-ended registered investment companies (i.e., mutual funds) or similar investment vehicles, each of which consists of internally diversified portfolios within their asset classes.

In the process of selecting the funds to be used as the Plan's investment alternatives, the Investment Fiduciary will first select the asset classes and investment styles ("asset classes") intended to satisfy the broad range requirement. At a minimum, the Plan's investment alternatives should provide participants the opportunity to invest in vehicles designed to maintain a stable principal value (i.e., cash equivalents), vehicles designed to primarily target domestic bonds, vehicles designed to primarily target domestic equities and vehicles designed to primarily target international equities. Once the asset classes are determined, the Investment Fiduciary will, utilizing the procedures described in Section III of this IPS, identify one or more funds to represent each of those asset classes.

The asset classes and the funds selected as the Designated Funds, along with their benchmarks, are identified in Exhibit A.

C. **Additional Designated Funds**

The Investment Fiduciary may also decide to offer funds in addition to those selections for the broad range requirements. These funds are also known as Designated Funds, and they may include, but are not limited to, those that target a specific sector or sectors, country or region, whose managers take greater than normal risk or whose managers tactically reallocate asset classes within their portfolio. These funds may be added to provide additional investment alternatives and accommodate participant interest.

In selecting these additional Designated Funds, the Investment Fiduciary will consider factors such as: the nature of the participant workforce; investment education, communication and advice programs; the needs and preferences of the participating employees and/or of certain groups of employees.

The additional Designated Funds are also listed in Exhibit A.

D. **Investment Education and Models for Participant Direction**

The plan will provide participants with general financial and investment information, including asset allocation models to educate and assist them in making their allocation decisions. Participants will be provided with a questionnaire that measures their individual risk tolerance and investment time horizon and may select a model portfolio based on the results of that questionnaire. Participants may then select from among the funds offered by the Plan to build their own asset allocation portfolio consistent with their individual risk tolerance and investment time horizon.

The asset allocation models are described in Exhibit B.

[Option II-E.
Plans offering Asset
Allocation Funds]

E. **Asset Allocation Funds**

To enable participants to benefit from the asset allocation expertise of investment professionals, the Plan will provide participants with five asset allocation funds. Those funds, and the purpose of each, are:

- Conservative: This fund seeks to maximize total investment return through income and secondarily through long-term growth of capital.
- Moderately Conservative: The fund seeks to maximize total investment return through income and secondarily through long-term growth of capital.
- Moderate: This fund seeks to maximize total investment return through growth of capital and income.
- Moderately Aggressive: This fund seeks to maximize total investment return primarily through growth of capital, but also through income.
- Aggressive: This fund seeks to maximize total investment return through growth of capital.

The purpose of the asset allocation funds is to provide participants with investment options professionally designed to take into account risk tolerances and investment time horizons. Additionally, the asset allocation funds will automatically be re-balanced periodically to maintain the strategic asset allocation.

The asset allocation funds are described in Exhibit B.

[Option II-F
Plans offering
Self-Directed Brokerage
Accounts]

F. **Brokerage Accounts**

The Investment Fiduciary may, from time to time, decide to offer participants the opportunity to invest in individual stocks, additional mutual funds and other investment alternatives through self-directed brokerage accounts. The Investment

Fiduciary will impose limits on the types of securities available through such accounts as listed in Exhibit F. The investment alternatives in the self-directed brokerage accounts are not classified as Designated Funds (nor are they considered as Designated Investment Options).

In offering self-directed brokerage accounts, the Investment Fiduciary will notify participants that the investment alternatives available through the self-directed brokerage accounts are nondesignated alternatives that have not been prudently selected, are not monitored, require investment expertise or advice to prudently manage and have greater risk of material loss.

[Options II-G
Plans Offering Mutual
Fund Window]

G. **Mutual Fund Window**

The Investment Fiduciary may, from time to time, decide to offer participants the opportunity to select from among a large number of mutual funds and similar investment vehicles through a mutual fund window selected by the Investment Fiduciary. The investment alternatives in the mutual fund window are not designated as investment options and, therefore, are not Designated Funds

The Investment Fiduciary will notify participants that the investment alternatives available through the mutual fund window are nondesignated alternatives that have not been prudently selected, are not monitored, require investment expertise or advice to prudently manage and therefore may have greater risk of loss than the Designated Funds.

[Option II-H
Plans offering
Employer Stock]

H. **Employer Stock**

The Plan will offer shares of the Plan Sponsor's common stock ("employer stock") as an investment alternative. The employer stock will be held in an employer stock fund, which will not be classified as a Designated Fund (nor is it considered as a Designated Investment Option). However, it is not appropriate for the employer stock to be selected and monitored under the general provisions of this IPS, as those provisions are designed for Funds that consist of a portfolio of diverse securities. Instead, the provisions of sections IV and V of this IPS will apply for that purpose, as well as for proxy voting and restrictions on participant direction.

[Option II-I RIA Managed Account Services]

I. RIA Managed Account Services

The Investment Fiduciary will select an investment adviser to provide investment management services to participants (the "RIA Management Firm"). The RIA Management Firm is an independent registered investment adviser under the Investment Advisers Act of 1940 and has acknowledged in writing that it is an ERISA fiduciary with respect to the Plan (as required by ERISA Section 3(38)). The Plan will provide the participants with information concerning the availability of the investment services, including the nature of the services, the cost of the services, and the credentials of the investment adviser. Participants will also be informed that they may select another investment adviser of their choice. The participants will individually decide whether or not to use an investment adviser and, if so, whether to use the adviser selected by the Plan. If participants use investment advisers, they will bear the cost of the service.

For participants who select the RIA Management Firm provided by the Plan as their investment manager, the adviser will establish the investment allocations for their accounts, will select the funds to be used for that allocation, and will direct the purchase and/or exchange of the funds needed to implement the investment program.

III. STANDARDS FOR SELECTION OF PORTFOLIO

A. **Overview of Portfolio and Performance Standards**

The Investment Fiduciary will engage in a process to prudently select, monitor and, where appropriate, remove Designated Funds. The Funds will be selected from among a universe of investment alternatives such that there is reasonable assurance that an adequate number of funds have been reviewed and, therefore, that the Designated Funds are representative of superior investment alternatives available to the Plan.

The Designated Funds will be regularly monitored and, where appropriate, will be removed. If a Designated Fund is removed, it will normally be replaced by a similar Designated Fund. However, the Investment Fiduciary may, in its discretion, determine that a removed Fund will not be replaced.

The following are the guidelines for the selection, monitoring, retention and removal of Funds.

B. **Selection of Funds**

1. Selection of Designated Funds

   For the selection of Designated Funds (other than cash equivalents and index funds), the Investment Fiduciary will evaluate a reasonable universe of mutual funds using the guidelines set forth in this section of the IPS. The Investment Fiduciary will evaluate the total returns of cash equivalents and index funds against their specific market benchmarks.

   a. Evaluation Guidelines. The Investment Fiduciary will initially create a peer group of funds for each targeted asset class consisting of mutual funds or other diversified investments ("funds") with similar investment styles, then screen the universe of funds based on the following evaluation guidelines:

   i. Operating Expenses. The expense ratio of the funds will be evaluated to consider the reasonableness and effect of the costs, with preference being given to low-cost funds unless the additional cost can be justified by other factors.

    ii. Sharpe Ratio. The investment performance of the funds, relative to the risk taken by the managers, will be evaluated.

    iii. Trailing Performance. The investment performance of the funds will be evaluated using weighted trailing annualized total returns.

    iv. Rolling Information Ratio. The consistency of risk-adjusted investment performance of the funds, relative to their benchmarks, will be evaluated.

    v. Rolling Performance Consistency. The total returns of the funds will be evaluated using rolling periods to minimize the end period dominance of recent performance history and to provide more comprehensive performance data to evaluate.

    vi. Rolling Selection Return. Each fund's returns will be compared to the market benchmarks of various investment styles to determine the custom portfolio benchmark that best explains the pattern and consistency of each fund's returns. The Investment Fiduciary will then compare each fund's performance to its custom portfolio benchmark to determine the value added or subtracted by its manager.

The specific evaluation guidelines ("fund evaluation measures") applied to each fund are listed in Exhibit C.

    b. Fund Warning Signs. As a secondary screening process in selecting the fund, the Investment Fiduciary will also evaluate certain factors, called "warning signs." Warning signs could be an indication of a fund's inability to consistently outperform its peers in the future and will be carefully considered by the Investment Fiduciary. When selecting between two funds that have similar results under the evaluation guidelines (listed above), preference will normally be given to the fund with fewer warning signs. The Investment Fiduciary will evaluate warning signs such as the following:

    i. High operating expenses

    ii. High individual holding concentration

    iii. High economic sector concentration

    iv. High performance volatility

    v. High portfolio turnover

vi. Low style purity
vii. High duration bet
viii. Low credit quality average
ix. Low manager tenure
x. Low asset base

The specific warning signs applied to each fund are listed in Exhibit D.

c. Fund Selection. For each peer group, the Investment Fiduciary will review a minimum of 2 funds that best satisfy the evaluation guidelines, with the Investment Fiduciary determining the relative weighting of any warning signs or other relevant considerations. The Investment Fiduciary will then select, from those finalists, one or more Designated Funds that the Investment Fiduciary determines to be most suitable for the Plan and the participants to provide a broad range of investment alternatives to the participants.

2. Selection of Additional Designated Funds
For the selection of additional Designated Funds, the Investment Fiduciary will use the same procedures and guidelines used for the selection of funds selected to satisfy the broad range investment options above, with the following exceptions:

a. The Investment Fiduciary normally will not consider the following warning signs as grounds for elimination when selecting additional Designated Funds:

i. Lack of internal diversification.
ii. Lack of investment style purity and consistency.
iii. Funds with highly volatile past performance relative to their peer group.
iv. Funds with high portfolio turnover relative to their peer group.
v. Funds with insufficient assets or portfolio management experience to adequately handle large cash flows and/or significant increases in fund assets.

b. Other than those exceptions, the Investment Fiduciary will use the same evaluation guidelines and fund selection criteria for reducing the universe of funds to a minimum of 2 alternatives within each selected peer group and for selecting among those alternatives.

[Option III B-3 Socially Responsible Investment Funds]	3. Socially Responsible Investment Funds The Investment Fiduciary may consider offering Designated Funds, which include the standard of socially responsible investing as a criteria for selecting the underlying securities for the Fund. However, the Investment Fiduciary must act solely in the interest of the participants and for the exclusive purpose of providing benefits to the participants. As a result, a Fund cannot be selected for its socially responsible investment standards unless the Fund is comparable to the other Funds that satisfy the Plan's general selection criteria.

C. **Investment of Accounts Without Participant Direction**

If a participant fails to provide the Plan with an investment direction, the Investment Fiduciary will direct the investment of the participant's account, until such time as the participant provides his or her first affirmative direction. In consideration of the risk tolerances, time horizons and investment needs of the average participant, and of the common investment allocations by fiduciaries of large retirement plans, accounts for participants who do not affirmatively select their investment alternatives will be invested to the moderate asset allocation portfolio or another appropriately diversified fund allocation. Such monies will continue to be invested in the moderate asset allocation portfolio, or another appropriately diversified fund allocation, until and unless the Investment Fiduciary decides to change this decision for all participants who have not provided investment directions or until the Investment Fiduciary determines that a different investment selection is appropriate for a participant. In making these decisions, the Investment Fiduciary is not responsible for inquiring into the specific goals or needs of a participant.

[If the asset allocation funds are not selected for inclusion in your plan, the reference in this section to the moderate asset allocation portfolio should be deleted and replaced with another portfolio containing a balance of equity growth and income.]

D. **Selection of Stock Brokerage Firm.**

The Investment Fiduciary has, in selecting its investment provider, reviewed the considerations for brokerage accounts for the Plan participants and has decided, based on that review, to utilize the brokerage account offered by the investment provider selected for the Plan. In making that decision, the Investment Fiduciary has considered factors such as: the expense structure of the brokerage accounts; the administrative needs of the Plan, including recordkeeping; adherence to Plan policies; and range of investment alternatives.

E. **Selection of Mutual Fund Window**

The Investment Fiduciary will select the provider for the mutual fund window. In making that decision, the Investment Fiduciary will consider factors such as: the expense structure of the mutual fund window; the administrative needs of the plan, including recordkeeping; the adherence of the provider to Plan policies; and the number and variety of the investment alternatives in the mutual fund window.

F. **Selection of RIA Management Firm and RIA Service Provider**

The Investment Fiduciary has established criteria for its selection of an investment adviser for the participants. In selecting the adviser, the Investment Fiduciary will consider factors including, but not limited to, the following:

- Expertise of candidates and their consistency with the objectives of this IPS;
- Qualification of the candidate as an investment manager pursuant to ERISA Section 3(38); that is, the manager is registered as an investment adviser under the Investment Advisers Act of 1940 or is registered as an invest

ment adviser under Section 203A(a)of the 1940 Act in the State where it maintains its principal place of business;

- The candidate agrees in writing that, in the capacity of an investment adviser, it will be an ERISA fiduciary to the Plan;
- Business structure, affiliations, financial condition, capitalization and assets under management of the candidate;
- The investment process proposed by the candidate;
- The identity, experience, and qualifications of professionals handling the accounts;
- Whether the candidate has adequate fiduciary liability or other insurance to protect the plan in the event of a fiduciary breach;
- Fee structure;
- Information provided by client references

Based on the application of these criteria to investment advisers who have established contractual relationships with the Plan's investment provider, the Investment Fiduciary will select the RIA Management Firm for the Plan.

The RIA Investment Manager will implement its investment decisions on behalf of participants with the Plan's investment provider through an intermediary service provider (the "RIA Service Provider"). The RIA Service Provider will enable the RIA Investment Manager to directly implement the investment programs on behalf of participants and thereby will facilitate the purpose of offering participant-level investment management.

IV. MONITORING OF INVESTMENT ALTERNATIVES

A. **Overview of Monitoring**

The Investment Fiduciary will periodically monitor and evaluate the specific investment alternatives to determine if they continue to be suitable and appropriate for the Plan and the participants.

B. **Monitoring of Designated Funds**

1. Procedures for Review of Investment Information. The Investment Fiduciary will obtain and review the following information, as well as any other information that the Investment Fiduciary finds valuable in fulfilling its responsibilities:

    The Investment Fiduciary will periodically obtain reports for all Designated Funds, which include a full and comprehensive review and evaluation of each Fund with respect to the portfolio and performance standards in this IPS. The Investment Fiduciary will meet at appropriate intervals to review this Investment Policy Statement, the investment structure and the investment alternatives offered by the Plan. While it is contemplated that the Investment Fiduciary will meet annually, that is a guideline and not a requirement.

2. To continue to be offered to the participants, a Fund will be expected to maintain an overall rating ("fund status") of above average, based on the evaluation guidelines (fund evaluation measures) in the section of this IPS on Standards for Selection of Portfolio. However, if a Fund is rated below average for one or two quarters, that normally will not be cause for the removal of the Fund. If a Fund is rated below average for three (3) or more quarters out of the past four (4) quarters as of the annual review date, it will normally, but not necessarily, be removed by the Investment Fiduciary. The Investment Fiduciary may keep the Fund as an investment alternative if the Investment Fiduciary determines in its discretion that it is prudent to do so. If a fund is removed, the Investment Fiduciary will normally replace the Fund with another similar fund, using the procedures in this IPS for the selection of a fund. However, the Investment Fiduciary may, in its discretion, determine that a removed Fund will not be replaced.

The criteria for determining a Fund's overall rating ("fund status") are listed in Exhibit E.

3. If a Fund is removed for future contributions, the following procedures will generally be followed by the Investment Fiduciary:

    a. The monies will ordinarily be transferred to the replacement Designated Fund, if one is selected by the Investment Fiduciary. Alternatively, the Investment Fiduciary may inform the participants of its intention to remove the Fund and permit the participants to direct the transfer of their monies from the Fund being removed. In that case, any monies remaining in that Fund at the time of its removal will be transferred by the Investment Fiduciary to the replacement Fund, if one is selected. Otherwise, the monies will be transferred to the most appropriate investment alternative, as determined by the Investment Fiduciary.

    b. The Investment Fiduciary may implement reasonable procedures, including blackout periods, to accomplish these changes.

    c. The Investment Fiduciary may decide to preclude the investment of additional participant money in a Fund, but not remove the Fund as an investment alternative in the Plan to the extent participants are already invested in that Fund (that is, investment in that Fund may be "frozen"). For example, the Investment Fiduciary may determine that, while another Fund better serves the needs of the Plan and its participants, the frozen Fund remains a prudent and suitable alternative for the participants who are invested in it and therefore restrict additional investments in that Fund for the administrative purposes of the Plan.

[Option IV-C
Asset Allocation Funds]

C. **Monitoring of Asset Allocation Funds**

The Investment Fiduciary will periodically obtain and review information necessary to determine whether the asset allocation funds are performing in a manner consistent with the objectives described in Section II, Investment Structure, of this IPS.

[Option IV-D
Brokerage Accounts]

D. Monitoring of Brokerage Accounts

The Investment Fiduciary will periodically monitor the self-directed brokerage accounts for proper operation as brokerage accounts, including accounting for transactions and recordkeeping. However, while the brokerage accounts are designated investment vehicles, the investment alternatives within the brokerage accounts are not designated by the Plan and, therefore, are not selected or monitored by the Investment Fiduciary. Instead, the self-directed brokerage accounts are intended to provide the electing participants with all of the investment alternatives that it is administratively feasible for the Plan to hold. As such, the investment alternatives available within the brokerage accounts are neither selected nor monitored by the Investment Fiduciary or other Plan fiduciaries.

[Option IV-E
Mutual Fund Window]

E. Monitoring of Mutual Fund Window

The Investment Fiduciary will periodically monitor the mutual fund window and its provider for proper operation of the window, including accounting for transactions and recordkeeping. However, while the mutual fund window is a designated investment vehicle, the investment alternatives within the window are not designated by the Plan and, therefore, are not selected or monitored by the Investment Fiduciary. Instead, the mutual fund window is intended to provide the electing participants with all of the investment alternatives that it is administratively feasible for the Plan to hold.

[Option IV-F
Company Stock]

F. Monitoring of Employer Stock

Consistent with the requirements of Title I of ERISA, the Investment Fiduciary will periodically review employer stock as an investment alternative to determine if it continues to be a suitable and appropriate investment for the Plan and the participants. In conducting that review, the Investment Fiduciary will take into account that the acquisition and holding of employer stock is exempt from the diversification requirements of ERISA. The Investment Fiduciary will report its findings and conclusion on that review to senior management of the Plan Sponsor, which will make the decision of whether to continue to offer employer stock as an investment alternative.

[Option IV-G
Monitoring of RIA
Management Firm and RIA
Service Provider]

G. **Monitoring of RIA Management Firm and RIA Service Provider**

The Investment Fiduciary will periodically monitor the RIA Management Firm to determine if its services continue to be suitable and appropriate for the Plan and the participants. The Investment Fiduciary will obtain and review updated information to ensure that the selection criteria continue to be satisfied, together with the following information, as well as any other information that the Investment Fiduciary finds material in fulfilling its responsibilities:

- Review of the performance of the portfolios of the RIA Management Firm for compliance with objectives of this IPS;
- Review of the investment results of RIA managed participant accounts versus appropriate indices or benchmarks;
- Verification of fee computation and transactions;
- Review of any significant changes in the RIA Management Firm's structure, investment processes and philosophy, and professional staff

The Investment Fiduciary will periodically monitor the RIA Service Provider's performance related to participant-level investment management services, including accuracy of transaction processing, accounting for transactions and payment of appropriate fees.

If a participant does not use the services of the RIA Management Firm, but instead appoints his or her own investment adviser, that adviser will not be monitored by the Investment Fiduciary.

V. OTHER PROVISIONS

A. **Proxy Voting**

The Investment Fiduciary will determine the proper voting of proxy proposals related to the Funds. Because the Funds are prudently selected and monitored, and underperforming Funds are removed, the Investment Fiduciary will usually vote in support of the management proposals in the proxies. However, the Investment Fiduciary will review the proxy statements for proposals that could be detrimental to the interests of the Plan and the participants and will vote the Plan's shares against those proposals. For example, the Investment Fiduciary will generally vote against proposals that:

1. Increase the expenses of the Funds.
2. Increase the risk of the investments in the Funds.
3. For Designated Funds, would result in a change to an investment style inconsistent with the objective and targeted asset class for which the Fund was chosen.

While the Investment Fiduciary is responsible for deciding on how to vote the Fund shares, it may delegate the ministerial tasks of implementing its voting directions and submitting the votes.

B. **Investment Fiduciary Discretion**

The Investment Fiduciary has the sole and absolute discretion to interpret, implement and amend this Investment Policy Statement, including any decisions to select, remove and replace investment alternatives for participant direction.

[Option V-C
Plans offering
Employer Stock]

C. **Issues Concerning Employer Stock**

The Plan Sponsor makes matching contributions and may make profit sharing contributions to the Plan by contributing to an employer stock fund investment alternative ("employer stock fund"). Participant interests in that fund will be allocated to the accounts of the participants in accordance with the Plan document and other policy that may

[Option V-CA
Matching and profit
sharing; participant may
not dispose of shares]

[Option V-CB
Matching and Profit
Sharing; Participant may
dispose of shares]

[Option C.C.
Employer stock
is investment option]

be adopted by the committee and/or Plan Sponsor. Participants may only exchange out of their employer stock in accordance with the terms of the Plan.

The Plan Sponsor makes matching contributions and may make profit sharing contributions by contributing to an employer stock fund investment alternative ("employer stock fund"). Participant interests in that fund will be allocated to the accounts of the participants. Participants may direct the sale of units allocated to their accounts.

The Plan permits participants to purchase units of an employer stock fund. Employer stock is included as an investment alternative in order to provide participants with a sense of ownership of their employer and to permit participants to participate in the growth of the Plan Sponsor. Such shares will be held in an employer stock fund investment alternative ("employer stock fund"), and participant interests in that fund will be allocated to the accounts of the participants.

1. The Investment Fiduciary will make every effort to honor buy and sell instructions from participants through the employer stock fund, consistent with restrictions of federal securities laws. The Investment Fiduciary will carry out those instructions in as efficient a manner as possible, taking into account the best interests of the participants, including such factors as execution costs.

2. The Investment Fiduciary will cause the Form S-8 prospectus relating to the Plan, and related materials, to be delivered to all participants in

accordance with federal securities laws. Additionally, all reports issued by the Plan Sponsor, which are normally provided to other shareholders of the Plan Sponsor, will be delivered promptly to all participants in the Plan. The Investment Fiduciary may also suspend trading in the employer stock fund if it becomes aware of non-public information about the Plan Sponsor that, if known, would affect an investor's decision to buy or sell the employer stock. Such trading may resume once a public announcement of such information is made.

Upon the Plan's receipt of proxy solicitation or tender offer materials, the Investment Fiduciary will ensure that the responsible fiduciary follows the procedures established for the distribution to participants of the proxy solicitation or tender offer materials. The procedures will provide for the confidentiality of information relating to the purchase, holding and sale of employer securities, and the exercise of voting, tender and similar rights, by the participants and beneficiaries. All shares on which proxies are not received shall be voted or tendered by the Investment Fiduciary in accordance with the terms of the Plan.

EXHIBIT A: DESIGNATED FUNDS AND BENCHMARKS

As of the effective date of this Investment Policy Statement (IPS), the Designated Funds and their respective benchmarks are:

Asset Class	Fund Name	Market Index	Peer Group
Cash		SB 3-month T-Bill Index	S&P Money Market Taxable
Bonds		LB Aggregate Bond Index	S&P Fixed Income General Intermediate
Large-Cap Stocks		S&P 500, S&P/ BARRA 500 Value or S&P/ BARRA 500 Growth Index, depending on the fund selected	S&P Equity Large-Cap Value or Growth, depending on the fund selected
Mid-Cap Stocks		Russell Mid-Cap, Russell Mid-Cap Value, or Russell Mid-Cap Growth Index, depending on the fund selected.	S&P Mid-Cap Value or Growth, depending on the fund selected
Small-Cap Stocks		Russell 2000, Russell 2000 Value or Russell 2000 Growth Index, depending on the fund selected	S&P Equity Small-Cap Value or Growth, depending on the fund selected
International Developed Equity		MSCI EAFE Index or MSCI Emerging Markets Free Index, depending on the fund selected	S&P Equity International or S&P Equity Emerging Markets, depending on the fund selected

EXHIBIT B: ASSET ALLOCATION MODELS

Asset allocation models will be offered to participants as a part of the Plan's investment education program. The asset allocation models will assist participants in allocating the investment of their accounts at the appropriate point on the risk/reward spectrum, as determined by each participant. A risk tolerance questionnaire designed for use with the models has been adopted by the Investment Fiduciary. Based upon an analysis of the completed risk tolerance questionnaire and other relevant criteria, the participant will be responsible for selecting an appropriate asset allocation model. The asset allocation models are as follows:

Strategic Asset Class	Conservative	Moderately Conservative	Moderate	Moderately Aggressive	Aggressive
Cash	15	10	5		
Short-Term Bonds	25	15	10	5	
U.S. Bonds	40	35	25	15	5
U.S. Large-Cap Stocks	10	20	30	35	40
U.S. Mid Cap Stocks	5	10	10	15	15
U.S. Small-Cap Stocks			5	5	10
International Stocks	5	10	15	25	30

The asset allocation models are designed to assist participants in making strategic asset allocation decisions, based on the participant's investment time horizon and risk tolerance.

[COMMENT: The asset allocation models are structured to consider and include the six asset classes listed above. To enable participants to obtain full advantage of the models and the related investment education services, the Investment Fiduciary should include at least one fund from each of the six asset classes.]

[The following is optional for Plans that include the asset allocation funds as investment options.]

In addition to asset allocation models in the investment education program, the Plan offers asset allocation funds to the participants. Similar to the models, the asset allocation funds have been strategically designed to afford participants with the opportunity to select an investment that matches their risk-and-reward profile, based on a questionnaire completed by the participant. However, this alternative enables the participant to select an investment option (that is, the asset allocation fund), rather than selecting individual funds to implement the model approach. Further, the asset allocation funds are periodically automatically re-balanced (while, in the model, the responsibility for re-balancing remains with the participants).

The asset allocation funds consist of the same asset classes and the same percentages described earlier in this Exhibit. The underlying fund within each asset class is an index fund for a common benchmark index for that asset class.

EXHIBIT C: FUND EVALUATION MEASURES

Each fund is evaluated on the basis of six evaluation measures (fund evaluation measures) that quantify the relative operating expenses, total returns and risk-adjusted performance of a fund within its peer group. The total returns of cash equivalents and index funds are evaluated against their specific market benchmarks. The evaluation methodology is not an attempt to predict a fund's future potential; it summarizes how well each fund has historically balanced expenses, returns and risk. The six evaluation measures together provide a systematic process to evaluate and monitor funds using generally accepted investment principles and modern portfolio theories. For each of the six evaluation measures, all funds are ranked using percentile rankings ranging from 1% (best) to 100% (worst) within their respective peer group to determine each fund's relative performance. Percentile ranks for each evaluation measure are translated into "batting averages" for presentation purposes. Batting averages range from 0.400 (best) to 0.100 (worst). The six evaluation measures are equally weighted to compute each fund's overall batting average within its peer group, which is used to determine each fund's status rating. This ranking system provides for appropriate comparisons of funds with similar objectives and investment styles. The fund evaluation measures are as follows:

Short-term Measures

- **Expense Ratio** (current) peer group ranking
- **Sharpe Ratio** (trailing 36-month) peer group ranking

Intermediate-term Measures

- **Trailing Performance** (3-year, 5-year and 10-year annualized total returns; weighted) peer group ranking
- **Information Ratio** (36 rolling 36-month information ratios) peer group ranking

Long-term Measures

- **Performance Consistency** (rolling 12-month total returns for the past 10 years) peer group ranking
- **Style Selection Return** (rolling 36-month style selection returns for the past 10 years) peer group ranking

EXHIBIT D: FUND WARNING SIGNS

The following fund screening criteria (fund warning signs) are evaluated in order to highlight exposure to potential risks that could possibly make the fund an unsuitable investment alternative. These criteria are evaluated and monitored to reveal potential risks and provide relevant information to assist the Investment Fiduciary in making prudent investment decisions.

- **High operating expenses** (equity, bond, hybrid):
  Rank each fund within its peer group based on recent operating expense data. Flag funds that have an operating expense ratio *above the peer group average.*

- **High individual holding concentration** (equity, hybrid):
  Flag equity and hybrid funds with more than 10% of assets in any one stock, OR more than 50% of assets in the top ten holdings (excluding real estate funds), OR less than 40 holdings (excluding real estate funds).

- **High economic sector concentration** (equity, hybrid):
  Flag equity and hybrid funds with *more than the greater of 25% of assets or 1.5 times the peer group average sector weight* in any one economic sector. The economic sector concentration flag applies only to the equity portion of a hybrid fund. Flag *economic sector* funds with *less than 75%* of assets invested in the *targeted economic sector.*

- **High performance volatility** (equity, bond, hybrid):
  Rank each fund within its peer group by 3-year average annualized standard deviation of monthly returns. Flag the funds in each peer group with a *standard deviation of returns in the highest 10% of their peer group.*

- **High portfolio turnover** (equity):
  Rank each equity fund within its peer group by portfolio turnover. Flag the funds in each equity peer group with *portfolio turnover in the highest 10% of their peer group.*

- **Low style purity** (equity):
  Rank each equity fund within its peer group by correlation with the market benchmark assigned to the fund's S&P style classification. Regress each equity fund's monthly returns against the monthly returns of its corresponding market benchmark using a single 36-month trailing period computation. Flag equity funds within the *lowest 10% of R-squared* for each peer group. The market benchmarks assigned to each peer group are identified in Exhibit A.

- **High duration bet** (bond, hybrid):
  Flag bond and hybrid funds with a *3-year average duration 1.5 or more years above or below the 3-year average duration of the peer group.* The high duration bet flag applies only to the bond portion of a hybrid fund.

- **Low credit quality average** (bond, hybrid):
  Flag bond and hybrid funds with a *current average credit rating below single A* (S&P ratings).

- **Low manager tenure** (equity, bond, hybrid):
  Flag funds whose portfolio managers have *less than one year* of tenure managing the fund.

- **Low asset base** (equity, bond, hybrid):
  Flag funds with less than $50 million in assets.

EXHIBIT E: FUND STATUS

Each fund with three or more years of performance history is evaluated and monitored on a quarterly basis and assigned an overall fund status rating according to the following criteria:

Above-Average Quality Fund:

- *Equity, bond and hybrid funds:* Overall fund batting average of 0.250 or higher
- *Index funds:* 5-year tracking error of 1.00% or lower (use 3 years if fund has less than 5 years of performance history).
- *Cash equivalents:* Expense ratio less than or equal to 0.80%.

Below-Average Quality Fund:

- *Equity, bond and hybrid funds:* Overall fund batting average less than 0.250
- *Index funds:* 5-year tracking error greater than 1.00% (use 3 years if fund has less than 5 years of performance history)
- *Cash equivalents:* Expense ratio greater than 0.80%.

Note: Overall fund batting average is based on the six individual fund evaluation measures listed in Exhibit C (weighted equally).

OPTIONAL
[Complete only if the Plan offers self-directed brokerage accounts]

EXHIBIT F BROKERAGE ACCOUNTS

- Because of the vast array of investment options available in self-directed brokerage accounts, it is impossible for the Investment Fiduciary to oversee these investments. Since securities purchased through the self-directed brokerage account are not selected and evaluated by the Investment Fiduciary, they are not designated investment alternatives. Instead, they offer the participants the opportunity to invest in all of the alternatives that it is administratively feasible for the Plan to offer. Consequently, participants who choose to invest through the self-directed brokerage account will be notified that investments in such accounts have not been prudently selected, and are not monitored by the Investment Fiduciary. Participants who invest through the self-directed brokerage account will be notified that they are taking on more responsibility and greater risk, and are solely responsible for the consequences of their investment decisions.

- The Investment Fiduciary may impose restrictions on the investments available through the self-directed brokerage accounts and on the types of transactions which may be made in those accounts. Those restrictions are contained in this Exhibit and in the Securities Restriction Schedule completed by the Investment Fiduciary (which is incorporated into and made a part of this Exhibit). The restrictions in this Exhibit are:

  - Securities eligible for trading in the brokerage accounts shall include only investment companies registered under the Investment Company Act of 1940 and equity; securities traded on a national securities exchange or over-the-counter. The Investment Fiduciary may further limit these options in the Securities Restriction Schedule. The ownership of the securities in the Brokerage Accounts may not be maintained outside the jurisdiction of the district courts of the United States.
  - Contributions directly from a participant to a brokerage account will not be accepted.

- Distributions directly from a brokerage account to a participant, IRA or another qualified plan are not permitted, other than certain in-kind distributions.

- The following investments and transactions are not available through the Brokerage Accounts: bonds, employer securities, margin accounts (or debt-financing of any kind), options and futures (including commodities), currencies and foreign securities, short sales, limited partnerships (other than publicly traded limited partnerships), tax-exempt securities, unit investment trusts, precious metals and certificates of deposit.

- In addition, the Investment Fiduciary may also impose other restrictions and limitations on the brokerage accounts. If additional restrictions are imposed, they will be listed below or on the Securities Restriction Schedule.

[NOTE: If a Plan offers self-directed brokerage accounts to its participants, the Investment Fiduciary for a Plan should consider the restrictions and limitations in this Exhibit and in the Securities Restriction Schedule, as well as other possible restrictions, and determine the proper policy for its Plan and participants. This Model Exhibit should be modified by the Investment Fiduciary to reflect those decisions.]

Appendix D
Form ADV

Form ADV of the Uniform Application for Investment Advisor Registration, is a requirement for money managers that charge a fee, and must be filed with the SEC to become a Registered Investment Advisor (RIA). Although registration with the SEC does not signify competence or training, Form ADV provides important information about the manager. Check this information against that which the manager gives to you in an interview to ensure that there are no discrepancies.

Note: The official term for money managers is Registered Investment Advisor, however we have chosen to use the term Money Manager throughout this book for clarity, since the term "advisor" is used for many positions and, because Registered Investment Advisor is rarely used outside of the industry.

Form ADV has two parts and provides basic background information on the manager's state registrations, disciplinary or legal problems, ownership, potential conflicts of interest with fees or commissions, financial condition, and the background of the firm's principals. Investors should keep in mind that the SEC never passes on the merits or accuracy of the information provided in the ADV, it simply requires that this information be filed and made available to the public. By reviewing Form ADV, the investor has an opportunity to do some basic background checking. Obvious areas of interest are prior employment of the firm's principals and their educational backgrounds. When legal action against a firm is discovered, investors should try to obtain copies of the court-file complaints. By checking with the SEC's enforcement division, the investor may uncover actions taken by the SEC against the manager for regulatory violations.

FORM ADV PART I

Registered Investment Advisors, money managers, must file a Form ADV, Part I, with the SEC and/or the states in which they do business and this must be updated and filed annually. Failure to do so may result in revocation of the manager's registration. This form contains information about the money manager and its business practices, as well as background information on the manager and persons who own or control the business. Form ADV, Part I also contains disclosure information about certain disciplinary events involving the manager and its key personnel. SEC rules require RIA's to report if they have filed bankruptcy in the last ten (10) years, had their license suspended or, violated any of the SEC's or Commodity Futures Trading Commission's regulations or statutes. Part I is a very lengthy document, which we have not provided as part of this chapter, however Part I and Part II can be accessed through the SEC's website at www.sec.gov, then type ADV in the "search" window on the home page.

FORM ADV PART II

By law the manager must provide Part II of the form (or equivalent disclosure) to prospective clients. While Part II is the only form (not Part I) that is legally required to be furnished to the public, it never hurts to request both parts during the due diligence process. Part II is often included with marketing materials and the management firm will send a copy to new clients. Managers are not required to file amendments to Part II with the SEC.

Part II provides more detailed information about the manager and the way the manager conducts business, such as:

- The manager's education and experience
- Services provided
- Procedures for account review
- Fee structure
- Types of clients
- Investments offered
- The manager's methods of analysis
- Sources of information
- Investment strategies

- Other financial industry activities and affiliations
- Any fines, securities violations or litigations

Again, the money management firm will provide Part II, as they are required to do so. If you would also like to review Part I, this will have to be requested from the manager. If the manager resists, this form can be obtained from the SEC, however this may be a red flag.

Appendix E

Glossary of Terms

12b-1 Fee is a fee charged by some mutual funds to cover promotion, distributions, marketing expenses, and sometimes commissions to brokers. This fee is generally included in the expense ratio and is disclosed in a fund's prospectus.

A Share is a class of mutual fund shares that carries a front-end load.

Absolute Return is the actual, raw-number return for a specified period of time.

Advance/Decline Line is the relationship between the number of stocks that are increasing in value and the number that are decreasing in value. The A/D line is a technical tool used to measure the market's overall direction.

Aggressive Growth Portfolio is a portfolio designed to generate the highest capital appreciation possible and is not risk-averse in its selection of investments. Aggressive growth portfolios are most suitable for investors willing to accept a high risk-return trade-off, as many of the stocks with high growth potential can also show considerable share price volatility. portfolios tend to have a high positive correlation with the stock market, and therefore often produce very good results during economic upswings and negative results during economic downturns.

Alpha is a measurement of the amount of reward earned for the risk taken. An alpha of 0.00 indicates that the risk versus reward relationship is equal to that of the benchmark. A positive alpha shows the portfolio achieved higher returns for the risk level assumed, when compared to the benchmark. A negative alpha means that the portfolio generated lower returns and/or experienced greater volatility (risk) when compared to the benchmark.

Asset Allocation is the mix of various asset classes and styles designed to meet an investor's objectives and risk tolerance.

Asset Weighted Blend is the blend of a portfolio's comparative benchmarks (indexes) in ratios equal to that of its representative individual investment styles. As an example, a portfolio made up of 30% large cap managers, 40% mid cap managers and 30% international managers would have an asset weighted blend comprised of a 30% weighting of the S&P 500, a 40% weighting of the S&P 400 and a 30% weighting of the MSCI-EAFE.

Attribution Analysis compares each segment of a portfolio (individual stocks, sectors, market cap, etc.) to its benchmark to determine where the manager adds value, i.e., is the manager making better sector calls and/or security selections than the benchmark and thus, adding value.

Average Capitalization is the total capitalization of the portfolio divided by the number of securities in a portfolio.

B Share is a class of mutual fund shares that carries a back-end load or surrender charge if redeemed prior to a specified period of time.

Balanced Index is a market index that serves as a basis of comparison for balanced portfolios. The composition of the balanced index used should mirror that of the comparative portfolio, i.e., a 60% weighting of the S&P 500 Index and a 40% weighting of the SLH Government/Corporate Bond Index. A balanced index is a more relevant comparative to a balanced portfolio than either a stock or a bond index alone.

Batting Average is a measure of a manager's ability to consistently outperform their benchmark. Divide the number of quarters that the manager outperformed the benchmark by the total number of quarters in a given period.

Beginning Value is the market value of a portfolio at its inception.

Benchmark Analysis is the process of determining how closely the manager's style matches that of the benchmark. This includes comparisons of market capitalization, style, standard deviation, beta, R-squared and tracking error.

Beta shows the level of volatility of a portfolio's return relative to the market's return or, the level of volatility of a manager's return relative to their benchmark's return. Each benchmark that is used (i.e., S&P 500, R2000 or MSCI) has a beta of 1.00. A portfolio that has a beta greater than 1.00 has experienced greater volatility than its corresponding benchmark; a beta of 1.00 means that the portfolio experienced volatility equal to that of its benchmark and, a beta of less than 1.00 means that the portfolio experienced less volatility than its corresponding benchmark.

Blackout period is a period of time when the participants or beneficiaries of a retirement plan are unable to direct, transfer or withdraw monies in their accounts.

Book Value of a company, as it appears on the balance sheet, is equal to the total assets minus liabilities, preferred stock, and intangible assets such as goodwill or, what the company's assets would be worth if the company were to be liquidated. Book value often differs substantially from the market price, especially in knowledge or information based industries, such as high-tech. Book value is of more interest to value investors than growth investors.

Bottom-Up Analysis is an investment strategy in which companies are considered based on their own merit, without regard to their sector or current economic conditions. This analysis includes a study of the company's management, history, business model, growth prospects and other company characteristics Bottom-up analysts are seeking companies that are superior to their peers and those that will outperform regardless of industry and economic circumstances.

Break Point is the dollar amount required to be invested in a specific mutual fund for an investor to become eligible for a discounted sales fee. These levels (the greater the investment amount, the larger the discount) may be achieved through a single purchase or a series of smaller purchases and includes the investments of family members.

Broker/Dealer is any individual or firm in the business of buying and selling securities for itself and others. Broker/dealers must be registered with the SEC. When acting as a broker, a broker/dealer executes orders on behalf of its client. When acting as a dealer, a broker/dealer executes trades for their firm's own account. Securities bought for the firm's own account may be sold to clients or other firms or, become a part of the firm's holdings.

Business Risk is that risk that is associated with the unique circumstances of a particular company and therefore the price of its securities.

C Share is a class of mutual fund shares that carries both a front-end load, which is generally only 1 to 2% and a higher expense ratio than A shares, usually equivalent to that of a B share. This higher expense, usually seen as a 12b-1 fee, provides for a higher pay-out (trail) to the selling broker.

Clearing Firm is an organization that works with the exchanges to handle confirmation, delivery and settlement of transactions (clearing). These firms play a key role in ensuring that executed trades are settled within a specified period of time and in an efficient manner. They may also be referred to as clearing corporations or clearing houses.

Company Risk is the risk that is specific to an individual company.

Comparative Universe consists of a group of professionally managed portfolios which are managed with a similar investment philosophy and/or objective as that of the portfolio being measured.

Comparative Rate of Return is a raw-number comparison between the manager or total portfolio's return and that of a specific benchmark. It is the same as "relative return." The return should be gross when compared to a specific benchmark and net when compared to an absolute return expectation.

Correlation Coefficient measures the correlation of movement between two variables such as different asset classes and styles. The range is between -1.00 and $+1.00$. Investments that move exactly together have the highest correlation coefficient, $+1.00$ and those that move in completely opposite directions to one another have the lowest correlation coefficient, -1.00. Zero or 0.0, indicates that they have no correlation or a random relationship to one another. The lower the correlation coefficient, the greater the diversification affects of mixing the assets.

CPI, Consumer Price Index, is maintained by the Bureau of Labor Statistics and measures the changes in the cost of a specified group of consumer products relative to a base period. Because it represents the rate of inflation, the CPI can be used as a general benchmark for gauging the maintenance of purchasing power.

Custodian is an agent, bank, trust company, or other organization that holds and safeguards an individual's, mutual fund's or investment company's assets. The custodian will physically maintain possession of securities owned by the plan, collect dividend and interest payments, redeem maturing securities, and effect receipt and delivery following purchases and sales. The custodian also performs regular accounting of all assets owned, purchased, or sold, as well as movement of assets into and out of the accounts.

Cyclical Market Cycles are short to intermediate market trends.

Default Risk, also called **credit risk** is the possibility that a bond issuer will default, failing to repay principal and interest in a timely manner. Bonds issued and backed by the federal government, have the lowest default risk, whereas bonds issued by corporations have greater risk as companies can declare bankruptcy. Municipalities occasionally default as well.

Directed Brokerage includes circumstances in which a board of trustees or other fiduciary requests that an investment manager direct trades to a particular broker/dealer, intending that the commissions generated be used or exchanged for specific services or resources. (Also see Soft dollar fees)

Discount Rate, also called the Federal Reserve Discount Rate, is the rate at which member banks may borrow short-term funds directly from a Federal Reserve Bank. The discount rate is one of the two interest rates set by the Fed, the other being the Federal funds rate.

Dispersion measures the consistency of performance results between accounts at a money management firm. Do accounts of like objectives and time of investment have the same or similar performance? This information will clarify the source and quality of the performance data, as well as reveal possible operational inconsistencies within the management firm's trading or account tracking disciplines.

Dollar-Weighted Rate of Return is calculated using the average dollars invested during a specified period, including cash added or withdrawn by the investor. The result shows the change in value of a portfolio.

Downside Capture Ratio compares a manager's percentage move to the downside to the appropriate benchmark, thus reporting how much of the benchmark's negative returns the manager captured during a down market. A number less than 100%, means that the manager is adding risk management value, not losing as much as the relative benchmark. A number greater than 100% means that the manager lost more than the benchmark during a down market.

Due Diligence is the process of investigating details of a potential investment or money manager, including the examination of operations and management, and the verification of material facts.

Duration is a measure of the change in the value of a fixed income security that will result from a 1% change in interest rates, stated in years. A 5-year duration means the bond will decrease in value by 5% if interest rates rise 1% and increase in value by 5% if interest rates fall 1%. Unlike maturity, duration takes into account interest payments that occur throughout the course of holding the bond; it is the weighted average of the maturity of all income streams within the bond or portfolio of bonds.

Efficient Frontier is based on the Modern Portfolio Theory and is the line that connects all optimal portfolio returns across all levels of risk.

Embedded Capital Gains represent accrued gains in a mutual fund portfolio. When the stocks that have these gains are sold and the portfolio manager cannot offset the gains with losses, capital gains will be distributed to the investor. This is a taxable event that the investor cannot control and, may not have benefited from depending upon the investor's holding period in the fund.

Emotional Risk is the risk associated with investor emotions. Fear often causes the investor to sell at the bottom and greed can cause the investor to buy at the top and/or abandon the concept of diversification.

ERISA, Employee Retirement Income Security Act of 1974, is the federal law that established legal guidelines for private pension plan administration and investment practices.

Excess Returns are a measure of those returns that are greater than those of the comparative benchmark during a specified time period.

Federal Fund Rate is the interest rate that banks charge each other for the use of Federal funds. It changes daily and is a sensitive indicator of general interest rate trends.

GIPS, Global Investment Performance Standards (formerly AIMR), are standards designed to promote full disclosure and fair representation in the reporting of investment results in order to provide uniformity in comparing manager results.

Gross Rate of Return is the total rate of return with no deductions, such as fees.

Hedge Fund is a fund, usually used by wealthy individuals and institutions, that uses aggressive investment strategies, including selling short, leverage, program trading, swaps, arbitrage, and derivatives. Hedge funds are exempt from many of the rules and regulations governing mutual funds and are generally unregulated.

HOLDRs (Holding Company Depository Receipts) are undivided interests in grantor trusts that hold the shares of companies identified by the issuer as representative of a particular industry or sector. HOLDRs are true pass-through securities conveying direct voting and dividend rights to the underlying securities and thus, investors receive proxy materials for all issues contained in the basket. Investors in HOLDRs can unbundle the basket into its component stocks and hold the individual securities. Once established, stocks in the HOLDRs remain relatively static with no mechanism to maintain the basket's size or focus.

Idiosyncratic Risks (see Unsystematic Risks)

Inflation Risk reflects he possibility that the purchasing power or value of a currency (dollar) will decrease due to inflation.

Information Ratio is a measure of a manager's performance, including return and risk, to that of a benchmark. It measures the consistency with which the manager's performance exceeds that of the benchmark. A higher ratio usually indicates better active management skills. Ratios from 0.50 to 0.75 are considered decent, with 1 being exceptional.

Interest Rate Risk reflects the possibility that the value of a security, especially a bond, will be reduced due to a rise in interest rates. This risk can be reduced by diversifying the durations of the fixed income investments.

Intrinsic Value is a company's fair value including its book value plus price per sales, enterprise valuation and other balance sheet information. It is a measure of a company's true value as opposed to its market price or book value.

Investment Policy Statement (IPS) is the formal description of the investor's goals, objectives, risk tolerance, time horizons and investment limitations. The IPS will act as a guide for portfolio design, asset allocations and manager selection.

Investment Risk reflects the possibility that the value of a security may be reduced due to changes in market conditions. This risk can be reduced by diversifying among investments with a low correlation to one another.

iShares are a family of Exchange Traded Funds (ETFs) that combine the characteristics of stocks with those of index funds. Each iShare closely tracks a specific market index, charging low management fees. The investor participates in the pool of securities that make up the tracking index and the iShare trades throughout the day like a stock. The investor can employ all trading techniques associated with stocks, such as market orders, limits, stops, short sales and margin.

Large-Capitalization stocks generally have a market capitalization of greater than $10 billion.

Liquidity Risk occurs when investments are difficult to sell on short notice without accepting a reduced price, impossible to sell due to contractual limitations or lack of a market or, there is a penalty for an early sale or withdrawal.

Managed Futures accounts are generally comprised of an individually managed account or co-mingled fund in which professional commodity manager's trade futures and forward contracts.

Market Risk describes risk that is common to an entire class of assets due to changes in economic conditions. Asset allocation and diversification among asset classes can reduce market risk, as different asset classes tend to underperform at different times. This is also called systematic risk.

Margin of Safety is the difference between the intrinsic value of a company and the cost of the stock.

Market Value is the price that a buyer is willing to pay for a given asset.

Median Market Cap (or Median Capitalization by Portfolio Weight) is the midpoint of market capitalization when the stocks in a portfolio are ranked in descending order by their capitalization. Half the stocks in the portfolio will have higher market capitalizations and half will have lower capitalizations.

Mid-Cap stocks generally have a market capitalization between $1.2 billion and $10 billion.

Modern Portfolio Theory (MPT) was developed by Harry Markowitz in 1952. It is based on the theory that markets are efficient, investors make rational investment decisions and that past results will continue into the future. The historic numerical data is combined into an overall investment strategy that seeks to construct an optimal portfolio at each level of risk.

Momentum Investing depends on the perceived strength behind a security's price movement. Momentum investors seek to take advantage of upward or downward trends in stock prices or earnings.

Net Asset Value (NAV) is the dollar value of a single mutual fund share, based on the value of the underlying assets of the fund minus its liabilities, divided by the number of shares outstanding.

Net Contributions refers to funds placed into a portfolio in excess of disbursements and withdrawals during a specified period.

Net Rate of Return is the gross return minus all applicable costs.

Nominal Rate is the stated interest rate of a bond or the actual return of a portfolio. This rate is not adjusted for inflation.

Party-in-interest is an individual who is in a position to exercise undue or improper influence over assets, such as an employer and a retirement plan.

Phantom Gains result from capital gain distributions made by a mutual fund that the investor has not benefited from in the form of NAV appreciation. This is a taxable event, which can be incurred by an investor, even if the value of the fund has gone down.

Price-to-Book Ratio is the company's market price per share divided by its book value per share. Book value is calculated using the firm's total assets minus the firm's liabilities, preferred stock value and intangible assets, such as good will, patents and franchises.

Price-to-Earnings Ratio (P/E) compares the price of the stock to the company's after-tax, twelve-month trailing earnings. The ratio is calculated by dividing the market price (price per share) by the earnings per share, or put another way, the cost an investor must pay for each dollar of the company's earnings.

Prime Rate is the interest rate that commercial banks charge their most creditworthy borrowers, such as large corporations.

Prohibited Transactions may be stated in an investment policy or required by certain state laws or ERISA, when applied to retirement plans. Fiduciaries must act in the sole interest of plan participants and beneficiaries and therefore, any action that is contrary to this requirement is considered a prohibited transaction.

Prudent Expert Act is the revised version of the Prudent Man Rule and required by ERISA to guide managers of pension and profit sharing portfolios. The main revision is that the fiduciary must act as someone who is familiar with matters relating to the management of money, not simply prudence.

Prudent Man Rule is the fundamental principle for professional money management, as stated by Judge Samuel Putnum in 1830: "Those with responsibility to invest money for others should act with prudence, discretion, intelligence, and regard for the safety of capital as well as income."

Prudent Investor Act (Rule) was established to provide investment standards for trusts and is the current standard by which most fiduciaries must act.

Qualified Plans are retirement plans that have a favorable tax treatment, but for the plan to maintain its tax-exempt status, it must stay in compliance with ERISA under the Internal Revenue Code.

Quartile is a ranking of comparative portfolio performance. The top 25% of portfolio managers are in the 1st Quartile, those ranking form 26% to 50% are in the 2nd Quartile, from 51% to 75% in the 3rd and the lowest 25% are in the 4th Quartile. The top and bottom 5% are generally excluded.

Rank refers to a ranking of performance in percentiles with the 1st percentile being the highest and the 99th being the lowest. The ranking evaluates a manager's performance in relation to other managers: a 10th percentile ranking means that this manager has performed better than 90% of managers in the comparative universe for a similar style.

R-squared measures the correlation between a portfolio and a benchmark and aids in predicting or analyzing the behavior of a portfolio. Values range from 0 to 1; the closer this relationship is to 1, the more the portfolio will behave like the benchmark.

Real Estate Investment Trust (REIT) is a corporation or trust that uses the pooled capital of many investors to purchase and manage income property (equity REIT) and/or mortgage loans (mortgage REIT). REITs are traded on major exchanges just like stocks.

Real Rate of Return is the rate of return after adjusting for inflation.

Registered Investment Manager (RIA) is an individual who has registered with the Securities & Exchange Commission (SEC) and holds himself or herself out to be an investment advisor. Registration is required of anyone who receives compensation and as part of their business, gives advice, makes recommendations, issues reports or furnishes analysis on securities either directly or through publications. RIA is not a credential. It simply means that an individual or a firm has submitted certain filings to the Securities and Exchange Commission and paid a modest fee. They can become registered without passing a test or demonstrating a degree of skill.

Reinvestment Risk is the risk associated with the potential decrease in income when a fixed income security matures or a dividend paying security is sold and must be reinvested at the then current interest rate. The replacement investment may not be able to earn the same rate of return as the security that it is replacing. This most commonly occurs when interest rates are falling.

Relative Return is a raw-number comparison between the manager or portfolio's return and that of benchmark that most closely replicates their style. The return should be stated as gross when compared to a specific benchmark and net when compared to an absolute return expectation.

Reversion to the mean occurs when segments of the markets return to their long-term average return following periods of over- or under performance.

Risk is the level of variability of returns of a portfolio, portfolio segment, or index and is measured using Standard Deviation.

Risk Budgeting is the process by which the overall acceptable portfolio risk is determined and then that "budget" is allocated across the various investment styles. This process is part of portfolio optimization, where is it the goal to achieve the best returns for a given level of overall portfolio risk. Institutional-type investors, such as large pension plans, use this approach in asset allocation and performance monitoring.

Risk/Return Quadrants describe the four areas or quadrants of a risk/return analysis graph. Risk (measured as standard deviation) is plotted on the "x" axis and return on the "y" axis. A manager or portfolio that is in the northwest quadrant indicates that there has been better return with less risk than the comparative index.

S&P 500 is the Standard and Poor's 500 Composite Stock Index. It is a capitalization-weighted index of 400 industrial, 40 public utility, 40 financial, and 20 transportation equities and its return includes dividend reinvestments. It is a widely accepted proxy for the domestic stock market; "the market." The S&P 500 is used as a benchmark for evaluating the performance of many equity portfolios.

Sector Risk is the risk associated with a single market sector.

Secular Market Cycles are long-term market trends.

Sharpe Ratio is a risk-adjusted performance measurement used to determine reward per unit of risk. It is calculated using standard deviation and excess return; the higher the Sharpe ratio, the better the portfolio's risk-adjusted performance.

Small Capitalization stocks generally have a market capitalization between $250 million to $1.2 billion.

Soft Dollar Fee is the portion of trading commissions incurred in the buying and selling of securities that is allocated for acquiring goods or services through a Directed Brokerage arrangement. Many soft dollar arrangements are effected through a brokerage affiliate of the consultant. Other soft dollar arrangements are effected through brokerages that, while acting as a clearing/transfer agent, also serve as the conduit for the payment of fees between the primary parties to the directed fee arrangement.

Standard Deviation measures the level of variability or volatility in the return of a portfolio or the market index when compared to its average. The higher the value, the greater the volatility (or risk) of the portfolio or index is.

Survivorship Bias refers to those managers that are included when reviewing universe rankings. Managers are not required to report performance data and therefore universe rankings can be suspect because managers with poor performance records tend not to report data for inclusion in these databases. This results in reporting biases for those who do choose to be included (the survivors).

Swapping is the tax management strategy of selling one security or mutual fund to capture losses and replacing it with a like security or fund.

Style Drift occurs when a manager places securities into a portfolio that are inconsistent with their stated investment philosophy and discipline. This practice is not acceptable in the consulting process, as asset allocations decisions are dependent upon style consistency within management firms.

Systematic risk (see market risk)

T-Bills are promissory notes issued by the U.S. Treasury and sold through competitive bidding, with a short term maturity date, usually 13 to 26 weeks. The return on T-bills has almost no variation, so it serves as a proxy for a "risk-free" investment.

Terminal Point Bias describes the perceived performance results when a specific ending point (terminal point), changes.

Time-Weighted Rate of Return is the rate at which a dollar invested at the beginning of a period would grow if no additional capital were invested and no cash withdrawals were taken. A manager cannot control the size or timing of money flowing in and out of an account and a time-weighted calculation eliminates the distortions caused by cash flows. It provides an indication of the value added by the investment manager, as it allows valid performance comparisons with other investment managers and market indexes.

Top-Down Analysis in an investment strategy that begins with an analysis of the overall economic picture and then narrows the search to sectors, industries and finally companies that are expected to perform well within this environment. This investing strategy focuses on the best sectors or industries in which to invest, and then searches for the best companies within those sectors or industries. Fundamental analysis of a specific security is the final step.

Total Return refers to the complete return earned by the portfolio, including income earned plus capital appreciation.

Tracking Error measures the amount by which the performance of the portfolio differs from that of the benchmark.

Trailing Returns refers to the returns generated for the most recently completed designated time period. For example, trailing twelve month returns are the returns for the twelve-month period ending on the final day of the last complete month.

Treynor Ratio (T) is a risk-adjusted performance measurement that relates excess return to systematic risk. This differs from the Sharpe ratio, which is calculated using total risk (standard deviation). The higher the Treynor ratio, the better the performance.

Universe defines the comparable peer group for a manager; managers with like styles and investment philosophies.

Unsystematic Risk, also called idiosyncratic risk, is risk related to the quality of an individual security.

Upside Capture Ratio compares the manager's percentage move to the upside to that of the appropriate benchmark. A number greater 100% indicates that the manager's returns are greater than those of the benchmark.

Weighted Capitalization means that the total market valuation of a given equity will determine its weighting within an index. The 100 largest companies of the S&P 500 are responsible for 80% of the index's performance.

Wirehouses are the larger broker/dealer firms whose branch offices are linked by a communications system that permits the rapid dissemination of pricing, information, and research relating to financial markets and individual securities. Although smaller retail and regional brokers currently have access to similar data, the term "wirehouse" dates back to the time when only the largest organizations had access to high speed communications.

Wrap Fee is a fee that bundles the services of the advisor or consultant with administrative costs, including custodianship of assets, reporting and brokerage transactions. In single contract accounts, the manager's fee is also included. The fee is calculated as a percentage of assets under management.

Yield Curve describes the shape of the line produced when yields are plotted on the "y" axis and maturity dates on the "x" axis for a similar type of bond, at a given point in time. Treasuries are generally used for comparisons.

Index